The Games That
Changed Baseball

The Games That Changed Baseball

Milestones in Major League History

JOHN G. ROBERTSON *and*
ANDY SAUNDERS

McFarland & Company, Inc., Publishers
Jefferson, North Carolina

LIBRARY OF CONGRESS CATALOGUING DATA ARE AVAILABLE

BRITISH LIBRARY CATALOGUING DATA ARE AVAILABLE

ISBN (print) 978-1-4766-6226-8
ISBN (ebook) 978-1-4766-2259-0

Front cover photograph: Jackie Robinson breaks the color barrier, April 15, 1947 (National Baseball Hall of Fame Library)

Printed in the United States of America

McFarland & Company, Inc., Publishers
Box 611, Jefferson, North Carolina 28640
www.mcfarlandpub.com

This book is dedicated to our mutual friend and fanatical baseball enthusiast John Dungey. John's unsurpassed passion for the grand old game, his remarkable in-depth knowledge of all aspects of the sport, and his unbridled zeal for anything and everything about the history of America's national pastime are unmistakable and endearing traits that have always been truly inspirational to us. We could not possibly have penned this work without his keen and unwavering interest in the project. Thank you, John!

Acknowledgments

As always, our thanks go to the many amateur baseball historians—amateur in the truest and noblest sense of the word; they do it for the love of the sport—who maintain the wonderful baseball information websites that have developed and proliferated on the Internet during the past two decades. Those caches of data really are a godsend. It certainly beats the crapshoot of having to travel to far-flung research libraries to discover what their microfilm collections may or may not contain. Special thanks go to the following people:

• Carl Madden, for his invaluable service as a volunteer proofreader, keenly alerting us to several typos that somehow escaped us despite numerous readings of the manuscript;

• Bruce Saunders for contributing his personal suggestions for historic MLB games that he felt ought be included within our list, and for his unofficial proofreading work on some chapters;

• Alan Stern, for alerting us to the controversial video-review situation that occurred at the Detroit–Kansas City game on Saturday, September 20, 2014;

• Dr. Terry Aitken, a New Zealand–born, Canadian physician who knows absolutely zilch about baseball, but did supply us with some insightful medical analysis about Doc Powers' untimely death in April 1909;

• John Horne from the National Baseball Hall of Fame Library in Cooperstown, NY, who helped provide the photographs for this book.

Table of Contents

Acknowledgments   vi

Preface   1

The 43 Most Historically Significant MLB Games

April 22, 1876 (First National League Game)   3

August 17, 1877 (First MLB Game-Fixing Scandal)   9

September 4, 1884 (Moses Fleetwood Walker's Last MLB Game)   15

April 19, 1890 (First Players' League Game)   20

April 27, 1893 (First Game Using the Modern 60'6" Pitching Distance)   29

April 24, 1901 (First American League Game)   33

October 1, 1903 (First Modern World Series Game)   37

September 23, 1908 ("Bonehead" Merkle Game)   46

October 3, 1915 (Final Federal League Game)   60

October 1, 1919 (Game One of the 1919 World Series)   67

April 14, 1920 (Babe Ruth's First Game as a New York Yankee)   73

August 16, 1920 (Ray Chapman Fatality)   77

May 16, 1921 (Fans Attain the Right to Keep Balls Batted into the Stands)   84

August 5, 1921 (First Radio Broadcast of an MLB Game)   88

July 6, 1933 (First MLB All-Star Game)   92

May 24, 1935 (First MLB Night Game)   96

August 26, 1939 (First Televised MLB Game)   101

April 15, 1947 (Jackie Robinson's MLB Debut)   105

August 19, 1951 (Eddie Gaedel Comes to Bat)   112

October 3, 1951 (The Shot Heard Round the World)   117

April 14, 1953 (First Milwaukee Braves Home Game) 120

September 24, 1957 (Last Game at Ebbets Field) 125

October 1, 1961 (Roger Maris's 61st Home Run) 133

April 12, 1965 (First Regular-Season MLB Indoor Game) 141

April 14, 1969 (First MLB Game in Canada) 148

October 13, 1971 (First World Series Night Game) 152

April 6, 1973 (Debut of the Designated Hitter) 157

April 8, 1974 (Hank Aaron's 715th Career Home Run) 161

April 9, 1974 (Debut of the San Diego Chicken) 167

October 21, 1975 (Game Six of the 1975 World Series) 173

September 9, 1979 (Bob Montgomery's Final Game) 177

October 26, 1985 (Game Six of the 1985 World Series) 182

October 3, 1995 (First Post-Season Game Featuring a Wild-Card Team) 186

June 12, 1997 (First Interleague Game) 190

September 8, 1998 (Mark McGwire's 62nd Home Run) 195

July 9, 2002 (All-Star Game Tie) 203

October 14, 2003 (Game Six of the 2003 NLCS) 208

August 7, 2007 (Barry Bonds' 756th Career Home Run) 215

June 2, 2010 (Jim Joyce's Blown Call) 222

May 25, 2011 (Buster Posey's Injury) 229

October 5, 2012 (First Wild-Card Play-In Game) 234

March 31, 2014 (First Use of the Video-Review Challenge System) 238

April 29, 2015 (First MLB Game Played with Zero Paid Attendance) 245

Appendix: Games That Didn't Quite Make the Cut 251

Notes 252

Bibliography 257

Index 261

Preface

"The exploits of Cy Young or Don Larsen, of [Sandy] Koufax, Catfish [Hunter], and Dennis Martinez would really amount to less in the public mind than the game of jacks played on porch fronts over the decades if not for the endurance of the institution of baseball. Today's Little Leaguers are at least the seventh generation to be following box scores in their local papers, and to have baseball to talk about with their elders. Baseball is America's great perennial, shooting up every spring and blossoming in the summer and ripening in the resplendent drama in the fall for every new class of citizens since before the Civil War."—baseball historian Michael Coffey

"You spend a good piece of your life gripping a baseball—and in the end it turns out that it was the other way around all the time."—MLB pitcher and author Jim Bouton

"The strongest thing that baseball has going for it are its yesterdays."—baseball historian Lawrence Ritter

With the aid of modern computer technology and an excellent database, virtually anyone, without too much exertion, can create accurate and unchallengeable baseball lists. For example, it would not be too terribly strenuous to compile a list of the top 100 triples hitters in Major League Baseball history, or the top 25 fielding averages by National League second baseman since the Second World War, or even the best World Series batting averages compiled by players named Smith. There's nothing to it, really. Numbers do not lie—and they are brutally blunt in their raw truthfulness. The bare facts of arithmetic are irrefutable.

However, compiling a list of anything to do with baseball history can be a challenge if the topic requires any degree of judgment. Deciding what should appear on a list of the "greatest games" or the "biggest blunders" or the "most dramatic events" in baseball history inevitably creates muddy waters simply due to the subjective nature of the endeavor. What is obviously memorable or tremendous to one observer might not even register in the mind of another fan of the grand old game due to age differences, knowledge of the sport's history, or some level of personal bias. Thus any list of the 43 most important/historically significant games in baseball history could never possibly attain anything close to unanimity. What constitutes "importance" is clearly very much a matter of personal opinion.

An amusing old adage states, "Opinions are like noses—everybody has one." We'll go along with that. Since our opinions are as meaningful or meaningless as any other fans' viewpoints, we boldly proffer here a compilation of 43 games that *we think* are the most important in baseball's long, colorful and illustrious history. Let's be clear about this: What follows is *not* a selection of the greatest MLB games ever played; it's a list of *the most historically significant* MLB games. There is an important difference. For example, no one can deny that Game Seven of the 1960 World Series was certainly thrilling, but it is not especially historically significant unless your name is Ralph Terry or Bill Maze-roski or you are a die-hard Pittsburgh Pirates fan. On the other hand, Game Six of the 1975 World Series was both thrilling *and* historically significant because of its undeniable positive impact on baseball's rejuvenation and surge in popularity in the years that followed. Similarly, most Opening Days are forgotten soon after the final pitch is thrown. However, the first Milwaukee Braves' home opener in 1953 provided an attention-grabbing harbinger that the traditional locales of MLB teams sometimes were not necessarily carved in stone. Likewise, Opening Day at Fenway Park in 1973 ushered in the profoundly game-changing designated hitter "position" in the American League. Both those games certainly possess clear historical merit.

This list we have compiled in this book was done so for your amusement, entertainment and enlightenment. Keep in mind that the list is not designed to be everything to everyone. We expect dissent. It represents merely only *our personal choices*—although we do firmly believe them to be valid and educated selections.

The games we have chosen span the entire 14 decades of professional baseball's history. They include contests that any baseball fan worth his salt ought to be familiar with, along with some games so obscure that they will be revelations to a great many readers. After beginning within a brainstormed list of about 130 candidates, the 43 selections that made the grade for this book did so for a wide variety of reasons: some obvious, some subtle. No bias was given for or against a particular era or decade. As it turned out, though, the decades of the 1880s and 1980s provided just one game apiece. Remarkably, the two games from 1974 that are included here occurred on consecutive days on opposite sides of the continent, but each represents a dramatically different reason for being significant. Curiously, two other games on our list were incapable of producing a winner, which must be a statistical anomaly considering how rarely tie games occur in MLB.

Each of the 43 games' respective claim to fame for historical importance will be recalled and discussed. The box score from each game will appear at the end of each chapter, if for no other reason than baseball box scores are an endless source of fascination and fun. (At least they are endlessly fascinating and fun to us.) Moreover, our success in tracking down hard-to-find, 19th-century MLB box scores from the archives of long-defunct newspapers such as the *Pittsburgh Commercial Gazette*, the *New York Clipper* and the *Boston Evening Transcript* was a very satisfying and happy accomplishment for us.

Our picks for the 43 most important games in baseball history are presented here in chronological order—not in a "countdown" format or any type of ranked system. You are free to rank them as you please based on any criteria of your choice. Since this book is a compilation of games rather than an ongoing narrative, there is no compelling reason to read the chapters in chronological order. Choose your favorites from the Table of Contents and tackle them first, if you so desire. Baseball remains the greatest game ever devised because it invites comparison and speculation and invokes passionate debate. Accordingly, you are invited to agree or disagree with our selections and compile a different set of rankings or lists based on your own personal preferences and criteria. We hope you are inspired to do so. To quote historian Bruce Catton, "Say this much for big league baseball—it is beyond question the greatest conversation piece ever invented in America."

The 43 Most Historically Significant MLB Games

April 22, 1876

Site: Jefferson Street Grounds, Philadelphia

Teams: Boston Red Caps vs. Philadelphia Athletics

Significance: First National League Game

Impact: MLB and Organized Baseball as modern fans know it is established

> "It was in 1876, the very year when Americans were observing their centennial as a nation, that a small group of men formed the National League of Professional Baseball Clubs. Few Americans were aware of it, fewer still would have believed that it would ever observe its centennial, and it would have been a rash individual who dared to predict that this National League would become a major institution in American life, one that commanded the attention of presidents and congresses and the loyalty of Americans. But that is exactly what happened."—Joel Zoss and John S. Bowman in *The National League*

> "Baseball is the very symbol, the outward and visible expression of the drive and push and rush and struggle of the raging, tearing, booming nineteenth century."—Mark Twain

> "In 1876 the crucial step was taken. Under the leadership of [Albert] Spalding and William A. Hulbert of Chicago, a new organization was formed [to replace the failed National Association] called the National League of Professional Baseball Clubs. A 'league' is a formal alliance among sovereign entities with set responsibilities, instead of an 'association' which implies voluntary compliance among a loosely tied membership."—*The Sporting News*, April 5, 1969, in an article by Leonard Koppett celebrating professional baseball's centennial

> "The National League was started by several teams from the National Association, which basically went belly-up with the birth of the NL. The new league went through many changes in its first few seasons. Some teams folded and some got kicked out. It's a wonder the league survived."—B. T. Grimes

The long-defunct *New York Clipper* holds a special place in baseball history. Strangely, it was not a daily newspaper or even a publication that focused on sports alone. The *Clipper* was a weekly entertainment journal founded in 1853 that specialized in covering various amusements in all their forms. Published on Saturdays, at its peak the *Clipper* had a circulation of 25,000, indicating its importance among the fashionable crowd in New York City and beyond.

The *Clipper* thoroughly covered theater, circuses, music, dance, and outdoor life. It also covered sports—presumably because its publisher considered sports to be a diversion or a form of recreation. Therefore mixed among the paper's Broadway scuttlebutt and coverage of minstrel shows were reports on bowling, billiards and chess. For baseball fans, the *Clipper* retains even more significance: It was the first newspaper in America to deem baseball a serious enough pursuit to merit extensive and scholarly coverage. Henry Chadwick, a transplanted English cricket player who became enamored with baseball as soon as he witnessed his first game, was the sport's foremost chronicler. He began enthusiastically writing about the exploits of New York City's top amateur baseball clubs in the *Clipper* in the 1850s at a time when the sport initially began to cast its grip on the attention of the public. Chadwick also developed the box score as an abbreviated way for fans to see how individual players had fared in a game. For his plentiful contributions to early baseball journalism, Chadwick earned himself a posthumous election to the National Baseball Hall of Fame in 1938. By 1894 the *Clipper* had discontinued its sports coverage and began focusing entirely on other forms of amusement. By 1924, after more than 70 years of existence, it was absorbed into the well-known entertainment trade paper *Variety*. Here is the verbatim account from the *New York Clipper* of the first game in National League history in its pages on April 29, 1876. A detailed report of the terrific game was sent to the *Clipper* by "special dispatch" from a correspondent in Philadelphia. Typical of the era, there was no byline given to the reporter, so it is impossible today to know the identity of the scribe who provided the *Clipper*'s coverage for this extremely historic game. It was an exciting, well-played clash at Philadelphia's Jefferson Street Grounds between the hometown Athletics and the visiting Boston Red Caps on Saturday, April 22, 1876. Dramatically, the game's outcome was not settled until the ninth inning. The NL was off to a tremendous start. Typical of baseball reports from the 1870s, the game's summary was written as one enormous paragraph using exasperatingly long sentences. Also (and sadly typically), it contained more than a few errors in players' names, it got the date of the game wrong, it included some factual impossibilities, and it featured antiquated and quirky terminologies that amuse and befuddle modern-day MLB researchers:

The first championship game between League clubs was played at Philadelphia on May [*sic*] 22, the contestants being the Athletics and the Bostons. The weather was favorable and the attendance large, over three thousand persons being inside the enclosure. O'Rourke, having widely reconsidered his determination not to play, made his first appearance this season with the Bostons, the Athletics presenting the same nine as in previous games. McLean, having been chosen umpire, proceedings commenced at 3:40 p.m. Both failed to score in the first inning, Meyerle being credited with a splendid hit to right centre for two bases. A wild throw by Sutton gave the Bostons a run in the second inning. The Athletics then tied the score by fine hits of Coons [*sic*] and Hall. The Bostons again went to bat, a difficult chance that Fisler declined to accept and which Fouser should have caught. O'Rourke's fine two-baser and Murnan's [*sic*] safe hit for a single, leading to the scoring two unearned runs in the third inning. The Athletics, after being retired in one-two-three order for three consecutive innings, managed to make three runs in the sixth inning, and thus tied their opponents' score: Fisler, Coons [*sic*] and Hall hit clean and hard for their bases, Josephs preferring to let Meyerle take his base on "called balls." The Bostons had previously earned a run in the fifth inning by the good batting and base-running of George Wright and Leonard. The score remained tied at four each during the sixth, seventh, and eighth innings, the Bostons then having had six men on the bases—three by errors of Force, Eggler and Sutton, two on "called balls," and one by a clean hit; a pretty double play by Eggler's quick return of a fly to Coons [*sic*] being a noteworthy feature of the Athletics' fielding. Force and Fisler made clean hits in the Athletics' seventh inning, and Hall's hot bounding hit was muffed by Leonard in the inning following, yet no runs were scored, the excitement continuing at fever heat. A change was made in the Athletics' field in the eighth inning, Sutton, in consequence of a rheumatic arm, being unable to throw and going to right field, Fouser to second base and Meyerle to third base. McGinley, the catcher of the Bostons, had his eye nearly closed n the seventh inning by a foul tip, but pluckily played his position throughout. In the last inning of the Bostons, Murnan [*sic*] and Schafer, in consequence of the double-play in the preceding inning, had another turn at the bat and made good of it by making a couple of runs, leading off as they did with safe single bases, and by desperate base-running they both came home after two men were out on Manning's hit, which Fouser failed to field; a neat double-play by Force, Fouser, and Fisler then closed the inning. The Athletics had now two runs to make in order to tie their opponents' score, and Knight led off well with a beautiful hit to left field on which he easily made second, and stealing to third, came home on Force's out to Parks. Eggler also hit in the same direction, but Parks failed to accept the difficult chance offered him, and the striker reached second base in safety. Fisler popped up a foul fly to McGinley, but Meyerle's hit was muffed by Schafer. Sutton, the next striker, proved unequal to the emergency, and a weak hit to Josephs closed the inning and the game, the Bostons winning 6 to 5. The game was sharply played throughout with the Bostons winning by their superior fielding and base-running.

The history-making game of April 22, 1876, was the culmination of overwhelming dissatisfaction with what some researchers deem to be baseball's first "major league": the National Association of Professional Base Ball Players (often abbreviated to the much simpler National Association). The NA operated for five tumultuous seasons from 1871 to 1875. Although it was unquestionably baseball's first professional league, the NA's ways of doing business left a lot to be desired. Such was the state of disarray in the NA that Major League Baseball does not consider the NA to be a true major league. (Some important reference sources, including SABR and Retrosheet, do give the NA top status, however, and have included their stats in MLB totals.)

The NA's origins came from the burgeoning amateur game which had strongly taken hold in the New York City area in the 1840s and 1850s. The National Association of Base Ball Players was founded to codify the rules and keep teams in line. Once strictly the governing body of amateur baseball, in 1869 the organization expanded to include a special subgroup of professional teams. The touring Cincinnati Red Stockings proved that baseball for pay was a viable proposition in both 1869 and 1870. By 1871, somewhat optimistically, enough teams were willing to try a new venture of a league consisting of entirely professional baseball teams, thus the NA was born on March 17, 1871.

In its five-year history, 25 different teams played under the NA banner, but never more than 13 in any single season. The league's first champions were the 1871 Philadelphia Athletics, but their championship was not without controversy. The Athletics finished the 1871 season with a record of 22–7. The Boston Red Stockings had a record of 22–10. The Red Stockings claimed at least a share of the championship because they had equaled Philadelphia's win total and the Athletics had not completed their full

Although he was much more famous as a longtime *Boston Globe* sports journalist, Tim Murnane participated in the first-ever National League game on April 22, 1876, as a member of the Boston Red Caps. Fame is fleeting, however. His surname is misspelled on this card printed to honor him as the president of the New England League (Library of Congress, Benjamin K. Edwards Collection).

schedule. Boston's claim to the title was dismissed, however. For the next four years, the Red Stockings copped the NA laurels. After the Red Stockings handily defeated the Athletics in an 1872 contest, one Boston newspaper reported that "half the city took a holiday to celebrate the victory."[1]

Overwhelming supremacy by one team is usually not a good thing for any new league, and Boston's superiority over its rivals was just one reason why the NA eventually dissolved after the 1875 season. The NA also placed teams in cities with insufficient populations to support them adequately. These metropolises included Fort Wayne, IN, Troy, NY, and Keokuk, IA. Boston was so thoroughly dominant that while they drew decent crowds at their home games, they were not a strong attraction on the road because they routinely thrashed the overmatched locals.

A lack of central authority also hampered the stability of the NA. The league was an association in the truest sense of the word. Teams were regarded as individual entities that voluntarily joined together to form a baseball league. Thus the NA's member clubs did not especially feel there was an obligation to the NA beyond their own narrow and specific interests. Accordingly, clubs often operated at odds with the well-being of the organization as a whole. Teams notoriously failed to make money-losing road trips when they were out of pennant contention. Games were cancelled on short notice without adequate reason. In one season nearly half of the NA's 232-game schedule was not played because teams lacked the funds to travel or simply dropped out of the league partway through the season. In 1875, six of the 13 teams that began play were gone before the season concluded.

Worse still, it was well established that gamblers corrupted many NA games just as they had in the prominent amateur leagues. John M. Rosenburg, in his book *They Gave Us Baseball*, wrote, "The poisonous effect of gambling had, in fact, seemed to reach new heights [in the NA] as poorly paid, unscrupulous, hard-drinking players often succumbed to the allure of easy money to fix or throw games." It was little wonder that confidence in the NA was rocky at best. By the conclusion of the 1875 campaign, fan interest in the NA was on the decline although baseball was booming on the amateur level everywhere on the continent. Professional baseball was in desperate need of a shakeup. Ironically, it was an underhanded player raid that gave birth to the National League.

Another problem associated with the NA was that the dominance by Boston and Philadelphia resulted in western alienation. William Hulbert, a coal magnate and brilliant baseball man who became president of the Chicago NA club in 1874, saw the powerful duo as a major impediment to the growth and stability of the league. Near the end of the 1875 season, he appealed to pitcher Albert Spalding's sense of regionalism to leave Boston and return to his home to ply his trade for the Chicago White Stockings in 1876. The doubling of Spalding's salary to $2,000 per season plus a 25 percent share of the gate did the trick. Hulbert then got Spalding to use his leverage on the Boston club to persuade three other Red Stockings star players (Ross Barnes, Cal McVey and Deacon White) to uproot and play for Chicago the next season too. Chicago newspapers got wind of the arrangement and published the story. This news traveled fast and was not especially well received in Boston. Fans still came in decent numbers to watch their Red Stockings thump their opponents—they went 71–8 in 1875 and did not lose a single home game— but the four "seceders" were mercilessly jeered at the ballpark and on the streets of Boston. Not satisfied with just pillaging the Red Stockings' roster, Hulbert also pried Cap Anson from the Philadelphia Athletics. Anson would become a beloved central figure in Chicago baseball for a quarter century. When rumors began to circulate that the NA would expel any players who jumped teams, Hulbert decided the next logical step was to break away from the NA and form a league of his own.

With the guidance of Harry Wright, an esteemed baseball pioneer who had also grown tired of how the NA conducted its affairs, Hulbert used his tremendous leadership skills to form the National League of Professional Baseball Clubs after the 1875 NA season had concluded. In one of his letters to Hulbert, Wright said in order for a new league to succeed and prosper, it must be run for the benefit of the clubs—not the players. The NL had to be structured as a business, teams had to play their entire schedules, and there needed to be a level of confidence that every game would be a money-making enterprise. Hulbert took Wright's counsel to heart. In early 1876 Hulbert summoned the owners of the Louisville, St. Louis and Cincinnati NA clubs to a secret meeting in Louisville to discuss his idea of a new league to replace the faltering NA. Hulbert had already drawn up a constitution for the NL. His sales pitch was this: For western teams to survive, a new league would have to start afresh. His listeners agreed. On February 2, 1876, Hulbert met with the representatives of the Philadelphia, Hartford, New York, and Boston clubs in New York City's Grand Central Hotel and sold them on the idea too. The NA was essentially dead—killed by the single-minded actions of William Ambrose Hulbert. Henry Chadwick, upon hearing the news, described the emergence of the new NL as a "coup d'état."[2]

Hulbert's constitution was applauded by all the club owners. It set standardized admission prices for all NL games at 50 cents, empowered umpires to eject rowdy players and spectators from NL ballparks, called for adequate police presence at NL games, and barred both open gambling activity and Sunday baseball. All NL contracts would bind players to their respective clubs and force them to adhere to NL rules. Players who engaged in match-fixing would be expelled for life. Any player suspended by one NL team could not be signed by another. Teams had to be located in centers that had a population of at least 75,000, and no two teams could be located within five miles of each other.

Hulbert was clearly the brains behind the new league and probably should have been acclaimed as the NL's first president. Instead he suggested that 38-year-old Morgan G. Bulkeley (the president of the Hartford Dark Blues) be the league's head man—at least on paper. Hulbert saw it as a clever way of placating the eastern teams' concerns about western domination of the new circuit. After one year, Bulkeley stepped down as NL president to focus on his lofty political ambitions. He would eventually be elected governor of Connecticut in 1888. In 1877 Hulbert formally took control of the NL and guided it during its formative years.

Eight teams began play in the NL's inaugural 1876 season. Perhaps symbolically, the first game was scheduled between the two dominant powerhouses of the defunct NA: Boston and Philadelphia. George Wright—Harry's little brother and the sport's premier shortstop—was the first man to come to bat in an NL game as the Boston Red Caps' lead-off hitter. He failed to reach base. The first pitch—thrown underhand because the rules forbade overhand deliveries—was tossed by Philadelphia's Alonzo (Lon) Knight, a mustachioed 5', 11" right-hander who later managed the Athletics. Tim Murnane, who later achieved considerable prominence as a Boston sports writer once his playing days had concluded, played first base for the Red Caps on Opening Day. Nobody wore a glove in the field and neither catcher wore a mask. William McLean, a local Philadelphian, was the sole arbiter of the first NL ballgame. (Until 1879 the home team was responsible for recruiting and hiring an umpire to officiate each league contest. In 1878 the standard rate

The first National League pennant winners were the 1876 Chicago White Stockings, who took the flag with a fine record of 52–14, six games ahead of the St. Louis Brown Stockings (Library of Congress).

of pay for an umpire was set by the NL at $5 per game. To ensure high standards and a degree of uniformity, the following year teams had to select officials from a pool of umpires approved by the NL.) The 3,000 fans' admission fees to Philadelphia's Jefferson Street Grounds for the April 22 game alone were nearly enough to cover two typical players' salaries for the entire season. Baseball could indeed be a profitable enterprise.

Of course that inaugural NL game was replete with a huge number of MLB "firsts." Boston's Jim O'Rourke got the first hit and first single with one swing of the bat. Philadelphia's Davy Force was credited with the first assist. Boston's Tim McGinley scored the first run. Philadelphia's Levi Meyerle belted the first double. (Two days later he also smacked the NL's first triple.) The game also provided the first MLB "last": It was the one and only MLB game ever played by Boston left fielder Bill Parks, whose career stats show him having more errors (one) than hits (zero). As the season progressed, more notable firsts entered the record books. On May 2, Ross Barnes of Chicago hit the league's first home run, an inside-the-park clout. (On the reverse side of that coin, Cincinnati pitcher Cherokee Fisher surrendered the first home run.) George Bradley of St. Louis pitched the first no-hitter on July 15 versus Hartford.

That first NL season lasted until October 21. Not surprisingly, the players acquired by the Chicago club after the final NA season decisively led the White Stockings to the first NL pennant. Chicago compiled an impressive 52–14 record—which translates to a .788 winning percentage—to win the flag by a comfortable six-game margin over Hartford. For the next quarter century, the NL would be the standard bearer for top-level professional baseball. Boston's exciting 6–5 victory on that sunny April afternoon in Philadelphia some 140 years ago provided an excellent starting point.

Boston 6 at Philadelphia 5

Game played on Saturday, April 22, 1876, at Jefferson Street Grounds

Boston	ab	r	Philadelphia	ab	r
Wright ss	4	2	Force ss	5	0
Leonard 2b	4	0	Eggler cf	5	0
O'Rourke cf	5	1	Fisler 1b	5	1
Murnane 1b	6	1	Meyerle 2b,3b	5	1
Schafer 3b	5	1	Sutton 3b,rf	5	0
McGinley c	5	1	Coon c	4	2
Manning rf	4	0	Hall lf	4	0
Parks lf	4	0	Fouser rf,2b	4	0
Borden p	3	0	Knight p	4	1
Totals	40	6	Totals	41	5

Boston	012 010 002—6
Philadelphia	010 003 001—5

ER–Boston 1; Philadelphia 2. 2B–Meyerle. U–William McLean. T–2:05.

August 17, 1877

Site: South End Grounds, Boston

Teams: Louisville Grays vs. Boston Red Caps

Significance: First MLB Game-Fixing Scandal

Impact: Established a precedent to apply severe penalties for players who fixed games and/or consorted with gamblers; established William A. Hulbert as a no-nonsense administrator who was determined to clean up professional baseball and make the new National League respectable

"Any professional base ball club will 'throw' a game if there is money in it. A horse race is a pretty safe thing to speculate on in comparison with the average ball match."—*Beadle's Dime Base Ball Player*, 1875

"The aim of baseball is to employ professional players to perspire in public for the benefit of gamblers."—*New York Times*

"Certainly nothing can be lost to the legitimate game by the conviction and punishment of the thieves and scoundrels who infest it and [who] by their presence as players bring disgrace and contempt upon it."—National League president William A. Hulbert

Though the vast riches of modern professional baseball are obvious, the sport's purist likes to think of baseball in naïve, Pollyana-esque imagery. He envisions small-town amateurs playing for the sheer enjoyment of the game, perhaps for the pride of their schools, their hometowns, or their counties. In his eyes corruption is a concept utterly foreign to America's national pastime. Most knowledgeable fans, however, are realistic and are well aware that baseball has been tainted with crookedness and scandals that date to almost the very beginning of the sport as an organized pastime.

As early as the 1850s, Henry Chadwick, baseball's first true chronicler, used his influential newspaper column in the *New York Clipper* to give credence to rumors of game-fixing among the top amateur clubs in New York City and to chastise those who might sully the pure sport. (A game between the New York Mutuals and Brooklyn Eckfords on September 28, 1865, played before at least 3,000 spectators in Hoboken, NJ, is the first known case where players admitted to fixing a high-level baseball game. Brooklyn won, 23–11, breaking open a tight game by scoring 11 runs in the very suspicious fifth inning.) If amateurs could be tempted to sell games during the sport's infancy, it was not much of a stretch to imagine semi-pros and full-fledged professionals padding their wallets by deliberately not doing their best on any given afternoon. The offers were undoubtedly plentiful, the money was too easy, and the temptation was often too great. Gambling and questionable play were so rampant at National Association and other pro-level games that it was not unknown for police to post warning signs outside a ballpark bluntly declaring, "No game played between these two teams is to be trusted."

Of course the most egregious scandal in baseball history was the Black Sox Scandal in which eight members of the superb 1919 Chicago White Sox famously conspired to throw that autumn's World Series against the underdog Cincinnati Reds. When the scandal came to light late in the 1920 season, it rocked professional baseball to its foundations. Significant changes were swiftly made in the structure of MLB to convince the American public that such an occurrence would never happen again. The guilty parties—and perhaps some innocent ones—were banned for life from any and all aspects of professional baseball. Hollywood movies and several scholarly books have told the sad tale of the eight men forever tainted as the 1919 "Black Sox": Joe Jackson, Eddie Cicotte, Lefty Williams, Swede Risberg, Happy Felsch, Chick Gandil, Buck Weaver and Fred McMullin.

The story of the 1919 Black Sox makes for compelling reading, but it was not the first wholesale game-fixing scandal to rock MLB. Forty-two years before the gang from Chicago deliberately booted the World Series for gamblers, a similar sellout took place during the National League's second season. The culprits were the high-flying Louisville Grays, who went from pennant favorites to bumbling also-rans in a short space of time. It was no accident. However, few followers of baseball today know very much about MLB's first gambling scandal. Even Eliot Asinof, whose *Eight Men Out* remains the premier account of the shady goings-on behind the 1919 World Series, barely acknowledged it when discussing the background to the famous Black Sox Scandal. In fact, Asinof made only a brief and inaccurate mention of what had happened four decades earlier.

The 1877 season was critical for the National League's survival. Its initial campaign had had its fair share of rocky moments. Two of the eight clubs from 1876—Philadelphia and New York—were expelled from the league for failing to make late-season road trips. It was a drastic yet wholly reasonable response to the clubs' thumbing their noses at the league, shirking their responsibilities to play a full schedule, and depriving the home teams of needed and expected gate receipts. Although the NL was reduced to a six-team loop for 1877, the circuit was in firm and capable hands. A new president, the energetic and youthful William Ambrose Hulbert, was at its helm. Learning from the plentiful mistakes of the poorly run National Association where he had been president of the Chicago club, the 44-year-old Hulbert was determined to make the new league a financial success.

Hulbert believed one important pillar in establishing the league's stability was to make each NL ballpark a place where everyone could attend a wholesome athletic contest without being accosted by drunks and tempted by gamblers. During the 1876 season, reports of rowdy inebriates were plentiful. Although Hulbert was not a teetotaler himself, he saw there was value in presenting a family-friendly image to the public. Decorum at NL games was the goal. "Ladies and children must be allowed to view the competition in a dignified atmosphere,"[1] Hulbert told his colleagues. Accordingly, Hulbert succeeded in having all alcoholic libations—including beer—banned from NL parks. No intoxicating beverages could be sold on any NL grounds or brought into the ballpark by the spectators. With the temperance movement starting to gain greater momentum across America, it was a wise public-relations move. Eradicating gambling from professional baseball was a whole other problem, however.

In the 1870s, organized gambling held a surprisingly tight grip on baseball. In Hoboken, NJ, for example, fans could partake in daily baseball pools. They were like the parlay cards that modern football fans find in sports books in Las Vegas. Realizing he couldn't hope to stop gambling on baseball completely, Hulbert nobly made a concerted effort to keep it as far from the gates of the six NL ballparks as humanly possible. Wagering booths at entrance gates and the brazen hawking of odds by bookies in the stands—once startlingly prevalent—were prohibited in the NL starting in 1877. "Ballplayers are to stay clear of anyone known to be tied in with gambling circles," warned Hulbert. "Such practices only detract from the magnificence of our teams."[2] Interestingly, Hulbert also insisted on uniform 50-cent admission prices for all NL games, although one could wait until the third inning and pay just a dime. He thought the steep price would ensure the league's players were paid decent salaries and thus make them less likely to fall prey to gamblers.

Throughout the early summer of 1877, the Louisville Grays looked to be the most magnificent of the six clubs in the close-knit NL. Led by captain and outfielder George Hall and nifty drop-ball pitcher Jim Devlin, the Grays vaulted to a solid four-game lead by August 13 with a 27–13 record. Because the schedule was just 60 games per team, Louisville looked like the solid favorites to capture the NL flag. After all, the Grays had been playing at a formidable .600 clip for most of the season.

Things went immediately awry, though, once the Grays embarked on an eastern road trip. Consecutive losses to the Boston Red Caps and the Hartford Dark Blues in the first two games were considered minor setbacks. (The Hartford club was drawing poorly at home, so their home dates were shifted to Brooklyn.) Devlin, a good-hitting pitcher who usually batted cleanup, uncharacteristically began to strike out frequently. He did so twice in the first of the suspicious games the Grays lost, 6–1 to Boston on Friday, August 17. Even though the Grays made eight errors, the unnamed reporter from the *Boston Evening Telegraph* declared the home team's victory as a game "well played by both clubs." Despite the loss to the Red Caps, Louisville still held a comfortable margin over the rest of the league's contenders.

But the Louisville losses continued to mount. On August 21 Hartford inflicted a shutout defeat on the Grays with a 7–0 trouncing. It was only the second time all season that Louisville had been kept off the scoreboard. Two days later those same teams played to a 1–1 tie that had to be called after 11 innings. Eyebrows were starting to be raised. It was well known that the Dark Blues had been the favorite in the Hoboken pool for each game—which was quite the opposite of what one would expect when a third-place team was facing the NL's front-runners. The Grays returned to Boston's South End Grounds, where they dropped a 3–2 decision to the Red Caps on August 25, leaving the teams tied in the NL standings. When the Boston club swept the final two games of the series, 6–0 and 4–3, the Grays fell out of first place for good. The *Louisville Courier-Journal* reported, "It is not known whether the players have been dissipating, keeping late hours, and having a jolly time generally, but tight or sober they should realize the fact that they've run afoul of the most humiliating set of reverses."[3] Back the Grays went to Brooklyn's Union Grounds for two more games versus Hartford, as the game-fixing scandal was about to break.

On the morning of August 31, Grays vice-president Charles E. Chase was eating breakfast at home when a telegram—sent by an anonymous person—arrived at his door. The message was from Hoboken. It stated that the Dark Blues were again mysteriously favored by 3:2 odds in the local baseball pools—and that something was clearly amiss with the Louisville team. Chase initially figured the message had no merit whatsoever and disregarded it. Later in the day, though, when the news reached him that Louisville had been defeated by a 6–3 score, he felt compelled to send his own wire to Grays manager Jack Chapman.

The loss was bad enough, but Chase was especially perplexed by a curious player substitution. Chase wanted to know why Al Nichols had played instead of regular Grays third baseman Bill Hague. Chapman replied that team captain George Hall had requested the change. Nichols was a Brooklyn lad, and Hall had thought it would be a positive gesture to allow him to play in front of his hometown fans. The answer seemed quite reasonable to Chase—but only temporarily.

Before the Grays' next game on September 6, another anonymous telegram arrived at Chase's home. This one was more specific than the previous warning: It stated the game set for that day "was to be crooked and Louisville [was] to lose"[4] with Nichols, Hall and Devlin making enough errors to ensure the defeat. That is precisely what happened. Chase was now understandably worried about the honesty of his team. He sent a wire to Chapman instructing him not to use Nichols in any more games.

The Grays finished their awful road trip by losing two of three games to last-place Cincinnati. Not only had the Grays dropped nine NL games to teams they probably should have beaten based on their early-season form, they also lost exhibition games to minor league clubs in Indianapolis, Pittsburgh and Lowell, MA. The pennant was lost, the team was in disarray, and tongues were wagging throughout Kentucky and organized baseball. Conversely, the Boston Red Caps were on a tear. They won 20 of their last 21 games to cruise to the NL pennant with a terrific 42–18–1 record. Eight of their wins had come against Louisville, which finished seven games in arrears of Boston, in second place with a 35–25 mark.

The *Louisville Evening News* sensed something was rotten with the faltering home-town team and was not afraid to spell out its suspicions to its readers with a large serving of sarcasm. Before the Grays' exhibition game versus an aggregate of local amateurs, the newspaper snarkily reported, "The Louisville Grays, alleged baseball players, have returned from their triumphal tour ... and will play the Amateurs on the Louisville grounds this afternoon. It will scarcely be profitable to throw the game to the Amateurs as the pennant does not depend on it."[5] Most everybody involved in baseball had their suspicions about the Grays' recent road trip. John A. Haldeman, a fine amateur player who worked as a reporter for the *Courier-Journal*, often served as the official scorer at Grays' home games. He had publicly accused both Hall and Devlin of tanking games. Furthermore, Devlin and Nichols were seen sporting fancy new wardrobes and dining at expensive local restaurants. NL president Hulbert had heard enough of the disturbing scuttlebutt. He sent a wire to Chase ordering him to launch an immediate investigation of his team.

Although the Grays were now in the midst of a six-game winning streak, Chase promptly summoned both Hall and Devlin to his office, where he informed the two players of his and Hulbert's suspicions of game-fixing. Neither came forth with a full confession, but Devlin mildly conceded that he had "performed carelessly against outside [non–NL] clubs."[6] Chase wired this information to Hulbert, who urged Chase to pursue the matter more forcefully. On the evening of October 4, the entire team appeared before Chase and the Grays' board of directors. Chase sternly demanded that each man sign an order directing the Western Union Telegraph Company to turn over duplicates of every telegram sent or received by the Louisville players during the 1877 season. "If you don't," warned Chase, "it will be considered an admission of guilt. I will suspend you from the club, and request Mr. Hulbert expel you from the league."[7] All the Grays except for short-stop Bill Craver gave in to Chase's ultimatum. Craver was promptly suspended for his defiance.

When Chase and Hulbert sifted through the telegrams, the evidence of game-fixing was irrefutable. Three Louisville players (Devlin, Hall and Nichols) had sold out to a coterie of New York City gamblers. They had thrown games and pocketed about $500 for their shady work. Undoubtedly they all had made additional sums of money by betting against their own team. Surprisingly, though, no evidence was ever found that directly implicated Craver in the game-fixing scandal. Whether the moody shortstop was guilty, merely insubordinate, or simply objected to his personal telegrams being read is open to speculation. Whatever Craver's motivation was for not cooperating with the investigation, he was tarred with the same brush as game-fixers Devlin, Hall and Nichols. On October 30, Craver and his three undeniably guilty teammates were expelled for life from the National League. Left in disarray by the magnitude of the scandal, the Louisville team was dissolved at the end of the 1877 season. The Kentucky city would not be represented in the NL again until 1892. Throughout the remainder of Hulbert's presidency, many friends and family members of the "Louisville Four" tried to persuade him to lift the players' suspensions so they could earn a living the only way they knew how. The resolute Hulbert refused even to consider the idea.

A few years later baseball impresario Albert Spalding witnessed a remarkable incident in Hulbert's office on a cold wintry, morning. Hulbert was sitting at his desk when the door was pushed open. In walked a shabbily dressed, underfed, sobbing individual. It was Jim Devlin. Spalding described Devlin as "the picture of abject misery." Devlin dropped to his knees, assuming a posture of humility. He begged Hulbert to remove the stigma from his name and reinstate him. "It is not on my account," the tearful Devlin explained, "but for the sake of my wife and family." Hulbert was emotionally moved by Devlin's appearance, but he would not reconsider his suspension. Hulbert pressed a $50 bill into the crying Devlin's palm. "That's what I think of you personally," he said to the disgraced ex-pitcher. "But damn you, you are dishonest. You have sold a game, and I can't trust you. Now go and never let me see your face again, for your act will not be condoned so long as I live."[8]

Exiled from baseball, both Devlin and Bill Craver got jobs as policemen for a short time. Devlin died in 1883 as a result of tuberculosis complicated by acute alcoholism. One newspaper editorial called Devlin's death at the young age of 34 "an instructive example of the fruits of crookedness."[9] Craver lived to 57, surviving mostly on a military disability pension until his death in 1901. George Hall died in 1923 at age 74. (Interestingly, Hall had been the NL's first home run champion by belting five for Boston in 1876. However, his role in the Louisville game-fixing scandal of 1877 made him the sport's first home-run king to fall from grace. He would not be the last.) Al Nichols—who holds the distinction of being the first English-born player in MLB history—spent his post-baseball career as a shipping clerk and inspector. Remorseful about his role in the game-fixing scandal, he made numerous unsuccessful attempts to be reinstated. He died at age 84 in 1936.

Every one of the banned players—collectively known in baseball history as the Louisville Four—outlived William A. Hulbert. The strong-minded NL president died of a sudden heart attack at age 49 on April 10, 1882. His obituary in the next day's *Chicago Tribune* declared, "There is not in America a player, club, officer or patron of the game who will not feel that the loss is irreparable." Hulbert's unexpected passing was indeed a severe blow to the NL and baseball in general. Nevertheless, the man whose high standards and expectations may have saved the National League in 1877 was sadly forgotten for many years. SABR biographer Michael Haupert lamented, "Despite the glowing tributes to Hulbert and the proclamations that he would never be forgotten nor would the game ever be the same without him, he faded into obscurity. No trophy bore his name, no event was dedicated to him, and for a long time no place could be found for him in the Hall of Fame."[10] Remarkably, Hulbert would not be enshrined in the Hall of Fame until 1995—113 years after his untimely death. (The impetus to finally get Hulbert his rightful place in Cooperstown came from his great-great-nephew, who began a letter-writing campaign to sports writers as a third-grader in 1965. It took 30 years to achieve a positive result.) Hulbert's absence from baseball's shrine for so many decades was truly both perplexing and utterly inexcusable.

Louisville 1 at Boston 6

Game played on Friday, August 17, 1877, at South End Grounds I

Louisville	ab	r	h	po	a	e		Boston	ab	r	h	po	a	e
Latham 1b	4	0	1	9	0	1		Wright 2b	5	0	0	2	1	0
Hague 3b	4	0	3	2	0	1		Leonard lf	4	0	0	0	0	0
Hall lf	5	1	1	0	0	1		O'Rourke cf	4	2	3	2	0	0
Devlin p	4	0	1	1	2	0		Murnane 1b	5	2	2	6	1	0

Louisville	ab	r	h	po	a	e
Shafer rf	3	0	1	0	0	1
Gerhardt 2b	3	0	0	4	5	2
Craver ss	3	0	0	3	4	1
Snyder c	3	0	0	5	3	0
Crowley cf	3	0	1	3	0	1
Totals	32	1	8	27	14	8

Boston	ab	r	h	po	a	e
Sutton ss	4	1	0	2	2	0
Bond p	4	0	2	0	7	1
Morrill 3b	4	1	1	4	1	0
Schafer rf	4	0	2	2	0	0
Brown c	4	0	1	9	2	2
Totals	38	6	11	27	14	3

Louisville	000 100 000—1
Boston	000 001 203—6

(Note: Even though Boston was ahead 3–1 after the top of the ninth inning was completed and had thus won the game, NL rules at that time permitted the home team to bat in the bottom of the ninth inning if they so desired. Boston chose to bat and scored three more runs.)

DP–Gerhardt-Latham; Brown-Murnane. 3B–Brown. LOB–Louisville 4; Boston 2. WP–Bond. U–J. G. Sumner. T–2:10.

September 4, 1884

Site: League Park, Toledo

Teams: Pittsburgh Alleghenys vs. Toledo Blue Stockings

Significance: Moses Fleetwood Walker's Last MLB Game

Impact: Walker was the last black player to appear in an MLB game until Jackie Robinson broke baseball's "color barrier" 63 years later.

> "Moses Fleetwood Walker was no ordinary man, and in the 1880s he was no ordinary baseball player."—David W. Zang, Fleet Walker's biographer

> "Get that nigger off the field!"—Cap Anson

> "Not to discount anything [Jackie] Robinson went through, but Walker suffered more. When you look at the fact that slavery had only been abolished less than 20 years before Walker [played in the majors], America was still getting used to that idea. For many (including Anson), having an African-American ballplayer on the same field was unfathomable. Whether they thought they were far superior or they still couldn't get used to the idea that slavery no longer existed, whites struggled with blacks being on the field."—Chris Stevens, *Bleacher Report*

If one asks a typical sports fan, "Who was the first black man to play major league baseball?" the vast majority will quickly give Jackie Robinson as the reply. Robinson was actually at least the third—and quite likely the fourth—of his race to participate in MLB play. However, scholarly baseball fans know that long before Robinson made his historic debut at Ebbets Field in 1947, he had been preceded by Moses Fleetwood Walker and his brother Welday. In fact, the pioneering Walkers were ahead of Robinson by 63 years.

John R. Husman, who penned Walker's life story for SABR's Biography Project, rightly asks (and then answers) the obvious question:

> Why then does the myth persist that Jackie Robinson was first? Could it be because Walker played so long ago that what he did no longer seems relevant? Or could it be because the league in which he played has not survived? Could it be that Robinson played within the memory of still living Americans and so is favored by them? I believe the answer is that Walker's action resulted in the segregation of major-league baseball. Robinson's, on the other hand, resulted in a completely opposite and positive outcome—the integration of the game. Both Walker and Robinson met and withstood the assault of racial bigotry. Their experiences were often painful and very similar but separated by 63 years. Their times were very different

and the results of their actions were very different. But without question, Moses Fleetwood Walker was the first.

To complicate matters further, fairly recent research into 19th century baseball has uncovered an even earlier candidate to the title of being the first black man to play in the majors. William Edward White, who was partly African American and partly white, had a one-game MLB career. On June 21, 1879, White appeared in his lone game with the Providence Grays of the NL. A substitute, White replaced injured first baseman Joe Start, went 1-for-4 at the plate and scored a run in Providence's 5–3 home win versus the Cleveland Blues. Why White's MLB career consisted of just one game is not known. Quite likely the Grays needed someone to fill in for Start as a one-game replacement. White fit the bill nicely because he was competent, local, and available. In 2004 researchers discovered, quite by chance, that White had been listed in the Milner, GA, census of 1870 as a nine-year-old mulatto boy whose mother was also of mixed race. If this information is indeed accurate, it would also make White the only former slave to play in an MLB game. Regardless of White's racial composition, Husman entirely dismisses his status in the debate about who was the first black major leaguer. Wrote Husman, "White, however, played and lived his life as a white man and faced none of the trials that Walker and Robinson did. Despite the retroactive application of genetic rules, I believe that if Mr. White said he was white, we should consider him white."

If White's status as the first black player in MLB history is to be dismissed, greater emphasis should indeed be placed on Walker's career and experiences. The son of a Methodist minister, Moses Fleetwood Walker was born in 1856. He was known to friends and family as "Fleet" at a very early age. His first experience with baseball probably occurred in Steubenville, OH, where he spent most of his childhood. The first record of Walker playing in anything close to an official game was in Oberlin, OH, where his father's church was located. Walker was a decent student whose grades began to slip when baseball became more of a priority. In 1877, as a 20-year-old, Walker enrolled at Oberlin College. Within a short time Walker was the catcher and leadoff hitter on Oberlin's prep-school team. At the time, baseball at Oberlin was limited to intra-school play; no varsity squad existed until 1881.

When Walker was finally able to test his talents against other, more sizable schools, he did not disappoint. After a 9–2 win over the University of Michigan, the vanquished players were so impressed by Fleet Walker, his brother Welday, and pitcher Harlan Burket—all future pros—that they were persuaded to transfer from Oberlin to Ann Arbor. During the spring of 1882, Walker's excellent catching skills helped lead Michigan to a 10–3 record.

During the summer of 1881, before he enrolled at Michigan to study law, Fleet Walker's exceptional baseball talents became known to semipro teams. Cleveland's White Sewing Machine Company team recruited Walker to catch for them in a game versus the Louisville Eclipse in Kentucky on August 21. The Eclipse was virtually a pro team; they would enter the American Association in 1882 as one of the league's charter members. Seven of their players in 1881 would be on major league rosters in 1882. When the Cleveland semipros arrived at the ballpark, Walker's appearance presented a problem. The *Louisville Courier-Journal* reported the following day that "players of the Eclipse Club objected to Walker playing on account of his color."[1] Typical of the day, the Cleveland club meekly withdrew Walker from their lineup and sat him on the bench. That solved the problem only temporarily: Walker's replacement behind home plate suffered an injury in the first inning and could not come out for the second frame. The crowd was open-minded enough to begin a clamor to get Walker into the game. At first the Eclipse players acquiesced, but Walker looked so skillful during his warmups that two Louisville players strenuously renewed their objections to Walker being allowed to play. With the game in jeopardy, Cleveland's third baseman offered to catch the game and Walker was ordered back to the bench. The Eclipse won the game, 6–3. The shabby treatment was but a taste of what was in store for Fleet Walker as he moved up the ladder in organized baseball.

In July 1882, between university semesters, Walker signed with a team in New Castle, PA, called the Neshannocks. Although the team was supposed to be an amateur outfit, there is no doubt that Walker and other mercenaries were paid for their services. The local newspaper, remarkably, made no reference to Walker's color during his time there, and heaped glowing praise upon him. Not only did it refer to Fleet as one of the best catchers in the country, but also commended him for his gentlemanly behavior on and off the field. In 1883 the lure of baseball for pay proved too great. Walker gave up the collegiate game and signed a contract with the Toledo club—sometimes referred to as the Blue Stockings—of the professional Northwestern League.

Before he ever caught an inning, Walker found himself the center of a controversy because of his race. At a pre-season meeting of club officials, the manager of the Peoria club presented a motion to bar black players from the league. The measure was obviously directed at Walker, whose skills were well known. It prompted some heated discussion but was summarily voted down. The *Toledo Blade* reported, "It is well known that the catcher of the Toledo club is a colored man. Besides being a good player, he is intelligent and has many friends. The motion which would have expelled him was fought bitterly."[2]

The basic question needs to be addressed: Why was organized baseball opposed to black players? There are at least three legitimate answers—at least they were legitimate in the minds of 19th-century baseball moguls and players. First, there was simple, unabashed bigotry against people of African descent. Slavery was within the living memory of most adult Americans in 1884. Having whites compete with and against people who were constitutionally considered less than human rankled a good segment of white society. Second, white players resented the prospect of competing against black players for already hard-to-come-by jobs. Excluding black players meant greater employment security for white players. Third, owners feared that white customers would balk at paying to see blacks play professional baseball. Moreover, they had concerns that blacks on the field would result in more blacks in the grandstands, which, in the long run, would dissuade whites from attending games. Thus, the easiest way to take care of all three problems was to ban the likes of Moses Fleetwood Walker.

Walker was permitted to play in the Northwestern League in 1883—and he shone, especially defensively. At one point *Sporting Life* gushed, "Toledo's catcher is looming up as a great man behind the bat."[3] Walker caught 60 of his team's 84 official league games plus most of the exhibition games Toledo played. The most noteworthy of those was a contest versus a National League club—Cap Anson's Chicago White Stockings—on August 10, 1883. Interestingly, Walker was hurt and was not supposed to play in the game versus the White Stockings. Nevertheless, when Anson's club arrived in Chicago, they learned that Toledo's star player was a black catcher, and Anson predictably went into a fit. According to newspaper accounts, Anson vowed that his team would not play against any team that had a black man on its roster. (Anson was better educated than most of his MLB peers. He spent two years at a prep school affiliated with the University of Notre Dame and studied for a semester at the University of Iowa. Racial tolerance was obviously something Anson never acquired: His favorite term for Negroes was "chocolate-covered coons.") To his credit, Toledo manager Charlie Morton decided to call Anson's bluff, figuring the Chicago manager would not risk forfeiting his club's share of what promised to be a large gate. Anson caved in and his White Sox played the August 10 game with Walker inserted into the Blue Stockings' lineup—but Anson vowed never again to play a team with a racially integrated roster.

The Toledo club's success in the Northwestern League prompted them to try their fortunes in the American Association in 1884. The AA was a legitimate major league from 1882 to 1891. Thus, on Opening Day, May 1, 1884, Walker became the first black man to play in an MLB contest (if William White is not considered). Ironically, the site was Louisville, where his presence three years earlier with the semipro club from Cleveland had created a racial problem. Walker faced torrents of abuse and played poorly in Toledo's 5–1 loss. Toledo was facing much stiffer competition in the AA than they had in the Northwestern League the previous summer. They won just one of their first 12 games. The vitriol directed towards Toledo's catcher barely subsided throughout Walker's short time as a big-leaguer. Two of his teammates were openly opposed to Walker being on the club. One was star pitcher Tony Mullane, one of the fastest pitchers in baseball. Thirty-five years later, in 1919, Mullane said in a newspaper interview with the *New York Age*,

> He [Walker] was the best catcher I ever worked with, but I disliked a Negro and whenever I had to pitch to him I used to pitch anything I wanted without looking at his signals. One day he signaled me for a curve and I shot a fastball at him. He caught it and came down to me.... He said, "I'll catch you without signals, but I won't catch you if you are going to cross me when I give you signals." And all the rest of that season he caught me and caught anything I pitched without knowing what was coming.[4]

Typical of all catchers in the 1880s, Fleet Walker wore precious little protective equipment, with the exception of a mask. He constantly suffered the usual nicks and bruises that were a day's work behind the plate in MLB. Occasionally he was too banged up to play. (During one stint when Fleet was unable to play, the Blue Stockings used his brother Welday as an outfielder, making Welday Walker the second black player in MLB history. Welday's MLB career lasted just five games. He batted .222. He and Fleet were never in Toledo's lineup at the same time.) Frequent injuries and inactivity—and the tougher competition of MLB opposition—began to affect Fleet's productivity. On Thursday, September 4, having played in just 42 games, Fleet Walker's MLB career came to an inglorious conclusion when he went hitless in Toledo's 4–2 home win over the Pittsburgh Alleghenys. Injuries had prevented him from playing in all but six of the Blue Stockings' games after July 12. The following day manager Charlie Morton received a letter from Richmond, VA, warning him not to bring Walker to Toledo's upcoming series in that city. It read,

> Manager Toledo Base Ball Club:
>
> Dear Sir: We the undersigned, do hereby warn you not to put up Walker, the Negro catcher, the evenings that you play in Richmond, as we could mention the names of 75 determined men who have sworn to mob Walker if he comes to the ground in a suit. We hope you will listen to our words of warning, so that there will be no trouble: but if you do not, there certainly will be. We only write this to prevent much bloodshed, as you alone can prevent.[5]

The threatening letter actually served no point. Fleet Walker had been released by the time the Blue Stockings visited Richmond to conclude their schedule in mid–October, but the missive does indicate the intense level of hatred that Walker's presence had inspired. In Walker's lone MLB season he batted .263—the third-best average on his club that finished in eighth place in a ten-team league.

Walker's professional baseball career was not over—only his MLB career. The following year he played for minor league teams in both Cleveland and Waterbury, CT. By 1887 Walker was catching for Newark of the International Association. The team's star pitcher was George Stovey, another black man, who won 33 games. On July 14, Walker and Stovey were not permitted to play in an exhibition game versus the Chicago White Stockings. With open hostility towards colored players growing, that very same day, the IA agreed not to approve the contracts of any further blacks, though those already in the league were permitted to continue. Walker's last pro team was the Syracuse club in the IA. When he was released on August 23, 1889, it marked the last time a black player was on the roster of a team in organized baseball until Jackie Robinson's stint with the Montreal Royals in 1946.

In his post-baseball career, Fleet Walker worked for the U.S. Post Office. He was convicted of mail theft in 1898 and spent a year in a federal prison. Upon his release, Walker later managed a hotel, an opera house, and a theater—often working alongside brother Welday. The creative Walker obviously had a wide variety of interests: He patented inventions for changing movie reels and for a new type of exploding artillery shell. For a time he and Wel-

One of the greatest baseball stars of the 19th century, Cap Anson, was also one of its most immovable racists. His influence combined with his opposition to black players in Organized Baseball helped draw MLB's "color line" that lasted until the middle of the 20th century (Library of Congress, Benjamin K. Edwards Collection).

day co-edited *The Equator*, a newspaper that dealt with black-specific issues. In 1908 Fleet wrote a book titled *Our Home Colony* in which he encouraged black Americans to immigrate to Liberia to escape the overt racism that pervaded the United States. Walker's biographer, David W. Zang, described the 47-page treatise as "certainly the most learned book a professional athlete ever wrote." Zang may very well be right. Here is a portion of the book's eloquent preface:

> No one could entertain higher regard for the American white man and his magnificent civilization than the writer; and it is the appreciation of this fact, along with the infancy of Negro freedom, that forces the conclusion upon our mind that it is contrary to everything in the nature of man, and almost criminal to attempt to harmonize these two diverse peoples while living under the same government.[6]

Fleet Walker died in 1924 in Steubenville, OH. His final resting spot in that city's Union Cemetery was unmarked for 67 years. Finally, in 1991, a 350-pound granite headstone was placed on Walker's grave thanks to fund-raising and awareness efforts at Oberlin College after the school discovered its historically significant alumnus from the 19th century. Sara Freeman, Walker's 74-year-old niece, was present for the ceremony, as was her 33-year-old son. Walker died when Freeman was just seven. But in an interview published in philly.com, she vividly recalled her late Uncle Fleet as being "a nice man with a flamboyant way about him."[7] Samuel Cooper, an Oberlin College official who spoke at the dedication of the monument, noted, "We're hopeful that what we're doing will bring more attention to a piece of baseball history without stepping on the image of Jackie Robinson."[8]

Despite being twice married, fathering three children, and having at least one grandchild, Moses Fleetwood Walker is thought to have no direct living descendants.

Pittsburgh 2 at Toledo 4

Game played on Thursday, September 4, 1884, at League Park and Tri-State Fairgrounds

Pittsburgh	r	h	po	a	e	Toledo	r	h	po	a	e
Swartwood rf	1	2	1	0	1	Barkley 2b	2	1	3	3	0
Eden cf	0	1	2	0	0	J. Miller ss	1	2	2	3	1
Doyle lf	0	0	1	0	0	Welch cf	1	2	5	0	0
Whitney 3b	1	1	3	3	0	Poorman rf	0	1	0	2	0
Faatz 1b	0	1	11	0	0	Mullane p	0	1	1	3	0
Forster ss	0	0	1	2	0	Meister 3b	0	1	0	1	0
Creamer 2b	0	0	1	2	0	Lane 1b	0	1	10	0	0
Neagle p	0	0	0	5	1	McSorley lf	0	0	1	0	0
D. Miller c	0	1	4	2	0	Walker c	0	0	5	1	0
Totals	2	6	24	14	2	Totals	4	9	27	13	1

Pittsburgh   000 100 010—2
Toledo   100 000 03x—4

Pittsburgh	IP	H	R	ER	BB	SO
Neagle L	8.0	9	4	2	1	2
Totals	8.0	9	4	2	1	2

Toledo	IP	H	R	ER	BB	SO
Mullane W	9.0	6	2	2	0	3
Totals	9.0	6	2	2	0	3

DP–D. Miller-Faatz. 2B–Faatz; Welch. 3B–J. Miller, Poorman. LOB–Pittsburgh 4; Toledo 4. U–Jack Holland. T–1:28.

April 19, 1890

Site: Olympic Park, Buffalo

Teams: Cleveland Infants vs. Buffalo Bisons

Significance: First Players' League Game

Impact: A players' union organizes a third major league, but it dissolves after just one season; the hated reserve clause remains a standard part of players' contracts; MLB clubs learn the folly of scheduling simultaneous games in the same city

"Like a fugitive slave law, the reserve rule denies [the player] a harbor or a livelihood, and carries him back, bound and shackled, to the club from which he attempted to escape."—John Montgomery Ward, a key figure in MLB's first players' union

"The Players' National League, as it stands today, rose out of necessity, and is an honor and monument to its organizers, stockholders, players, and officials."—John Montgomery Ward

"Contrary to most historians' treatment, the Players' League was not doomed from the start; in fact, it was a highly viable product which ultimately fell apart due to naïveté, and the victory of profit over principle on the part of some of its members."—PL historian Ethan M. Lewis

Major League Baseball fans have endured multiple labor disputes since 1972 that have tested their loyalty to teams and their love for the professional game as a whole. In some MLB locales, the sport's magnates are still trying to coax back disenfranchised fans lost during the aborted 1994 season.

None of the disruptions of the past 40-plus years, however, was as damaging to professional baseball's image as the season-long Brotherhood Rebellion of 1890. Though it is largely unknown to today's fans, Organized Baseball was turned inside-out that year when players from the two established major leagues ignored their contracts, created their own league, and waged war on their former employers. In the end, nobody profited and MLB barely survived the catastrophic 1890 season.

Professional baseball was riding a tremendous crest of popularity in the 1880s. Attendance in both major leagues (the National League and American Association) was booming. The 1889 season was an especially banner one. Nineteenth-century baseball historian Daniel M. Pearson wrote,

In that year both the National League and American Association staged two close, exciting pennant races which represented a fitting culmination to baseball's expansion in the 1880s. Baseball captured the attention of thousands of urban dwellers as it never had before. It had definitely become the national game by 1889, and it had become recognized, especially in New York City, as a valuable and necessary feature of modern urban culture. In some way, the 1889 season was modern baseball's borning [*sic*] cry.[1]

However, clouds of discontent were looming: The players were grumbling about the hated reserve clause in their contracts. This fascinating gimmick bound each player to his club even after his contract expired. Some ballplayers compared their lot in life to indentured servitude. Players' salaries were kept artificially low because they either had to re-sign with their old clubs or quit professional baseball altogether. In 1887, Deacon White and Jack Rowe decided to challenge the system by attempting to leave their team in Pittsburgh to play for Buffalo. The reaction of management was swift and crystal clear: Frederick Stearns, the owner of the Detroit Wolverines, publicly declared that White would play for Pittsburgh or "he'll get off the earth."[2]

The Players' Brotherhood began in 1885 as a benevolent association. It mainly concerned itself with helping players in financial trouble and improving the often tenuous relations between management and players. In 1888, when club owners tried to impose an inflexible set of salary limits upon the players, the Brotherhood provided a united front for player resistance. Its leader, chosen by the players, was John Montgomery Ward, a one-time superstar pitcher who had switched positions and become the popular shortstop of the New York Giants. (Ward is the only player in MLB history to record 100 wins as a pitcher and collect 2,000 hits as a batter. He also has the third-best career WHIP, behind only Addie Joss and Ed Walsh. On June 17, 1880, while pitching for the Providence Grays, Ward pitched the second perfect game in MLB history.) Ward was one of the few players of his era who had attended and graduated from college. He practiced law in the off-season. In 1887 Ward penned a scholarly article for *Lippincott's Magazine* titled "Is the Baseball-Player a Chattel?" that questioned the legality of the reserve clause and espoused a somewhat Marxist view of baseball as a business. He wrote, "Every dollar received by the club [in selling a player] is taken from the pocket of a player; for if the buying club could afford to pay that sum as a bonus, it could just as well have been paid to the player in the form of increased salary. The whole thing is a conspiracy, pure and simple, on the part of the clubs by which they are making money rightfully belonging to the players."[3]

After the 1888 season, Ward and many other top players were taken on an around-the-world exhibition tour to promote baseball in uncharted waters. It was organized by Chicago's club president, Albert Goodwill Spalding. Spalding was a former pitcher for the White Stockings. Along with running the White Stockings, Spalding also ran a sporting goods company that bore his name. Every ball used in NL games was manufactured in Spalding's' factory. In 1888 he was the owner most trusted by the players—which was not saying a whole lot.

While the group was touring overseas, the NL enacted the pay-cutting "Brush Classification Plan" (named after tight-fisted Indianapolis Hoosiers owner John T. Brush), which fixed salaries at five different levels based on the skill and drawing power of each player plus his deportment on and off the field. The best players—rated Grade A—would receive the less than princely remuneration of $2,500 a year. Spalding undoubtedly had been aware of what his fellow owners planned to do while his tour was visiting far-flung locales thousands of miles away, so he was correctly perceived as a willing collaborator by the players. With NL teams now nervily charging players for their uniforms and forcing them to contribute 50 cents per day to cover meal money during road trips, player-owner relationships were approaching rock bottom. Ward noted that they would improve once the NL moguls "could only get over the idea that they owned us."[4]

The remarkably multi-talented John Montgomery Ward is the only man in MLB history to win 100 games as a pitcher and collect 2,000 hits (mostly while playing shortstop). Ward is most historically significant, however, as a formidable players' rights advocate and the driving force behind the short-lived Players' League (National Baseball Hall of Fame Library, Cooperstown, New York).

The Brotherhood became the first baseball players' union on July 14, 1889. The date coincided with the 100th anniversary of Bastille Day, which was probably not a coincidence. Eradicating the loathsome reserve clause was high on the Brotherhood's agenda. "Players have been bought, sold, or exchanged as though they were sheep instead of American citizens,"[5] declared the Brotherhood's Manifesto. The union also wanted the end of the robber-baron-type owners who ran the NL. "There was a time when the [National] League stood for integrity and fair dealing. Today it stands for dollars and cents. Once it looked to the elevation of the game and an honest exhibition of the sport; today its eyes are on the turnstile. Men have come into the business for no other motive than to exploit it for every dollar in sight."[6]

Brotherhood representatives' meetings with the club owners achieved nothing. The NL president at the time was Nick Young, but Spalding's domineering presence made him the de facto leader of the league. Spalding and his fellow owners refused to consider amending the reserve clause. During the 1889 season, the Brotherhood secretly began organizing its own league. Although Frank H. Brunell of the *Chicago Tribune* had written an article about the proposed Brotherhood League on September 7, most of the baseball public was unaware of the union's ambitious plans until the *New York Times* broke the major story on September 23 under the headline "Ball Players Revolt." At the end of the 1889 season, more than 100 players walked out on their contracts with their NL or AA clubs and vowed their loyalties to a new

Albert Goodwill Spalding, shown here as an old man, was a fine pitcher in the 1870s, but became more noteworthy as a wealthy sporting goods mogul and frugal team owner in the 1880s. Like his fellow owners, he was a staunch opponent of players' rights. Spalding's "treachery" during the 1889 World Tour was perhaps the final straw in the Players Rebellion of 1890 (Library of Congress, George Grantham Bain Collection).

circuit—the Players' League (officially and confusingly dubbed the Players' National League)—which would begin play in the spring of 1890. Fifteen of the rebels were future Hall of Fame members. In contrast, only four future Hall of Famers were left on the NL clubs' rosters—although three rookies who would become Cooperstown inductees (including Cy Young) were elevated to the NL to fill the many voids created by the rebels' departure. "A one-league monopoly was always the ambition of the controlling spirits of the National League," wrote John Montgomery Ward. "To make it the central figure in the baseball world has been their aim for years, and to this end they have directed every effort."[7]

Initially the owners did not take the Brotherhood seriously. But when the PL awarded eight franchises and began constructing ballparks in seven of the NL's eight cities, the NL owners began to panic. They threatened the "insurrectionists" and "anarchists" who jumped to the PL with lawsuits and injunctions. Spalding headed a "war committee" that promised to drive the PL out of business. Ward tried arranging a truce with the American Association, but the AA's owners balked at dealing with organized labor.

Seven of the eight PL clubs operated in direct competition with NL clubs in the same city; only the Buffalo club was located in a virgin market. PL supporters, such as

St. Louis railroad magnate Will Johnson, saw this as no obstacle, though. "The [PL] players will have the sympathy of the people with them," he declared. "No man living that I know of feels friendly to the [NL] bosses. The selling and trading of players, as though they were so many cattle, is all wrong, and the time has come when the players must take the bull by the horns and do something for themselves."[8] Will Johnson was the brother of Albert L. Johnson, the owner of the Cleveland PL club.

Buoyed with the optimistic dreams of a financial bonanza based on MLB revenues of 1889, the PL unveiled its unique profit-sharing plan: Beyond their contractual salaries, the players on the top four teams were to receive the first $10,000 in any profits the PL made. The next $80,000 in profits would be divided among the owners. The next $80,000 beyond that would be evenly split among the players. Any profits accruing beyond that lofty amount would be equitably shared among the owners and the players. PL players were also encouraged to buy shares in their teams and thus become part owners. In stark contrast, NL rules proscribed players from owning any shares in their teams.

The PL opened its gates for business for the first time on Saturday, April 19, 1890, with all eight teams in action. In one of the four contests on Opening Day, the Buffalo Bisons—a team that featured a gangly, 27-year-old catcher named Connie Mack who had invested his life savings of $500 in the PL franchise—clobbered the curiously named Cleveland Infants, 23–2, in front of a good crowd at Buffalo's Olympic Park. (Mack would lead the PL in one painful category: He was hit by pitches 20 times. It was the only offensive category he ever topped in his 11-year playing career.) Eight of the nine Bisons scored at least two runs in the rout. Leadoff hitter John Irwin scored five times. Cleveland made seven errors, so only seven earned runs counted against the Infants' luckless hurler, Henry Gruber, who batted in the eighth spot that day. Gruber endured the full eight innings despite allowing 17 hits in the terrible beating, as was customary at the time. The Infants' lineup featured all-time greats Ed Delahanty and Pete Browning. The huge win was a deceptive result for the home team. Buffalo would finish at the bottom of the PL standings with a dismal 36–96 record, a whopping 46½ games in arrears of the first-place Boston Reds. Cleveland would struggle mightily too and limp home in seventh place.

According to a story in the April 26 edition of *The Sporting News*, the four PL games on the first Saturday drew about 26,000 fans, while the NL games drew approximately 17,000 spectators. "The Brotherhood teams have scored the first blood and the first knockdown," declared *The Sporting News*. The *New York Times* concurred. It claimed the PL team in Gotham had outdrawn the previous season's World Series winners on Opening Day by at least a 2:1 ratio. There were no games the next day as the PL, like the NL, refused to schedule games on Sundays. The AA had no such qualms about defiling the Sabbath.

Journalists were divided on who was right and who was wrong in what baseball historians would later describe as the Brotherhood War of 1890. Henry Chadwick, baseball's most respected writer, sided with management. Chadwick claimed the Brotherhood Rebellion was a "revolutionary manifesto" and thought the rebels were ingrates. The *Cincinnati Enquirer* agreed. It claimed Ward had instigated the labor trouble primarily to boost his legal career. Newspapers in NL cities enjoyed demeaning Ward with nicknames such as "Judas." (Ward preferred a different biblical allusion: He sought to portray the PL as David battling the Goliath NL.) *The Sporting News*, however, allied itself with the players—a courageous act considering how much Spalding advertising the popular and prestigious weekly baseball publication carried. There was probably local resentment of Spalding in St. Louis, where *TSN* was published, as Spalding often spoke unkindly about the Missouri city. Not surprisingly, the American Federation of Labor eagerly supported the Brotherhood and invited the players to join its ranks.

One PL franchise was placed in New York City, home of the 1889 NL champions. As America's largest city, it was considered a key battleground by both sides. Competition was especially savage there. It was also a time of high confusion. New York's clubs in the NL and PL were both nicknamed the Giants. Amazingly, the two Giants' teams played in adjacent ballparks—often simultaneously. Cagey fans quickly discovered that some seats offered decent views of both games.

Fans who did watch games in multiple leagues were quick to notice something: The balls used in PL games were livelier than the balls Spalding's company produced for NL play. The PL had hoped that greater offense would equate to more customers passing through the turnstiles. Fans who liked spectacular defensive feats got their share of thrills too. There were seven triple plays executed by PL clubs in the league's 529 official games—a remarkable total. In contrast there were just two triple plays in more than 2,400 MLB games in 2012. There was one no-hitter thrown in the PL, albeit an unofficial one. Silver King of the Chicago Pirates tossed an eight-inning gem on June 21 versus Brooklyn but lost, 1–0.

The New York City baseball crowds tended to divide themselves along social lines. The upper and middle classes generally supported New York's NL team at

COPYRIGHTED, 1887.

GOODWIN & CO., NEW YORK.

Cornelius McGillicuddy (better known as Connie Mack) was baseball's most beloved manager of all time, remarkably guiding the Philadelphia Athletics for 50 seasons. He also played catcher for Buffalo in the first Players' League game in 1890 (Library of Congress, Benjamin K. Edwards Collection).

the Polo Grounds, while the working populace attended PL games at Brotherhood Park. PL attendance was promising at first, but fan interest began to wane as the inter-league bickering increased over the summer. Attendance dipped to dangerously low levels everywhere. Pittsburgh's pitiful NL team won just 23 of 136 decisions and attracted a mere 16,604 spectators all season. All three leagues suffered from the pig-headed stupidity of scheduling games in direct competition with each other in the same city. In Chicago alone, the city's NL White Stockings and PL Pirates had 48 dates when both teams were playing at home simultaneously. Philadelphia and Brooklyn had teams in all three major leagues—and 32 instances when all three teams were playing home games at the same time—resulting in severely divided loyalties and patronage. In *Slide, Kelly, Slide*, Marty Appel's terrific biography of King Kelly, the author noted,

> The season went on with one eye on the pennant race, and one eye on the small gates. With two games in each city at once, 2,000 [spectators] was a good crowd. As the [PL] players had a stake in the profits, they no doubt counted the house and talked about their concerns while on the bench. In a Players' League game in Brooklyn, where Ward was the manager, only 80 people showed up to watch visiting Buffalo. It was hard to put a good face on the situation.

The perils of head-to-head scheduling of games between competing leagues were well remembered a decade later. The debacle was an error the National League and the American League generally learned from even in the most intense period of their rivalry to win the hearts of spectators. On most days the AL and NL magnates were smart enough to avoid making fans choose between two simultaneous games in the same city.

Spalding tried to cajole some PL stars into returning to the NL. Boston's enormously popular King Kelly was promised $10,000 and a three-year deal if he would come back. Although he was nearly bankrupt, Kelly declined. "I can't go back on the boys,"[9] he loyally said. Of course, Spalding was disappointed with Kelly's principled decision, but Spalding was so impressed with the star catcher's unwavering loyalty to the PL that he offered him a personal $1,000 loan—which the cash-strapped Kelly gladly accepted. Cap Anson, who had stayed loyal to the NL, was not surprised by Kelly's refusal to abandon the Brotherhood. Anson said money easily slipped though Kelly's fingers, but it was friendship and loyalty that counted most to him. Similarly, Buck Ewing, the catcher on New York's PL Giants, was offered part ownership of the Cincinnati NL club if he quit the Brotherhood. Like Kelly, Ewing refused the enticing offer.

To make his league look like the more popular circuit, Spalding gave his sporting-goods customers thousands of free passes to White Stockings' home games. When the PL clubs mocked him for "papering the house," Spalding posted spies outside the rival parks to count actual paid admissions to PL games. He then published these figures to show that the PL was also chronically dishonest in reporting its attendance totals.

Years later, an embarrassed Spalding wrote, "If either party ever furnished to the press one solitary truthful statement about attendance figures [for 1890], a monument should be erected to his memory."[10] David Nemec, an expert on 19th-century baseball, echoed Spalding's sentiments in 1997. "Reliable attendance figures for the 1890 season should be available one day," he wrote. "Try Doomsday. Each of the three major leagues lied through its teeth."[11]

Despite numerous bold statements from Ward that the PL had replaced the NL as the premier professional baseball circuit in America, there were signs that the PL was struggling financially too. The Brooklyn club—Ward's own team—was the target of legal action by the company that had built its home grounds. It had placed a lien on Eastern Park for $5,000 to secure payment on unpaid construction bills dating back to March. *The Sporting News* noted in its September 6 issue that such dire news was completely contrary to the wholly positive comments Ward had been making about both his club's ledgers and the PL's finances in general, and "will cause many a liberal-thinking critic to wonder how much truth there is in the statements of the average baseball magnate."

White Stockings club secretary Jonathan Brown was especially adroit at manipulating minuscule crowd numbers. One afternoon when fewer than 50 people watched a Chicago home game, Brown informed a reporter the attendance was "twenty-four eighteen." When the scribe was safely out of earshot, Spalding asked Brown how he had concocted such a preposterously exaggerated figure. "Don't you see? There are 24 fans on one side of the grandstand and 18 on the other," said Brown assuredly. "If he reports 2,418, it will be on his conscience, not mine."[12] At another NL game, *The Sporting News* comically reported the dismal attendance to be "fifty-two people (including the ballplayers), six babies, and seven yellow dogs."[13]

Traditionally the statutory holidays on the baseball calendar were responsible for attracting the largest crowds every season. In 1889, some 200,000 fans had attended MLB games on the Fourth of July. In 1890 the number dropped dramatically to just 116,000—a decline of 42 percent. In Brooklyn, home attendance for all three of the city's MLB teams in 1890 did not equal what the AA Bridegrooms alone had drawn the year before when they had the borough's baseball fans entirely to themselves and a pennant winner on the field. "Too many cooks spoil the soup,"[14] succinctly concluded the *Brooklyn Daily Eagle*. Clearly the inter-league squabbling had soured a large portion of America's baseball fans to the dangerous point of ambivalence.

The final PL game took place in Chicago on Saturday, October 4,

Such was the universal popularity of King Kelly that Albert Spalding reputedly offered him $10,000 during the tempestuous 1890 season to return from the Players' League to the National League. Kelly declined the offer (Library of Congress).

fittingly in drizzly and disheartening conditions with the Giants playing the hometown Pirates in a meaningless affair. *The Sporting News* described the scene:

> That gurgling noise heard yesterday afternoon at 5 o'clock was the death rattle of old baseball. When Umpire [Lon] Knight called the game at the end of the fifth inning, the few mourners who were present at the last rites silently arose and passed out with bowed heads and the air of men burdened with grief. It was somehow a fitting end to this sorry baseball season of 1890. The rain drizzled down intermittingly, the fog hung so low that the players looked like creatures of a mirage.... Looking through the haze a man could imagine himself adrift in a mighty sea, with the fog waves tumbling at him. The players were dim blurs of white and black.... The game amounted to nothing and ended in a [2–2] tie.[15]

For the record, Boston won the Players' League's only championship, finishing the 140-game schedule with a 6½-game lead over second-place Brooklyn. Cleveland's Pete Browning won the league's batting title with a .373 average.

By the end of the tumultuous season, all three major leagues were perilously close to financial ruin. With the daily fudging of turnstile counts irretrievably skewing the true attendance figures—baseball historians will never know for certain—the fledgling PL may have drawn more fans than the NL in 1890 and definitely did not lose as much money as the older league. (It certainly outdrew the AA, which would exist as a major league circuit for only one more year.) PL historian Ethan M. Lewis claims the Brotherhood's losses totaled about $125,000 while the NL clubs may have lost nearly $500,000 over the course of the tumultuous season.

Nevertheless, in a post-season peace meeting between the NL and PL, Spalding, in a daring act of bravado, demanded unconditional surrender from the Brotherhood. Having endured more losses than its backers were willing to accept, the Brotherhood suddenly lost its vigor to put up any further fight. The players' naïveté and inexperience as businessmen were exploited by the more worldly NL magnates. Many PL players were frightened that their careers would be imperiled if they remained in the rebel camp. Even though they may have had the more prosperous league and the moral high ground, the Brotherhood caved in and capitulated.

Ward was thoroughly disappointed by the lack of backbone shown by the PL's players and its bankrollers after the 1890 season sputtered to its end. He bitterly told *The Sporting News,*

> The Players' League had the call when the season closed, but the ridiculous and needless weakening by the local backers has placed it in an embarrassing position, while the National League magnates have been benefitted.... When they started in with this fight they knew very well what to expect, and they have no right to squeal now. There are lots of players who have put their all into the Players' League who are willing to play for almost nothing next season to continue the fight if necessary. No, I am not in favor of consolidation. I think with a non-conflicting schedule, two clubs can live in New York and Brooklyn, and also in Boston, Philadelphia and Chicago.... I think both sides could make money and the public would be better pleased.[16]

By mid–November it was obvious that the PL was kaput. *The Sporting News* gave it something akin to an obituary when its November 22 edition declared, "The Players' League is dead. Goodbye, Players' League. Your life has been a stormy one. Because of your existence many a man has lost thousands of dollars. And before long all that will be left is a sad, discouraging memory." With the PL relegated to history, the Brotherhood collapsed shortly thereafter and the rebels meekly returned to their old NL or AA clubs, often signing for substantially less than they had earned in 1890. The reserve clause remained a standard part of major league baseball contracts for the next 85 years. Because the caliber of play in the PL was at least on par with the NL or AA—if not better—its statistics properly count as part of the official records of MLB.

For many years MLB's owners cited the example of the Brotherhood War of 1890 to prove the following points: the reserve clause is essential to the professional game, unions have no place in sports, players cannot stick together as businessmen the way owners can, and owning a baseball club can be either a profitable or a risky endeavor. These key concepts and assumptions became entrenched in the minds of all MLB owners long after the Players' League was relegated to the history books.

The Players' League did, however, leave one silent but large monument for decades: New York City's famous Polo Grounds was originally Brotherhood Park, the home ballpark for the PL's version of the Giants. Once the circuit folded, Brotherhood Park became the new home, in 1891, of the NL Giants who re-christened it as the newest incarnation of the Polo Grounds. To lessen the chance of fire damage and to increase spectator capacity and comfort, the Polo Grounds was rebuilt with steel and concrete in 1911 and served as the Giants' home until the team moved to San Francisco after the 1957 season. The expansion New York Mets called the Polo Grounds home in 1962 and 1963 while awaiting the construction of Shea Stadium. Once the Mets had their shiny new home, the last tangible vestige of the long-forgotten, insurrectionist, ambitious, short-lived Players' League was demolished by a wrecking crew in 1964.

Cleveland 2 at Buffalo 23

Game played on Saturday, April 19, 1890, at Olympic Park

Cleveland	ab	r	h	Buffalo	ab	r	h
Stricker 2b	4	0	2	Irwin 3b	4	5	1
Delahanty ss	4	0	2	Hoy cf	5	3	2
Browning lf	4	1	0	Rowe ss	4	2	2
Twitchell rf	4	0	0	Wise 2b	3	3	4
Tebeau 3b	4	1	1	White 1b	4	2	1
Larkin 1b	4	0	1	Beecher lf	3	0	1
McAleer cf	3	0	1	Rainey rf	4	4	2
Gruber p	3	0	0	Mack c	4	2	2
Brennan c	3	0	1	Haddock p	4	2	2
Totals	33	2	8	Totals	35	22	17

Cleveland	000 001 010—2
Buffalo	360 425 03x—23

2B–Tebeau; Haddock, Wise. HR–Rainey. T–2:25.

April 27, 1893

Site: League Park I, Cincinnati

Teams: Chicago Colts vs. Cincinnati Reds

Significance: First Game Using the Modern 60'6" Pitching Distance

Impact: After a decade of pitcher-dominated games, the pitcher's advantage no longer exists

> "Up until 1892 the pitching mound [sic] was a neighborly fifty feet away from home plate, giving a wallbreaker like [Giants fireballer Amos] Rusie what was finally deemed an unfair advantage. Accordingly, in 1893 the mound was hauled back to its present sixty feet six inches. The National League's batting average promptly jumped from .245 in 1892 to .280 in 1893 and then to .309 a year later. (To this day, psychological studies of pitchers come up with persecution disorders dating back to 1893.)"—Donald Honig in *Baseball America*

The MLB single-season pitching record for most strikeouts in a season is not held by Nolan Ryan, Sandy Koufax, Randy Johnson, Rube Waddell, Bob Feller, J. R. Richard, or Walter Johnson. It is held by someone the vast majority of baseball fans have likely never heard of: Matt Kilroy. As a 20-year-old, rookie left-hander, Kilroy set the unapproachable mark of 513 whiffs for the 1886 Baltimore Orioles of the American Association. (The AA held major-league status from 1882 to 1891.) In that dominating season, Kilroy actually compiled a losing record of 29–34 for a last-place club. As the Orioles' ace, Kilroy pitched the staggering total of 583 innings and threw 66 complete games. No other pitcher on the Orioles that season accrued more than 209 innings.

The top seven seasonal strikeout totals in MLB history all occurred in a short span from 1884 to 1886, when pitchers held a clear advantage over batters. Beginning with the 1884 season, pitchers in the National League were first permitted to throw overhand. They could also do so from a running start if they so chose. Most did. Hoss Radbourn of the 1884 Providence Grays won 59 games with that approach. Midway through the 1885 season, the AA followed suit and allowed pitchers free rein to deliver the ball however they liked.

Most importantly, the pitchers from that era were distinctly closer to home plate than their modern counterparts. Despite author Donald Honig's quote at the beginning of this chapter, there was no "pitcher's mound" on 19th-century baseball diamonds; the mound was a 20th-century innovation. All pitches in the 1800s were delivered from ground level, where the batters were positioned. Instead of a mound there was a "pitcher's box" chalked on the infield. Over the years its distance from the plate varied. Pitchers had to deliver the ball without stepping beyond the front line of the box. In Kilroy's record-setting 1886 season, the AA rules set the front of the pitcher's box 50 feet from home plate.

Baseball repeatedly tinkered with pitching rules and distances in order to find a happy balance to make the pitcher-batter confrontation competitive. With offensive outputs understandably dwindling, baseball's rules were changed for the 1887 season. Four strikes were required for a strikeout. The four-strike rule lasted for just one season, but in 1887 the back line of the pitcher's box was set 55'6" feet from home plate. It was the point from where the pitcher now had to start his delivery. The following year the pitcher's box vanished from baseball diamonds forever—although the archaic term "getting knocked out of the box" still exists to describe a pitcher who was ineffective and yanked from the game, as does the term hitting a dribbler "back to the box."

Although most baseball historians cite 1901 as the beginning of the modern era of MLB because of the emergence of the American League as a major circuit, it can be argued that the 1893 season was the true turning point that separated MLB's early days from the game today's fans recognize. The key change in the playing rules for 1893 put pitchers 60'6" from home plate. The blazing fastball of imposing New York Giants and Future Hall of Fame hurler Amos Rusie—whom baseball writers dubbed the "Hoosier Thunderbolt" because he hailed from Indianapolis—is largely considered responsible for inspiring the new rule. Rusie, a solidly built, 210-pound right-hander who stood 6'1", was the Nolan Ryan of the last decade of the 19th century. He was downright scary to face from such a short distance.

According to baseball historian Jack Kavanagh, Rusie "personified sheer power pitching of the 1890s."[1] Although largely forgotten today, Rusie was probably New York City's first true baseball superstar. Among Rusie's admirers was Lillian Russell, the leading Broadway actress of the time, who requested a chance to meet the Giants' renowned flamethrower. Of course it is impossible to know how fast Rusie's speed balls travelled through the air 12 decades ago, but some baseball scholars estimate them to have been somewhere in the mid–90-mph range. Years after Rusie retired, Chicago outfielder Jimmy Ryan offered this testimony about the Hoosier Thunderbolt's fearsome fastball:

Words fail really to describe the speed with which Rusie sent the ball. He was a man of great height, great width, prodigious muscular strength and the ability to put every ounce of his weight and sinew on every pitch. The distance was shorter then, Rusie had the whole box to move around in, instead of being chained to a slab; and the Giant simply drove the ball at you with the force of a cannon. It was like a white streak tearing past you.[2]

Rusie's fastball was both impressive and occasionally wild, a combination that rightly instilled fear in many opponents. From 1890 to 1892, Rusie struck out 969 overmatched batters—quite a feat considering foul balls did not count as strikes in Rusie's era. Mastering control over his pitches was not necessarily a high priority for Rusie. Often his seasonal walk total approached his strikeout tally.

Rusie also hit more than his share of batters with pitches; he usually attained double digits in that stat each season. (Twenty-six hit batsmen in 1890 was Rusie's apex of wildness.) Combined with his frightening speed, Rusie's sporadic lack of control likely added to batters' reluctance to dig in against him. In a game in versus Baltimore in 1897—well after the new pitching distance was established—Rusie solidly beaned Hughie Jennings, another future Hall of Famer, with a rising fastball that today would be considered an illegal "quick pitch." (Rusie faked a pickoff throw to first base and then fired a pitch toward the plate. Jennings was flattened as the surprise pitch struck him near the temple. There was no balk rule on the books in 1897—it would be added to baseball's rules a year later—so Rusie's fake-throw/quick-pitch stunt was perfectly legal.) Nineteenth-

Fireball pitcher Amos Rusie, the "Hoosier Thunderbolt," was New York City's foremost baseball superstar of the 1890s. His speed and occasional wildness was downright terrifying to batters in the era before the 60'6" pitching distance and the establishment of the pitcher's mound and the balk rule (National Baseball Hall of Fame Library, Cooperstown, New York).

century ballplayers were certainly a tough lot, though. Jennings somehow managed to finish the final six innings of the game, but collapsed shortly afterwards. According to some sources, Jennings was comatose for four days.

How the quirky new pitching distance of 60'6" was actually established is something of a mystery. Some baseball historians believe the extra six inches resulted from a misunderstanding of the written instructions given to NL groundskeepers at the beginning of the 1893 season. Others believe it was a case of simple arithmetic: Five feet was simply added to what used to be the distance of the back line of the pitcher's box. Whatever the case, 60'6" became the standard pitching distance across all professional and amateur leagues. Moreover, pitchers were now required to toe a 12-inch-by-4-inch rubber slab placed at that distance from the back corner of home plate. No more running deliveries were allowed. (Two years later, in 1895, the size of the pitching rubber was increased by six inches to 24 inches, presumably to give the pitchers a little more horizontal latitude.)

The game obviously became better for the previously overmatched batters. For the first time in a decade, they had a decent chance to regularly put the ball into play. The desired result was achieved: Offensive numbers jumped significantly. On Opening Day 1893 in Cincinnati—with a lineup that featured Charles Comiskey playing first base—

the Reds soundly beat the Chicago Colts, 10–1, at League Park. Three other NL games played that Thursday afternoon saw scores of 7–2, 4–2 and 7–5. Runs and hits soon became more plentiful. Fans were grateful for a fairer contest between the pitcher and the batter, as it clearly made the action more compelling. Pitchers still shone on occasion, though. Bill Hawke of the Baltimore Orioles tossed the first no-hitter from the new pitching distance on August 16, 1893, in a 5–0 shutout victory over Washington. Overall, though, pitchers were certainly less effective and dominant than before the longer pitching distance was established. In 1893, Ted Breitenstein of the St. Louis Browns was the top NL hurler with an ERA of 3.18. It was more than a run greater than Cy Young's league-leading 1.93 ERA had been a year earlier. Hugh Duffy of the Boston Beaneaters led all NL batters in 1893 with a lofty .363 average. The previous season's leader was Dan Brouthers, who had batted just .335.

The pitching distance in MLB has remained unchanged for more than 120 years and there are no plans afoot to change it. The oddball distance remains a remarkable testament to the sport's rule-makers' ability to find a happy medium that favored neither the batter nor the pitcher too much. But should baseball fans totally discount the remarkable statistics from the pre–1893 days of the level-to-the-ground pitcher's box? No, says 19th-century baseball histo-

Baseball historians most frequently think of Hughie Jennings as the animated manager of the Detroit Tigers during the early years of the 20th century. Jennings had previously been a fine player in the 19th century, batting .401 for Baltimore in 1896. In the season following that stellar performance, Jennings was severely injured by an Amos Rusie fastball (Library of Congress, Harris and Ewing Collection).

rian Jonathan Stilwell. In a piece that appeared in a 2010 SABR newsletter, Stilwell frankly admits, "The pre-modern era deserves its own category for ranking, as the rules and standards were constantly evolving during these years." But he also states, "These pitchers' careers are gems worth knowing about. The modern baseball fan should understand this era and admire these pitchers, not ignore it and put its stars on a forgotten shelf."[3]

Somewhere in baseball's Valhalla, Matt Kilroy, Amos Rusie and Hoss Radbourn surely agree with those sentiments.

Chicago 1 at Cincinnati 10

Game played on Thursday, April 27, 1893, at League Park I

Chicago	ab	r	h	Cincinnati	ab	r	h
Caruthers rf	3	1	0	Latham 3b	4	3	2
Dahlen ss	3	0	1	Holliday cf	3	0	1

Chicago	ab	r	h		Cincinnati	ab	r	h
Ryan cf	4	0	1		McPhee 2b	4	1	2
Anson 1b	2	0	0		Vaughn c	5	1	0
Lange lf	3	0	0		Henry rf	5	2	1
Dungan 2b	4	0	1		Duffee lf	3	0	0
Parrott 3b	4	0	1		Smith ss	4	0	2
McGill p	0	0	0		Comiskey 1b	5	2	1
McGinnis p	3	0	0		Jones p	0	0	0
Kittridge c	3	0	0		Mullane p	5	1	2
Totals	29	1	4		Totals	38	10	11

Chicago	000	100	000—1
Cincinnati	040	020	31x—10

U–Emslie.

April 24, 1901

Site: South Side Park, Chicago

Teams: Cleveland Blues vs. Chicago White Stockings

Significance: First American League Game

Impact: A viable second major league is born, creating the modern version of MLB recognizable to contemporary baseball fans

> "Both before and since the founding of the American League at the turn of the [20th] century, there had been attempts to set up another major league, but only the American League has held its own with the National League. Today baseball fans who root for one or another of the American League teams tend also to identify with that league as a whole, and it can fairly be said that the friendly—if sometimes intense—rivalry between these leagues is as indigenous as apple pie and Mom."—Joel Zoss and John S. Bowman in *The American League: A History*

> "By 1900, baseball had grown from a children's game to a brawling pastime for big-city workers to a full-fledged industry, and the names and deeds of its greatest heroes had become familiar in every American home. But jealously and greed among the [National League's] owners, and a host of other ills—rowdy fans, dirty play, dissension among the players, and domination by a handful of seemingly invincible teams—threatened to destroy all that had been built."—Geoffrey C. Ward

> "Ban Johnson was the most brilliant baseball man the game has ever known. He was more responsible for making baseball the national game than anyone in the history of the sport."—Will Harridge, AL president from 1931 to 1959

It was raining in Detroit, Washington and Boston on April 24, 1901, but passable baseball weather showed itself in Chicago. Because of the inclement conditions elsewhere, the visiting Cleveland Blues (sometimes called the Bluebirds that season) and the Chicago White Sox had the stage all to themselves and thus played the first game in American League history that Wednesday afternoon at Chicago's South Side Park. "The American League has been launched as an act of popular favor," the May 4, 1901, edition of *The Sporting News* declared, "and never had any craft a more auspicious christening."

In that inaugural AL contest, the hometown White Sox prevailed before about 9,000 excited spectators. Aided by six bases on balls issued by Cleveland pitcher Bill Hoffer, Chicago jumped out to an insurmountable 8–0 lead after two innings and coasted to an

8–2 triumph. The game took just 90 minutes to complete. Hoffer, who had last pitched in the majors for the 1899 Pittsburgh Pirates, would go 3–8 in 1901 and vanish from MLB thereafter. Opening Day was a harbinger of how things would unfold during the 1901 season: Cleveland would struggle mightily throughout the schedule and finish in seventh place in the eight-team league, while Chicago would take the AL's inaugural pennant in a truly memorable and milestone season for MLB. In 1901 the White Stockings were managed by 31-year-old Clark Griffith, who had been instrumental in persuading many of the NL's stars to jump leagues after the 1900 season concluded. Doing double duty, Griffith would also win 24 games as a pitcher in the AL's debut season and lead the circuit with five shutouts and a winning percentage of .774. A fine hurler who relied more on finesse and guile than power, Griffith had won 152 games for the NL's Chicago Colts/Orphans franchise from 1893–1900. Teammate Jimmy Callahan called Griffith the cagiest pitcher who ever lived.

The American League was the baby of Byron Bancroft (Ban) Johnson, one of the most important figures in baseball history. He first gained fame as a sportswriter in Cincinnati, where he grew to dislike how the National League and most of its club owners ran their businesses. Photographs of Johnson invariably show him to be grim-faced but determined, much like a stern school principal. One contemporary of Johnson said he "looked like he had been weaned on an icicle." "The American League was Johnson's gift to baseball," wrote A. D. Suehsdorf. The baseball historian elaborated,

> As boss, Johnson found no task too large or too small to merit his attention. He located millionaires to bankroll his teams, came down hard on rowdies and roughhousing on the field, appointed managers, arranged trades, and apportioned players. He arranged schedules to spread travel costs equitably, interpreted rules, levied fines and suspensions, issued statistics, and even recruited William Howard Taft as the first President to throw out an Opening Day ball. One of his most important contributions was to enforce respect for umpires as symbols of baseball's integrity. He did it all with little grace and no humor. Johnson was hot-tempered, bull-headed, imperious, and uncompromising, not unlike many other tycoons of his time. But he was successful.[1]

In 1894, Johnson and his friend Charles Comiskey—who had recently been deposed as manager of the National League's Cincinnati Reds—took the reins of the financially troubled Western League. Johnson appointed himself president and embarked on micromanaging every aspect of the resurrected circuit. Within a very short time, the WL was the best-run of the plentiful minor professional leagues that dotted the North American continent. Increased attendance at WL games by women and children was especially noteworthy. Johnson's prestige skyrocketed. Foreseeing even greener pastures, in 1900 Johnson renamed the WL the American League.

At the turn of the 20th century, the time was ripe for a second major league. In 1900, Frank Richter, the editor of *Sporting Life*, bluntly criticized the NL moguls' methods of conducting their affairs. He claimed their personal ambitions were blinding them to the damage they were doing to the professional game as a whole. Richter accused the NL's owners of "gross individual and collective mismanagement." He further stated that the league was marred by the owners' "fierce factional fights, their cynical disregard for decency and honor, their open spoliation of each other, their deliberate alienation of [the] press and public, their flagrant disloyalty to friends and supporters, and their tyrannical treatment of players."[2] It was hardly a ringing endorsement of how the magnates of the top echelon of the national pastime went about their business. Yet the game still held its firm grip on the public's interest. At one point the *Boston Globe* assured its readers they would still get plenty of baseball coverage, even if "emperors may be shot down by the dozen, gigantic political frauds may be exposed, [and] steamships may collide and go down with all hands on board."[3]

The NL had operated as a monopoly since 1892. A cumbersome 12-team league was contracted to eight teams after the 1900 season. Johnson correctly sensed that there was a void to be filled—especially in Cleveland, Baltimore and Washington, three of the four cities that had suddenly lost their NL teams. Accordingly, in 1901 Johnson declared the AL a major league and began raiding the established NL teams' rosters. Baseball historian David Nemec wrote of the period, "In 1901, for the first time in a decade, there were two major leagues. Two years were to pass before they learned to coexist peacefully. In the meantime it was all-out war."[4]

At the time, the NL had a salary cap of $2,400 per player. Many of the NL's underpaid stars were only too glad to walk away from their NL contracts—the reserve clause be damned!—and sign with Johnson's fledgling circuit. Among the 100 or so notable star players who jumped leagues were Cy Young, Clark Griffith, Hugh Duffy, Jimmy Collins, Willie Keeler, John McGraw and Ed Delahanty. Such marquee names plying their trade in the new circuit gave the AL instant credibility. The most important acquisition for the AL, however, was Napoleon Lajoie, the game's best second baseman. Lajoie was a hugely popular fan favorite as a member of the NL's Philadelphia Phillies for his slick fielding and unparalleled offensive production. Johnson encouraged Philadelphia Athletics owner Connie Mack to make Lajoie an offer he could not refuse—a $6,000 annual salary. Lajoie did not have to be asked twice to join the A's. The Phillies, of course, were outraged, as was the entire NL establishment. In 1902, when a state court ruled that Lajoie could play professional baseball in Pennsylvania only for the Phillies, Johnson orchestrated Lajoie's transfer to the AL team in Cleveland as the battle for the hearts of fans continued.

With player raids becoming commonplace, the sport's two top leagues operated as bitter enemies throughout the 1902 season. In the five cities that had both NL and AL franchises (Boston, New York, Philadelphia, St. Louis, and Chicago), the AL team consistently drew larger crowds to its home games in every case. This trend was likely due to a combination of more competitive play (and perhaps better quality games) and cheaper admission prices at AL parks. NL teams charged 50 cents for general admission. In contrast, the ticket price for an AL game was just a quarter.

The atmosphere at AL parks was almost certainly more appealing than what routinely was on display at NL playing grounds. Realizing that respectable folks were turned off by uncivil behavior in the stands, Johnson insisted on well-policed facilities and the suppression of rowdyism. Johnson was obviously onto something as baseball fans favorably responded to the new league. The AL drew more than 2.22 million fans to its games in 1902, compared to 1.68 million fans who attended NL games that same season.

Johnson was especially harsh toward out-of-control players and managers who disrespected his league's umpires. An umpire in the NL often relied only on his own reputation and field presence to acquire respect, as he could expect little backing from his league. On the other hand, an AL umpire could consistently count on Johnson's unwavering support. Johnson disliked showboat arbiters, however. "A good umpire is the umpire you don't even notice. He's there all afternoon, but when the game is over you don't remember his name."[5] Fiery John McGraw of the new Baltimore Orioles, who had run roughshod over intimidated NL umpires for years as a player, found that Johnson's no-nonsense approach was not at all to his liking. Problems soon arose between the two

One of the major coups achieved by the American League in 1901 was Nap Lajoie's defection from the National League Phillies. Lajoie was the AL's first true superstar (Library of Congress, Harris and Ewing Collection).

men. After Johnson suspended McGraw for abusing AL umpires, McGraw took his act elsewhere. He headed back to the NL to manage the New York Giants in July 1902. Thus, inadvertently, Johnson started an NL dynasty. Not surprisingly, McGraw and Johnson became lifelong enemies.

By the 1903 season, most unbiased observers had to admit the AL was providing the superior product on the diamond. Deep down the NL moguls knew it too—and it was the NL that was asking for peace. In fact, many NL owners favored a merger between the two warring leagues. Johnson knew he had the upper hand, so he was not particularly interested in combining the AL and NL into a single organization. However, he did know that the ongoing player raids were harmful to baseball as a whole. A peace settlement was arranged that left the two leagues as distinct entities, but bound the clubs to respect the player contracts of both leagues. This set the stage for a golden era of MLB and the possibility of post-season play to determine an overall championship club. On their own initiative, the owners of the Boston AL club and Pittsburgh NL club—MLB's two league champions—arranged the first World Series in October 1903. After a year's hiatus, it became an annual spectacle in 1905. Johnson was appointed president of the AL for life and given an annual $25,000 salary by his league's happy owners.

Johnson remained the most powerful figure in MLB until 1919. That year's Black Sox Scandal caused an irreparable rift between him and his old pal Charles Comiskey when Johnson refused to investigate Comiskey's complaints that the World Series was fixed. After several highly publicized disagreements in the 1920s with the new generation of AL club owners that he could no longer hand-pick, and particularly with MLB's all-time biggest autocrat—Commissioner Kenesaw Landis—Johnson bitterly and unwillingly stepped down from AL presidency at the end of the 1927 season. In one of his last acts as AL boss, Johnson formally congratulated the New York Yankees via telegram for convincingly vanquishing the NL "enemy" Pittsburgh Pirates in the World Series in four straight games. Johnson died in St. Louis on March 28, 1931, at the age of 66. (Ironically, Johnson's successor, E. S. Bernard, had died earlier that same day.) Johnson was posthumously elected to the Hall of Fame in 1937.

It is not an overstatement to declare that Ban Johnson, by the sheer will of his personality and his drive to succeed, in the course of just a few years transformed the American League and all of professional baseball into a thriving enterprise. The solid foundation of the 21st-century game can be directly attributed to Johnson's actions in the first decade of the 20th century. In his book about MLB's great pioneering figures, *They Gave Us Baseball*, author John M. Rosenburg declared, "An ordinary man would have quailed at the thoughts of overcoming so many obstacles. But Ban Johnson was no ordinary man."[6]

Cleveland 2 at Chicago 8

Game played on Wednesday, April 24, 1901, at South Side Park

Cleveland	ab	r	h		Chicago	ab	r	h
Pickering rf	4	0	1		Hey cf	3	0	1
McCarthy lf	4	0	1		Jones rf	3	2	0
Genins cf	4	0	1		Mertes lf	4	2	1
LaChance 1b	4	1	0		Shugart ss	4	2	1
Bradley 3b	2	0	1		Isbell 1b	4	1	1
Beck 2b	3	0	1		Hartman 3b	3	0	0
Hallman ss	3	1	0		Brain 2b	3	0	1
Wood c	3	0	2		Sullivan c	4	1	2
Hoffer p	3	0	0		Patterson p	3	0	0
Totals	30	2	7		Totals	31	8	7

Cleveland	000 100 100—2	7	2
Chicago	350 000 00x—8	7	1

Cleveland	IP	H	R	BB	SO
Hoffer L(0–1)	8.0	7	8	6	1
Totals	7.0	7	8	6	1

Chicago	IP	H	R	BB	SO
Patterson W(1–0)	9.0	7	2	2	0
Totals	9.0	7	2	2	0

E–LaChance, Hallman; Hartman. DP–Cleveland 1; Chicago 1. 2B–Beck. LOB–Cleveland 3, Chicago 5. U–Tommy Connolly. T–1:30.

October 1, 1903

Site: Huntington Avenue Baseball Grounds, Boston

Teams: Pittsburgh Pirates vs. Boston Americans

Significance: First Modern World Series Game

Impact: Established the World Series as the climactic event of every MLB season

> "I always thought the first pitch of the World Series was one of the most delicious moments in all sports—a moment to be eagerly awaited, to be thoroughly enjoyed, and later to be savored like a rare wine."—Joe Falls in the October 21, 1972, edition of *The Sporting News*

> "The best thing that ever happened for baseball is the world's championship series between the two pennant winners, Pittsburgh and Boston. Nothing that has been done for the game in recent years has stirred up the interest than have these games."—J. Ed Grillo, *Cincinnati Commercial-Tribune*

> "That was probably the wildest World Series ever played. [There was] arguing all the time between the teams, between the players and the umpires, and especially between the players and the fans. That's the truth. The fans were part of the game in those days. They'd pour right out onto the field and argue with the players and the umpires."—Tommy Leach, as quoted in *The Glory of Their Times*

The modern World Series owes its very existence to Barney Dreyfuss, although few contemporary baseball fans have probably ever heard of him. It was not until 2008—76 years after his death—that Dreyfuss was rightfully enshrined in the National Baseball Hall of Fame, proving that he was unappreciated even by those who ought to know better.

Dreyfuss was the owner of the National League's Pittsburgh Pirates for 32 years. He was the personification of the American success story. A Jew who wanted to flee his homeland to avoid conscription in the German army, the bright, 19-year-old Dreyfuss arrived in the United States with just a few dollars in his pockets, some training as a bookkeeper and bank clerk, a limited grasp of English, and an invitation to work at his cousins' bourbon distillery in Paducah, KY. By applying himself at his job and also in night-school classes, Dreyfuss mastered the English language and became a successful businessman in a very short time.

Dreyfuss was a workaholic. A concerned physician advised him that it would be good for his overall well-being if he were to take up some type of recreation to relieve stress. Baseball was suggested. Dreyfuss immediately took a liking to the American game. The orderliness of batting lineups and the geometry of the diamond likely appealed to his heightened sense of organization. Dreyfuss played for a while on local amateur teams, but he found even greater joy in organizing and running ball clubs that he stocked with workers from his family's distillery. By 1892 Dreyfuss had graduated from running amateur baseball outfits to being part-owner of the NL's Louisville Colonels. When the NL voted to contract from 12 teams to eight for the 1900 season, Louisville was one of the four clubs to vanish. Dreyfuss had anticipated the move and had shrewdly bought 50 percent ownership of the Pittsburgh Pirates. He moved the best Louisville players to Pittsburgh—among them were Fred Clarke, Honus Wagner and Deacon Phillippe—and masterfully created the nucleus of a superb team.

Dreyfuss was among the first owners to recognize that the expanding popularity of professional baseball in the first decade of the 20th century meant that 19th century ballparks were becoming outdated, insufficient, and quite often embarrassing in their shortcomings. The Pirates' home grounds—Exposition Park—was especially awful. Located near the Allegheny River, it had lousy drainage and was prone to flooding. Important games in Pittsburgh were sometimes played with outfielders covering their positions in ankle-deep water. Critics justifiably denounced Exposition Park as "Lake Dreyfuss."

Dreyfuss used his clout and wealth to build a more suitable stadium for his team—Forbes Field. Opened in 1909, it was one of the first steel-and-concrete MLB ballparks. The days of wooden firetraps housing MLB teams were coming to an end—and not a moment too soon.

Dreyfuss was also one of the first owners to keep detailed statistics of every player, thus developing a better understanding of each player's weaknesses, strengths, and overall value to his team. Upon Dreyfuss' death at age 66 in 1932, his obituary in the *New York Times* said he had gained "the distinction of being the most thoroughly schooled baseball man to be found among club owners."[1] John Heydler, president of the NL at the time, claimed that Dreyfuss had "discovered more great players than any man in the game and his advice and counsel always were sought by his associates."[2]

However, Dreyfuss' most enduring contribution to MLB is the annual championship series that he grandiosely named the "World Series." As the 1903 season entered its final month, it was likely that Dreyfuss' Pirates would win their third consecutive NL pennant while the Boston Americans (sometimes called the Pilgrims) would cop the American League flag. Although the two leagues had operated separately and as bitter enemies since 1901, a tenuous peace had been declared in January 1903, with a "National Agreement" mainly to stop clubs from engaging in costly and disruptive inter-league player raids. "The contract-breaking, the player-jumping from league to league, the bickering and the name-calling that took place in baseball's infancy soured the fans to such an extent that the attendance in both leagues suffered drastically,"[3] wrote baseball historian Joseph L. Reichler of the era.

Although many of the NL's longstanding owners wanted nothing to do with the upstarts from the AL, Dreyfuss saw the cessation of hostilities as both an opportunity to make a lot of money and give fans what they wanted—an undisputed champion of Major League Baseball. In August, Dreyfuss penned a friendly missive to Pilgrims owner Henry Killilea which stated, "The time has come for the National League and American League to organize a World Series. It is my belief that if our clubs played a series on a best-of-nine basis, we would create great interest in baseball, in our leagues, and in our players. I also believe it would be a financial success."[4]

What Dreyfuss suggested was not intended as an annual event. It was merely a special truce-binding deal that would showcase MLB's two greatest teams that particular October. Killilea was delighted to accept the challenge. He had nothing to lose. NL owners and fans had denounced the AL as an inferior product since 1901. A victory by the Pilgrims over the mighty Pirates would put to rest any notions that the AL was a second-tier league. Killilea took Dreyfuss' letter to AL president Ban Johnson, who cherished the opportunity as well. Killilea informed Johnson that Boston manager Jimmy Collins was confident his pitching staff, led by the reliable Cy Young and Bill Dinneen, "would stop Honus Wagner, Fred Clarke, and those other batters."[5] Johnson needed no further convincing. He ordered the Pilgrims to defeat the Pirates.

Dreyfuss and Killilea met in Pittsburgh in early September to finalize their plans. A few bugs had to be worked out. Killilea thought a best-of-seven series would suffice, but Dreyfuss maintained that a nine-game series would determine a trucr champion. Dreyfuss got his way. It was also agreed that neither team could use any player acquired after August 31. The biggest stumbling block was money, of course. While the NL players' contracts ran through October 15, the AL players' contracts expired on September 30. Extending those players' services into October would require some negotiations. Dreyfuss

In 1903 Barney Dreyfuss, the owner of the Pittsburgh Pirates, challenged the AL champion Boston Pilgrims to the first World Series. In this photograph from 1913, Dreyfuss is on the right, seated next to National Commission president Garry Herrmann (Library of Congress, George Grantham Bain Collection).

suggested the players be given 70 percent of the gate receipts. The Pirates' players approved, but the Pilgrims unrealistically wanted the players to get 100 percent of the gate. Eventually the Pilgrims settled for the 70 percent of the gate receipts plus two extra weeks of pay. A two-man umpiring system—one arbiter from each league—would work the games. They were each paid the princely sum of $100 per contest. The Series would open in Boston with three games, move to Pittsburgh for the next four, and return to Boston for the eighth and ninth games if they were necessary. The final agreement for the inaugural World Series worked out by Killilea and Dreyfuss was just one page long.

However, some Boston players failed to get the memo. One September 25 the Boston morning newspapers had reported that the squabble over how the World Series profits would be split was irreconcilable and the Series had been cancelled. Although there were a handful of games left on Boston's schedule—the Pilgrims had the luxury of playing their final 21 games at home!—they had already clinched the AL pennant with plenty of room to spare. (Boston would finish atop the AL with an excellent 91–47 record, 14½ games ahead of second-place Philadelphia.) With the league title sewed up, pitcher Cy Young and catcher Lou Criger had been given permission to go home. When a last-minute deal was brokered to save the World Series, panicked player/manager Jimmy Collins had to track down his formidable Young-Criger battery. He found them, in the nick of time, at a railroad station near the Pilgrims' ballpark. They were just a few minutes away from catching a train to take them to their respective winter homes in the Midwest.

Freddy Parent, Boston's shortstop, lucidly recalled in a 1968 *Sports Illustrated* interview when he was 92 years old, "We didn't have much communication with management in those days."[6]

Pittsburgh entered the 1903 World Series with unexpected pitching problems. The Pirates, who had won six consecutive games by shutout in June to begin a 15-game winning streak, now suddenly found themselves in a weakened state on the mound. Righthander Sam Leever had developed a sore arm but gamely tried to pitch through it. Lefthander Ed Doheny had serious mental health issues. At one point in the season he convinced himself he was being followed by detectives. To give the imaginary sleuths the slip, Doheny went back home to Massachusetts for a time. A sub-headline in the *Pittsburgh Post*'s July 29 edition unsympathetically said of Doheny, "His Mind is Thought to be Deranged." For a while Doheny returned to the Pirates and compiled a very good 16–8 record. However, on September 22, he was granted a leave of absence from the club which turned out to be permanent. (Doheny's personal problems climaxed during the World Series. On October 10 a visiting physician was summarily ejected head-first from Doheny's house. The next day Doheny attacked a male nurse with a cast-iron stove leg. Doheny's troubled wife summoned police. Doheny held them off for a while, threatening to kill anyone who tried to capture him. Eventually the volatile situation was defused and Doheny was promptly shipped off to a mental institution in Danvers, MA, where he lived until his death in 1916.) Honus Wagner, heralded by *The Sporting News* that season as the game's best all-around player, was nowhere near his best entering October. He was quietly laboring with thumb and leg injuries that had kept him out of nine games in September.

The greatest National League star of the first decade of the 20th century was Honus Wagner, who won eight NL batting titles. Playing injured in the 1903 World Series, his statistics were far below his normal production. Wagner ignominiously struck out to end the Series (Library of Congress, George Grantham Bain Collection).

Optimism ran high in Pittsburgh despite the Pirates' lineup troubles. A headline in the October 1 *Pittsburgh Gazette* startlingly claimed, "Pirates in Fine Shape to Face Boston Americans." NL president Harry C. Pulliam exuded the utmost confidence in his league's champs. He said, "While the Bostons have a good team, the Pirates outclass them at every point, I think. They are the greatest aggregation of ballplayers that ever stepped onto a field."[7] Nevertheless, given Wagner's nagging injuries and the prominent gaps in Pittsburgh's starting pitching, the healthier Boston club seemed more likely to triumph. The September 30 edition of the *Boston Globe* neutrally and diplomatically declared the Series to be a toss-up.

Excitement pervaded both cities as the baseball fans knew something extraordinary was about to occur. The September 30 *Boston Post* giddily proclaimed, "Tomorrow at Huntington Avenue, what is expected to be the greatest series in the history of baseball will begin. Interest all over the city and by all classes is at fever heat. In the downtown hotels and sporting resorts last evening, nothing else was talked of."

The first modern World Series game took place at Boston's Huntington Avenue Baseball Grounds on Thursday, October 1, 1903. There was an overflow crowd, to say the least. One of the most famous baseball photos of that era shows the chaos before Game One as unrestrained fans swarmed onto the field to try to find some vantage point from which to watch the historic game. Other photos in the next day's Boston newspapers showed policemen using night sticks and rubber hoses to drive back the crowd. The tiny ballpark was simply too confined to accommodate everyone who wanted to see the historic contest, even though ticket prices for grandstand seats were raised to $1 apiece, double the cost of a regular-season game. Even standing room passes cost 50 cents. The official attendance was 16,242, but thousands more were probably present. There was considerable grumbling from patrons that the cost of a scorecard at the ballpark—a virtual necessity to follow the action in that era—had tripled from a nickel to 15 cents.

However, it was the Pirates who prevailed rather easily, 7–3, in the first game. Cy Young started well, as expected, for Boston. The first two Pirates were retired without too much trouble. Leadoff hitter Ginger Beaumont flied out to center fielder Chick Stahl. Next up was Fred Clarke, who harmlessly popped out to catcher Lou Criger. The home fans predictably cheered wildly. Young got two quick strikes on Tommy Leach … and then the wheels suddenly fell off. Leach connected for a ground-rule triple to right field. (Any fair batted ball that rolled into the spectators standing in the outfield behind outstretched ropes was deemed an automatic three-bagger.) Honus Wagner promptly drove home Leach with a solid base hit to left field to record the first RBI in World Series history, giving the visitors a fast 1–0 lead.

The boisterous pro–Boston crowd grew sullen and concerned. The Pirates were not through with their first-inning rally. Wagner, who had swiped 46 bases during the regular season with an ungainly yet powerful running style, easily stole second base when Criger seemed unusually slow in releasing his throw to second baseman Hobe Ferris. Ferris himself, usually a sure-handed infielder, botched Kitty Bransfield's routine grounder to extend the visitors' inning. With Wagner on third base, Bransfield broke for second base on the next pitch—which Criger threw wildly into center field. Wagner trotted home easily and Bransfield advanced to third base. Pittsburgh led, 2–0. A good many people looked suspiciously at Criger, who had committed just ten errors in 661 fielding chances in 1903. Boston baseball writer Tim Murnane—who had played for the Boston Red Caps in the first-ever NL game back in 1876—said Criger "looked like a fur overcoat in July."[8] Grumbling about the possibility of a rigged outcome was heard throughout the stands. Eventually Young surrendered four runs (three unearned) before the side was retired. The *Pittsburgh Post* reported that the hometown crowd was largely silent, while the traveling band of 300 Pirate rooters who had made the trip to Boston were "indulging in the wildest kind of antics."[9] Barney Dreyfuss was among the most vocal.

Entering the bottom of the seventh inning, Pittsburgh held a commanding 7–0 lead.

The usually dominant Denton True ("Cy") Young pitched the very first inning of World Series play on October 1, 1903. When he gave up four runs in that frame, a few eyebrows were raised (Library of Congress).

The Pilgrims could not recover from the early deficit and lost, 7–3. The game took one hour and 55 minutes to play. Deacon Phillippe was the winning pitcher for Pittsburgh, striking out ten Boston batters. Both he and Young went the distance. Remarkably, Phillippe would pitch five complete games in the Series totaling 44 innings—two World Series records that will surely stand forever. When the Series concluded, Dreyfuss rewarded Phillippe for his stalwart work by giving him ten shares of stock in the Philadelphia Traction Company, the business that operated most of the trolley lines in Pittsburgh.

Young took the loss bitterly and sought redemption. "I am deeply disappointed," he said. "Those Pittsburgh fellows can hit the ball. I had my usual speed and my curves broke as sharp [*sic*] as ever. I want another chance at them. I think I can turn the tables."[10]

Was the first modern World Series game ever played tainted by dishonesty? We will never know for certain. However, crookedness would be totally incongruous with Cy Young's career. He was so virtuous and respected throughout baseball that he was routinely cheered in rival teams' ballparks. Such was Young's reputation for fairness and honesty that on a handful of occasions when the game's umpire was either delayed or absent, Young was called upon to call balls and strikes. He was that honest!

To Pittsburgh fans, the relatively easy win in the opening game created a sense that the World Series would be a romp. John H. Gruber of the *Pittsburgh Post* wrote, almost with a tinge of arrogance, "There is gloom in old Boston town tonight, and the gloom is intensified by the knowledge that Pittsburgh has the faster team in every respect. The work put up by the National League champions simply made the Boston men look like counterfeit money. Local fans cannot see how their team is going to win a game, let alone a series."[11]

NL president Harry C. Pulliam shared the Pirates fans' sense of joy. "Today held the happiest hours of my baseball life," he told *The Sporting News*. "I saw the champions of my [National] League show their superiority over their rival champions of the American League. No matter how the remaining games of the world's championship series terminate, Pittsburgh's baseball team, the greatest in the country, cannot be deprived of the glory earned on the diamond here."

After four games, confidence in the Pirates' chances to win the Series seemed wholly justified. Under threatening skies the following day, Boston played quite well and won Game Two, 3–0, as Bill Dinneen gave up just three singles for the victors in front of fewer than 10,000 fans. (The significant drop in attendance was attributed to the home team's poor play in Game One. Quietly, though, suspicions about the game's honesty may have been a contributing factor as well.) Still, even with their depleted pitching staff and Wagner at less than top form, Pittsburgh won both Game Three and Game Four of the World Series—but then they were completely outclassed the rest of the way. Not once in the final four contests did the Pirates hold the lead. Boston won three consecutive games in Pittsburgh by scores of 11–2, 6–3, and 7–3. The Series concluded back in Boston on Tuesday, October 13, with Bill Dinneen whiffing Honus Wagner on a full count to complete a dominant 3–0 shutout. Tim Murnane, writing in the *Boston Globe*, declared that when Wagner swung at and missed Dinneen's final offering, the roar from the jubilant Boston crowd sounded like "a thousand lions doing their prettiest."[12]

In the eight games, Boston outscored Pittsburgh, 39–24. Wagner slumped badly in the final four games of the Series. He was just 1-for-14 at the plate in those contests after going 5-for-13 in the first four games, giving him a disappointing overall .222 batting average for the World Series—hardly representative of the numbers usually put up by the man who was far and away the NL's best hitter in the first decade of the 20th century. Boston supporters joyously jeered the Pittsburgh star by mockingly showering the field with confetti whenever he came to bat. Freddy Parent recalled 65 years later, "Wagner was hurt and wouldn't speak to me on the field or right after the Series. I'm afraid he choked."[13] Wagner would get just one more opportunity to play in a World Series. Six autumns later, in 1909, his Pirates beat Ty Cobb's Detroit Tigers in seven games. Wagner had a much better outing than he had in 1903. This time he batted .333, drove in seven runs, and stole six bases. In 1957, *The Sporting News* selected the greatest MLB players of all time by position. To no one's surprise, Wagner was chosen as the shortstop. The publication noted that Wagner, who had died in 1955, had no serious rival for the honor.

Dinneen was Boston's pitching star of the 1903 World Series. He won three games, including two by shutout. Happy Boston fans triumphantly carried Dinneen off the field on their shoulders. A dead arm ended Dinneen's pitching career in late August of 1909. Less than three weeks later, Ban Johnson gave him a one-month trial as an AL umpire. It was a very successful career switch; Dinneen enjoyed a 28-year career as an arbiter. Half a century after his 1903 post-season heroics for Boston, Dinneen made a special appearance at Game Two of the 1953 World Series to throw out a ceremonial ball, which he did with surprising snap for a man in his 70s. The occasion was the 50th anniversary of the World Series. Barney Dreyfuss' idea had indeed caught on and thrived.

How had Boston managed to turn a 1–3 series deficit into a 5–3 triumph? Parent explained, "We just couldn't get started. We didn't get the breaks in those first four games. We were hitting the ball hard—and we were a hitting team—but it would go straight to someone, or one of the Pittsburgh players would come up with a sensational catch. [Pirates first baseman] Kitty Bransfield caught one that I hit. As I ran past him, he himself said he was a lucky SOB. After we started getting the breaks, we could have beaten them 50 games easy."[14] (Like Dinneen, Bransfield would also have a second MLB career as an umpire. His tenure was brief, lasting through the 1917 season only. Curiously, all of Bransfield's 156 umpiring assignments were on the bases.)

Despite less than ideal weather for many of the eight games, and the lingering suspicion that the first game may have been fixed, more than 100,000 fans paid to watch the historic battles of the 1903 World Series—about the same total number of spectators who had attended Boston's home games throughout the entire regular season. Gate receipts for the Series exceeded $55,000, a fantastic sum for the era. Most everyone agreed the World Series had been a smashing success on all levels and ought to be an annual climax to every MLB season. Seventy-five years after that groundbreaking first World Series was played, Joseph L. Reichler opined,

> It is almost impossible to picture baseball without this spectacular climax to the season, for what would the pennant races mean if the goal were not a place in the World Series? It is quite conceivable that without the tremendous popular interest in the World Series, Major League Baseball would not have survived the destructive influence of wars and depressions. Certainly baseball minus a World Series would lose its vibrancy.[15]

Regardless of the prestige, the vast media attention, and the enormous sums of money now associated with the Fall Classic, the 1903 World Series will always retain its historic importance as the start of something special. Misters Dreyfuss and Killilea, with great foresight, had established a championship structure for MLB that would guide the sport through many tumultuous times.

Pittsburgh 7 at Boston 3

Game played on Thursday, October 1, 1903, at Huntington Ave. Baseball Grounds

Pittsburgh Pirates	ab	r	h	rbi		Boston Americans	ab	r	h	rbi
Beaumont cf	5	1	0	0		Dougherty lf	4	0	0	0
Clarke lf	5	0	2	0		Collins 3b	4	0	0	0
Leach 3b	5	1	4	1		Stahl cf	4	0	1	0
Wagner ss	3	1	1	1		Freeman rf	4	2	2	0
Bransfield 1b	5	2	1	0		Parent ss	4	1	2	1
Ritchey 2b	4	1	0	0		LaChance 1b	4	0	0	2
Sebring rf	5	1	3	4		Ferris 2b	3	0	1	0
Phelps c	4	0	1	0		Criger c	3	0	0	0
Phillippe p	4	0	0	0		O'Brien ph	1	0	0	0
						Young p	3	0	0	0
						Farrell ph	1	0	0	0
Totals	40	7	12	6		Totals	35	3	6	3

Pittsburgh   401 100 100—7 12 2
Boston   000 000 201—3 6 4

Pittsburgh Pirates	IP	H	R	ER	BB	SO
Phillippe W (1–0)	9.0	6	3	2	0	10
Totals	9.0	6	3	2	0	10

Boston Americans	IP	H	R	ER	BB	SO
Young L (0–1)	9.0	12	7	3	3	5
Totals	9.0	12	7	3	3	5

E–Leach (1), Wagner (1), Ferris 2 (2), Criger 2 (2). 3B–Pittsburgh Leach 2 (2, off Young 2); Brans-
field (1, off Young), Boston Freeman (1, off Phillippe); Parent (1, off Phillippe). HR–Pittsburgh
Sebring (1, 7th inning off Young 0 on, 1 out). SF–LaChance 2 (2, off Phillippe 2). HBP–Ferris (1,
by Phillippe). SB–Wagner (1, 2nd base off Young/Criger); Bransfield (1, 2nd base off Young/
Criger); Ritchey (1, 2nd base off Young/Criger). CS–Leach (1, Home by Young/Criger). HBP–
Phillippe (1, Ferris). U–Hank O'Day (NL), Tom Connolly (AL). T–1:55. A–16,242.

September 23, 1908

Site: Polo Grounds V, New York

Teams: Chicago Cubs vs. New York Giants

Significance: "Bonehead" Merkle Game

Impact: Baserunning rules are confirmed that require runners to advance to forced bases on walkoff hits; the lives of Fred Merkle and Harry Pulliam take irrevocably negative turns

> "Fred Merkle experienced something that made Bill Buckner's 1986 World Series nightmare seem like a quick dance in the spring rain."—ESPN's Keith Olbermann, discussing the infamous Merkle game on its 105th anniversary in 2013

> "When Bridwell shot that long single, I started across the grass for the clubhouse. Matty was near me. When Evers began shouting for the ball, he noticed something was wrong. Matty caught me by the arm and told me to wait a minute. We walked over toward 2B, and Matty spoke to [umpire] Emslie. 'How about this, Bob, is there any trouble with the score of the play?' 'It's all right,' said Emslie. 'You've got the game. I don't see anything wrong with the play.' Matty then took me by the arm and we walked to the clubhouse confident that we had won the game."—Fred Merkle, recalling the events of September 23, 1908

> "During his 16 years in the majors, he played for the Giants, Brooklyn Robins (Dodgers), Chicago Cubs and New York Yankees. With Merkle, each of these teams advanced to the World Series, totaling six times. Throughout his career, he displayed a blend of speed and power. He had eight seasons with 20 or more stolen bases and a solid .273 career batting average in an era dominated by pitching and defense. Teammates and opponents considered Merkle one of the smartest players in the game. Merkle was the only player who Giants manager John McGraw consulted on strategic decisions."—an excerpt from the commemorative plaque at Fred Merkle Field in Watertown, WI

    The most controversial game in the history of MLB occurred on Wednesday, September 23, 1908, at New York City's Polo Grounds during a heated pennant race between two National League archrivals. The major parties involved were a wily Chicago Cubs veteran infielder; an unfortunate, naïve, teenage rookie substitute for the New York Giants; two well respected but beleaguered umpires; a reluctant, harried and moody league president; and a large supporting cast of characters. In the end, the letter of the law was held to a higher standard than commonplace baseball tradition. It was a keystone ruling that greatly affected the final NL standings of 1908—and it all came about because of the force-play rule.

    Baseball rules pertaining to the scoring of runs are fairly simple. A team scores a run when a batter becomes a baserunner and safely advances to all four bases before three outs are made against his team. There are some important exceptions, however. Regardless of how fast a runner may be, no run can score if the third out of the inning is due to a batter not reaching first base safely. This scenario occurs if the batter strikes out, if the batter is retired at first base on a ground ball, if the batter hits a ball that is caught in the air, if the batter is called out for interference—or if any baserunner is retired for the third out on a force play.

What's the definition of a force play? A force play occurs whenever a runner is forced to leave his base and advance to the next base because of the batter becoming a baserunner. It is a ground ball on which a runner is retired by a member of the defensive team, who is in possession of the ball, by touching the base ahead of the oncoming runner who is forced to advance. (A tag on the runner is not necessary to record an out, but it is permitted, of course.) Most players learn these things at a very young age playing youth baseball and accept them without question. It is a rare player today who actually makes the effort to read the sport's rule book to study its finer points. It was equally as rare for a player in 1908 to do so, even one playing in the major leagues.

Occasionally some thoughtful fans wondered about the implications of the force-play rule. One submitted the following question to the *Chicago Tribune*'s popular baseball question-and-answer column. It appeared in print on Sunday, July 19, 1908. "In the last half of the ninth with the score tied, two men out and a runner on third, the batter hits to left field and the runner scores. The batter, seeing the runner score, stops between home and first. The ball is thrown to the first baseman who touches his base before [the] runner reaches it. Can [the] runner [from third base] score on this?" The columnist, citing what was then Rule 59, correctly said no.

From 1901–1913, three teams dominated the National League: the Pittsburgh Pirates, Chicago Cubs, and New York Giants. None of the other five NL clubs won a pennant during that long stretch. The Honus Wagner-led Pirates were baseball's most dominant club from 1901–1903. They won a fourth pennant in 1909. The New York Giants copped the laurels in 1904 and 1905. The Chicago Cubs started a dynasty beginning in 1906 when they won the remarkable total of 116 games while losing just 36. (Somehow, though, the Cubs managed to lose the 1906 World Series to the light-hitting AL champion Chicago White Sox in six games in a startling upset.) The Cubs repeated as pennant winners in 1907, this time emerging victorious in the World Series versus Ty Cobb's Detroit Tigers. The 1908 NL pennant chase would quickly become a three-team battle featuring the only clubs that had won pennants during the 20th century. None of the other five NL clubs finished within 15 games of the dominant threesome, and throughout the exciting and memorable season Pittsburgh, New York and Chicago continually leapfrogged each other in the standings, with none of the frontrunners ever being more than six games out of first place.

One the morning of July 17, with most teams having played about 80 games, the Pirates were atop the NL standings, half a game ahead of the Giants and two ahead of the Cubs. After August 19, the Pirates still led the NL field with the Giants one game in arrears and the Cubs 4½ games back. By September 11 the Giants had vaulted into the top spot with Pittsburgh 1½ games behind and the Cubs just two games off the pace. No other team was within sight of the leaders. In fact, three teams—Boston, Brooklyn, and St. Louis—had already been mathematically eliminated from pennant contention. Every game that featured a matchup between the three contenders was obviously going to be critical. Fans in all three cities followed the results carefully. Newspapers would create batter-by-batter results in their extensive coverage of the pennant chase. Crowds gathered in front of saloons, newspaper offices, and elsewhere to get up-to-the minute results on all the key NL contests.

Johnny Evers' heads-up play on September 23, 1908, caused Fred Merkle to be retired on a force out. New York Giants manager John McGraw always maintained his team had been swindled out of the 1908 NL pennant. In more peaceful times, Evers and McGraw enjoy a friendly chat (Library of Congress, George Grantham Bain Collection).

One of those important games was played at Pittsburgh's Exposition Park on Friday, September 4. The Pirates edged the Cubs, 1–0, that afternoon in ten innings. As it turned out, the most remarkable part of the game was a critical call that was not made in the bottom of the tenth. Years later, Cubs shortstop Johnny Evers declared, "It was 19 days earlier, at Pittsburgh, when we really won that game in New York."[1]

A native of Troy, NY, Johnny Evers is likely known to today's fans mostly for being part of the Tinker-to-Evers-to-Chance double play combination during the Chicago Cubs' glory years. It was not an especially prolific twin-killing threesome. Research has shown that they were never better than fourth in the NL in double plays in any given season. Nevertheless they were made famous in "Baseball's Sad Lexicon"—a short poem by baseball scribe Franklin P. Adams written in 1910, and created only because he had a few lines to fill in his column—thus providing the Cubs' infield threesome with a unique brand of immortality. Individually, Evers was a terrific ballplayer. Baseball historian David Shiner, in his SABR biography of Evers, said of the Cubs' truculent infielder,

Johnny Evers was considered one of the Deadball Era's smartest and best all-around players, but he was just as well known for his fiery disposition. The star second baseman's nickname, "The Human Crab," was origi-nally bestowed due to his unorthodox manner of sidling over to ground balls before gobbling them up, but most baseball men considered it better suited to his temperament than his fielding. A 5'9", 125 lb. pepper-pot with a protruding jaw that came to be a symbol of the man, for he was always jawing about something, Evers developed a reputation as a troublemaker by squabbling regularly with teammates, opponents, and especially umpires. "They claim he is a crab, and perhaps they are right," said Cleveland Indians manager Joe Birmingham. "But I would like to have 25 such crabs playing for me. If I did, I would have no doubts over the pennant. They would win hands down."

Because Evers' off-putting personality made him a bit of a loner, he did not socialize much with teammates or anyone else. That gave him plenty of time and solitude to read baseball's rule book. During one perusal he noticed that the force-play rule had no time limit attached to it, nor did it give any exemption to game-winning hits. At the time, it was customary at all levels of baseball that a game ended when the winning run crossed home plate in the bottom of the ninth inning or the bottom of an extra inning, regardless of what trailing runners did or did not do. Seemingly nobody enforced the rule that a trailing runner, if forced to advance by the base hit, had to advance at least one base to nullify a potential force play. Evers made a mental note of the situation and vowed to make an issue of it if such a scenario ever arose.

It arose for the first—but not last—time on September 4, 1908. In the first game of a two-game series, the Cubs were battling the Pirates in a 0–0 deadlock at Pittsburgh's Exposition Park. In the bottom of the tenth inning, the Pirates loaded the bases with two outs. On what appeared to be a game-winning hit to center field, the runner at first base, Warren (Doc) Gill, left the diamond without bothering to touch second base. Evers, standing on second base, called for the ball to be relayed to him while the Pirates celebrated their apparent extra-inning triumph. When he got the ball Evers immediately stepped on the bag and demanded that Hank O'Day—the only umpire working that day's game—rule the play a force out, which, strictly according to the rules, would nullify the run and end the inning. Since Gill's maneuver was completely customary in those days, O'Day refused to make the force-out call that Evers was seeking despite the fact that Evers was technically correct.

Evers also had historical precedent on his side, although he was likely unaware of it. Nine years earlier, in a Western League game contested on June 11, 1899, the very same play occurred. St. Paul trailed Indianapolis, 12–11, in the bottom of the ninth inning. Facing Doc Newton with two out, St. Paul's pitcher, Chauncey Fisher, singled to bring home teammate Frank Shugart with the tying run and advance catcher Harry Spies to third base. Eddie Burke then lined a single to George Hogriever in center field to drive in Spies with the apparent winning run. Before running to second base, however, Fisher stupidly stopped to congratulate Burke for his hit. Hogriever noticed Fisher's gaffe and sprinted to second base with the ball in his hand. Hogriever appealed to umpire Al Manassau to call Fisher out on the force play and nullify the run. He did—but not until the crowd had streamed on the field and players from both teams had left the diamond, wrongly believing St Paul had won the game. When the umpire was unable to clear the field and resume play, the game was ruled a 12–12 tie.

In the wake of the trouble that occurred 19 days later at the Polo Grounds, O'Day would later claim in the Pittsburgh game that he was focused on the run crossing home plate rather than anything that did or did not occur at second base. (At the very least, it was a persuasive argument to end the antiquated one-umpire system that was still used frequently in MLB solely to save money.) The Pirates won, 1–0, and moved within a half-game of league-leading New York. The loss put Chicago two games in arrears. Umpire O'Day was a former MLB pitcher. He had starred on the New York Giants' pennant-winning team of 1889, compiling a 9–1 record in limited service. In 1890 he won 22 games for the Players' League Giants.

A pitcher for the New York Giants championship team of 1889, Hank O'Day clearly did not favor his old club when he ruled Fred Merkle out on a force play on September 23, 1908, turning a 2–1 Giants win into an abandoned 1–1 tie. Nineteen days earlier, O'Day had not ruled Pittsburgh's Doc Gill out on the same play because he claimed he did not see Gill's baserunning error. O'Day's Hall of Fame plaque specifically mentions his role in the most famous force play in MLB history. O'Day is pictured here at the 1916 World Series, second from the right (Library of Congress, George Grantham Bain Collection).

Years later Evers recalled in an interview, "That night O'Day came to look me up [at the team's hotel], which was an unusual thing in itself. Sitting in a corner in the lobby, he told me that he wanted to discuss the play. O'Day then agreed that my play was legal and that under the circumstances, a runner coming down from first and not touching second on the final base hit was out."[2] Whether this alleged meeting between O'Day and Evers actually occurred is anyone's guess. O'Day was almost as reclusive as Evers so it is difficult to imagine that the umpire would make such an extraordinary visit. Be that as it may, the incident at Exposition Park on September 4 undoubtedly had a profound effect on the umpire, as events 19 days later at the Polo Grounds clearly demonstrated. Although Evers had failed to persuade O'Day to rule Gill out on a force play, he had succeeded in planting seeds of doubt in the mind of one of the NL's foremost arbiters.

Pittsburgh owner Barney Dreyfuss figured the NL pennant would come down to a two-team race between his club and the Cubs. Dreyfuss told *The Sporting News*' Pittsburgh correspondent that the Giants' pitching staff was too weak overall to successfully challenge for the NL championship. Dreyfuss was wrong. The Giants embarked on an 11-game winning streak to keep the three-team race very much alive.

As the calendar approached the end of September, baseball fever engulfed New York City. Joe Vila wrote in the September 24 edition of *The Sporting News*,

New York is baseball mad just now and thousands of wild-eyed fans are rooting for the Giants. After making the St. Louis Cardinals look cheap, the Giants faced the Pittsburghs in a double-header last Friday. The biggest crowd that ever sat around a diamond saw these battles, both of which were won in easy style by [manager John] McGraw's Hustlers. The increased seating capacity at the Polo Grounds enabled perhaps 27,000 fans to see the fun.... The Pittsburghs played as if they were half scared to death, and when the day was over everybody wondered how Dreyfuss's team ever got up so high.

The Giants' winning streak, however, ended with a 6–2 Pirates victory on September 19. Pittsburgh won the next game too, 2–1, before leaving town. On September 22 the Cubs arrived in New York City for a four-game series. On Tuesday the clubs played a doubleheader. Chicago won both hard-fought games by scores of 4–3 and 3–1. The suddenly cold Giants' four-game losing skein meant the two teams were in a virtual tie for first place, with the Pirates just 1½ games back.

A single game was scheduled for Wednesday, September 23. Fred Tenney, the Giants' regular first baseman, woke up that morning with a case of lumbago. He was unable to play; it was the only game the stalwart Tenney missed in the entire 1908 season. Manager John McGraw was forced to insert Fred Merkle into the Giants' lineup in Tenney's place. Merkle would bat seventh, between Moose McCormick and Al Bridwell. Although Merkle had some experience under his belt as a substitute, this would be his first MLB start. He was 19 years old and eager to show that he belonged in the majors. In his 35 appearances with the Giants thus far, Merkle had impressed the sportswriters with his baseball smarts. Merkle, declared Sid Mercer of the *New York Globe*, was a "fellow who uses intelligence in everything he does."[3] In a brief report on the Giants rookie a few weeks earlier, *Sporting Life* said Merkle showed "plenty of pepper ... and good judgment on the bases."[4] Based on what Merkle had shown so far in 1908, McGraw had the utmost confidence in his substitute first baseman.

Neither team's pitcher was completely fit on September 23. Christy Mathewson of the Giants complained to McGraw that he was tired. He had a right to feel worn out. Statistically, the 1908 season was perhaps Mathewson's greatest. He started 44 games, completed 34 and finished nine others that he did not start. Mathewson compiled a tremendous 37–11 record while pitching 390⅔ innings. Jack Pfiester, a Cubs' left-hander,

MERKLE, N. Y. NAT'L

Despite enjoying a fine career spanning 20 MLB seasons, Fred Merkle will never be separated from his baserunning gaffe that may have cost the New York Giants the 1908 NL pennant (Library of Congress, Benjamin K. Edwards Collection).

was battling a sore tendon in his pitching arm. It was sheer agony for Pfiester to throw his curve ball, but manager Frank Chance needed him on the mound because of his reputation as a "Giant killer." Pfiester would throw mainly fastballs to the Giants the entire game.

Through the first four innings the teams exchanged zeroes on the scoreboard as Mathewson and Pfiester generally stifled the offenses. The Cubs had made two errors, but timely double plays had gotten them out of trouble each time. In the top of the fifth inning there was a scoring breakthrough. With one out and no runners on base, Joe Tinker came to the plate. Tinker always fared well against Mathewson. Earlier in the game he had launched a line drive that was heading toward right field. Merkle made a skillful grab to retire the Cubs' shortstop. This time Tinker rapped a fastball for an inside-the-park home run. Outfielder Mike Donlin made a mess of the play when he tried to use his leg to stop the ball from skidding past him. Tinker circled the bases easily when the ball eluded Donlin's grasp—and his leg.

The Giants rallied in the bottom of the sixth inning to level the game. Buck Herzog reached first base on an infield single and advanced to second on a throwing error. Roger Bresnahan laid down an excellent sacrifice bunt to move Herzog to third base. Mike Donlin atoned for his clumsy fielding with a base hit that scored Herzog. The game was tied, 1–1. No further scoring occurred in the frame, but there was a moment of comic relief to break the growing tension: While running to second base on a ground ball, Donlin inadvertently collided with base umpire Bob Emslie and knocked the arbiter's hairpiece askew.

Heading into the bottom of the ninth inning, the Cubs were happy to be still in the game. They had sent just 30 batters to the plate to face Mathewson—three above the minimum. Defensively they had committed three errors. Yet they were locked in a tie game. The Giants had managed only four hits themselves as the bottom of the ninth inning began. Cy Seymour led off the home half of the ninth with a groundout to Johnny Evers, but Pfiester surrendered a single to Art Devlin that enlivened the partisan crowd.

Moose McCormick, the next batter, slapped what could have been an inning-ending double–play ball to Joe Tinker. After Tinker tossed the ball to Evers, Devlin broke up the play with a hard slide. Typically, Evers raged at Devlin, but it was a completely legal play. McCormick was at first base with two outs. The next batter was Fred Merkle, as darkness began to settle over the Polo Grounds. In his three previous trips to the plate, Merkle had twice grounded out weakly and drawn a walk. Pfiester got two quick strikes on Merkle, but the teenager smacked a fair ball into right field. It may have been possible for Merkle to try to stretch the play into a double, but he cautiously stopped at first base. It was the sensible thing to do as McCormick advanced to third base on the play. The Polo Grounds was in bedlam.

Al Bridwell, the eighth hitter in the lineup, was next to bat. Although he had made good contact in three previous at-bats, Bridwell was hitless. Before Bridwell stepped into the batter's box, he motioned to Merkle to take a smaller lead at first base. There was no point in risking a pickoff. Merkle retreated closer to the bag. The first pitch from Pfiester was a belt-high fastball. Bridwell made solid contact. It was a clean single that flew into center field. It nearly struck base umpire Emslie, who flopped to the turf to get out of the way.

Chaos broke loose. McCormick easily trotted home with the apparent winning run in a 2–1 triumph for the home team. Bridwell reached first base. The excited fans poured

Top: Harry ("Moose") McCormick was the New York Giants baserunner who was deprived of scoring the winning run on September 23, 1908, because of Fred Merkle's mistake. *Bottom:* Al Bridwell connected for the apparent game-winning hit in the Merkle game, only to have it nullified on the delayed force play (Library of Congress, George Grantham Bain Collection).

onto the field. Merkle did what hundreds of runners had done before him in similar circumstances: As soon as Merkle saw McCormick score, he veered off the basepath before touching second base and headed in the direction of the Giants' clubhouse, located in right-center field. Johnny Evers, probably not believing that the Warren Gill situation was repeating itself in so short a time, stood at second base and hollered at center fielder Art Hofman to retrieve the ball.

Amid the hoopla of the apparent dramatic victory, some Giants sensed trouble was brewing. Third base coach/pitcher Joe McGinnity first became attuned to it. He ran onto the field and intercepted Hofman's throw before it got to Evers. He threw the ball among the encroaching mob of fans, who according to *Chicago Tribune* reporter Charles Dryden, "had swarmed up on the diamond like an army of starving potato bugs."[5] Meanwhile Mathewson was desperately trying to get Merkle's attention so he could direct him to touch second base. A ball—not necessarily *the ball*—was relayed to Evers, who stepped on second base. He looked for a decision from base umpire Emslie. Frank Chance joined Evers in arguing the point. Neither Emslie nor plate umpire O'Day ruled on the play immediately. A wedge of policemen led them to a safe place under the grandstand where they figured out what to do. Emslie, a Canadian who had been an MLB umpire since 1890, was in no position to make any call. He had not seen whether or not Merkle had made it to second base as he was sprawled on the ground trying to elude Bridwell's line drive. Plate umpire Hank O'Day would have to make the decision—the same Hank O'Day who had denied Evers' similar argument 19 days earlier in Pittsburgh. After due deliberation, O'Day ruled Merkle out on a force play. Accordingly McCormick's run did not count. Furthermore, he ruled that the crowd on the field and impending darkness made further play impossible. The game ended in a 1–1 tie. If necessary, the teams would have to replay the entire game at the end of the season to break a tie in the standings. The umpires left the Polo Grounds under a police escort. On his way out of the ballpark, Emslie shouted the news to the journalists: Merkle failed to touch second so McCormick's run was nullified.

At least that is one passable version of the story. No film of the sequence of events exists. There are no known photographs either. In the days and years that followed, countless varied descriptions would be related by fans and players alike as to what actually happened following Bridwell's hit. Author Cait Murphy, in her book *Crazy '08*, cleverly likened the events at the Polo Grounds that day to those in the classic 1951 Japanese movie *Rashomon*, in which numerous eyewitnesses to a crime surprisingly report vastly different accounts about what really occurred. The next day's newspapers had wildly varying versions of which Cubs player made the putout at second base and what happened to the ball that Bridwell hit. Just about all of the stories, however, were quick to blame Fred Merkle for his baserunning oversight. (W.W. Aulick of the *New York Times* blamed the outcome on Merkle's "censurable stupidity.")[6] Merkle swiftly acquired the unflattering nickname "Bonehead"—an unfair label he could never shake in the 48 years he had left to live. From time to time, even Johnny Evers changed his account of what transpired. In one version he ran onto the outfield grass to retrieve the ball himself and returned to second base to record the putout singlehandedly. In other versions of that day's climactic at-bat, Evers recalled a succession of Cubs teammates relaying the ball to him. Merkle claimed years later that umpire Emslie had assured both Mathewson and him that McCormick's run would count. Mathewson later said that Merkle was already in the shower by the time the force out was made. Hank O'Day would later say that any controversy about the Cubs using another ball to put out Merkle was utterly irrelevant. He claimed he had ruled Merkle out as soon as McGinnity interfered with Hofman's throw to Evers. Hooks Wiltse, a Giants pitcher who was coaching first base for the home team that fateful afternoon, said years afterward in an interview, "There is no doubt that Merkle missed touching second base. Still, nobody knows whether the Cubs ever got the official baseball into second base to force Merkle because of the mass confusion."[7] Wiltse, who has never received one iota of blame for MLB's most infamous baserunning debacle, conveniently omitted that he had not reminded Merkle to advance to the next base before leaving the diamond.

Murphy brilliantly summarized, "Somewhere an objective reality exists. The evidence is persuasive that in 1908 there was a city called New York, and that on September 23, 1908 something called baseball was played in a curious place known as the Polo Grounds, and that something out of the ordinary happened late that afternoon. But it is not possible now, any more than it was at the time, to know what that reality is. One thing is, however, as close to an objective truth as it is possible to come in baseball's *Rashomon* moment: Merkle never touched second [base]."[8] Murphy concludes that was the case because umpire O'Day ruled Merkle out—and any umpire would have

Bob Emslie was the base umpire in the famous Merkle game in 1908. Although Emslie was stationed closer to second base than partner Hank O'Day when the critical incident occurred, Emslie was in no position to make a call (Library of Congress, George Grantham Bain Collection).

to be absolutely certain of the situation to make that call in those critical circumstances. Moreover, O'Day had been certain because he was looking for such an omission after what had occurred in Pittsburgh nearly three weeks earlier.

This is the verbatim report that O'Day wrote and sent to NL president Harry Pulliam, confirming that McGinnity's interference with Hofman's throw was of paramount importance to his ruling on the field:

New York, Sept 23/08
Harry C. Pulliam, Esq.
Pres. Nat. League

Dear sir,

In the game to-day at New York between New York and the Chicago Club. In the last half of the 9th inning, the score was a tie 1–1. New York was at the Bat, with two Men out, McCormick of N. York on 3rd Base and Merkle of N. York on 1st Base; Bridwell was at the Bat and hit a clean single Base-Hit to Center Field. Merkle did not run the Ball out; he started toward 2nd Base, but on getting half way there he turned and ran down the field toward the Club House. The Ball was fielded in to 2nd Base for a Chgo. Man to make the play, when McGinnity ran from the Coacher's Box out in the Field to 2nd Base and interfered with the Play being made. Emslie, who said he did not watch Merkle, asked me if Merkle touched 2nd Base. I said he did not. Then Emslie called Merkle out, and I would not allow McCormick's Run to score. The Game at the end of the 9th inning was 1–1. The People ran out on the Field. I did not ask to have the Field cleared, as it was too dark to continue play.

Yours respt.
Henry O'Day[9]

Here's how Joe Vila, a well-known New York City baseball scribe, described the chaotic Merkle incident on the front page of the October 1, 1908, edition of *The Sporting News*:

Riot at Polo Grounds

The mob came back on Wednesday, and before the sun set there was an old-time riot such as used to prevail when [former notorious Giants owner] Andy Freedman was in the limelight. It was caused by the stupidity of Fred Merkle. It was in the last of the ninth with two men out and runners on third and first bases (Merkle on the latter bag), when Bridwell drove the ball past Evers into center field. The man on third hiked for the plate with what looked like the winning run, but Mr. Merkle, losing his head, never went to second base, but made a beeline for the clubhouse thinking the game had been won. Evers called to Hofman to throw the ball to second base for the force-out, but McGinnity, who wasn't in the game at all, rushed out onto the field and intercepted the throw. Mathewson, meanwhile, hustled after Merkle and told him to run to second base. The crowd was all over the field by that time, and McGinnity, in a tussle with several Chicago players, threw the ball into the crowd back of third base.

Not knowing just what was in the wind, a wild-eyed mob surrounded umpires O'Day and Emslie, but luckily the regular police who had been sent to the battlefield by [New York City police] Commissioner Bingham kept the judges of play from being killed, perhaps. Chance yelled to O'Day that Merkle was the third man out and the run did not count.

The ball by this time had been thrown to Evers while Merkle was fighting his way through another mob to the bag. Half a dozen fights were soon going on, and it looked as if somebody would be seriously injured. The cops took the umpires under the grandstand where O'Day ruled that the run did not count and that the game was a tie—1 to 1.

Of course, everybody put up a fearful howl, except the Cubs and [Cubs owner] Charley Murphy.

The Giants, of course, figured they had been cheated out of a legitimate 2–1 win. Manager McGraw furiously likened the umpires' verdict to highway robbery. Another NL umpire, Bill Klem, who in 1908 was only a few years into a Hall of Fame career, said the force-out call on Merkle was "the rottenest decision in the history of baseball."[10] Although the rule book made no exceptions, Klem believed the force-play rule was meant to apply only to batted balls that stayed within the infield and where the putouts were made quickly. He did not think it should apply to potential game-winning hits when the ball ended up in the outfield. Of course the game was formally protested by the Giants. *The Sporting News* was so sure the Giants would eventually be awarded the victory that its box score of the game shows it as a 2–1 New York win with Bridwell getting credit for a hit. The *Boston Globe* ran the same result. (As it turned out, the force out actually deprived Bridwell of a single. Evers was credited with a putout. The strange and uncertain sequence of events surrounding how Evers got the ball caused the *Chicago Tribune* to liberally credit assists on the play to center fielder Hofman, shortstop Joe Tinker, and third baseman Harry Steinfeldt. The *Tribune*, of course, reported the game as a 1–1 tie.)

Faced with a monumental decision, the capable NL president took his time to make a final ruling on the Giants' protest. Pulliam deeply hoped the tie game would not affect the overall standings. It was not to be. Weighing common practice against the letter of the law, eventually Pulliam courageously ruled that the force-play rule still applied on game-ending situations, thus McCormick's run did not count. "Much as I deplore the unfortunate ending of a brilliantly played game as well as the subsequent controversy, I have no alternative than to be guided by the law," wrote Pulliam in his official announcement. "I believe in sportsmanship, but would it be good sportsmanship to repudiate my umpires simply to condone the undisputed blunder of a player?"[11] Pulliam was sullen by nature and sensitive to criticism. Troubled by the Merkle controversy and a ticket-scalping scandal that surfaced during the 1908 World Series, the idealistic and gentlemanly Pulliam suffered a nervous breakdown during the winter meetings following the 1908 season. He was granted a year's leave of absence to regain his mental health, but returned to his presidential duties on June 28, 1909. Exactly one month later, in his apartment on the third floor of the New York Athletic Club, Pulliam took his own life with a self-inflicted pistol shot to the head. He was only 40 years old at the time of his unexpected suicide. Both the NL and AL cancelled their full schedules of games on August 2—the day of Pulliam's funeral—as a gesture of respect and mourning.

Umpire Hank O'Day was excoriated by Giants fans for years—even though his call was technically correct and properly upheld by Harry Pulliam. The Merkle controversy made O'Day even more reclusive than he had been before. "Look at O'Day," said AL umpire Silk O'Loughlin. "He is one of the best umpires, maybe the best today, but he's sour. Umpiring does something to you. The abuse you get from the players, the insults from the crowds, and the awful things they write about you in the newspapers take their toll."[12] O'Day would be posthumously elected to the Hall of Fame in 2013, 86 years after he umpired his last MLB game and 78 years after his death. His plaque in Cooperstown acknowledges the courage it took for O'Day to make the unpopular but correct call against Fred Merkle. Of the handful of umpires enshrined in the Hall of Fame, O'Day's plaque is the only one that makes reference to a specific decision in a game.

What is often overlooked in all the hullaballoo and debate about the Merkle incident is that the NL season was far from over when it occurred. There were still two weeks of games on the 1908 slate, and it was still very much a three-team race for the title. The Giants beat the Cubs the following day, 5–4, but suffered a huge setback when they lost both ends of a home doubleheader to lowly Cincinnati on September 25. Overall, the Giants won 11 of 16 games after the famously controversial 1–1 tie. A three-game sweep over the Boston Doves kept the Giants tied for the NL lead. The Cubs had done even better. They had gone 8–2 in their final ten games and finished with five straight triumphs. One of the wins was a makeup game versus Pittsburgh on October 4. (The Pirates had stayed in the hunt by spectacularly winning 13 of 15 games.) Chicago upended Pittsburgh, 5–2, to mathematically eliminate the Pirates from any chance of taking the pennant. Pittsburgh finished the 1908 season with 98 wins and 56 losses. Both the Cubs and Giants had 98 wins and 55 losses after 153 decisive results. To determine the 1908 National League champions, the tie game from September 23 would have to be replayed at the Polo Grounds on Thursday, October 8.

Predictably, tension and emotions ran high in the days leading to the replay. The Giants seriously considered boycotting the game as they genuinely felt they had already won the contest on September 23 and, by extension, the pennant. However, McGraw thought such a move would smack of cowardice and reflect badly on the team. On October

The replay of the tied Merkle game drew an enormous crowd to the Polo Grounds. The photograph shows a small fraction of the hopeful hometown rooters. They would go home disappointed (Library of Congress, George Grantham Bain Collection).

8, everyday life in Chicago and New York came to a standstill as baseball fans were glued to batter-by-batter reports from the Polo Grounds. The Giants scored a run in the first inning to excite the overflow and high-strung crowd, but the Cubs eventually prevailed, 4–2. The victors were quick to leave town. McGraw, unwilling to accept the circumstances surrounding his team's defeat, had medals struck for his Giants that proclaimed them to be the real NL champions of 1908. Nevertheless, Chicago beat the Detroit Tigers in five games in the World Series. The Cubs have not won another in more than a century of trying. They claimed their most recent NL pennant back in 1945 when the Second World War had siphoned the most talented ballplayers away from the diamond.

Fred Merkle would become a mainstay at first base for the Giants beginning in the 1910 season. Although he played on five NL pennant winners, he never tasted ultimate victory as a World Series winner. Merkle put up with cruel taunts the rest of his days. "Goodbye, Fred. Don't forget to touch second base," was a common way people bid farewell to him. Merkle severed all ties with baseball in his middle-age years after a young player he was coaching referred to him as "Bonehead." In 1950 Merkle was persuaded to attend a Giants old-timers' event at the Polo Grounds. He received a standing ovation. He died six years later in Florida at the age of 67.

Whether or not Merkle deserves his status as a goat is a topic that has been debated for years. Baseball historian David Nemec has his own opinion on who was truly to blame for the Giants' 2–1 win turning into a controversial 1–1 tie: Giants manager John McGraw! Nemec wrote in a special SABR publication on the 100th anniversary of the incident,

Merkle's failure to touch second [base] haunted him for the rest of his life, but the real goat should have been John McGraw. The 19-year-old Merkle was only following a lax custom—runners as late as 1908 often did not bother to touch the next base on a "sudden death" hit. But on September 4, some three weeks before Merkle's boner, Johnny Evers had endeavored to have Warren Gill of the Pittsburgh Pirates called out by O'Day on a nearly identical play. O'Day demurred at the time but later that night, after debating the issue with Evers in a Pittsburgh hotel lobby, he realized that Evers had a valid argument. Since the Gill incident was widely reported, it ought to have been incumbent upon McGraw to remind his players of what Evers had tried to engineer against the Pirates, particularly when a repeat attempt was an imminent possibility with two out in the ninth and Giants runners at the corners.

From a historical perspective, the Merkle incident was also terribly costly to Christy Mathewson in a key statistical department. He was deprived of a pitching win he certainly deserved to have. That missing victory would give him 374 wins for his career—thus breaking the tie for third place on MLB's all-time list with Grover Cleveland Alexander.

Baseball's rule regarding force plays remains as it did in 1908. (It's now rule 4.09, if you care to look it up.) On potential game-winning hits, umpires are instructed to make sure that all runners properly advance to the next base if they are in a force-play situation—and to be prepared for a delayed force play by the defensive team if trailing runners wrongly assume the game is over as soon as the lead runner touches home plate.

The passage of more than a century has caused the harsh lesson of "Merkle's Boner" to be lost on some modern players, however. Proving that history does indeed repeat itself, on July 1, 2013, a game in the Class A Midwest League between the Lansing Lugnuts and the visiting Great Lakes Loons featured a costly Merkle-like play. With two men out and the bases loaded, an apparent game-winning single for the Lugnuts by Chris Hawkins was nullified when the runner at first base, Santiago Nessy, prematurely joined the celebration instead of advancing to second base. The Loons alertly retired the careless Nessy on a force play while Nessy whooped it up on the infield without even thinking of advancing to second base. Unlike the Merkle play, video evidence exists of the Lugnuts-Loons game, and it clearly shows Nessy cavalierly stopping on the basepath well before he got anywhere near second base. The Lugnuts eventually lost the game in ten innings. The game was played one day before the anniversary of Hank O'Day's death in 1935 and four weeks before his enshrinement in Cooperstown.

"From Lugnut to Lughead," declared a report on the Yahoo! Sports website. Some commenters gleefully saw Nessy's comeuppance as poetic justice for one of those excessive celebrations that now typically follow most walkoff wins at every level of baseball. Scholarly fans were equally quick to chide Nessy for not knowing about Merkle's 1908 baserunning gaffe and ignorantly repeating it. Although "Lughead Nessy" does not quite have the ring of "Bonehead Merkle," somewhere in the hereafter Johnny Evers was smiling contentedly and Fred Merkle now had earthly company.

Chicago 1 at New York 1
(game called after nine innings due to darkness
and spectators on the field)

Game played on Wednesday, September 23, 1908, at Polo Grounds V

Chicago	*ab*	*r*	*h*	*rbi*		*New York*	*ab*	*r*	*h*	*rbi*
Hayden rf	4	0	0	0		Herzog 2b	3	1	1	0
Evers 2b	4	0	1	0		Bresnahan c	3	0	0	0
Schulte lf	4	0	0	0		Donlin rf	4	0	1	1
Chance 1b	4	0	1	0		Seymour cf	4	0	1	0
Steinfeldt 3b	2	0	0	0		Devlin 3b	4	0	1	0

Chicago	ab	r	h	rbi		New York	ab	r	h	rbi
Hofman cf	3	0	1	0		McCormick lf	3	0	0	0
Tinker ss	3	1	1	1		Merkle 1b	3	0	1	0
Kling c	3	0	1	0		Bridwell ss	4	0	0	0
Pfiester p	3	0	0	0		Mathewson p	3	0	0	0
Totals	30	1	5	1		Totals	31	1	6	1

Chicago   000 010 000—1 5 3
New York   000 001 000—1 6 0

Chicago	IP	H	R	ER	BB	SO
Pfiester	9.0	6	1	0	2	0
Totals	9.0	6	1	0	2	0

New York	IP	H	R	ER	BB	SO
Mathewson	9.0	5	1	1	0	9
Totals	9.0	5	1	1	0	9

E–Steinfeldt, Tinker 2. HR–Tinker. SH–Bresnahan, Steinfeldt. HBP–McCormick (by Pfiester). LOB–Chicago 3, New York 7. U–O'Day, Emslie. T–1:30. A–20,000 (estimated).

October 3, 1915

Site: Weeghman Park, Chicago

Teams: Pittsburgh Rebels vs. Chicago Whales

Significance: Final Federal League Game

Impact: Ended the Federal League's attempt to establish itself as a viable third major league

> "Even a remarkably close race in which six of the eight clubs had a shot at the Federal League flag could not obliterate the hard fact of failing attendance. The Chicago Whales captured the pennant on the final day of the season only by .001 percentage points over St. Louis. Pittsburgh finished third, just half a game out."—Marc Okkonen, Federal League historian

> "Of all the fiascos that have taken place in [pro] baseball's 100 years, the Federal League episode will have to assume a position near the top. For two wild years—1914 and 1915—the FL operated as a third major league before it collapsed in an avalanche of bitter words and lost millions."—Bill Fleischmann in *The Sporting News*, April 5, 1969

> "The Sporting News has always held to the view that the Federal League could not live and prosper and that it could never hope to accomplish its purpose of forcing recognition from Organized Ball."—*The Sporting News*, October 7, 1915

Perhaps the greatest pennant race in MLB history occurred in a league that no longer exists and few contemporary fans have ever heard of. As the 1915 Federal League season wound down to a thrilling climax, its championship was not decided until the final two innings of the last game on the league's schedule. The sensational conclusion left the fans of the upstart circuit with happy memories they would have to cherish because the FL disbanded shortly thereafter.

Few baseball fans today know much about the FL's brief existence as one of the sport's major leagues. It is doubtful there is anyone alive who can honestly recall attending an FL game, and Edd Roush, the last surviving FL veteran, died in 1988 at age 94. Nevertheless, for two seasons the FL scared the bejeezus out of Organized Baseball, created a bidding war that players loved and owners feared, and threatened to upend the stability of the major leagues. In the end, the FL died awash in red ink. But on its final day of play, its great pennant race of 1915 absolutely riveted the baseball-loving city of Chicago.

Chicago's Wrigley Field is one of baseball's grand old cathedrals. With its cozy confines, natural grass, and ivy-covered outfield walls, it represents old-time baseball. To those with a broad knowledge of baseball history, Wrigley Field is also a tangible link to the Federal League—a third major league that operated in 1914 and 1915. Like other upstart sports organizations, it failed to survive and ended up costing its backers tens of thousands of dollars.

The FL actually began in 1913 as a six-team loop with no affiliation to either the major or minor leagues. Teams were placed in Indianapolis, Cleveland, St. Louis, Chicago, Pittsburgh and Covington, Kentucky. Recently retired Cy Young managed the Cleveland club. As a so-called outlaw league that year, its moguls were careful not to infringe on existing major league player contracts.

Using mostly unwanted free agents to stock their teams, five Federal League clubs made money in 1913. Only Covington finished in the red. In fact, the unprofitable franchise was shifted to Kansas City in mid-season. Emboldened by their short-term success, the FL owners opted to expand in 1914. More importantly, they declared the FL a major league to rival the older and more established American and National Leagues.

Armed with large bankrolls, FL owners tried to lure established major league stars away from their present clubs. This was easier said than done because of the standard "reserve clause" written into every major league contract. This interesting legal instrument bound each player to his club in perpetuity. Anyone who violated his contract risked being blackballed from Organized Baseball if the FL collapsed. Few players in 1914 were willing to take such a gamble. Still, FL president James A. Gilmore—known to sports journalists as "Fightin' Jim" for his truculent attitude toward the moguls of Organized Baseball—was optimistic. "We'll break up the baseball trust and the National Commission," he said. "We'll free every ballplayer in the United States."[1]

Otto Stifel, the owner of the St. Louis Terriers, said the FL just wanted to compete with the NL and AL on equal terms. He figured his Terriers had just as much right to compete for the support of St. Louis' baseball fans as the Cardinals or the Browns. "Baseball is not sacred or different from the rules which apply to any business," he declared. "There may not be room in a country town for three grocery stores or three meat mar-

James A. Gilmore was the capable and enthusiastic magnate who was responsible for the upstart Federal League's challenge to Organized Baseball in 1914 and 1915. After the FL folded, Gilmore never again had any connection to baseball (Library of Congress, George Grantham Bain Collection).

kets or three churches for that matter, but that doesn't prevent anyone from investing his money where he thinks he has an opportunity. This is a free country and the law of competition is upheld by the Sherman Antitrust Act."[2]

Eight FL teams operated in 1914. Buffalo, Baltimore and Brooklyn joined the league while Cleveland withdrew. (Ever sympathetic to revolutionary causes, 54-year-old John Montgomery Ward, the chief figure behind the players' revolt of 1890, obtained an executive position with the Brooklyn Tip-Tops.) New ballparks were built while old ones were refurbished. Admission prices ranging from 25 cents for bleacher seats to $1 for boxes were standardized across the league.

Great excitement abounded at the 1914 FL home openers. An enthusiastic crowd of nearly 28,000 attended the Baltimore Terrapins' first game on April 13, an exciting 3–2 triumph over the Buffalo Buffeds. The impressive turnout was reputed to be the largest gathering ever to see a baseball game in that city. Jack Quinn, whose MLB career began in 1909 and would remarkably last until 1933, was the winning pitcher. Those fans at the Terrapins' game sadly missed the professional debut of local prospect Babe Ruth, who was pitching an exhibition game for the then-minor league Baltimore Orioles at an adjacent ballpark. (The mere presence of the FL caused the Orioles to abandon Baltimore and relocate to Richmond, VA, in mid-season.) *The Sporting News* optimistically declared in its April 16 edition, "The Federal League season, so far as Baltimore is concerned, is going to be a big success judging from the start it got here on Monday."

Similarly, the following afternoon in Chicago, some 20,000 fans crammed into brand new Weeghman Park, at the intersection of Clark and Addison Streets, to watch the Whales (sometimes called the Chifeds) defeat the visiting the Kansas City Packers, 3–2. Weeghman Park would eventually be renamed Wrigley Field. The overflow crowd witnessed an unusual sight: During the game, Packers pitcher Chief Johnson was served

Members of the Buffalo and Brooklyn Federal League clubs jointly participate in a flag-raising ceremony at Brooklyn's Washington Park during the 1914 season (Library of Congress, George Grantham Bain Collection).

with an injunction by the Cincinnati Reds for breaking his NL contract. FL president Gilmore and other FL officials were slapped with lawsuits too. These were the first shots fired in a bitter two-year legal battle.

Despite the ongoing litigation, the FL got through the 1914 season with each team successfully playing its 154-game schedule just like those in the NL and AL. Baseball historian Marc Okkonen declared, "The caliber of play in the FL during the 1914 season was sometimes criticized by more cynical observers with an axe to grind, but in general was considered equally as appealing as that of the established major league clubs."[3] The FL offered to pit its pennant-winning Indianapolis Hoosiers against the winner of the AL-NL World Series, but was flatly turned down.

Outfielder Bennie Kauff of Indianapolis, dubbed by some journalists as the "Ty Cobb of the Federal League," was the circuit's offensive star in 1914, batting .366 and stealing 75 bases. Arguably the best FL pitcher was Buffalo's badly misnamed Gene Krapp, who compiled a sparkling 1.19 ERA. Before the 1915 season, the Indianapolis franchise was shifted to Newark, NJ to tap into nearby New York City's baseball market.

The 1915 season is best remembered for dozens of NL and AL players jumping their contracts for more lucrative deals in the FL, where the reserve clause had been outlawed. Defectors decimated both the NL champion Boston Braves and AL kingpin Philadelphia Athletics. Walter Johnson initially signed an FL contract with the Chicago Whales, but a change of heart—and a substantial pay raise—persuaded him to return to the Washington Senators. (Johnson's reversal was not quick enough, however, to prevent him from being featured on the cover of the April 1915 issue of *Baseball Magazine*, pen in hand, alongside the caption, "Why I signed with the Federals.") Ty Cobb and Tris Speaker both used the FL as bargaining leverage to negotiate better contracts from the Tigers and Red Sox, respectively.

Nearing the end of a Hall of Fame pitching career, Eddie Plank left the familiar surroundings of the Philadelphia Athletics after the 1914 season and signed with the St. Louis Terriers of the Federal League, where he won 21 games (Library of Congress).

However, it was painfully clear that three major leagues could not operate profitably. Attendance dipped everywhere—especially at FL games. (If official attendance records for the FL exist, they are not easily acquired.) Bleacher-seat prices in the FL were slashed to a mere dime in a last-ditch attempt to lure indifferent fans. Not even a terrific, hard-fought, five-team pennant race put enough people into the seats to pay the bills.

An antitrust lawsuit was launched by the FL against the AL and NL, claiming the established major leagues operated as an illegal monopoly. The court delayed making a ruling, thus further clouding the FL's tenuous future. No decision was rendered until

This attractive card shows the complete home schedules for the 1915 Philadelphia A's (who would finish dead last in the AL) and the 1915 Philadelphia Phillies (who would win the NL pennant). Philadelphia was one of the few established MLB cities that did not have to compete with an upstart Federal League franchise (Library of Congress).

1922, when the FL was only a memory. The judge who eventually ruled that MLB was not a trust in the traditional sense of the term was Oliver Wendell Holmes. Another federal judge, Kenesaw Mountain Landis, had conveniently delayed the ruling until the FL was a mere footnote to baseball history.

With financial losses mounting, the FL moguls pulled the plug on their league after the 1915 campaign. Players who had "jumped" their contracts were permitted to rejoin their old AL and NL clubs without fear of retribution, but their salaries generally returned to 1913 levels. Outfielder Edd Roush and player-manager Bill McKechnie both got their start in the FL and went on to enjoy Hall of Fame careers.

For one player, though, the FL did not end in 1915. Rupert Mills of the Newark Peppers, who had studied law at Notre Dame, had signed a special ironclad contract that paid him through the 1916 season—even if the FL went bust. To fulfill his obligations to the Newark club, Mills arrived at vacant Peppers Park every day and engaged in a strenuous workout regimen, proving that he was ostensibly ready to play for a non-existent team in a defunct league. By mid-summer, Peppers co-owner Patrick Powers bought Mills out of his contract to end the charade.

Before it collapsed, the FL had one last, glorious hurrah. The Pittsburgh Rebels and Chicago Whales met in a doubleheader on Sunday, October 3, 1915, at Weeghman Park to decide the floundering circuit's final pennant winner. With the St. Louis Terriers winning their final game, 6–2, against the Kansas City Packers, and Pittsburgh taking the first game versus Chicago 5–4 in 11 innings, everything now rode on the second game of the Whales-Rebels twin bill. Eric Lutz, a Federal League scholar, described the scene:

> Weeghman Park, the new steel-beam and concrete baseball cathedral on Clark and Addison, swelled to accommodate the some 35,000 fans in attendance. They filled all 21,000 seats of the stadium, spilled out into the aisles and even onto the field between the dugouts and foul poles, sometimes packed in ten to

The managers of the Federal League's Buffalo Buffeds (Larry Schlafly) and Brooklyn Tip-Tops (Lee Magee) pose for a photograph before a 1915 game. Magee was fired after 117 games and replaced by John Ganzel (Library of Congress, George Grantham Bain Collection).

fifteen deep. Others watched from the rooftops across Waveland and Sheffield, while more loitered in the streets below.[4]

With darkness impending, it was unlikely the full nine innings would be played. Through the first five innings, the two teams competed at a brisk pace and were dead-locked 0–0 as Chicago's Bill Bailey and Pittsburgh's Elmer Knetzer shut down the offenses. In the bottom of the sixth inning, doubles by Max Flack and Dutch Zwilling sparked a three-run rally for the home team as the faithful at Weeghman Park went wild. (Note to trivia buffs: Zwilling was the FL's all-time home run leader with 29.) Pittsburgh went down in the top of the seventh without scoring. Umpires Bill Brennan and Jim Johnstone, two former NL arbiters—it wasn't only players who jumped to the FL!—conferred and decided the game could not continue in the waning light. The 74-minute game was over and the Chicago Whales were the final Federal League champions, by one mere percentage point over St. Louis, as the final FL standings for 1915 indicate (see below). Pittsburgh's loss dropped the Rebels into third place. In the history of MLB, there has never been a tighter pennant race.

1915 Federal League: Final Standings

Team Name	G	W	L	T	PCT	GB
Chicago Whales	155	86	66	3	.566	-
St. Louis Terriers	159	87	67	5	.565	-
Pittsburgh Rebels	156	86	67	3	.562	0.5
Kansas City Packers	153	81	72	0	.529	5.5
Newark Peppers	155	80	72	3	.526	6
Buffalo Blues	153	74	78	1	.487	12
Brooklyn Tip-Tops	153	70	82	1	.461	16
Baltimore Terrapins	154	47	107	0	.305	40

The FL finale was Johnstone's last MLB game. Brennan returned to umpire NL games for one more season, but he had to wait until 1921 to be reinstated. Brennan was allegedly the umpire in a 1914 FL game that featured the most comical home run in MLB history. According to the story—which first appeared in a book of baseball anecdotes published in 1952—Brennan's partner failed to show up for a Brooklyn-Chicago game. As was customary for the time, Brennan positioned himself behind the pitcher to do double duty, calling balls and strikes and plays in the infield. It was a sultry summer day, and, in order not to have to periodically walk all the way to the home team's dugout to replenish his supply of baseballs, Brennan stupidly stacked a large quantity in a pyramid just off to the side of the mound. The inevitable happened, of course: Sometime during the game Brooklyn's catcher, Grover Land, smacked a line drive into Brennan's cache of extra balls, scattering them everywhere. The Chicago infielders scrambled madly about the infield, picking up one ball after another, throwing them around the infield for apparent putouts. After each tag, Brennan ruled Land safe, claiming that the wrong ball was being used. Land eventually circled the bases on a hit that traveled no more than 70 feet from home plate. The miffed Whales put the game under protest. It's a great story, but it has several flaws in it, as pointed out in Rob Neyer's *Big Book of Baseball Legends*: The light-hitting Land never hit a home run in his seven-year MLB career, there is no record of a protest being filed pertaining to such a play, and no researcher has ever been able to find a verifiable primary-source account of such a remarkable happening.

At the end of the season, the Federal League moguls attempted to make peace with Organized Baseball but were thoroughly rebuffed. During the 1915 World Series, FL kingpins proffered the idea of having some of their better teams join the ranks of both the NL and AL and expand them to ten teams each. With the latter teams' moguls and league presidents not in a conciliatory mood, this plan was clearly not going to happen. On October 14, 1915, *The Sporting News* reported that AL president Ban Johnson "refused to entertain any offers from the Feds except absolute surrender." In the previous week's edition of *TSN*, the weekly baseball journal was prophetic: "We have reason and basis for making a prediction, and that prediction is that the Federal League has staged its last pennant race. There is cumulative evidence that it is done and unless we are greatly mistaken the coming winter will see its formal burial."

FL president James Gilmore, whose strong leadership qualities were frequently said to be on par with those of Ban Johnson, completely disassociated himself from baseball after his league collapsed. He died, virtually forgotten, at age 71 in a veterans' hospital in March 1947. One FL figure who stayed in the news in the coming years, for all the wrong reasons, was Newark Peppers owner Harry Sinclair. He was one of the major principals in the Teapot Dome kickback scandal that sullied Warren Harding's abbreviated presidency in the early 1920s.

Pittsburgh 0 at Chicago 3

Game played on Sunday, October 3, 1915 (D) at Weeghman Park; game terminated due to darkness

Pittsburgh Rebels	ab	r	h	rbi		Chicago Whales	ab	r	h	rbi
Berghammer ss	3	0	0	0		Zeider 2b	3	0	0	0
Wickland lf	2	0	0	0		Flack rf	3	1	1	1
Lennox ph	1	0	0	0		Zwilling cf	3	1	1	1
Oakes cf	3	0	0	0		Wilson c	3	0	1	1
Konetchy 1b	3	0	1	0		Pechous 3b	3	0	2	0
Rheam rf	2	0	0	0		Mann lf	3	0	0	0
Mowrey 3b	2	0	1	0		Weiss 1b	1	0	0	0
Yerkes 2b	1	0	0	0		Fischer ph	1	0	0	0
Berry c	2	0	0	0		Beck 1b	0	0	0	0
Knetzer p	2	0	0	0		Doolin ss	2	1	2	0
Allen p	0	0	0	0		Bailey p	1	0	0	0
Totals	21	0	2	0		Totals	23	3	7	3

Pittsburgh	000 000 0—0 2 0	
Chicago	000 003 x—3 7 1	

Pittsburgh Rebels	IP	H	R	ER	BB	SO
Knetzer L(18–15)	5.2	7	3	3	0	2
Allen	0.1	0	0	0	0	0
Totals	6.0	7	3	3	0	2

Chicago Whales	IP	H	R	ER	BB	SO
Bailey W(9–20)	7.0	2	0	0	1	8
Totals	7.0	2	0	0	1	8

E–Weiss (2). 2B–Flack (20); Zwilling (32). SH–Bailey (7). SB–Doolin (15). HBP–Cicotte (1, Rath); Lowdermilk (1, Daubert). LOB–Pittsburgh 1; Chicago 3. U–Bill Brennan, Jim Johnstone. T–1:14. A–34,212.

October 1, 1919

Site: Redland Field, Cincinnati

Teams: Chicago White Sox vs. Cincinnati Reds

Significance: Game One of the 1919 World Series

Impact: To keep MLB scandal-free, Judge Kenesaw Mountain Landis becomes the autocratic Commissioner of Baseball and bans the eight Black Sox from Organized Baseball for life

> "The throwing of a World Series seems today a barely conceivable adventure, but in the atmosphere in which the 1919 World Series was played, it was indeed believable. Given the impunity in which games had been thrown [in the past], and the purblind attitude of the game's authorities, sabotaging an event as august as the World Series was merely the crescendo climax to all that had gone before."—Donald Honig in *Baseball America*

> "The Reds beat the greatest ball team that ever went into a World's Series. But it wasn't the real White Sox. They played baseball for me only a couple or three of the eight days."—Chicago White Sox manager Kid Gleason, as quoted in the *Chicago Tribune*, following his team's surprising defeat in the 1919 World Series

> "The White Sox didn't give us the battle I expected."—Cincinnati Reds manager Pat Moran, quoted in the *Chicago Tribune*

> *I'm forever blowing ball games,*
> *Pretty ball games in the air.*
> *I come from Chi.*
> *I hardly try.*
> *Just go to bat and fade and die.*
> *Fortune's coming my way.*
> *That's why I don't care.*
> *I'm forever blowing ball games,*
> *For the gamblers treat me fair.*

> —baseball journalist Ring Lardner's parody of the popular song "I'm Forever Blowing Bubbles," which he used to accuse and mock the crooked Chicago White Sox players during the 1919 World Series

The 1919 Chicago White Sox were not the first MLB team to throw ballgames for the benefit of gamblers, and they certainly were not the last team either. A previous chapter chronicled the underhanded misdeeds of the largely forgotten Louisville Grays, who willfully lost the 1877 National League pennant. Ballplayers were not an especially well paid lot during the first century of professional play, so on some level one can readily understand the temptations of easy money that could be made by an underpaid outfielder deliberately misplaying a fly ball or an aggrieved pitcher grooving soft tosses to opposing batters.

Even amateur contests were known to have been "bought" by gamblers. Sometimes games were fixed based on good intentions. The result of one of the sport's earliest recorded contests—the alleged debut of Alexander Cartwright's rules on June 18, 1846, on the Elysian Fields of Hoboken, NJ—is considered questionable by some cynical baseball historians. Curiously, Cartwright's Knickerbockers Club was trounced, 23–1, by a group of cricketers who were largely unfamiliar with baseball before the game started. The conspiracy theory is that the Knickerbockers conveniently and deliberately took a dive that afternoon to encourage interest in the new sport among their opponents. If that indeed was the case, the plot worked beautifully.

Laying down in MLB games was once considered sportsmanlike—provided the circumstances were just right. On June 3, 1918, Dutch Leonard of the Boston Red Sox pitched a no-hitter against the Detroit Tigers at Navin Field. With Boston comfortably holding a 5–0 lead with two outs in the bottom of the ninth inning, Detroit's Donie Bush deliberately whiffed on obviously wild swings to ensure the opposing pitcher's rare no-hitter was achieved. That would be absolutely scandalous behavior today, but in 1918 it was somehow deemed both proper and laudable. "Donie Bush a Sportsman," trumpeted the headline in the next day's *Detroit News*.

Author Mark S. Halfon, in his 2014 book *Tales of the Deadball Era*, recounts another game—this one played on September 15, 1917—in which Boston Red Sox pitcher Babe Ruth carried an 8–0 lead into the bottom of the ninth inning versus New York. Instead of trying to earn a shutout, Ruth instead deliberately took it easy and allowed the Yankees to get a handful of hits and score three runs solely for the entertainment of the numerous flag-waving soldiers at the Polo Grounds who would soon be shipped overseas to experience the hell of trench warfare. "No one objected," wrote Halfon. "No one thought to object." Even more egregious was the late-season debacle known as the "Good Samaritan game"—a common occurrence in which Team A (whose position in the final standings was assured) would play half-heartedly to allow Team B to win and move up a notch in the standings. Sometimes this shady help was provided free of charge; other times cash or merchandise was gratefully delivered to the helpful opponents.

Although the line that separated outright fixes from shenanigans that were considered acceptable was extremely blurry, some players unabashedly crossed it to throw games for profit. Take the case of right-handed pitcher Jack Taylor. In 1902 Taylor led the National League in ERA. In 1903 he completed a second consecutive 20-win season for the Chicago Cubs, who finished third with an 82–56 record. The Cubs played the seventh-place White Sox in their first-ever City Series. (For many years it was an annual post-season matchup between Chicago's two MLB clubs if neither happened to be playing in the World Series. The last one was played in 1942.) Taylor pitched four times in the 1903 City Series. He won his first outing, 11–0, but oddly proceeded to lose his next three games 10–2, 9–3 and 4–2, to a prohibitive underdog White Sox team. Chicago's AL club was not exactly known for its offensive punch; it had won just 60 games during the 1903 regular season. Cubs president James Hart was more than a trifle suspicious of Taylor's efforts (or lack thereof) and swiftly traded him to St. Louis. When Taylor returned to Chicago as a member of the Cardinals in 1904, he was genuinely surprised when he encountered hostility from his one-time fans. "Why should I have won?" he explained to the Cubs rooters. "I got $100 from Hart for winning and I got $500 for losing!"

It was an outright and shameless admission of game-fixing, but Taylor faced no disciplinary action, at least not for a while. Taylor's new employers, the Cardinals, accused him of dumping a July 30, 1904, game versus Pittsburgh for the benefit of a local gambler. Taylor claimed he was not dishonest that particular afternoon, just horribly drunk. Taylor was slapped with a $300 fine for misbehavior, which is thought to have gone unpaid. For good measure, Taylor was also accused of throwing games in the 1904 St. Louis City Series! Because of the scuttlebutt out of St. Louis, in February 1905, the National Commission (MLB's pre-commissioner oversight body) belatedly got around to investigating Taylor's shabby performance in the 1903 Chicago City Series. It conveniently concluded that Taylor's blatant declaration of a fix had been made in jest. Ultimately the Cubs greatly profited from dumping the corrupt Taylor. They got future Hall of Famer Mordecai (Three Finger) Brown in the trade with St. Louis. Still, MLB's refusal to ban an admitted game-fixer sent a clear message to other players that crookedness would likely go unpunished. "In a culture of permissiveness that hung over the sport like a wet tarpaulin," author Halfon concluded, "willing ballplayers crossed into a netherworld of deceit and fraud."

Therefore, by the time the 1919 World Series rolled around, game-fixing had become

MLB's dirty little secret. Given that the participants in the 1919 World Series were the underpaid Chicago White Sox, it made a fix almost inevitable. In an age of parsimonious team owners, Charles Comiskey of the White Sox was among the stingiest. Although it was not specifically guaranteed in his contract, reliable pitcher Eddie Cicotte, a 13-year MLB veteran, had allegedly been promised a bonus if he won 30 games in 1919. After Cicotte attained his 27th win on September 1, Comiskey ordered manager Kid Gleason to use him sparingly so he could not easily earn the extra money. After making eight starts in July and nine more in August, Cicotte started just five games in September. He finished the season 29–7. Then there was the issue of the dirty duds: Comiskey wanted to charge the players for laundering their uniforms! The players balked and wore distinctly soiled uniforms until Comiskey was shamed into laundering them. Then he had the cost of the service deducted from the White Sox players' paychecks.

First baseman Chick Gandil, an unsavory character who was going to retire at the end of the season anyway, recognized the unhappiness among his White Sox teammates as a situation that could be perfectly exploited by gambling interests, if one was so inclined. Gandil was indeed inclined. He let it be known among his underworld cronies that he and a few other White Sox might be agreeable to laying down in the upcoming World Series if the price was right. Sleepy Bill Burns, an ex-MLB pitcher, and Abe Attell, the former world featherweight boxing champion, started the ball rolling. With the help of the bankrolls of Sport Sullivan, a prominent Boston gambling figure, and Arnold Rothstein, an even bigger New York gambler, the financial arrangements were made. Each crooked player was to receive $5,000 for his non-efforts. Gandil recruited shortstop Swede Risberg, outfielders Happy Felsch and Shoeless Joe Jackson, and pitchers Lefty Williams and Eddie Cicotte. Third baseman Buck Weaver sat in on the discussions but refused to have anything to do with the fix. Substitute Fred McMullin accidentally overhead the fixers' nefarious plans. He demanded to be in on the shenanigans too, even though his playing time in the World Series was expected to be very limited. The smart players asked for their money up front. Outfielder Shano Collins, second baseman Eddie Collins and catcher Ray Schalk were not even asked to participate. They were perceived by Gandil as being too clean or too competitive to willingly be part of any fix. Pitcher Red Faber was also deemed to be incorruptible. The dishonest Sox got a break when Faber, who would win 254 games for Chicago in his long career—the second-highest total in team history—was sidelined with the flu. Had he been healthy, the 31-year-old Faber certainly would have gotten at least one of the starts that fell to Cicotte or Williams.

As usual, the World Series was big news across North America. It was especially anticipated in the United States as the first major postwar sporting championship. The day the 1919 World Series opened, the *Philadelphia Bulletin* published this ironic eight-line poem:

> Still, it really doesn't matter,
> After all, who wins the flag.
> Good clean sport is what we're after,
> And we aim to make our brag
> To each near or distant nation
> Whereon shines the sporting sun
> That of all our games gymnastic
> Base ball is the cleanest one!

Game One was played on Wednesday, October 1, 1919, at Cincinnati's Redland Field. Rumors of a rigged outcome abounded. The day before the game, the realistic and

Left: Eddie Cicotte was a 29-game winner for the 1919 White Sox. However, his disenchantment with owner Charles Comiskey prompted him to join the conspirators in throwing that fall's World Series to the Cincinnati Reds (Library of Congress, George Grantham Bain Collection). *Right:* In the days leading up to the infamous 1919 World Series, ex–MLB pitcher Sleepy Bill Burns acted as one of the go-betweens between the crooked Chicago White Sox and gambling interests (Library of Congress, Benjamin K. Edwards Collection).

justifiable betting odds that initially favored the vaunted White Sox anywhere from 2–1 to 3–1 suddenly dropped to about even money. Those familiar with baseball fixes sensed something was terribly amiss before the first pitch was thrown. "You couldn't miss it," one gambler recalled years later. "There was just an odor about it."[1]

In the top of the first inning the White Sox got a leadoff hit from Shano Collins but no runs. The fix was assured with the very first Reds batter who stepped into the box in the home half of the first inning: Morrie Rath was hit by a pitch by Eddie Cicotte. That was the signal to the wise guys that the fix was definitely in. (A fine control pitcher, Cicotte had hit just two batters in 306⅔ innings all season.) Rath scored on a sacrifice fly. By the end of the fourth inning—the frame in which Cicotte was yanked from the mound by White Sox manager Kid Gleason—the underdog Reds held a commanding 6–1 lead. (Getting knocked out of the box was a rarity for Cicotte; he had completed 30 of the 35 games he started in 1919.) That surprising Reds' lead would grow to 9–1 on 14 hits before the lopsided game was over 102 minutes after it began. The White Sox got six hits. Interestingly, Gandil got two of them while Fred McMullin, the "fixer" who was not even expected to play in the Series, got a pinch-hit single. Although the White Sox made just one official error, there were head-shaking plays from the visitors that did not appear anywhere in the game's box score. Cicotte's pitches clearly lacked their usual snap. White

Sox runners seemed a tad slow on the basepaths. Chicago's outfielders reacted a trifle lethargically in their pursuit of batted balls. Those fans who had seen the White Sox decisively romp to the AL title saw the difference. They knew the AL champs were playing well below their capabilities. But no one with any clout dared say anything. The quaint illusion that MLB games were always honestly contested affairs had to be maintained by the baseball establishment.

Over the next week, there were several plot twists in the 1919 World Series fix. At one point, because they had received only a small fraction of the dirty money they had been promised, the crooked White Sox turned the tables on the gamblers by playing to win. Down four games to one in the best-of-nine series, the White Sox won the sixth

The 1919 Chicago White Sox were managed by Kid Gleason, a former MLB pitcher. There is no evidence that Gleason knew of the World Series fix in advance—though he must have suspected it once the games versus Cincinnati began (Library of Congress, National Photo Company Collection).

and seventh games. Before Game Eight, Lefty Williams was told in no uncertain terms that his wife would be harmed if he did not do his darnedest to lose. Williams gave up four straight hits and did not make it out of the first inning. The Reds won the final game of the 1919 World Series in a cakewalk, 10–5.

The scandal took nearly a year to be exposed to the public, although knowledgeable baseball fans who saw the Series knew in their hearts from the get-go it had not been played honestly. "It wasn't subtle,"[2] Daniel Okrent of *The Sporting News* said in an interview 75 years later. A comedic conspiracy trial followed. Shano Collins, the "clean" White Sox outfielder, was listed as the wronged party in the indictments, having allegedly been defrauded out of his winner's share of the World Series money. Confessions to the Grand Jury made by Cicotte and Jackson were somehow mislaid. A verdict of not guilty was rendered. The "Black Sox" may have been innocent in the eyes of the law but they were not perceived as such by anyone who read the sports pages.

To restore the public's faith in MLB, panicky owners had hired a showboat federal judge, Kenesaw Mountain Landis, for the newly created position of Commissioner of Baseball. (The owners likely figured Landis was owed a favor; his delay in ruling on the Federal League's antitrust suit against them had forced the FL out of business in 1915.) Landis was invested with autocratic powers and given the job for life. Landis' first duty was to deal harshly with the disgraced players. The seven openly crooked White Sox— and Buck Weaver, an honest player whose crime was not reporting the fix to his manager—were barred from professional baseball at all levels forever. Those bans still stand today.

Chicago 1 at Cincinnati 9

Game played on Wednesday, October 1, 1919, at Redland Field

Chicago White Sox	ab	r	h	rbi		Cincinnati Reds	ab	r	h	rbi
Collins S. rf	4	0	1	0		Rath 2b	3	2	1	1
Collins E. 2b	4	0	1	0		Daubert 1b	4	1	3	1
Weaver 3b	4	0	1	0		Groh 3b	3	1	1	2
Jackson lf	4	1	0	0		Roush cf	3	0	0	0
Felsch cf	3	0	0	0		Duncan lf	4	0	2	1
Gandil 1b	4	0	2	1		Kopf ss	4	1	0	0
Risberg ss	2	0	0	0		Neale rf	4	2	3	0
Schalk c	3	0	0	0		Wingo c	3	1	1	1
Cicotte p	1	0	0	0		Ruether p	3	1	3	3
Wilkinson p	1	0	0	0						
McMullin ph	1	0	1	0						
Lowdermilk p	0	0	0	0						
Totals	31	1	6	1		Totals	31	9	14	9

Chicago	010 000 000—1 6 1	
Cincinnati	100 500 21x—9 14 1	

Chicago White Sox	IP	H	R	ER	BB	SO
Cicotte L (0–1)	3.2	7	6	6	2	1
Wilkinson	3.1	5	2	1	0	1
Lowdermilk	1.0	2	1	1	1	0
Totals	8.0	14	9	8	3	2
Cincinnati Reds	IP	H	R	ER	BB	SO
Ruether W (1–0)	9.0	6	1	0	1	1
Totals	9.0	6	1	0	1	1

E–Gandil (1), Kopf (1). DP–Chicago 2. 2B–Cincinnati Rath (1, off Cicotte). 3B–Cincinnati Ruether 2 (2, off Cicotte, off Lowdermilk); Daubert (1, off Wilkinson). SH–Felsch (1, off Ruether); Rath (1, off Cicotte); Roush (1, off Wilkinson); Wingo (1, off Lowdermilk). SF–Groh (1, off Cicotte). HBP–Rath (1, by Cicotte); Daubert (1, by Lowdermilk). CS–E. Collins (1, 2nd base by Ruether/ Wingo); Gandil (1, 2nd base by Ruether/Wingo); Daubert (1, 2nd base by Cicotte/Schalk); Duncan (1, 2nd base by Wilkinson/Schalk). SB–Roush (1, 2nd base off Cicotte/Schalk). HBP–Cicotte (1, Rath); Lowdermilk (1, Daubert). U-HP–Cy Rigler (NL), 1B–Jim Evans (AL), 2B–Dick Nallin (AL), 3B–Ernie Quigley (NL). T–1:42. A–30,511.

April 14, 1920

Site: Shibe Park, Philadelphia

Teams: New York Yankees vs. Philadelphia Athletics

Significance: Babe Ruth's First Game as a New York Yankee

Impact: The first game in the transformation of Babe Ruth from a pitcher/outfielder to a full-time outfielder; the 50-home-run season is realized; the Yankees dynasty is born

> "No club except the Yankees could give me the amount of money I received for him [Ruth]. Naturally I got as much money as I could. It was such an enormous amount that no club would be justified in refusing it for any player it ever had, or ever will have. I think the Yankees are taking a big gamble, though. If he holds up for them for a couple of seasons, and continues his great hitting, they will more than get their money back. It is something of a risk, though, for no one can get insurance against a player being injured on the ball field."—Boston Red Sox

owner Harry Frazee, explaining the sale of Babe Ruth to the New York Yankees in the January 15, 1920, edition of *The Sporting News*

"Everybody interested in or connected with baseball in New York City has been building castles in the air for the Yankees with Babe Ruth the foundation. It would be a terrible state of affairs, therefore, if Ruth should fail to come through this year with the usual home run wallops, wouldn't it? But stranger things have happened."—Joe Vila in the January 22, 1920, edition of *The Sporting News*

"The talk about the great hitter being a drag on, rather than an asset to, a ball club is inspired by the attitude which certain Boston newspapers have taken on the deal. Last summer when Ruth was slamming the ball out of the lot with startling regularity, he was lauded by the scribes who are now seeking to belittle him. He was "Our Own Babe" in Boston in those days, and never was there a hint of the dissension on the club being traceable to him. Now that he has been sold, he is being branded as a trouble-maker and a braggart whom [Yankees manager] Miller Huggins will find exceedingly difficult to handle. Wonder if these scribes, who have experienced such a sudden change of heart, ever heard of the fable of the fox and the grapes?"— Joe Vila in the January 15, 1920, edition of *The Sporting News*

In 2014, a survey of baseball historians and scholarly fans was conducted by pollster Graham Womack to determine and rank the most important baseball figures of all time. Voters were presented with the names of 190 players, owners, managers, umpires, broadcasters, writers, statisticians, and executives on their ballots, from which to choose just 25. (They were also free to submit write-in candidates if they so desired.) When all the votes were counted, George Herman "Babe" Ruth finished at the top of the heap, appearing on 259 of 262 ballots—98.85 percent. (What the three dissenting voters were thinking is anyone's guess!) Jackie Robinson finished a close second, selected on 257 ballots. A century after Ruth made his MLB debut, nearly 80 years after he played his last MLB game, and more than 65 years after his death from cancer at the young age of 53, Ruth's impact on the sport still resonated. "It is difficult to overstate Babe Ruth's importance to baseball,"[1] Womack noted in summarizing the poll's results. Indeed it is.

During the 1919 MLB season, George Herman "Babe" Ruth swatted the astonishing total of 29 home runs for the Boston Red Sox, establishing a new seasonal home run record. Ruth was a bit of an odd case. Certainly he could hit, but he was primarily employed as a left-handed pitcher for Boston's AL club from 1914–1918. Quite the superb hurler he was! Had the Cy Young Award existed in 1916, Ruth's record of 23–12 with a 1.75 ERA would have made him a top candidate for the prize. During his tenure in Boston, Ruth also established a record streak of 29 shutout innings in World Series competition that lasted for more than 40 years.

But it was his hitting that made Babe Ruth the talk of the baseball world. In 1918, while still primarily a pitcher, he belted 11 home runs, good enough to tie for the AL lead in that category. Ruth's power hitting was such a formidable weapon that the Red Sox reduced his mound appearances in 1919 and positioned him in right field to get his bat into virtually every game. (Red Sox outfielder Harry Hooper, in his interview with Lawrence S. Ritter for *The Glory of Their Times*, claimed it was his persistent prodding that finally convinced the Red Sox brass to make Ruth a full-time outfielder.) Ruth's 29 homers were twice the total anyone else in the AL managed. (Gavvy Cravath was second best with 12. Four others had ten apiece.) Ruth was now the biggest star in baseball— and the New York Yankees wanted him badly.

Boston Red Sox owner Harry Frazee was a part-time baseball man, but his true love was the theater. Producing Broadway shows was expensive, so Frazee freely parted with the most attractive assets he had for their cash value: baseball stars in Red Sox uniforms.

The most frequent buyer was Colonel Jacob Ruppert, co-owner of the New York Yankees. The Yankees were trying to establish themselves as New York City's top baseball attraction. This was a daunting proposition with the storied Giants doing great business in the National League. Ruppert figured his best tactic to compete with the Giants was to buy the best players available, put them on display in Yankees uniforms, and let the fans of New York decide where the best entertainment value was. Frazee was open to all offers. Although the Red Sox were the most dominant team in MLB in the 1910s, Frazee was quick to break up the club for quick infusions of cash. Harry Hooper recalled years later,

> Harry Frazee became the owner of the Red Sox in 1917, and before long he sold off all our best players and ruined the team. Sold them all to the Yankees—Ernie Shore, Duffy Lewis, Dutch Leonard, Carl Mays, Babe Ruth. Then Wally Schang and Herb Pennock and Joe Dugan and Sam Jones. I was disgusted. The Yankee dynasty of the Twenties was three-quarters of the Red Sox of a few years before. All Frazee wanted was the money.[2]

Ruth began grumbling about his salary during and after the 1919 campaign, in which Boston finished in sixth place after having won the World Series three of the previous four seasons. Ruth was to be paid $10,000 a year through 1921, but he figured his value to the Red Sox as their top gate attraction merited some serious renegotiations. Frazee must have figured the sale of Ruth to New York was a good way to get rid of a malcontent player while getting a huge windfall at the same time. The deal was worked out before the end of 1919, but it was not formally announced until January 6, 1920. Although there was talk of Ruth being bought by the Yankees during the tail end of the 1919 season, the magnitude of the finances

Few baseball historians would rank Babe Ruth anywhere other than at the top spot on a list of the most important players in MLB history. His years with the New York Yankees elevated the team from mediocrity to absolute dominance of the American League. He singlehandedly made the home run fashionable (Library of Congress).

involved was banner news. Ruth's $20,000 salary demand was not an issue for the Yankees, as they happily forked over $100,000 to Frazee and provided him with a sizable personal loan of $350,000. Boston newspapers were split about the deal. Some said Ruth had become an egomaniac and would present a problem for the club's overall well-being had he been kept. The New York papers, on the other hand, were quite thrilled that the heretofore pennant-less Yankees were now a serious threat to contend for the top laurels in the AL. The *New York Times* was bold enough to suggest another record-smashing year was at hand for the Babe: "The short right field wall at the Polo Grounds should prove an easy target for Ruth next season and, playing seventy-seven games at home, it would not be surprising if Ruth surpassed his home run record of twenty-nine circuit clouts next summer."[3]

MLB had experienced record-breaking attendance in 1919 and expected more of the same in 1920, given the hype around Ruth's signing with the Yankees. Ruth, as a star attraction in America's biggest city, was sure to generate huge crowds in the Polo Grounds, where the Yankees were merely tenants, and Ruth was bound to be an attraction at the other seven AL ballparks. Once Ruth proved his capacity to draw crowds, a stadium the Yankees could call their own would surely be erected.

But first the Yankees would have to begin their 1920 season on the road with trips to Philadelphia and Boston. Ruth's first official game with New York came at Philadelphia's Shibe Park on Wednesday, April 14, 1920. Ruth batted fourth and played center field. The Athletics won, 3–1. It was a game that Ruth would have liked to forget—and it is one seldom discussed in Yankees lore. Ruth did get two base hits in four official at-bats, but he misplayed a fly ball in the bottom of the eighth inning that scored two unearned runs to provide the home team's wining margin. It was a highly inauspicious and embarrassing start for the greatest player in New York Yankees history. The Athletics would finish last in the AL 1920 with a 48–106 record. Here's how Philadelphia correspondent James C. Isaminger described the costly error in the April 22 edition of *The Sporting News*:

> In the eighth inning with runners on second and first with two out, [Joe] Dugan sent a long liner to center. Ruth ... stepped back a stride or two and clutched the ball. But it seemed as if the Babe wanted to get out of the glare of the sun too precipitately. He turned quickly to one side, and with that motion the ball fell out of his hands for a rank muff. Two runs crossed the plate and the Macks won 3–1.

In that same issue of *TSN*, Joe Vila reported, "Ruth's error was played up in the metropolitan papers as if it were the turning point in a World's Series."

The Yankees took the next game versus the Athletics and proceeded to Fenway Park, where they lost three straight games to the Red Sox, thus starting the 1920 campaign poorly at 1–4. In New York's much-awaited home opener on April 22, the Yankees beat the Athletics, 8–6, but Ruth was not much of a factor. He injured his back chasing after a curveball in batting practice. He was bandaged up and played center field for the top of the first inning. He batted once, struck out weakly on three pitches, and promptly left the game. Ruth was replaced in center field by Frank Gleich, who would play a grand total of 29 MLB games and bat an anemic .133. Except for Gleich's friends and relatives, such a development was probably not exactly what the majority of the 22,000 folks who paid their way into the Polo Grounds had come to see. Ruth did not return as a regular for another week.

It is fair to say that Ruth managed to overcome his stumbling and bumbling start to his first week in Gotham. During the 1920 season he nearly doubled his one-season home run record with a spectacular total of 54. (As a team, the Yankees hit 115 home runs in 1920. The next best team total was the St. Louis Browns' 50. In other words, Ruth himself whacked more home runs than any of the other seven AL teams!) At one point in August, Ruth's batting average was .392; he finished the year with a lofty .376 mark. His remarkable .847 slugging average was not surpassed until the lamentable PED era. Attendance at Yankees' home games skyrocketed. They became the first MLB team to surpass the seven-figure mark in attendance, drawing nearly 1.3 million fans in 1920. The Yankees' expensive and flamboyant star was going to be worth every penny of Colonel Ruppert's money—and then some!

New York 1 at Philadelphia 3

Game played on Wednesday, April 14, 1920, at Shibe Park

New York Yankees	ab	r	h	rbi	Philadelphia Athletics	ab	r	h	rbi
Gleich rf	4	0	0	0	Witt cf	4	0	2	0
Peckinpaugh ss	4	0	0	0	Strunk rf	2	0	0	0
Pipp 1b	3	1	2	1	Walker lf	4	1	3	0
Ruth cf	4	0	2	0	Griffin 1b	3	1	1	0
Lewis lf	4	0	1	0	Dugan 2b	4	0	0	0
Meusel 3b	4	0	0	0	Galloway ss	4	0	0	0
Pratt 2b	4	0	2	0	Dykes 3b	3	0	0	0
Ruel c	3	0	0	0	Perkins c	3	1	1	1
Shawkey p	2	0	0	0	Perry p	3	0	0	0
Totals	32	1	7	1	Totals	30	3	7	1

New York	100 000 000—1	7 1
Philadelphia	000 010 02x—3	7 1

New York Yankees	IP	H	R	ER	BB	SO
Shawkey L(0–1)	8.0	7	3	1	1	6
Totals	8.0	7	3	1	1	6

Philadelphia Athletics	IP	H	R	ER	BB	SO
Perry W(1–0)	9.0	7	1	1	1	6
Totals	9.0	7	1	1	1	6

E–Ruth (1), Galloway (1). DP–Philadelphia 2. Dugan-Galloway, Dykes-Griffin. HR–New York Pipp (1, 1st inning off Perry 0 on), Philadelphia Perkins (1, 5th inning off Shawkey 0 on). HBP–Shawkey (1). SH–Strunk (1); Griffin (1). U–Bill Dinneen, Dick Nallin.

August 16, 1920

Site: Polo Grounds V, New York

Teams: Cleveland Indians vs. New York Yankees

Significance: Ray Chapman Fatality

Impact: Resulted in the end of the "dead ball" era; baseballs replaced more frequently during the course of a game

> "In the course of an average nine-inning baseball game, there are approximately 200 to 250 balls thrown by pitchers. There have been roughly 1,200 games played each season … since big-league baseball began in 1871. That adds up to about one-quarter-of-a-million balls hurled toward the plate annually. All told there have been more than 25 million pitches thrown to batters [as of 1989]. Only one of them killed a man."—Mike Sowell, in the prologue to his book *The Pitch That Killed*

"I heard the sound when the ball crushed [Chapman's] skull and I saw him fall. I didn't want any closer view than that."—Larry Gardner, the only teammate of Ray Chapman's who did not rush onto the field to check on the fallen ballplayer's well-being

"It was long ago made very apparent to me that I was one of those individuals fated not to be popular. It used to bother me some.… Evidently I didn't impress people favorably at first sight.… I can explain most of my troubles on the grounds of unpopularity.… For my own part, I have long since ceased to care what people think about me."—Carl Mays, in an interview published in the November 1920 issue of *Baseball Magazine*

"The unfortunate death of Ray Chapman is a thing that I do not like to discuss. It is a recollection of the most unpleasant kind which I shall carry with me as long as I live."—Carl Mays, from the same interview

Injuries are an inevitable reality in sports. Fatalities, thankfully, are relatively rare. Since Major League Baseball began in 1876, only one player—perhaps two—has died from an on-field mishap.

The debatable baseball-caused death was that of Maurice "Doc" Powers of the Philadelphia Athletics. The fatal injury occurred in the first game ever played at Philadelphia's newly minted Shibe Park on Monday, April 12, 1909. Powers, a veteran catcher, had been complaining of stomach pains prior to the game. Sometime during the game, Powers collided with a brick wall chasing a foul popup. The incident was so innocuous that it merited absolutely no mention in any Philadelphia newspaper the following day. Powers became ill in the seventh inning but resolutely remained in the game until its conclusion, an 8–1 Athletics win over Boston. The *Philadelphia Inquirer* commented the following day, "The only thing that occurred to cast a shadow over the joy of the fans was the seizure of Doc Powers with acute gastritis in the seventh inning." Despite playing with terrible discomfort, Powers managed to connect for a base hit and score a run. Still complaining of abdominal pain once the victory was safely in the books, Powers collapsed in the Athletics' clubhouse. He was taken to Philadelphia's Northwest General Hospital, where an operation discovered Powers had twisted, gangrenous intestines. Powers developed peritonitis and did not survive a second operation. He died on April 26, four days after his 39th birthday. Powers' official cause of death was an invaginated intestine.

Whether Powers' run-in with the brick wall had any bearing on his overall health is a matter of speculation. Medical professionals severely doubt it; trauma is not known to cause that type of intestinal condition. Moreover, Powers' obituary in the April 27, 1909, edition of the *New York Times* made no mention of any on-field injury; instead it attributed his death solely to gangrene. A recent scholarly article penned by Robert D. Warrington for a 2014 SABR publication indicates that it is unclear where or when the "injury theory" of Doc Powers' death actually began. At the time, Powers' demise was more often wrongly attributed to his eating sandwiches before and during the game! Be that as it may, the one absolutely undisputed fatal MLB injury occurred more than 11 years later. The unfortunate victim was Ray Chapman, the Cleveland Indians' likable 29-year-old shortstop. He was struck by a wild pitch thrown by New York Yankees submarine hurler Carl Mays.

On the hazy afternoon of Monday, August 16, 1920, Chapman and his teammates began an important three-game series at the Polo Grounds against the surging New York Yankees. Cleveland, leading the American League, won the opening game, 4–3, before 21,000 fans. One of the spectators was Dan Daly, Chapman's 16-year-old brother-in-law. The game's result was overshadowed by a tragedy that became the focus of the baseball world for quite some time.

Chapman, playing his 111th game of the 1920 season, led off the top of the fifth inning with Cleveland in front, 3–0. In his two previous plate appearances that afternoon, Chapman had laid down a sacrifice bunt and popped up another bunt to first baseman Wally Pipp that resulted in a double play. On the mound for New York was their ace, 28-year-old Carl Mays. A right-handed, submarine-style pitcher with a famously nasty reputation, Mays was vying for his 100th career win. Chapman had an unorthodox right-handed batting style. He crowded the plate and went into an exaggerated crouch. Afterwards, Mays told a *New York Times* reporter, "Chapman was one of the hardest men to pitch to in the league. I always dreaded pitching to him because of his crouching position at the bat. It is the most regrettable incident of my baseball career. And I would do anything if I could undo what has happened."[1]

With the count at 1–1, Mays delivered a rising pitch toward the inside corner of the plate. Mays later claimed that the ball, scuffed and discolored from use, inexplicably "sailed" on him. There is no film of the incident, so different versions of what happened conflict with each other. Many witnesses maintained that Chapman never moved as

Cleveland Indian Ray Chapman is the only player in MLB history to die indisputably from an on-field injury. Chapman was fatally injured by a pitch thrown by Carl Mays of the New York Yankees on August 16, 1920. Chapman's untimely death was the impetus for umpires removing soiled and discolored baseballs from the game and replacing them with pristine white ones (National Baseball Hall of Fame Library, Cooperstown, New York).

the ball whizzed toward him. Cleveland player-manager Tris Speaker theorized that Chapman's spikes may have dug into the batter's box too firmly, as did some baseball writers. Yankees manager Miller Huggins and Cleveland's Ray Caldwell—a gritty, veteran pitcher who was struck by lightning during a game in 1919 and finished it!—both claimed that Chapman actually moved into the fateful pitch. Whatever the case, the ball violently crashed into the left side of Chapman's unprotected head.

The *New York Times* reported on August 17, "The crack could be heard all over the park. Spectators gasped as they turned their heads away." Cleveland coach Jack McAllister later described the noise as "an explosive sound." Yankees infielders mistook the sickening sound for the ball hitting Chapman's bat. Mays fielded the ball and was about to throw it to first baseman Pipp. Mays stopped his throwing motion when he noticed Pipp had his attention transfixed toward home plate. Frantic shouts for a doctor from plate umpire Tommy Connolly, a veteran arbiter in his 23rd MLB season, alerted the oblivious pitcher to the grim situation he had created. Chapman was sprawled beside home plate with blood gruesomely streaming from his left ear, nose and mouth. Two physicians quickly descended to field level from the Polo Grounds' lower stands.

At one point Chapman rose to his feet and attempted to walk without assistance to the visitors' clubhouse located in distant center field. The fans applauded his apparent swift recovery. However, Chapman's knees buckled as he approached second base and he was helped the rest of the way by two teammates. Once inside the Indians' clubhouse, Chapman, barely able to speak, mumbled to Indians trainer Percy Smallwood to retrieve a cherished personal item—a ring given to him by his wife. Shortly afterward, Chapman fell out of consciousness and was transported to nearby St. Lawrence Hospital in Manhattan.

While Chapman was being attended to on the field, Mays drew umpire Connolly's attention to the baseball. He indicated that a prominent scuff mark was the reason the ball had sailed on him. Connolly casually replaced the ball with another and mixed the lethal one among the others in his ball bag. To the best of anyone's knowledge, it was never retrieved as evidence and quite likely ended up back in play. As a grisly historic artifact, the ball was lost forever.

Few witnesses at the Polo Grounds initially realized the true seriousness of the situation. The next day's *New York Times*, which was published around midnight, simply noted that "Chapman was so badly injured that it isn't likely that he will be able to play again this season." After a short delay, the ballgame continued. Harry Lunte ran for Chapman and replaced him at shortstop when the side was retired. The Indians somehow refocused on the game and Tris Speaker scored a run in that fateful fifth inning. Despite the awful happening, the visitors, led by the excellent pitching of spitballer Stan Coveleski, held their 4–0 lead going into the bottom of the ninth inning. Cleveland catcher Steve O'Neill, who would later manage the Indians, hit one of his 13 career home runs in the third inning, a solo shot. New York scored three times in the home half of the ninth to make the game close before their late rally fell a run short.

Chapman's skull had been severely fractured by the pitch. Along with causing a 3.5-inch depression on the left side of his skull, the severe impact of Mays' pitch caused a fracture on the right side of Chapman's head too. The shock of the injury had lacerated both sides of his brain. Blood clots had formed too. Back in Cleveland, Kathleen, his wife of ten months who was pregnant, was notified about her husband's serious cranial injury. (Chapman had married into money in October 1919 in what one Cleveland newspaper had described as the city's "social event of the fall." Kathleen was the pretty daughter of millionaire industrialist Martin B. Daly. Unsubstantiated scuttlebutt circulating around the Indians' organization had Chapman retiring from baseball after the 1920 season to work alongside his father-in-law.) She boarded the next train bound for New York City. Doctors tried to postpone operating on her husband until she arrived, but Chapman's slowing pulse rate necessitated quick action. Emergency surgery began at 12:50 a.m. and lasted about 70 minutes. Initial reports had Chapman doing better. His breathing was steadier and his pulse rate had improved. His concerned teammates, somewhat relieved by the optimistic signs, were told to return to their hotel. Nevertheless, Chapman died at 4:40 a.m. Kathleen fainted upon learning the devastating news.

"Ray Chapman is dead!" screamed a 72-point, front-page headline in the August 17 edition of the *Cleveland News*. The opening paragraph of the story said, "The dots and dashes spelling out the doleful and heart-rending message came over the wire from New York shortly before 6 o'clock Tuesday morning. Although the news was somewhat anticipated … it came like a thunderbolt from the sky."

Baseball fans across the continent were understandably stunned. Widespread sorrow engulfed the Ohio city. "Lawyers forgot to talk of cases, ministers found it hard to concentrate on their work, politicians neglected their interests for the time being, workmen stood at their tools, and all thought of Chapman and his loss," the newspaper reported.

Known for his cheerful disposition, Chapman was arguably MLB's most popular player in 1920—the polar opposite of Carl Mays. In 1918 he led the AL in both walks and runs. His 52 stolen bases in 1917 established a Cleveland club record that stood until Miguel Dilone's 61 in 1980. Renowned statistician Bill James figured that Chapman was apace for attaining Hall of Fame credentials had he lived and played long enough.

Cleveland mayor William S. Fitzgerald issued the following public statement in the wake of the tragedy at the Polo Grounds: "Ray Chapman, I believe, represented the American ideal of a baseball player. He was a clean, high-principled sportsman, typical of those who have kept the game of baseball on a high plane, and made it worthy to be the national game of the United States."[2]

Mays learned of Chapman's death at 10 a.m. from Mark Roth, a team secretary with the Yankees. Mays immediately went to New York's district attorney and made a formal statement. He was swiftly exonerated. Most sports writers agreed that Mays was blameless, despite his overall unpopularity among his peers. Some scribes even argued that plate umpire Connolly could have legitimately called the fatal pitch a strike because Chapman was leaning over the plate.

Months later in his long interview with *Baseball Magazine*, Mays theorized what might have happened with the fateful and fatal pitch:

> I can explain this unfortunate accident on only two grounds: First, that for some unknown reason, Chapman failed to see the ball at all. Second, that he saw it but fell into that curious state of mind which a ballplayer sometimes encounters in which he is said to be hypnotized by the ball. It is true that [August 16] was a fairly dark day, but my speed is not of the Walter Johnson variety, and I think it very improbable that Chapman failed to see the ball. It is conceivable that he misjudged it, but I think it more likely that he was momentarily hypnotized. Chick Fewster, one of our own men, was hit on the head this spring by Jeff Pfeffer of the Brooklyn Club and very seriously injured. Chick has explained his unfortunate experience by saying that he saw the ball very clearly, but couldn't seem to get out of the way. Frank Chance, I have heard, used to suffer from the same mental peculiarity.... Of course this is idle speculation, for just what happened in Chapman's mind will never be known.
>
> One thing I am sure of: Nobody who saw that accident was more surprised than I. At first I thought the ball had struck the bat [and I] fielded it.... When I looked and saw that Chapman had been hit instead, you could have knocked me down with a feather.

Fellow AL ballplayers, however, were less forgiving. Knowing Mays' well-earned reputation for throwing beanballs, the Indians drafted a petition suggesting a general walkout if Mays went unpunished. Four other teams reputedly agreed. No suspension was ever handed down, and AL president Ban Johnson effectively quashed a players' uprising with the threat of fining any club $1,000 for participating in a walkout. Chapman's death seemed to have no adverse effect on Mays' pitching. The embattled pitcher tossed a dominant, 10–0 shutout versus Detroit in his next start, exactly one week after he threw the deadly pitch. Mays, however, chose not to travel to Cleveland when the Yankees played there in September. It has been argued by some fans that Mays has career statistics worthy of the Hall of Fame, but his connection with the Chapman tragedy and his generally unpleasant demeanor have kept him out of Cooperstown. Mays did not take kindly to any hint that he had beaned Chapman deliberately. Consider this gem of belligerence: "It is terrible to consider the case at all," Mays once tersely declared, "but when any man, however ignorant, illiterate or malicious, even hints that a white man in his normal mind would stand out there on the field of sport and try to kill another, the man making that assertion is inhuman, uncivilized, [and] bestial."[3]

The next day's game was postponed, although that came as news to several thousand fans who gathered at the Polo Grounds on Tuesday utterly unaware that Chapman had died overnight. After AL officials sadly informed them of the reason for the game's postponement, many fans dropped by the 153rd Street funeral parlor operated by mortician James F. McGowan to pay their respects to the fallen ballplayer. The press reported that about 3,000 sad people showed up there in the short period before Chapman's corpse was sent by train to Cleveland for burial. Mays was not among them, having been advised by the Yankees to keep a low profile. The Indians and Yankees split the two remaining games in the series. Tris Speaker did not play in either of the games; he had accompanied Chapman's young widow, her teenage brother, and her husband's coffin back to Ohio.

Some 2,000 mourners were present at Chapman's funeral at St. John's Roman Catholic Cathedral in Cleveland on Friday, August 20. Another 3,000 people who wanted to attend the rites were turned away. Earlier at the private visitation, two of Chapman's teammates had collapsed with grief. One was Tris Speaker, who appeared haggard and aged. He had lost 15 pounds in the four days since the fatal incident at the Polo Grounds. According to some sources, Chapman's grave is the most visited at Cleveland's Lake View Cemetery even though assassinated U.S. President James Garfield and famous billionaire oil magnate John D. Rockefeller are also interred there.

New York Yankees submarine-style hurler Carl Mays threw the fatal pitch that killed Ray Chapman at the Polo Grounds on August 16, 1920. The unpopular Mays had a nasty reputation and was widely excoriated for his role in the tragedy. Mays was quickly exonerated of any criminal responsibility. Mays outwardly seemed unaffected by the mishap. He threw a complete-game shutout in his next outing (Library of Congress, George Grantham Bain Collection).

Chapman's death fundamentally changed how MLB games were conducted. To prevent similar calamities, umpires were instructed to replace scuffed balls frequently with fresh white ones to increase their visibility. No longer could an entire MLB game be contested with just four or five balls. Several dozen were now needed. The days of games being finished with scarred, soft, misshapen baseballs suddenly came to an end. Batting helmets, however, would not be worn with any regularity until the late 1950s. They were not made mandatory in MLB until the 1970s.

Immediately following Chapman's death, the Indians and their supporters both went into a prolonged funk. ("Cleveland fans too deep in grief to care what happens," claimed one headline in *The Sporting News*.) After losing seven of their next nine games to fall into third place, the Indians rebounded spectacularly. They finished the 1920 campaign atop the AL standings, two games ahead of the soon-to-be-disgraced Chicago White Sox, to win Cleveland's first AL pennant. In October, with the emerging Black Sox scandal pushing Chapman's death into the recesses of memory, the Indians soundly defeated the Brooklyn Robins five games to two in the best-of-nine World Series.

Cleveland was also fortunate to find a superb replacement for Chapman at shortstop. After backup shortstop Harry Lunte injured himself, smooth-fielding Joe Sewell, an inexperienced, 21-year-old Alabamian, was elevated from the minor-league New Orleans Pelicans in mid–September to take his place. He tripled in his first plate appearance and surprisingly blossomed into baseball's toughest man to strike out, whiffing just 114 times in a solid, 14-year MLB career. Sewell's remarkable batting eye and reliable glove propelled him to the Hall of Fame in 1977. Sewell's SABR biographer, Bill Johnson, rightly described the youthful shortstop's timely rise to the big leagues as "opportunity from horrifying tragedy."

Six months after Ray's untimely passing, in February 1921, Kathleen Chapman gave birth to a daughter, Rae, and later remarried. Suffering from depression, she committed suicide by poison in April 1928. Eight-year-old Rae tragically died of the measles 359 days later.

Despite the tragic death of Ray Chapman, the Cleveland Indians won the 1920 pennant and the World Series. This photograph was likely taken early in the 1920 season, as Chapman is pictured second from the left (Library of Congress).

Cleveland 4 at New York 3

Game played on Monday, August 16, 1920, at Polo Grounds V

Cleveland Indians	ab	r	h	rbi		New York Yankees	ab	r	h	rbi
Jamieson lf	5	0	2	0		Ward 3b	4	0	0	0
Chapman ss	1	0	0	0		Peckinpaugh ss	4	0	0	0
Lunte ss	1	0	0	0		Ruth rf	4	1	1	0
Speaker cf	4	1	0	0		Pratt 2b	3	1	1	0
Smith rf	4	0	0	0		Lewis lf	4	0	0	0
Gardner 3b	3	1	1	0		Pipp 1b	3	0	0	0
O'Neill c	4	2	3	2		Bodie cf	4	1	2	2
Johnston 1b	4	0	1	0		Ruel c	3	0	2	1
Wambsganss 2b	4	0	0	0		Mays p	2	0	0	0
Coveleski p	3	0	0	1		Vick ph	1	0	1	0
						Thormahlen p	0	0	0	0
						O'Doul ph	1	0	0	0
Totals	33	4	7	3		Totals	33	3	7	3

Cleveland	010 210 000—4 7 0	
New York	000 000 003—3 7 2	

Cleveland Indians	IP	H	R	ER	BB	SO
Coveleski W(19–9)	9.0	7	3	3	2	4
Totals	9.0	7	3	3	2	4

New York Yankees	IP	H	R	ER	BB	SO
Mays L(18–9)	8.0	7	4	2	1	3
Thormahlen	1.0	0	0	0	0	0
Totals	9.0	7	4	2	1	3

E–Ward (13), Ruel (5). DP–New York 1. Pipp. 2B–New York Bodie (21). HR–Cleveland O'Neill (3, 4th inning off Mays 0 on). SH–Chapman (41); Coveleski (7); Ruel (7). HBP–Chapman (2). U–Tommy Connolly, Dick Nallin. T–1:55. A–21,000.

May 16, 1921

Site: Polo Grounds V, New York

Teams: Cincinnati Reds vs. New York Giants

Significance: Fans Attain the Right to Keep Balls Batted into the Stands

Impact: Faced with a legal decision favoring a spectator, MLB teams begin permitting fans to keep balls hit into the stands

> "Altruism and foul balls seldom have gone together. A beer in one hand, a guy in a business suit thinks nothing of trampling through a row of fourth-graders to catch a foul, then hoist it to the cameras for a moment of adulation. In baseball, that little sphere made in Haiti for $1.95 is everything."—from an *Orlando Sentinel* article, September 16, 1986

> "Around the turn of the century in this country, fans tossed foul balls back into play. But this is America, and, as with all things in America, the case of the fan keeping a foul ball was decided in court."—from the same article

If you've ever been fortunate enough to catch—or at least corral—a baseball at an MLB game, you have a strong-willed fan named Reuben Berman to thank for your legal right to keep your souvenir. On the afternoon of Monday, May 16, 1921, the aforementioned Berman, a 31-year-old businessman, became embroiled in a dispute at the Polo

Grounds grandstand that eventually led to a successful court challenge against a long-standing practice at MLB parks—one that required fans to return baseballs promptly to stadium personnel. The court's verdict has come to be known in baseball circles, quite properly, as "Reuben's Rule."

For years, MLB teams employed ushers or stewards whose main job was to retrieve baseballs that had been fouled off or thrown into the stands during games. Although it may not necessarily have been good for public relations, to the teams the policy made perfect financial sense; the balls were their property and they were entitled to have them returned. For many years soiled and discolored balls were used in games until they were too misshapen or battered for further use. Parsimonious owners, of course, tried to keep balls in the game as long as possible. Even after the game balls had served beyond their usefulness in actual competition, they could always be recycled for batting practice until they were battered beyond recognition. The team employees responsible for chasing down these wayward baseballs could be intimidating or physically rough in their retrieval efforts. Non-compliant fans—who faced the possibility of ejection from the premises and possible arrest—often worked together to hide balls until the gendarmes gave up their penny-pinching quest to locate them for their employers. Some teams simply gave up the practice of retrieving balls altogether. The Chicago Cubs, as early as 1916, permitted fans to keep any ball that ended up in the stands. They were the exception. Most MLB teams stubbornly stuck to the wholly reasonable principle that the baseballs they provided for a game remained their property regardless of where they ended up.

On that fateful day—May 16, 1921—a foul ball ended up in the hands of Reuben Berman, a New York Giants fan, who had come to the Polo Grounds to watch his favorite NL club battle the underdog visitors from Cincinnati. It was an unremarkable game on the field. Neither team's starting pitcher made it past the fifth inning. A home run was hit by Cincinnati outfielder Charlie See—the only one he would hit in 202 MLB games in his largely forgettable three-year career. See would be released by the club in early July. The Reds scored all four of their tallies in the top of the fifth inning, only to witness the hometown Giants rally for five runs in the bottom of the frame to retake the lead they would not relinquish. Something else that would not be relinquished—an official National League baseball—became much more historically important than the home team's 7–4 victory that day.

One of about 8,000 spectators who had paid his way into the ballpark that day, Berman had a box seat near field level and was enjoying the game with a group of friends. Sometime during the contest, Berman ended up with a foul ball in his grasp. "A burly attendant showed up, as was the custom, to get Berman's souvenir," said Tom Heitz, a librarian at the National Baseball Hall of Fame in Cooperstown, NY. "But Reuben tossed it over his head, and it disappeared into the crowd."[1] For his act of playful defiance, Berman was escorted into the nether regions of the Polo Grounds and given a stern lecture by security personnel. He was frankly told he was lucky he was not being arrested for theft. His ticket price was refunded and he was swiftly booted from the ballpark.

Berman felt he had been publicly humiliated by the whole ordeal. He was especially peeved at what he perceived as the arrogance of the Polo Grounds staff. Thoroughly disgusted, he decided to take the Giants to court over how he was treated. He sought the remarkable total of $20,000 in damages for "mental and bodily stress." In 1986, Berman's nephew Leonard told an interviewer from the *Orlando Sentinel*, "My uncle was a lovable guy, but he was very firm in his thinking. When he believed in something, he let you know."

Not too surprisingly, the Giants thought Berman's lawsuit was absurd. According to the court papers in *Berman v National Exhibition Company*, the baseball club contended that Berman's refusal to relinquish the baseball to the Polo Grounds usher constituted "disorderly and ungentlemanly conduct," and all the embarrassment laid on Berman, including ejection from the ballpark and the further threat of arrest, was "entirely the plaintiff's own fault." However, in a somewhat surprising decision for the time, the Supreme Court of New York County ruled in Berman's favor—to a point. The decision stated that the team should have let Berman keep the wayward baseball as a souvenir. Berman was awarded just $100 in compensation for his ordeal. Nevertheless, a legal precedent had been set: An American court of law had established that a ticket-holding baseball fan had a right to keep a foul ball. Immediately the Giants changed their policy. Fans were now welcome to keep baseballs hit into the stands as long as they did not chase them onto the field. Undoubtedly management did so reluctantly.

News of the decision apparently spread slowly. In Pittsburgh that same season, three fans were arrested for refusing to give up their souvenir foul balls. Eventually the city told the policemen assigned to duty at Forbes Field to stop arresting fans in such cases, forcing the Pirates to change their policy too. As late as 1922, an 11-year-old boy attending a game in Philadelphia was arrested and spent a night in jail for refusing to give up his prized baseball. A sympathetic judge quickly dismissed the charges against the feisty lad and commented, "Such an act on the part of a boy is merely proof that he is following natural impulses. It is a thing I would do myself."[2]

Teams quickly realized that the possibility of obtaining an actual game-used baseball was another enticement to get fans to come to the ballpark. Within a few years of "Reuben's Rule" being enforced at the Polo Grounds, all MLB teams caved to public pressure and allowed lucky fans to keep any and all baseballs that came their way. Interestingly, the Cubs reversed their policy in 1930 and had a non-compliant fan arrested. That was the last known case of an MLB team trying to retain foul balls as its property. However, many minor league teams on tighter budgets refused to comply for years. Some teams offered to buy foul balls back from fans or provided them with discounts on future tickets in return for surrendering baseballs. Only about half the major league teams in Japan permitted fans to keep foul balls as late as 1997. When Reuben Berman died at age 87 in 1977, his contribution to the ballpark experience of millions of baseball fans was known only to the most scholarly of them.

One YouTube moment from 2014 showed the happy residue of the Reuben Rule: a boy embracing his father at an afternoon Braves-Padres game. "In a span of 10 seconds you can see the son becoming a baseball fan for life," declared one blogger. "After the father catches a ball, he holds it triumphantly over his head in a Rocky-like pose. His son rushes to give him a bear hug. His dad then gives the souvenir ball to his son. You gotta love this."

But all is not skittles and beer when it comes to fans and foul balls. According to a September 2014 story posted on sourcefed.com, a remarkable number of spectators are injured each year at MLB games by the hurtling spheroids:

At two out of every three Major League Baseball games, a fan is hit by a ball propelling into the stands.

According to sources at Elias Sports Bureau Inc., the spectators are hit more often than batters are by bad pitches.

While there are safety nets behind home plate, they do not protect a majority of the people attending the game. MLB requires each team to be responsible for their own stadium's safety precautions, but MLB does not have a policy that mandates exactly how high and wide nets must be.

MLB has yet to see this issue as a serious problem. According to MLB's executive vice president, John

McHale, "There is no epidemic of foul ball damage yet that would warrant some sort of edict or action by the commissioner's office."

Most stadiums currently issue warnings to fans via signage and announcements, but that can only do so much. Patrons can be easily distracted by everything that is happening around them, and could possibly not see the ball heading straight towards their bodies before it is too late.

While making nets bigger might crush some fans' dreams of catching a foul ball from their favorite player, serious incidents, like when a seven-year-old Cubs fan at Wrigley Field received a fractured skull after a foul ball to the head, could be avoided.[3]

The odds against any one individual getting a foul ball or a home run ball are, of course, extremely long. Don't tell that to Zack Hample, though. The baseball fan/sports writer has made something of a career of snagging more than 7,000 baseballs at MLB and minor-league parks as of 2014. (That figure is slightly misleading as it includes balls captured during batting practice and special events such as the Home Run Derby at the MLB All-Star Game.) In 1999, when Hample had a mere 3,000 balls in his vast collection, the 22-year-old wrote the helpful guidebook, *How to Snag Major League Baseballs.* There was obviously a large audience eager to learn how Hample does it. It was the eighth-best selling American sports book of the year.

One of the 7,000 baseballs corraled by Hample includes Alex Rodriguez's 3000th career hit on June 19, 2005; a home run to right field. Hample elected to return the ball to Rodriguez. In exchange, the New York Yankees donated $150,000 to "Pitch in for Baseball," a charity to collect new and used baseball equipment for distribution to underserved communities in the United States and abroad.

Cincinnati Reds 4 at New York Giants 7

Game played on Monday, May 16, 1921, at Polo Grounds V

Cincinnati Reds	ab	r	h	rbi	New York Giants	ab	r	h	rbi
Bohne 3b	4	1	2	1	Burns lf	3	0	0	1
Bressler 1b	4	0	1	1	Bancroft ss	4	1	1	1
Roush cf	3	0	1	1	Frisch 2b	3	2	1	1
Duncan lf	3	0	1	0	Youngs rf	3	2	1	1
Fonseca 2b	4	0	0	0	Kelly 1b	4	0	2	0
See rf	4	1	2	1	King cf	2	0	0	0
Crane ss	3	1	0	0	Walker ph, cf	2	0	0	0
Wingo c	4	0	0	0	Rapp 3b	4	0	0	0
Coumbe p	2	1	1	0	Snyder c	3	1	1	0
Napier p	0	0	0	0	Toney p	0	0	0	0
Kopf ph	1	0	0	0	Brown ph	1	1	1	0
Rogge p	0	0	0	0	Ryan p	2	0	0	0
Hargrave ph	1	0	0	0					
Totals	33	4	8	4	Totals	31	7	7	4

Cincinnati	**000 040 000—4 8 2**
New York	**200 050 00x—7 7 0**

Cincinnati Reds	IP	H	R	ER	BB	SO
Coumbe L(0–3)	4.1	5	7	5	4	1
Napier	1.2	1	0	0	0	1
Rogge	2.0	1	0	0	1	1
Totals	8.0	7	7	5	5	3

New York Giants	IP	H	R	ER	BB	SO
Toney W(5–2)	5.0	6	4	4	1	0
Ryan SV(1)	4.0	2	0	0	1	0
Totals	9.0	8	4	4	2	0

E–Duncan (4), Fonseca (8). DP–New York 1. Rapp-Frisch-Kelly. 2B–Cincinnati Bressler (4, off Toney); Roush (4, off Ryan), New York Brown (1, off Coumbe). 3B–New York Frisch (5, off Coumbe). HR–Cincinnati See (1, 5th inning off Toney 0 on 0 out). SF–Roush (1, off Toney). SB–Burns (3, 2nd base off Coumbe/Wingo). CS–Snyder (1, 2nd base by Coumbe/Wingo). U–Bill Brennan, Bob Emslie. T–1:42. A–8,000.

August 5, 1921

Site: Forbes Field, Pittsburgh

Teams: Philadelphia Phillies vs. Pittsburgh Pirates

Significance: First Radio Broadcast of an MLB Game

Impact: Fans not present at the ballpark could now follow the game's every pitch instantaneously

"I watch a lot of baseball on the radio."—U.S. President Gerald R. Ford

"A few forward-thinking owners saw radio as a positive promotional device that could sell baseball to new customers, including women working in the home. It might also charm children, spawning the next generation of fans. Since the games were played during the day, women and children were the major groups in the radio audience."—an excerpt from James R. Walker's *The Baseball-Radio War 1931–1935*

"Listening to a baseball game is all well and good. But add a cool bottle of pop, some hot roasted peanuts and a ballpark hot dog, and the sights, sounds and smells of teams warming up on a freshly manicured field and it's magic … one of life's cosmic experiences."—a Westinghouse ad promoting the joys of listening to an MLB game on the radio while attending it in person

"It turned out radio's intimacy made it and baseball an ideal match. Radio's portability helped too; at home, in the car, at the office, a transistor radio under the pillow. Still, it took years for many teams to recognize the marketing ability of broadcasting games. It was 1938 before major league games were regularly broadcast in New York City, the country's largest market."—B. T. Grimes

Radio sets were still a bit of a rarity in American homes in the early 1920s. What was broadcast on Pittsburgh station KDKA on the afternoon of Friday, August 5, 1921, was even more of a novelty. In fact, it was something entirely new over the airwaves: a live, play-by-play description of an MLB game directly from Forbes Field! The few local listeners—probably fewer than 1,000—who got to hear announcer Harold Arlin's voice were part of history. As a bonus they got to hear Arlin's batter-by-batter account of an excellent baseball game.

Arlin was a 25-year-old radio foreman for Westinghouse who doubled as the night-time studio announcer for KDKA. He got the radio gig without having any broadcasting credentials. (Who did in 1921?) Arlin simply applied for the position out of curiosity when Westinghouse advertised it. Arlin worked solo on that historic afternoon from a box seat behind the Pittsburgh Pirates' dugout along the first-base side of Forbes Field's grandstand. His microphone was actually a jerry-rigged telephone that relayed his voice back to the station. As was the policy of most radio stations in the early 1920s, Arlin was not permitted to identify himself over the air. (The reason for the anonymity? Radio station owners feared their announcers would become popular celebrities and egomaniacs—and subsequently demand high salaries.) That autumn Arlin would be the announcer of another sports radio first: On October 8, 1921, he called the first college football game ever broadcast on the radio, a clash between West Virginia and Pitt.

Years later Arlin recalled that the August 5, 1921, ballgame was supposed to be a one-time experiment, nothing more. The historic broadcast was not even mentioned by the Pittsburgh correspondent in the August 11 edition of *The Sporting News* in which the game's box score appeared. There were no plans for future games to be carried. In fact, most of the staff at KDKA did not think baseball on the radio was an especially appealing idea. It lacked the capacity to keep a listener glued to his set, they theorized.

However, KDKA had luck on its side. That first game was a terrifically entertaining one for the folks at home; it featured 13 runs and 21 hits and a dramatic late-inning rally to seal the victory for the hometown team. Pittsburgh, the first-place NL club at the time, scored three runs in the bottom of the eighth inning to break a 5–5 deadlock and upend their intra-state rivals from Philadelphia, 8–5. The Phillies were in the NL cellar. Undoubtedly, some people in the radio audience were experiencing the thrills and drama of MLB for the first time in their lives and new fans were created. That was the magic and power of baseball broadcasts on this exciting new medium that no one had foreseen.

The experiment was obviously a success. As it turned out, the brain trust at KDKA who had dismissed the viability of radio broadcasts of baseball was dead wrong. The public was utterly enthralled by baseball on the radio. They could not get enough of it. The pace of the game, which allows for reflection and speculation, was perfect for radio. KDKA had a small epiphany and agreed to broadcast Pittsburgh Pirates games on an occasional basis for the next few years. However, KDKA did not establish regular coverage of the team until 1936. Albert "Rosey" Rowswell was the colorful voice of the Pirates once they became a mainstay on the air and remained so until his death in February 1955. A superfan who had not missed a Pirates home game since 1909, Rowswell was so much of an unabashed homer that Commissioner Landis once kiddingly berated Rowswell for his biased commentary. Landis told Rowswell that his descriptions of games were so one-sided that there were people in Pittsburgh who did not know the name of any other NL team except the Pirates. It mattered little to Pittsburgh fans. They admired Rowswell's unbridled enthusiasm for a team that went 33 years between pennants and generally ended up at or near the bottom of the NL standings. WWSW-FM secured the rights to Pirates' games in the 1940s and held them until 1955, when KDKA once again became the flagship station for the Pirates with Bob Prince replacing the deceased Rowswell. It retained those exclusive radio broadcasting rights until 2006.

By the end of the 1921 season, KDKA and WJZ of Newark, NJ, had collaborated to broadcast the best-of-nine World Series from New York City's Polo Grounds. Grantland Rice and Tommy Cowan called the action between the Giants and the Yankees, despite the fact that neither announcer was actually at the ballpark. Instead they recreated the games in a radio studio based on telegraphed reports. Occasionally sound effects were added to the broadcasts for heightened drama. It was a new version of an old system. For years newspaper offices and saloons had done the same thing at World Series time, with the ticker-tape accounts of the action replicated on gigantic scoreboards or announced through bullhorns—or a combination of the two. It was not uncommon for enormous crowds to attend one of these charming recreations. Silent newsreel footage exists of a massive crowd in New York City, unable to obtain tickets for the 1922 Fall Classic, assembled by the thousands in front of a mechanical scoreboard erected for the occasion. By the end of the decade, radio's phenomenal growth had rendered this quaint

tradition obsolete. One no longer needed to venture to a public gathering place to keep abreast of the happenings during a World Series game. Radio now brought that luxury into Americans' homes, creating a new, broader fan base and a new source of revenue for MLB teams.

Radio was strongly opposed by some owners, however; they believed the free broadcasts would keep paying customers at home instead of coming through the turnstiles. Some teams broadcast only road games for that reason. Occasionally curious arrangements were jointly made between two teams in the same city, such as the one the Boston Braves and Red Sox had for a time. Both teams agreed to broadcast only home games because they believed that if the Braves broadcast a road game it would dissuade Bostonians from buying tickets to see the Red Sox at Fenway Park the same day. New York City's MLB teams believed in more draconian measures for a few seasons during the 1930s. They stopped their radio broadcasts altogether—even forbidding visiting teams from broadcasting. Eventually every MLB team saw the wisdom in broadcasting every game. The benefits were many: New baseball fans were created; women and children were educated about the game's rules, strategies and subtleties; and grateful fans could follow their teams throughout the entire season without having to travel. In numerous cases, longtime and faithful broadcasters became symbols of the teams for which they called games.

Harold Arlin, baseball's first radio broadcaster, lived to be 90 years old. He died in 1986. According to Arlin's obituary in the *New York Times*, he spent five years at KDKA, where he became internationally famous (once the station loosened its restrictive rules pertaining to broadcaster anonymity) because KDKA's powerful signal could be heard across the Atlantic. Famous for his interviews of athletes and Hollywood stars, Arlin became a star himself. *The Times* of London called Arlin the "best-known American voice in Europe."[1]

Philadelphia 5 at Pittsburgh 8

Game played on Friday, August 5, 1921, at Forbes Field

Philadelphia Phillies	ab	r	h	rbi	Pittsburgh Pirates	ab	r	h	rbi
Rapp 3b	4	0	0	0	Bigbee lf	4	0	0	1
Smith 2b	4	1	1	0	Carey cf	4	0	0	0
LeBourveau lf	3	3	2	0	Maranville ss	3	0	0	0
Walker rf	2	0	1	1	Whitted rf,1b	3	3	2	0
Konetchy 1b	4	0	2	2	Barnhart 3b	3	2	1	1
Williams cf	4	1	2	2	Tierney 2b	2	1	1	1
Parkinson ss	4	0	1	0	Grimm 1b	2	0	1	2
Peters c	3	0	2	0	Rohwer pr, rf	1	1	1	1
Ring p	2	0	0	0	Brottem c	4	1	2	1
Monroe ph	1	0	0	0	Carlson p	1	0	0	0
					Zinn p	3	0	2	1
Totals	31	5	11	5	Totals	30	8	10	8

Opposite, top: **Pioneer announcer Harold Arlin called the first MLB game on radio on August 5, 1921. On that afternoon, listeners to KDKA in Pittsburgh could follow the action, batter by batter, without having to be in the ballpark. Arlin became the first of many beloved MLB broadcasters. In this photograph, Arlin (on the right) is shown with another Pittsburgh broadcasting favorite—Bob Prince (National Baseball Hall of Fame Library, Cooperstown, New York).** *Opposite, bottom:* **Fans in Saint George, Utah, gather in the street to follow the 1940 World Series via a broadcast coming from a local radio shop. Before the age of television, such sights were commonplace in communities all over North America (Library of Congress).**

| Philadelphia | 103 000 010—5 11 0 |
| Pittsburgh | 020 012 03x—8 10 1 |

Philadelphia Phillies	IP	H	R	ER	BB	SO
Ring L(8–12)	8.0	10	8	8	4	3
Totals	8.0	10	8	8	4	3
Pittsburgh Pirates	IP	H	R	ER	BB	SO
Carlson	3.0	5	4	4	2	1
Zinn W(5–4)	6.0	6	1	0	1	3
Totals	9.0	11	5	4	3	4

E–Rohwer (2). DP–Pittsburgh 1. Maranville-Tierney-Grimm. 2B–Pittsburgh Zinn (2, off Ring); Whitted (18, off Ring). 3B–Pittsburgh Barnhart (11, off Ring). HR–Philadelphia Williams (11, 3rd inning off Carlson 1 on 2 out). SH–Peters (1, off Carlson); Walker 2 (5, off Carlson, off Zinn); Ring (3, off Zinn); Tierney (9, off Ring). SF–C. Bigbee (2, off Ring). HBP–Grimm (2, by Ring). CS–Maranville (8, 2nd base by Ring/Peters). U–Cy Rigler, Charlie Moran.

July 6, 1933

Site: Comiskey Park I, Chicago

Teams: National League All-Stars vs. American League All-Stars

Significance: First MLB All-Star Game

Impact: The start of a mid-season MLB tradition; it remains the most meaningful of pro sports' All-Star Games

> "Arch [Ward] called me one day and asked me to have dinner with him. I didn't know he had anything in mind other than a sociable dinner until he sprang the All-Star Game idea on me, and I was flabbergasted at first. The idea was sound enough since that was the first year of the World's Fair in Chicago and Arch wanted to make an All-Star Game one of the highlights. His sales pitch was that it would be a wonderful thing for baseball. I told Arch I would submit the proposition to the owners. The American League owners finally agreed after considerable discussion that it would join strictly as an attraction for the 1933 Fair. At first the National League opposed it, but finally agreed to play the game for only one year. The game turned out to be so wonderful and so well accepted by the fans that the owners quickly agreed to continue the game and it became a solid fixture."—AL president Will Harridge, recalling how MLB's All-Star Game originated, as quoted in *Professional Baseball: The First 100 Years*

> "It's amazing that fans want to see me play. What is society coming to?"—John Kruk, discussing his election to play in the 1993 All-Star Game

"[Baseball] is an American tradition rich in legends, folklore and history, a never-ending story where every game is a new nine-inning chapter and every player has the chance to be the hero. Through the years, every franchise has had its share of superstar players that stand out above the rest. They are the ones that bring the fans out to the ballpark and only one game brings them all together at once: the All-Star Game." So begins Baseball-Reference.com's description of the history of the MLB All-Star Game—the oldest mid-season gathering of any major sports league's finest players.

The annual MLB All-Star Game began as the idea of a Chicago sports writer, Arch Ward, who saw a unique opportunity to bring together the best MLB players—merely as a one-time event—in conjunction with his city's 1933 World's Fair. Given the initial game's immediate and unqualified success, Ward had correctly gauged what MLB fans desired.

There had been other occasions before where MLB stars had gotten together to play special games for the benefit of causes. The most important of these occurred in 1911, when grief-stricken American Leaguers played a mid-season benefit game for the widow and children of superstar Cleveland pitcher Addie Joss, who had died of meningitis in April of that year at the age of 31. The death of the immensely popular Joss was a blow to MLB. Every AL team with the exception of the Chicago White Sox (whose travel schedule did not permit its stars to attend) sent its best-known players to Cleveland to form an All-Star team and play the hometown Indians in a special exhibition game on July 24. The game sold out quickly, even though the cost of the best seats—$1 apiece—was double that of a typical AL game in 1911. Among those who participated were Ty Cobb, Bobby Wallace, Walter Johnson, Home Run Baker, Tris Speaker, Smokey Joe Wood, Sam Crawford and Gabby Street. Washington manager Jimmy McAleer volunteered to run the All-Star squad for the afternoon, noting, "The memory of Addie Joss is sacred to everyone with whom he ever came in contact. The man never wore a uniform who was a greater credit to the sport than he."[1] The affair sold out quickly and raised about $13,000 for Joss' dependents. The game ended in a 5–3 victory for the All-Stars. Whether the crowd of more than 15,000 fans that packed tiny League Park came mainly to support a good cause or for the rare chance to see so many future Hall of Famers at once, or a combination of the two, we can never know for certain. However, the Addie Joss Benefit Game positively demonstrated that having some sort of All-Star Game would be appealing to baseball fans.

More than two decades went by. The Great Depression was adversely affecting attendance at all levels of baseball. MLB was not immune. Ticket sales were dipping to dangerously low levels even in places where baseball was practically an institution. *Chicago Tribune* sports editor Arch Ward pitched the idea to have the best players from each major league play a special game in conjunction with the Chicago's World's Fair, with its gate receipts going to charity. It seemed like a good gimmick to regenerate interest in the national pastime. At the very least it couldn't hurt. AL president William Harridge was enthusiastic about the concept, as were the eight AL member clubs. The National League was less so. However, with a little bit of persuasion, the NL moguls finally agreed to allow their best players to participate as a onetime experiment. The NL players wore special uniforms with NATIONAL LEAGUE proudly emblazoned across the front of their tops. The AL players dressed a little bit differently; each wore his individual club uniform. An enormous crowd of 49,200 fans showed up at Comiskey Park on the afternoon of Thursday, July 6, 1933, to watch what the local newspapers billed as the "Game of the Century." Both NBC and CBS broadcast the game on their full radio networks. To add to the festivities, John McGraw came out of retirement for one day to manage the National Leaguers. Venerable Connie Mack did the honors for the AL. Both Mack and McGraw selected their teams' lineups; prior to the game, the two managers quaintly posed for news photographers jointly holding a bat, as if they were about to choose up sides for a sandlot game.

The inaugural All-Star Game could not have been scripted better. Thirty-eight-year-old Babe Ruth—MLB's most celebrated player—hit a two-run homer just inside the right-field foul pole in the third inning to extend the AL's lead to 3–0. He also made a terrific catch in the eighth inning to rob Cincinnati's Chick Hafey of what seemed to be a game-tying home run. The NL had eroded the home side's lead to 3–2 with a pair of runs in the sixth inning. Frankie Frisch hit a solo home run in that frame. The AL got the run back in the home half of the sixth and held on for a 4–2 triumph. Because the two leagues used slightly different baseballs, the first half of the game was played with AL balls. NL balls were used in the second half. (The NL ball had slightly higher seams.) Similarly, the four-man umpiring crew shifted positions when the NL balls were introduced. Bill McGowan of the AL started behind the plate. Bill Klem of the NL finished the game calling balls and strikes. The game took 127 minutes to play.

Aside from Ruth's home run, the 1933 event, of course, provided a plethora of All-Star Game firsts. Pepper Martin of the St. Louis Cardinals was the first batter. (He grounded out.) Lefty Gomez of the New York Yankees threw the first pitch. Charlie Gehringer was the first man to reach base (via a walk). Babe Ruth was the first player to strike out. (He was caught looking in the first inning.) Chick Hafey got the first hit—a single in the top of the second inning. Ironically, light-hitting pitcher Gomez drove in the first run with an RBI single in the bottom of the second inning. Lou Gehrig made the first error, uncharacteristically dropping Dick Bartell's foul pop-up in the fifth inning. (Bartell immediately hit another pop fly in foul ground which Gehrig caught to redeem himself!) Gomez was the first ASG winning pitcher. Bill Hallahan of the St. Louis Cardinals was the first ASG losing pitcher. Lefty Grove would have gotten the first ASG save, but that stat did not officially exist in 1933.

Generally the game received rave reviews, except for the error-laden radio commentary inflicted on the home audience. *The Sporting News* editorialized in its July 13 edition, "Why dyed-in-the-wool fans will not desert the parks to sit beside the loudspeaker to get their thrills in baseball was amply illustrated in the broadcasts of the All-Star Game … at Chicago [on] July 6. The announcers had difficulties naming the teams, often confusing the Nationals with the Cubs and the Americans with the Yankees. Few of them apparently knew the players well enough by sight to name them when they came to bat, and twisted batting orders never were straightened out." NBC's Graham McNamee—a pioneer radio broadcaster whose voice exuded excitement but whose knowledge of MLB often left a lot to be desired—was specifically chided for his goofs and overall ignorance. His plentiful blunders included saying that AL shortstop Joe Cronin was part of a double play turned by the NL; insisting the score was 3–1 when it was actually 3–0; announcing it was the fourth inning when it was actually the fifth; claiming Earl Averill was batting for Cronin when he was batting for General Crowder; and wrongly declaring Lou Gehrig would not be charged with an error on a dropped foul ball "because no runner advanced on the play." Hal Totten of CBS did not fare much better. "There's a big right-hander warming up for the Americans in the bullpen," he told his audience. "I believe it is Rick Ferrell." (Ferrell played the entire game as the AL's catcher.)

TSN gave the game itself high overall marks. Under the headline "Fans' Rousing Support Stamps All-Star Game as Big Success," the paper's lengthy coverage of the inaugural ASG began,

> While the game between the All-Stars of the American and National Leagues at Comiskey Park on July 6 didn't provide a lot of things each club hoped it would, the contest did demonstrate to the magnates, some of whom were loathe to grant permission for the staging of the event, that the fans were enthusiastically in favor of such a game and wanted it made an annual affair for the same cause. The net proceeds, approximately $45,000, will be turned over to the Association of Professional Ball Players as a nucleus for a fund for a home for aged and indigent players.
>
> Every available seat was taken, and had the capacity been 100,000 it is believed all tickets would have been sold. The contest attracted practically all the notables of the game and aroused more enthusiasm among the fans and players than any similar event—even the World Series. The opportunity to witness such

a contest was considered an invaluable privilege and the demand is almost universal that the All-Star Game be staged every year. There is talk that next year's game will be held in New York.

The game itself was dominated by Babe Ruth, whose home run in the third inning scored two runs and gave the Americans a lead that was never overcome.

Indeed, the contest proved so popular that plans were immediately made to hold an All-Star Game every summer at approximately the halfway point in the season, with the two leagues taking turns hosting the event. As predicted by *TSN*, the second ASG was played in New York City; the Polo Grounds hosted the 1934 event. With the exception of 1945, when wartime travel restrictions made the game unworkable, the ASG has been in played each MLB season since 1933. From 1959 to 1962 there were two ASGs played each summer as a means to raise money for the players' pension fund. However, the added game seemed to be overkill and, in many fans' eyes, diminished the novelty of the event. In 1963 the ASG returned to a once-a-year format.

Imitation is the sincerest form of flattery. MLB's All-Star Game has been mimicked by the NHL, NBA, NFL, MLS, and numerous other sports leagues. Despite the copycats, baseball's showcase has remained the most important of them all largely because it has never varied from its original format: the natural rivalry of the NL versus the AL. While other leagues' all-star events fade from memory quite quickly, some of the most memorable moments in MLB history have occurred in All-Star Games. The ASG's luster has undoubtedly dwindled with the introduction of regular-season interleague play in 1997. The decision in 2003 to have the game's winner from that year onward get home-field advantage in the World Series has certainly been contentious. Nevertheless, MLB's Mid-Summer Classic is far and away the best All-Star Game of the bunch.

National League 2 at American League 4

Game played at Comiskey Park I on Thursday, July 6, 1933

National League	ab	r	h	rbi	American League	ab	r	h	rbi
Martin 3b	4	0	0	1	Chapman lf, rf	5	0	1	0
Frisch 2b	4	1	2	1	Gehringer 2b	3	1	0	0
Klein rf	4	0	1	0	Ruth rf	4	1	2	2
Waner rf	0	0	0	0	West cf	0	0	0	0
Hafey lf	4	0	1	0	Gehrig 1b	2	0	0	0
Terry 1b	4	0	2	0	Simmons cf, lf	4	0	1	0
Berger cf	4	0	0	0	Dykes 3b	3	1	2	0
Bartell ss	2	0	0	0	Cronin ss	3	1	1	0
Traynor ph	1	0	1	0	Ferrell c	3	0	0	0
Hubbell p	0	0	0	0	Gomez p	1	0	1	1
Cuccinello ph	1	0	0	0	Crowder p	1	0	0	0
Wilson c	1	0	0	0	Averill ph	1	0	1	1
O'Doul ph	1	0	0	0	Grove p	1	0	0	0
Hartnett c	1	0	0	0					
Hallahan p	1	0	0	0					
Warneke p	1	1	1	0					
English ph, ss	1	0	0	0					
Totals	34	2	8	2	Totals	31	4	9	4

National League   000 002 000—2 8 0
American League   012 001 00x—4 9 0

National League	IP	H	R	ER	BB	SO
Hallahan L	2.0	2	3	3	5	1
Warneke	4.0	6	1	1	0	2
Hubbell	2.0	1	0	0	1	1
Totals	8.0	9	4	4	6	4

National League	IP	H	R	ER	BB	SO
Gomez W	3.0	2	0	0	0	1
Crowder	3.0	3	2	2	0	0
Grove3.0	3	0	0	0	3	
Totals 9.0	8	2	2	0	4	

E–Gehrig. DP–Bartell-Frisch-Terry, Dykes-Gehrig. 2B–Traynor. 3B–Warneke. HR–Ruth, Frisch. SH–Ferrell. SB–Gehringer. LOB–National League 10, American League 5. U–Bill Klem, Bill Dinneen, Cy Rigler, Bill McGowan T–2:05. A–47,595.

May 24, 1935

Site: Crosley Field, Cincinnati

Teams: Philadelphia Phillies vs. Cincinnati Reds

Significance: First MLB Night Game

Impact: Impending darkness no longer impacts MLB games

> "There is no chance of night baseball ever being popular in the bigger cities. People there are educated to see the best there is and will stand for only the best. High-class baseball cannot be played at night under artificial light."—Clark Griffith, owner of the Washington Senators

> "No pun intended, but there was electricity in the air—on the field, in the stands and in the dugout. Ballplayers did not get blasé. They got fired up too."—Billy Sullivan, the Cincinnati Reds' first baseman, recalling MLB's first-ever night game

> "The theory that the players cannot see the ball well under artificial lights was shot to pieces by the staging of some of the finest defensive plays seen here this season."—Jack Ryder of the *Cincinnati Enquirer*, reporting on the game

> "In retrospect, it is difficult to comprehend the aversion of Organized Baseball to the night game when so much interest and enthusiasm were expressed whenever and wherever it was played. Certainly some innovative and venturesome club owner or general manager would seize the initiative and pioneer on this new frontier. But it did not happen immediately."— night baseball historian Oscar Eddleton

If you seek a monument to the Great Depression, look at the light fixtures at any ballpark anywhere in the world. Baseball under the lights was a technological inevitability to be sure, but it took the crippling effects of the Great Depression to make it desirable to MLB. Many enterprises died out during the horrible economic blight that ravaged most of the Western world for the better part of a decade. Night games saved baseball in many small locales and proved the profoundly conservative sport could be open to change when absolutely necessary.

The United States of America in 1933 was a dramatically different place than it had been in 1928. Here is one telling economic factoid: American consumers in 1933 spent only about one-third the sum on new clothing that they had just five years earlier during the prosperous 1920s. With money tight, suddenly the shirt or the dress with the small hole in it was not as unsightly or disposable as it had once been. That statistic is truly symbolic of the times. People learned to live with less, extend what they had to the nth degree, and prioritize their meager finances to make ends meet. Luxury items were generally off-limits to most common folks. Certainly people still needed welcome escapism from the hard times of everyday life—movie attendance actually increased during the

1930s—but it became a more difficult proposition to make people spend their dimes and quarters at baseball parks. Professional baseball at every level felt the pinch.

A quick check of attendance figures shows the extent to which MLB was hurt by the Great Depression. In 1928 about 4.9 million fans passed through the turnstiles in NL ballparks. In 1934 the figure slid to about 3.2 million paying customers—a decline of nearly 35 percent in six years. The Cincinnati Reds were especially struggling to put fannies in Crosley Field's seats. They drew just 206,773 fans for the entire 1934 season—an average of just 2,651 per game. The Reds were not even at the bottom of the heap in fan support in MLB. The St. Louis Browns attracted just 115,305 customers in 1934. That was actually an improvement over the pitiful total of 88,113 souls who had bought tickets to see their home games in 1933. Some MLB teams were facing bankruptcy. In the minors it was worse. In the face of unprecedented financial hardships, entire leagues threw in the towel. Other circuits survived but instituted rash cost-cutting measures such as using just one or two baseballs per game no matter how misshapen or soiled they became.

Any new gimmick that might attract more fans to games would be welcome by baseball's magnates. How about night baseball? It was already being done in the minor leagues to some extent, where desperate measures were being adopted to prevent insolvency. By 1934, 15 of 19 minor leagues had at least one ballpark featuring artificial lights. In some cases, attendance for night games was triple what it was for day games. In many cases the lights were solely responsible for saving minor league clubs from financial ruin.

Few fans realize that the first baseball game ever played under artificial lights occurred way back in 1880. Thomas Edison had invented the incandescent lamp just the previous year, so this baseball game under the lights was a spectacular means of proving how artificial light would be changing the world in the near future. On Thursday, September 2, two amateur teams representing prominent Boston department stores, Jordan Marsh and Company and R. H. White and Company, engaged in a remarkable night baseball game at Nantasket Bay on the seaside resort of Hull, MA. That particular contest was merely a sidelight to an elaborate lighting display staged by the Northern Electric Light Company of Boston to demonstrate the feasibility of illuminating large areas—including entire cities.

The venue for the game was the lawn in the rear of Nantasket's Sea Foam House. Three wooden towers were specially erected some 100 feet apart. At their summits were placed 12 electric lamps reputedly having a combined strength of 30,000 candle-power. Three electric generators powered each tower. The *Boston Post* reported the next day, "when the lamps were lighted after dark the effect was fine. A clear, pure, bright light was produced, very strong and yet very pleasant to the sight."[1] It must have seemed otherworldly to those who experienced light in the darkness for the first time.

The quality of baseball played that evening was not especially great; the game was called after nine innings with the score knotted, 16–16, in order for the players to catch the last boat back to Boston. Some 300 curious onlookers witnessed the spectacle. The *Post*'s correspondent reported the game was played "with scarcely the precision as by daylight."[2]

In recounting the game more than a century later in a superb scholarly article for SABR titled "Under The Lights," researcher Oscar Eddleton commented, "It would make a good story to be able to state that night baseball became an instant success following the debut at Nantasket Bay and that the professional leagues began to consider its possibilities with interest and enthusiasm. Such of course was not the case. Actually, another

50 years passed before the moguls of Organized Baseball finally decided to give the arc lights a serious try."[3] Indeed there were a handful of other exhibition night games in the 19th century that were basically dismissed by the sport's moguls as mere novelty events. Skeptics doubted that high-quality baseball at the MLB level could be played in anything but natural sunlight.

One man was determined to push the benefits of nighttime baseball. He was an inventor from Holyoke, MA, named George F. Cahill. He had already invented a pitching machine, but his new passion was portable lighting for ballparks. He obtained a patent for his invention and travelled wherever some team wished to give his light towers a try, hopeful that they would make him a fortune. On June 19, 1909, Cahill's lights were used at the Cincinnati Reds' ballpark to illuminate a game between two local lodge teams. Some 3,000 fans showed up for the event. The lights were said to have impressed Reds owner Garry Herrmann, who was among the throng, but nothing further came of them. A month later, on July 7, 1909, a Class B Central League game in Grand Rapids, MI, was also played under the lights. Local newspaper coverage said both teams' outfielders had trouble judging fly balls, but batters had no trouble at all swatting pitches under the arcs. Grand Rapids beat Zanesville, OH, 11–10. The game was deemed to be an exhibition because Central League rules stated that no official game could start less than two hours before sunset.

Cahill was persistent. In 1910 he hoped to persuade the American League that night baseball was both viable and profitable. On August 27 of that year, Cahill staged a night game at brand-new White Sox Park in Chicago with the approval of team president Charles Comiskey. More than 20,000 fans turned out to watch the Logan Square and Rogers Park amateur teams play nine innings beneath 20 137,000-candle-power arc lights. As in Cincinnati, the experiment was absolutely successful but Cahill could not sell his idea to MLB.

More than a decade went by before another serious attempt was made to play a meaningful game under artificial lights. It occurred on June 24, 1927, when the Lynn and Salem clubs of the Class B New England League played an exhibition game sponsored by the General Electric Employees' Athletic Association. The seven-inning contest was played at General Electric Field in West Lynn, MA. Lynn emerged victorious, 7–2. The game itself featured several spectacular catches. The large, enthusiastic crowd was estimated at more than 5,000—and it included Claude B. Johnson, the president of the New England League. He was so pleased with the game that he predicted that within five years all leagues would have night baseball—including the majors. Goose Goslin of the Washington Senators was also on hand for the contest and expressed a keen desire to play a night game.

The turning point for night baseball came in 1929. Late that year, E. Lee Keyser, the president of the Des Moines club in the Class A Western League, announced his intentions at the National Association meeting to open the 1930 season with a night game. The schedule-maker did not co-operate with Keyser's attempt to become a baseball pioneer. Des Moines opened its 1930 season on the road. By the time of the home opener under the lights versus Wichita on May 2, 1930, it had been beaten to the punch by the Independence, KS, club of the Class C Western Association. Independence defeated Muskogee, 13–3, in the first professional game (that actually counted in the league standings) under artificial lights on Monday, April 28, 1930. About 1,000 fans turned out for the game on a less-than-ideal, drizzly night. "I don't remember having much trouble with the lights," recalled Des Moines catcher Sherman Walker. "They were pretty good—although I do remember you'd get a shadow which gave you the impression it was only half a ball."[4] Within a short time, the novelty of night baseball was being hailed as the economic savior in many minor leagues.

Still MLB was slow to react. It was not until 1934 that Cincinnati Reds general manager Larry MacPhail sought permission from the NL to play a night game in 1935. During his involvement with the Columbus club of the American Association, MacPhail had seen the tangible financial benefits of night play. Still there was great trepidation among the other NL teams. Eddleton wrote,

> The idea of playing major league baseball under artificial lights was still repugnant to most of the National League executives who regarded the night game as a risky experiment. This sentiment is clearly reflected in the report of the matter in the 1935 Spalding's Baseball Guide.
> With great reluctance, however, MacPhail was granted permission to play seven night games at Cincinnati in 1935 ... provided [the visiting teams] consented. The National League's concession to Cincinnati was justified as an attempt to assist a franchise that was in perilous financial condition.[5]

Accordingly, the first night game in MLB history was played at Cincinnati's Crosley Field on May 24, 1935, with an attendance of 20,422—about eight times the Reds' average home crowd in 1934. President Franklin D. Roosevelt was included in the festivities. From a seat in the White House, FDR pushed a button that activated more than one million watts of electric power from 632 lamps. Artificial light flooded the field, turning night into day. NL president Ford Frick threw out the ceremonial first ball, after which the Reds defeated the visiting Philadelphia Phillies, 2–1, behind the six-hit pitching of Paul Derringer. Cincinnati's Billy Myers led off the bottom of the first with a double— the only extra-base hit in the game—and scored the first run on an RBI groundout two batters later. Cincinnati extended its lead to 2–0 in the bottom of the fourth inning with two consecutive singles and another scintillating RBI groundout. The Phillies got one run back in the top of the fifth. Al Todd singled and later scored on yet another fielder's-choice groundout. That was the last run of the ballgame. It took just 95 minutes to complete. Fittingly, George F. Cahill, the original promoter of night baseball, was present for the historic contest. Although there was some grumbling from traditionalists—and the game had certainly been short on offensive thrills—there was no denying it had been a smashing success.

Remarkably, the momentous occasion received surprisingly little coverage in *The Sporting News*. (Perhaps the inevitability of MLB night games made it not as newsworthy as one might think.) In the May 30 edition of the esteemed weekly trade paper, Cincinnati correspondent Tom Swope did not get around to mentioning MLB's historic first night game until about two-thirds of the way into his lengthy column. When he finally discussed the game he wrote,

> Night ball went over with a bang on its opening here the evening of May 24 with presidents Ford Frick of the National League and William Harridge of the American League both in attendance and high in their praise of the contest which saw Paul Derringer pitch his fifth victory of the season in scoring a 2–1 triumph over the Phillies.
> With 20,422 customers in attendance on a cool night and the efficiency of the lights handicapped somewhat by mist and fog, it appears the Cincinnati club has tapped a fine source of revenue by going in for electric light baseball.
> Before the next night game is played with the Pittsburgh Pirates on May 31 ... the efficiency of the lights will be increased by better focusing. Warmer weather should also help make games under the lights more attractive.

Cincinnati's Crosley Field was the venue for the first night game in MLB history on May 24, 1935. This photograph was taken during the Reds-Phillies game that night. The attendance was about nine times what the Reds typically drew for a daytime home game in 1935. Night baseball may have saved several MLB teams and entire minor leagues from bankruptcy during the Great Depression (National Baseball Hall of Fame Library, Cooperstown, New York).

Sam Breadon, the owner and president of the St. Louis Cardinals, was also impressed by what had occurred in Cincinnati. Breadon boldly told *TSN*,

> I am thoroughly sold on night games as a means of increasing patronage and adding to the income of the National League clubs. It has been proven that parks can be lighted in such a manner as to transform them into daylight conditions, and the risk of injury to the players is no greater than in the afternoon. I actually believe that within three years every club in the two major leagues will be playing night games.

Breadon was hopeful that the Cardinals could quickly install lights at Sportsman's Park. There was one problem, though: The Cards were only tenants there. The St. Louis Browns owned the ballpark, and any renovations had to be initiated by the AL club.

The interest in the groundbreaking contest was obvious. Although it did not merit front-page news in *TSN*, the paper did report a buzz of radio activity surrounding the game, including play-by-play accounts on local Cincinnati and Philadelphia radio stations and over the entire Mutual network. There were numerous on-air interviews with various baseball dignitaries who showed up at the Crosley Field for the event. *TSN* noted that while Ford Frick "was in his element" happily fielding interviewer Bob Newhall's queries, William Harridge "found it rather embarrassing to answer questions about night ball since the American League had not favored it."

Within a few years MacPhail moved on to Brooklyn, where he had lights installed at Ebbets Field in 1938. Attendance improved there too. Philadelphia Athletics owner/

manager Connie Mack, always short on cash, had lights installed at Shibe Park in 1939, becoming the first AL club to embrace the idea of night games. Within five short years more than half of all MLB parks had installed floodlights for night games. With the notable exception of Wrigley Field in Chicago, which steadfastly resisted night baseball until 1988, the longest holdouts were Fenway Park in Boston (1947) and Briggs Stadium in Detroit (1948). The slow but determined progress of night baseball had eventually won over the hearts and minds of baseball's fans and its power-brokers despite the barriers of apathy, skepticism, hostility, and fear of innovation.

Philadelphia 1 at Cincinnati 2

Game played on Friday, May 24, 1935, at Crosley Field

Philadelphia Phillies	ab	r	h	rbi	Cincinnati Reds	ab	r	h	rbi
Chiozza 2b	4	0	0	0	Myers ss	3	1	1	0
Allen cf	4	0	1	0	Riggs 3b	4	0	0	0
Moore rf	4	0	1	0	Goodman rf	3	0	0	1
Camilli 1b	4	0	1	0	Sullivan 1b	3	1	2	0
Vergez 3b	4	0	1	0	Pool lf	3	0	1	0
Todd c	3	1	1	0	Campbell c	3	0	0	1
Watkins lf	3	0	0	0	Byrd cf	3	0	0	0
Haslin ss	3	0	1	0	Kampouris 2b	3	0	0	0
Bowman p	2	0	0	1	Derringer p	3	0	0	0
Wilson ph	1	0	0	0					
Bivin p	0	0	0	0					
Totals	32	1	6	1	Totals	28	2	4	2

Philadelphia	000 010 000—1 6 0	
Cincinnati	100 100 00x—2 4 0	

Philadelphia Phillies	IP	H	R	ER	BB	SO
Bowman L(0–3)	7.0	4	2	2	1	1
Bivin	1.0	0	0	0	0	1
Totals	8.0	4	2	2	1	2

Cincinnati Reds	IP	H	R	ER	BB	SO
Derringer W(5–2)	9.0	6	1	1	0	3
Totals	9.0	6	1	1	0	3

E–None. DP–Cincinnati 1. Riggs-Kampouris-Sullivan. 2B–Cincinnati Myers (3). SB–Myers (6). U–Bill Klem, Ziggy Sears, Babe Pinelli. T–1:35. A–20,422.

August 26, 1939

Site: Ebbets Field, Brooklyn

Teams: Cincinnati Reds vs. Brooklyn Dodgers

Significance: First Televised MLB Game

Impact: Fans not at the ballpark could see a live MLB game for the first time

"Watching a baseball game on television is like chasing the great white whale in a goldfish bowl. It trivializes everything: men two inches high, a ball the size of a bee. It is like looking at the heavens through a dime-store telescope."—novelist Ward S. Just

"Never was a sport more ideally suited to television than baseball. It's all there in front of you. It's theatre, really. The star is the spotlight on the mound, the supporting cast fanned out around him, the mathematical precision of the game moving with the kind of inevitability of Greek tragedy—with the Greek chorus in the bleachers!"—Vin Scully

In 1939 a new technological wonder called television was in its infancy. Few people had one. Radio was still king. There were perhaps 400 television sets in the metropolitan New York City area at the time. Not until the middle of the 1950s would it be unusual to find an American household without a TV set.

Because there were basically no expectations for this medium, early television was a laboratory where new ideas for programming could be tested. On May 17, 1939, Baker Field, the baseball diamond of Columbia University, had the honor of being the site for the first-ever televised baseball game. The combatants facing the Columbia Lions were the Princeton Tigers. The visitors won, 2–1. Station W2XBS broadcast the game using just one camera. According to engineers, its signal was sent out from the Empire State Building and was capable of being received up to 50 miles away. There were obvious shortcomings in that first baseball telecast, though. The ball was almost impossible to see—especially the pitchers' deliveries—and the camera had trouble keeping up with sudden action. A *New York Times* editorial later criticized the poor picture and opined that "television is no substitute for being in the bleachers." The magazine *Variety*, meanwhile, quipped that without the radio-style commentary, the broadcast would have been

Legendary broadcaster Red Barber is shown at the microphone in this 1955 photograph. Barber called the first MLB game ever televised. He worked solo as he broadcast both halves of a Reds-Dodgers doubleheader at Ebbets Field in 1939 (Library of Congress, *New York World-Telegram and Sun* Collection).

the equivalent of a "42nd Street flea circus."[1] Nevertheless, the station considered its experimental broadcast a success. Next up would be a telecast of an MLB game.

Three months later, on August 26, 1939, with some of the problems from the May telecast ironed out, the first televised MLB game was broadcast on W2XBS (later called WNBC-TV) from Ebbets Field in Brooklyn. The Cincinnati Reds were facing off against the Brooklyn Dodgers in a Saturday doubleheader, and both games would be televised. Why was Brooklyn the site of this historic development? Red Barber explained in his autobiography that he wanted to be the first announcer to broadcast a game on the exciting new medium—and he also knew that Dodgers general manager Larry MacPhail loved to be credited with achieving "firsts." Barber wrote, "In being around Larry MacPhail, it became rapidly apparent to me that one of the things he dearly loved was to be first, so it was obvious to me that if you wanted to get him to do something, all you had to do was show him how he could be first in it."[2] Accordingly, with Barber's prodding, MacPhail agreed to allow NBC's cameras into Ebbets Field for the late-season Saturday twin bill between the soon-to-be NL pennant winning Cincinnati Reds and the third-place Dodgers.

In its preview of the Reds-Dodgers doubleheader on August 26, the *New York Times* noted the historic milestone almost as an afterthought: "Adding significance to the occasion is the fact that the double feature will mark the first time in major league history that a ball game has been televised. Both games are to be carried by television by NBC."

Among those watching the historic event were attendees at the 1939 World's Fair in New York City. In the fairground's RCA Pavilion, screens measuring nine inches by 12 inches showed the two games, complete with on-the-spot commentary. What better way to exhibit the wondrous new technology than by televising America's national pastime? Famed radio announcer Red Barber was thrilled to have the honor of calling the game, and it was indeed quite a challenge for him. Seated in an upper-deck seat behind third base, Barber had no monitor to consult, thus he had no idea what the viewers were seeing. The action on the field was filmed with two cameras. One was located near the visitors' dugout and was primarily there to show throws coming to first base. The other was set up in the upper tier of seats behind home plate to give the viewers a panoramic look at the entire field—and Barber had no idea which camera's pictures were being shown to the television viewers at any given time. Moreover, Barber's communication with director Burke Crotty was lost early on in the telecast and never was reconnected properly. The trooper that he was, Barber stalwartly plodded on despite the technical difficulties and the utter novelty of the situation. The Reds won the first game of the doubleheader, 5–2. All of Cincinnati's scoring came in the top of the eighth inning when the Reds parlayed three hits, two walks, and two errors into five runs and turned a 0–2 deficit into a victory. Bucky Walters threw a complete-game two-hitter for the win. The Dodgers came back with a solid 6–1 triumph in the second game to earn a split.

The telecast lasted just a little over four hours, including Red Barber's post-game interview on the field with Dodgers manager Leo Durocher and the standard 20-minute break between games of a doubleheader. Play proceeded at a fast-moving pace, typical of ballgames of that era. As well as calling the play-by-play, Barber had to ad-lib three live commercials to placate each of the Dodgers' regular radio sponsors, who understandably insisted on being plugged during the telecast. For Proctor & Gamble, he held up a bar of Ivory Soap. For General Mills, he poured Wheaties into a bowl, sliced in a banana, poured milk on top of the flakes, and gleefully proclaimed, "Now that's the breakfast of champions." For Socony, Barber put on a Mobil gas station cap and raised a can of oil. "There was not a cue card in sight,"[3] Barber proudly recalled years later.

Those who had seen the university ballgame via television in May noticed a few improvements in the MLB telecast from Ebbets Field. Most noticeable was that the ball was clearly more visible coming from the pitcher's hand—at least it was to some viewers. Television's positive relationship with MLB had been born and the public was eager for more, as Harold Parrott's report in the August 31, 1939, issue of *The Sporting News* certainly indicated. Nevertheless, the landmark event did not merit front-page coverage in *TSN*, just a brief column on page three with other baseball minutiae:

New Dodger Stunt: Twin-Bill Televised Intense Interest Reflected by Public's Reaction to First Experiment of Kind in Majors

Brooklyn, NY—Baseball got its first taste of television here last week—and liked it. The Ebbets Field double-header between the Dodgers and the Reds, August 26, was televised by the National Broadcasting

Company's elaborate equipment, and the public's response to the innovation was described as instantaneous and amazing.

Red Barber, the regular radio broadcaster for the Dodgers, left his usual microphone in charge of Al Helfer to do the sound effects over the air with the television. The experiment was under the direction of Alfred P. Morton, vice-president of the NBC in charge of television. The two huge television truck units were pulled up outside the third-base line at Ebbets Field, and the transmission of the two games went off without a hitch.

Two cameras handled the images. One was planted in the upper tier for a general view of the field, and the other was down on the playing level to get close-ups of the action at the plate. The players were clearly distinguishable, but it was not possible to pick out the ball. Those close-up images left a much better impression than did the general view of the field. Writers, officials, and players viewed the reception of the telecast over a special receiving set installed in the Ebbets Field press room.

The public received the experiment enthusiastically. The Television Building at the World's Fair, which showed pictures of the game, had to shut its doors, so great was the crowd, and a Broadway theater, which advertised the reception of the televised action of the Reds and the Dodgers, was swamped by the inquisitive.

Gordon White of the *New York Times* also gave the groundbreaking broadcast (which the headline writer dubbed "radio camera") a generally favorable review in its August 27 edition. Below are White's remarks, which must be considered the first-ever critique of a professional sport's telecast:

GAMES ARE TELEVISED
Major League Baseball Makes Its Radio Camera Debut

Major league baseball made its television debut here yesterday as the Dodgers and Reds battled through two games at Ebbets Field before two prying electrical "eyes" of station W2XBS in the Empire State Building. One "eye" or camera was placed near the visiting players' dugout, or behind the right-hand batters' position. The other was in a second-tier box back of the catcher's box and commanded an extensive view of the field when outfield plays were made.

Over the video-sound channels of the station, television-set owners as far away as fifty miles viewed the action and heard the roar of the crowd, according to the National Broadcasting Company.

It was not the first time baseball was televised by NBC. Last May at Baker Field, a game between Columbia and Princeton was caught by the cameras. However, to those who, over the television receivers, saw last May's contest as well as those yesterday, it was apparent that considerable progress has been made in the technical requirements and apparatus for this sort of outdoor pick-up, where the action is fast. At times it was possible to catch a fleeting glimpse of the ball as it sped from the pitcher's hand toward home plate.

The public's favorable response to the experimental broadcast from Ebbets Field prompted the Dodgers to televise at least one game per week starting in 1940. The Second World War—which began in Europe less than a week after the landmark baseball telecast—severely curtailed the development of commercial television for a few years, but by 1947 the World Series would be televised for the first time. On that Saturday afternoon in late August of 1939, who could have foreseen the new medium's significant impact on the sport—both positively and negatively—and its enormous influence on how MLB would conduct its business by the end of the century?

Cincinnati 5 at Brooklyn 2

Game played on Saturday, August 26, 1939, at Ebbets Field

Cincinnati Reds	ab	r	h	rbi	Brooklyn Dodgers	ab	r	h	rbi
Werber 3b	4	1	1	1	Coscarart 2b	3	0	0	0
Joost 2b	3	1	1	1	Lavagetto 3b	2	0	0	0
Goodman rf	3	0	0	1	Walker cf	4	0	1	0
McCormick 1b	4	0	2	2	Parks lf	4	0	0	0
Lombardi c	4	0	0	0	Camilli 1b	3	0	0	0
Craft cf	4	0	0	0	Phelps c	3	1	1	0

Cincinnati Reds	ab	r	h	rbi		Brooklyn Dodgers	ab	r	h	rbi
Bongiovanni lf	3	1	0	0		Moore rf	2	1	0	0
Bordagaray lf	1	0	0	0		Durocher ss	3	0	0	0
Myers ss	3	1	0	0		Hamlin p	2	0	0	0
Walters p	3	1	1	0		Tamulis p	1	0	0	0
Totals	32	5	5	5		Totals	27	2	2	0

Cincinnati 000 000 050—5 5 1
Brooklyn 020 000 000—2 2 2

Cincinnati Reds	IP	H	R	ER	BB	SO
Walters W(21–9)	9.0	2	2	0	5	1
Totals 9.0		2	2	0	5	1

Brooklyn Dodgers	IP	H	R	ER	BB	SO
Hamlin L(15–10)	7.1	4	5	1	2	2
Tamulis	1.2	1	0	0	0	1
Totals	9.0	5	5	1	2	3

E–Lombardi (8), Phelps 2 (8). DP–Cincinnati 1. Walters-Lombardi-McCormick. PB–Lombardi (13). 2B–Cincinnati McCormick (32). SH–Goodman (18). SB–Joost (1). U–Bill Stewart, Bick Campbell, George Magerkurth.

April 15, 1947

Site: Ebbets Field, Brooklyn

Teams: Boston Braves vs. Brooklyn Dodgers

Significance: Jackie Robinson's MLB debut

Impact: MLB's "color line" is broken

"Robinson, at 26, is reported to possess baseball abilities which, were he white, would make him eligible for a trial with, let us say, the Brooklyn Dodgers' Class B farm [team] at Newport News, if he were six years younger..."—*The Sporting News*, November 1, 1945

"[I] guess I'm just a guinea pig in this noble experiment. Maybe I'm doing something for my race."—Jackie Robinson, as quoted in an article by Al Parsley of the *Montreal Herald*

"Having Jackie on the team is still a little strange, just like anything else that's new. We just don't know how to act with him. But he'll be accepted in time. You can be sure of that. Other sports have had Negroes. Why not baseball? I'm for him if he can win games. That's the only test I ask."—an unnamed Brooklyn Dodgers veteran quoted in *The Sporting News*, April 23, 1947

In 1906, Sol White, a standout player with the 19th century Cuban Giants, wrote in his book titled *History of Colored Baseball*,

In no other profession has the color line been more rigidly drawn than in baseball. Colored players are not only barred from white clubs; at times exhibition games are canceled for no other reason than objections raised by a Southern player. These Southerners are, as a rule, fine players, and managers refuse to book colored teams rather than lose their services.

"The colored player suffers great inconveniences while traveling. All hotels are generally filled from garret to cellar when they strike a town. It is a common occurrence for them to arrive in a city late at night and to walk around for several hours before finding lodging.

Years later, when Jackie Robinson read White's words, he bitterly commented, "With minor modifications it was [still] true in 1945 when I was on the Kansas City Monarchs of the Negro National League."

Jack Roosevelt Robinson was unquestionably one of the most important social figures in American history. As an athletic pioneer for his race, he was at the forefront of bridging the eras of segregation and integration. MLB was such an important institution in the United States that once its unwritten racial barrier fell, it was a certainty that the rest of society would eventually be integrated too—although it was slow and painful in coming in numerous quarters.

Born in Cairo, GA, in 1919, Robinson was the youngest of five children. His father abandoned the family in 1920. Shortly thereafter Robinson's mother moved her family to Pasadena, CA. Strong-willed, she worked tirelessly at a variety of odd jobs to make ends meet. At a young age Robinson learned to stand up for himself. He was bloodied on occasion, but he never backed down from any perceived insults. Jackie's older brother, Mack, was an accomplished athlete, a silver medalist at the 1936 Berlin Olympics, finishing $4/10$ of a second behind Jesse Owens in the men's 200-metre final. Mack was the inspiration for Jackie to pursue his own greatness in athletics. An outstanding athlete first at Pasadena Junior College and later at UCLA, Jackie lettered in track, football and basketball. Baseball was his least promising sport, although he was renowned as a daring base runner. He batted below .100 in his lone season on the UCLA varsity team.

Robinson left UCLA before graduating. He was playing semipro football when Pearl Harbor was attacked. He was drafted into the United States Army in early 1942. On July 6, 1944, while riding on an army bus, Robinson refused the driver's demand that he move to the rear of the vehicle. He was court-martialed by a zealous officer who inflated the charges to include public drunkenness even though Robinson was a non-drinker. The charges were eventually reduced to two counts of insubordination, but Robinson was acquitted by an all-white panel of officers. The court-martial proceedings prevented Robinson from joining his all-black tank unit overseas. After being transferred to Camp Breckenridge in Kentucky, Robinson was encouraged to contact the Kansas City Monarchs of the Negro American League by the team's former catcher and ask for a tryout. Robinson was given an honorable discharge from the Army in November 1944. The Monarchs were interested in Robinson's services and signed him to a contract that paid him $400 per month in 1945.

Robinson played 47 games at shortstop for the Monarchs and batted .387. He found life in the Negro leagues to be somewhat foreign and unsettling. Their haphazard schedules and the moguls' open acceptance of gambling interests contrasted to the well-organized sports culture he had experienced at UCLA. On April 15, Robinson and five other black players were invited to a special Boston Red Sox tryout at Fenway Park. It was basically a sham, held only to appease a vocal city councilor named Isadore Muchnick, who demanded that his city's AL team at least look at black players. It was hardly a welcoming experience: Robinson and his colleagues were heckled by Red Sox executives in the grandstand and were not invited back. No black player wore a Red Sox uniform until 1959.

One MLB general manager was more broad-minded: Branch Rickey of the Brooklyn Dodgers. Rickey knew there were numerous black players who were talented enough to ply their trade in the majors. Known as MLB's foremost tightwad, Rickey saw integration as being both good for business and for the Dodgers' pennant chances. Rickey also had a personal motivation for integration. As Ohio Wesleyan University's baseball team's manager at the turn of the century, Rickey had seen his best player, a black student, frequently denied lodging in hotels when the squad travelled. He thought such discrimination was unfair and inhumane. He intended to rectify the situation by scouting the Negro leagues for a suitable candidate to integrate professional baseball.

Rickey chose Robinson from a list of potential candidates that included Roy Campanella. Robinson was not the best player in the Negro leagues. Satchel Paige and Josh Gibson each had better claims on that title. Rickey chose Robinson because he believed that Robinson's temperament and experience in the military would serve him well in the racial conflicts that were bound to arise. Robinson and Rickey met for three intense hours at Ebbets Field on August 28, 1945. Rickey tested him with a barrage of racist insults to see if Robinson had the courage to maintain his poise and not fight back. Robinson vowed to turn the other cheek for three years if he were given the opportunity to play in the white pro leagues. Rickey believed him and assigned Robinson to the Dodgers' top farm team—the Montreal Royals. Montreal was conveniently located outside America's borders and was known for its generally cosmopolitan attitudes. It was the ideal home for Robinson's debut among white baseball players and fans. The stunning, formal announcement was made on October 23. For the first time in more than 60 years, a black man was under contract to a team in Organized Baseball.

Many people viewed Rickey's move as a gigantic publicity stunt. *The Sporting News* thought it merited only page-four coverage in its November 1 issue. "It is quite conceivable that the story has received far more attention than it is worth," wrote New York correspondent Dan Daniel, whose displeasure with Rickey was obvious. "Robinson has not been signed by the Dodgers, and insofar as can be discerned, never will play for the Brooklyn club." Daniel's column in *TSN* included a verbatim exchange with Rickey that had certain comical aspects to it.

"Why did you sign a Negro?" the incredulous scribe asked.

"I want to win," replied the Brooklyn GM, considering the question to be absurd.

W. G. Bramham, the president-treasurer of the National Association of Professional Baseball Leagues—the governing body responsible for overseeing Organized Baseball's white minor leagues—had some interesting observations on Robinson's contract with Montreal and Branch Rickey's efforts in the field of racial integration which were printed in that same issue of *The Sporting News*:

After an unremarkable career as an MLB catcher, Branch Rickey found his true calling being the scenes in baseball. It was he, as the Brooklyn Dodgers' general manager, who sought out a talented black player to integrate MLB (Library of Congress, George Grantham Bain Collection).

My personal views do not enter into the picture, but I have no hesitancy in stating them.... There is no law in baseball to prohibit the employment of a member of the Negro race in professional baseball. That is a matter, insofar as our rules are concerned, which is left entirely within our leagues and their clubs.

In my opinion that if the Negro is left alone and aided by his unselfish friends of the white race, he will work out his own salvation in all lines of endeavor.

It is those of the carpet-bagger stripe of the white race, under the guise of helping, but in truth using the Negro for their own selfish interests, who retard the race.

The Negro is making rapid strides in baseball, as well as other lines of endeavor. They have their own forms of player contracts, and, as I understand it their organizations are well officered and are financially successful. Why should we raid their ranks, grab a player and put him, his baseball associates, and his race in a position that will inevitably prove harmful?

Whenever I hear a white man, whether he be from the North, South, East or West, broadcasting what a Moses he is to the Negro race, right then I know the latter needs a bodyguard. When the Negro needs counsel, guidance or assistance from his white friends, he will let it be known and will be found meeting with a ready response unaccompanied by ostentation or trumpeting.

TSN credited Bramham, a 71-year-old judge who resided in Durham, NC, with being "influential in assisting the Negro to better his situation in many ways." He was described as "an outstanding fighter for the Negro cause" during his 40 years in Durham, as he had fought for years to have Negroes installed in his city's police force and "helped the Negroes form their own separate fire department." According to *TSN*, Bramham was "kept awake for two nights after Robinson's signing by the continuous ringing of his telephone. Newspaper men, radio commentators, baseball officials, and others called from all over the country" seeking his views on Jackie Robinson's contract with the Royals.

Jack Horner of the *Durham Morning Chronicle* noted, "Some people seem to think that Rickey is interested in Robinson as a gate attraction for the Negro populace." Horner further speculated, "The general impression in this Southern city is that the Negro player will be so uncomfortable, embarrassed, and out of place in Organized Baseball that he will soon get out on his own accord. I believe it will be a long time before the Negro is accepted in the southern leagues."

J. Alvin Gardner, president of the Texas League, concurred with Horner. "I'm positive you'll never see any Negro players on the teams in Organized Baseball in the south as long as the Jim Crow laws are in force."

In its November 1 edition, *TSN* printed a wide variety of comments and opinions from baseball writers across America. Most were surprisingly supportive and open-minded, even those in Southern cities.

Ed McAuley of the *Cleveland Press* foresaw Robinson having problems with both his white opponents and teammates. "The position of the Negro in Organized Ball still is an aspect of great social question," he wrote. "I'm not so sure that Organized Ball's dugouts, seldom operated on the highest level of mental maturity, are the places to seek the answer."

Bill Corum of the *New York Journal-American* wrote, "Two obligations are imposed by the inevitable bringing of Robinson, or some other Negro star, into baseball: One is for baseball and the fans to accept the fact with common sense. The other is for the Negro race to behave with equal good sense."

Dan Parker of the *New York Mirror* opined, "Why a good, respectable Negro athlete shouldn't fit in just as well into Organized Baseball as he does into college football, basketball, boxing and cricket (to drag an ally into the argument) is something I have never been able to figure out in view of the record of amicable interracial relations in these sports."

Nat Low, a writer for the *Daily Worker*, a New York City Marxist publication, succinctly declared, "It banishes the scourge of Jim Crow from our great national pastime."

Smith Barrier of the *Greensboro* (NC) *Daily News* stated, "I don't see anything wrong with the signing of Jackie Robinson." Frank Spencer of the *Winston-Salem* (NC) *Journal* agreed. "If he is qualified, then give him an opportunity." W. N. Cox of the *Norfolk* (VA) *Virginian-Pilot* took a pragmatic, bottom-line approach. "The mainspring in this question is the Negro ballplayer's ability to deliver on the line of competition. I guarantee that if Jackie Robinson hits homers and plays a whale of a game for Montreal that the fans will soon lose sight of his color."

Beyond the American border, the Montreal newspapers—both English and French—seemed tickled that their city was going to be the grand stage for Rickey's very public social experiment. Paul Parizeau of *Le Canada* noted, "As far as the black race is concerned, Mr. Rickey and [Royals president Mr. Hector] Racine are pioneers in fair play in baseball, and Montreal continues to be the paradise of the minorities as it has been for years and years. However, we doubt if their action will be appreciated in many American cities for feeling against Negroes is so acute." Marcel Desjardines of *La Presse* wrote, "There are some places where the experiment could be tried, but not without risking protests of all kinds and even regretful incidents. It is in itself an indirect testimony to the liberal viewpoint of our people, especially those who follow sports events." The lone voice of concern came from Lloyd McGowan of the English-language *Montreal Star*, who cautioned, "Should Negro Robinson beat out Stan Breard, French-Canadian shortstop favorite, for his place on the Royals next spring—well, that might be another story, and a mighty big one too."

The Royals' 1946 spring training in Florida proved to be an adventure for Robinson and his teammates. On three occasions exhibition games were quashed by local authorities because of municipal laws prohibiting interracial sporting events. When Robinson did get to play, he starred. He got four hits in his first game. It was quickly discovered by Montreal manager Clay Hopper, a white Mississippian who was less than thrilled to be managing an integrated team, that Robinson was better suited for second base than shortstop. When the season finally began, Robinson excelled for the Royals. He batted .349 to lead the circuit and was named the International League's MVP. His daring base running was especially engrossing. Some fans came to the ballpark hoping to see Robinson fail, but many more came to see the excitement he brought to the game. Counting both the Royals' home and road attendance, more than one million fans paid to see Robinson play in 1946—an extraordinary total for the minor leagues.

It was obvious that Robinson would be promoted to Brooklyn for 1947—he was too good not to be in the majors. Many Dodgers, especially those who hailed from Southern states, were not ready or anxious for a black teammate. A petition was drafted and circulated during spring training in 1947 demanding that Robinson not be added to the team. Some Dodgers threatened to quit or demanded to be traded. Manager Leo Durocher—who, just prior to Opening Day, would be suspended by MLB for the entire 1947 season for consorting with unsavory characters—put a stop to the dissent as soon as he got wind of it.

With Durocher sidelined, Clyde Sukeforth managed the Dodgers for the first two games of 1947 before Burt Shotton took over the reins. On Opening Day at Ebbets Field on April 15, 1947, the Boston Braves were the visitors. Robinson could not displace Eddie Stanky at second base for the Dodgers, but he was penciled in at first base and batted second in the lineup. The game was not a sellout. "Of the crowd of 26,623 fans who attended the Flatbush opener, 14,000 were Negroes," reported *The Sporting News*. Newsreel cameras were there to capture the historic moment of Robinson entering the field for the top of the first inning wearing a Brooklyn Dodgers uniform bearing the number 42.

The first batted ball of the game was a grounder to Dodgers third baseman Spider Jorgensen. He threw to Robinson for the putout—and a black man figured in an MLB scoring stat for the first time since September 4, 1884. Robinson's first MLB at-bat in the bottom of the first inning was unproductive; facing Braves ace Johnny Sain, he grounded out to third baseman Bob Elliott. Robinson flied out to left fielder Mike McCormick in the third inning and hit into a double play in the fifth. Batting in the seventh inning with Stanky on first base and nobody out, Robinson's sacrifice bunt was bungled by Braves first baseman Earl Torgeson; Robinson reached second base on his throwing error. Eventually Robinson scored the game's winning run in the Dodgers' come-from-behind, 5–3 victory. Robinson, still new to playing first base, was replaced by Howie Schultz in the top of the ninth inning. In his eight innings at first base, Robinson had made 11 putouts and committed no errors.

Newspaper photographers had fun capturing candid shots of Rachel Robinson, Jackie's wife, suffering through every play in the grandstand. Recalling Jackie's first game three months later in an interview that ran in the July 9 issue of *The Sporting News*, Rachel said, "I felt that if Jackie could only get one hit it would be a boost to his morale. I knew that Jackie himself was tense and nervous because that's the way I felt and I pick it up from him. It's a sympathetic reaction, I guess."

Despite going a disappointing 0-for-3 at the plate on Opening Day, Robinson's debut with the Dodgers was a triumph on many levels far beyond baseball. MLB's nonsensical but longstanding unwritten rule that barred black players had crumbled into dust. Thirteen-year-old future television talk-show host Larry King was one of those in attendance that memorable Tuesday afternoon. More than half a century later he recalled, "I was sitting up there [in Ebbets Field] that day. When he [Robinson] came out of that dugout we knew we were part of history."[1]

Robinson would endure endless insults and harassment aplenty in his first few years as a Brooklyn Dodger—fans in Philadelphia and Cincinnati were especially vitriolic with their racially charged barbs—but Robinson's cool demeanor and undeniably great skills proved that not only could blacks play at the MLB level, they could provide the core of excellent teams.

Slowly the other 15 MLB teams began to notice to wealth of baseball talent that had been stupidly bypassed for six decades. Eleven weeks after Robinson's debut, on July 5, 1947, Larry Doby integrated the American League with a pinch-hitting appearance for the Cleveland Indians, with considerably less fanfare than surrounded Opening Day at Ebbets Field. (Doby struck out on three pitches—or perhaps five pitches, reports vary—versus Earl Harrist of the Chicago White Sox.) Indians owner Bill Veeck explained, "Robinson has proved to be a real big leaguer, so I wanted to get the best available Negro boy while the getting was good. Why wait?"[2] Upon hearing about Doby, Branch Rickey called Veeck "progressive and forward-thinking" and noted that race in MLB was slowly becoming a non-issue. "In the near distant [*sic*] future I look for this thing to take its natural course. The signing of a Negro will be no more than the news of a white boy."[3] Doby suffered the same indignities as Robinson. Some Indians teammates refused to shake his hand. One refused to lend him his first baseman's mitt. "The only difference [was] that Jackie Robinson got all of the publicity," Doby recalled late in his life. "You didn't hear much about what I was going through because the media didn't want to repeat the same story."[4]

Doby knew that although he was a baseball pioneer in his own right, Jackie Robinson had made his journey a little less bumpy. "I had the greatest respect for Jack," said Doby years later. "He was tough and smart and brave. I once told him, 'If not for you, then probably not for me.'"[5] Both Doby and Robinson are enshrined in the Hall of Fame.

The Dodgers comfortably won the 1947 NL pennant with a 94–60 record and Jackie Robinson was named the first-ever MLB Rookie of the Year. A total of 1,807,526 people passed through the turnstiles at Ebbets Field that historic year—200,000 more than any other NL team drew in 1947. It was the best single-season attendance total the Dodgers ever attained in Brooklyn.

Boston 3 at Brooklyn 5

Game played on Tuesday, April 15, 1947, at Ebbets Field

Boston Braves	ab	r	h	rbi	Brooklyn Dodgers	ab	r	h	rbi
Culler ss	3	0	0	0	Stanky 2b	3	1	0	0
Holmes ph	1	0	0	0	Robinson 1b	3	1	0	0
Sisti ss	0	0	0	0	Schultz 1b	0	0	0	0
Hopp cf	5	0	1	1	Reiser cf	2	3	2	2
McCormick rf	4	0	3	0	Walker rf	3	0	1	0
Elliott 3b	2	0	1	0	Tatum pr, rf	0	0	0	0
Litwhiler lf	3	1	0	0	Vaughan ph	1	0	0	0
Rowell lf	1	0	0	0	Furillo rf	0	0	0	0
Torgeson 1b	4	1	0	0	Hermanski lf	4	0	1	1
Masi c	3	0	0	0	Edwards c	2	0	0	1
Ryan 2b	4	1	3	2	Rackley pr	0	0	0	0
Sain p	1	0	0	0	Bragan c	1	0	0	0
Cooper p	0	0	0	0	Jorgensen 3b	3	0	0	1
Neill ph	0	0	0	0	Reese ss	3	0	1	0
Lanfranconi p	0	0	0	0	Hatten p	2	0	1	0
					Stevens ph	1	0	0	0
					Gregg p	1	0	0	0
					Casey p	0	0	0	0
Totals	31	3	8	3	Totals	29	5	6	5

Boston   000 012 000—3 8 1
Brooklyn   000 101 30x—5 6 1

Boston Braves	IP	H	R	ER	BB	SO
Sain L(0–1)	6.0	6	5	3	5	2
Cooper	1.0	0	0	0	0	0
Lanfranconi	1.0	0	0	0	0	2
Totals	8.0	6	5	3	5	4

Brooklyn Dodgers	IP	H	R	ER	BB	SO
Hatten	6.0	6	3	1	3	2
Gregg W(1–0)	2.1	2	0	0	2	2
Casey SV(1)	0.2	0	0	0	0	1
Totals	9.0	8	3	1	5	5

E–Torgeson (1), Edwards (1). DP–Boston 1. Culler-Ryan-Torgeson, Brooklyn 1. Stanky-Reese-Robinson. 2B–Brooklyn Reiser (1); Reese (1). SH–Culler (1); Masi (1); Sain 2 (2); Robinson (1). HBP–Litwhiler (1); Neill (1); Edwards (1). U–Babe Pinelli, Al Barlick, Artie Gore. T–2:26. A–26,623.

August 19, 1951

Site: Sportsman's Park III, St. Louis

Teams: Detroit Tigers vs. St. Louis Browns

Significance: Eddie Gaedel Comes to Bat

Impact: A famous publicity stunt blurs the line between entertainment and competition

> "The most beautiful thing in the world is a ballpark filled with people."—Bill Veeck

> "He was, by golly, the best darn midget who ever played big-league ball. He was also the only one."—Bill Veeck, recalling Eddie Gaedel, in his autobiography

> "The American League office does not approve the contract submitted by the St. Louis American League club for the services of Edward Gaedel on the basis that his participation in American League championship games, in our judgment, is not in the best interests of baseball."—American League President Will Harridge's dim view on Bill Veeck's midget pinch-hitter, as reported in the August 29, 1951, edition of *The Sporting News*

> "Organized Baseball should have a commissioner so I could appeal this decision. Harridge is ruining my baseball career. This is a conspiracy against all short guys. This is a strikeout against the little people."—Eddie Gaedel, reacting to the AL president's edict that banned midgets

To baseball scholars, the year 1951 is special. Of course there was the thrilling National League pennant race between the Brooklyn Dodgers and New York Giants, decided by Bobby Thomson's famous homer. That same year, Joe DiMaggio's magnificent career with the New York Yankees ended, but Mickey Mantle played his rookie season.

Baseball historians also remember 1951 for another reason: On August 19, during the second game of a Browns-Tigers doubleheader at Sportsman's Park in St. Louis, Eddie Gaedel made his only big league plate appearance. Gaedel was the most remarkable pinch-hitter in baseball history simply because of his stature: He was a 3'7" midget!

Gaedel's appearance in an MLB game was the brainchild of Bill Veeck, baseball's most colorful and creative owner. Born in 1914, Veeck was brought up in baseball surroundings. Veeck's father was president of the Chicago Cubs. Bill Jr., quickly learned to love all aspects of the game. After William, Sr.'s death, Veeck became the Cubs' treasurer. One valuable lesson he learned when counting the team's gate receipts was that it did not matter whose money was being spent at the ballpark or why, as long as it was entering the team's coffers. Accordingly, Veeck became an odd combination of a traditionalist and a maverick who would do anything to bring paying customers through the turnstiles.

In his meandering through the minor and major leagues as a baseball entrepreneur, Veeck discovered that a good team combined with excellent marketing could draw extremely well. In their World Series-winning season of 1948, Veeck's Cleveland Indians attracted more than 2.62 million fans to Municipal Stadium—an astonishing number at the time when few MLB teams drew a million fans per year. (That impressive figure stood as a Cleveland club attendance record until 1995.) After acquiring ownership of the pitiful St. Louis Browns in July 1951, Veeck realized his hapless club was destined for another last-place finish. Since he could not advertise winning baseball, Veeck desperately needed gimmicks more than ever. Inspired by "You Could Look It Up," James Thurber's hilarious fictional story from 1941 about a midget pinch-hitter's at-bat in a minor league game, Veeck decided to copy the stunt in a real MLB game.

Veeck was the undisputed leader in promotional ideas to attract fans to the ballpark. He was the first owner to feature regular promotions that were sometimes more than a little bit offbeat. The odder the idea, the more likely Veeck was to embrace it. In the past, the pioneering Veeck had enticed fans through the turnstiles of his minor league and major league ballparks with giveaways of orchids, razor blades, and automobiles. On "Grandstand Managers Night"—which took place just six days after the Gaedel game— he let the hometown fans dictate strategy to Browns manager Zack Taylor with the aid of yes/no placards to answer such questions as whether or not to replace the pitcher. (Specifically, the placard read, "Shall we jerk the bum?") St. Louis won the game, 5–3. However, the Eddie Gaedel stunt was easily Veeck's most memorable.

Years later Veeck recalled, "After a month or so in St. Louis we were looking around desperately to draw a few people into the ballpark, it being perfectly clear by that time that the ball club wasn't going to do it unaided. What can I do, I asked myself, that is so spectacular that no one will be able to say he had seen it before? The answer was perfectly obvious: I would send a midget up to bat."[1]

Before the Sunday doubleheader with the Tigers, Veeck told reporters he had planned what he called a "Festival of Surprises," but would not divulge any specifics. Veeck enigmatically stated that anyone who bought a ticket to see the Tigers-Browns twin bill would see an unforgettable sight. Even with St. Louis 37 games out of first place, 18,369 curious fans—the largest home crowd for a Browns home date in four years— took the bait and paid their way into the ballpark to see something special. They got it.

The first game, won by Detroit, 5–2, proceeded without anything out of the ordinary happening. Between games Gaedel jumped out of a giant papier-mâché cake as part of a promotion to salute the 50th anniversary of both the American League and Falstaff Brewing (the team's radio sponsor). Veeck later claimed that Falstaff's marketing people—"romantics all"—were in favor of any sort of publicity stunt he might devise, but the Browns' owner did not even tell them the details of his master plan. "They were so anxious to find out what I was going to do that they could hardly bear to wait out the two weeks." Veeck added, "I was rather anxious to find out what I was going to do too."[2]

Gaedel inspired a few laughs when he dramatically popped out of the oversized birthday cake. He was wearing elf shoes with curled-up toes. He disappeared into the Browns' clubhouse. When the home team's lineup was posted for the second game, Jim Delsing, who had gotten three hits and scored a run in the first game, was miffed that he was out of the Browns' starting nine for the second game. He recalled, "I went up to Zack Taylor, who was manager, and he said, 'Cool it. You'll be all right.'"[3]

Detroit batted in the top of the first inning of the second game and did not score. Still nothing happened. The fans were puzzled. Where was Veeck's promised "unforgettable sight?" They did not have to wait much longer.

When the Browns batted in the bottom of the first inning, Veeck's plan unfolded. The public-address announcer informed the crowd that Eddie Gaedel would pinch-hit for right fielder Frank Saucier. Gaedel, clad in a tiny St. Louis uniform bearing the number ⅛, strode to the plate carrying a miniature bat. The crowd predictably erupted with hoots and laughter.

Behind the plate was umpire Ed Hurley who was in his fifth season as an AL arbiter. Perplexed, he reputedly exclaimed, "What the hell?"[4] when he saw Gaedel approaching the batter's box. Believing the midget to be a momentary distraction, Hurley brusquely ordered Gaedel off the field. However, Veeck was prepared for such an objection, so manager Taylor quickly produced a valid American League contract (paying Gaedel $100 per game, the standard daily rate for stunt actors at the time) making the midget an official member of the Browns. Hurley scanned his lineup card. Sure enough, Gaedel was listed as a potential St. Louis substitute. Hurley briefly huddled with first-base umpire Art Passarella, who had been working AL games since 1941, to consider their options. They had none. With Gaedel's paperwork thoroughly in order, Hurley grudgingly allowed him to take his turn at bat.

Gaedel dug into the right-handed hitter's batter's box and assumed what one writer called "a classic Joe DiMaggio stance." Veeck's plan had the added benefit of discomfiting the Tigers. Catcher Bob Swift, a notorious prankster himself who would twice serve as Detroit's interim manager in the mid–1960s, requested time to discuss strategy with pitcher Bob Cain. Swift nearly doubled over laughing as he trudged to the mound.

Cain, also amused by his diminutive opponent, rejected a sensible suggestion to pitch to Gaedel underhand. He simply told Swift he would do his best to find Gaedel's tiny strike zone. Swift offered one piece of undeniably sage advice to Cain: "Keep it low."[5] Swift returned to his position behind the plate. He initially sat in the catcher's box, but eventually changed his mind and kneeled on his shin guards to receive Cain's deliveries. Even then Swift was taller than Gaedel. To make his puny strike zone even smaller, Gaedel went into a crouch.

According to *Los Angeles Times* columnist Bob Christie, who attended the game as a 13-year-old, at least two Tigers were utterly oblivious to the goings-on. "Pat Mullin, the Tigers' left fielder, and Johnny Groth, the center fielder, were not aware that the Browns' half of the inning had started," Christie wrote in a 1991 retrospective piece on the 40th anniversary of the game. "They stood talking to each other in left-center field while Cain pitched to Gaedel."[6] Mullin later explained, "We thought he was still warming up, and we couldn't see the midget at the plate. If that kid had somehow got the bat on the ball, neither one of us was in a position to catch it."[7] [Authors' note: The passage of time must have played tricks with Christie's memory of some details. According to the box scores of the Tigers-Browns doubleheader, Mullin was actually Detroit's left fielder in the second game, although he was the center fielder in the first game. Although Groth played 118 games for Detroit in 1951, he was not in the Tigers' lineup in either game.]

It was, ahem, a short at-bat for Gaedel. Cain threw four pitches—all of them high. Gaedel never lifted the bat from his shoulder—largely out of fear. According to one tale, Veeck had warned Gaedel that a sniper would put a bullet through his head if he swung at a pitch. (In James Thurber's work of fiction, the midget tapped a 3–0 pitch into fair territory—contrary to his manager's orders—causing his team to lose the game.)

After the fourth ball, Gaedel slowly trotted to first base, pausing twice to doff his cap to the cheering crowd. "It must have taken him a full minute to get there,"[8] recalled one amused fan. Manager Taylor replaced him with pinch-runner Delsing. "Then I knew what he was talking about—why I wasn't starting the second game."[9] Delsing remembered. Gaedel patted Delsing on the rump and headed toward the Browns' bench. "I felt like Babe Ruth out there,"[10] he later admitted. It was the greatest moment in Gaedel's life, but his professional baseball career was over. Delsing did not score. The Tigers won the game, 6–2, to sweep the doubleheader. The losing pitcher, right-hander Duane Pillette—who had to endure the indignity of a chimpanzee sitting on his lap as part of the entertainment between games—believed he and the rest of the Browns were distracted by the stunt. "I pitched as bad [*sic*] as I ever did in my life," he recalled. "None of the players knew what was going on."[11]

The next day a photograph of Gaedel in the batter's box appeared in newspapers across the continent. (Veeck had tipped off Bob Broeg of the *St. Louis Post-Dispatch* about his planned stunt the night before to ensure that at least one news photographer would be on hand to capture the momentous occasion. Photojournalists generally did not give high priority to Browns home games.) Gaedel told reporters he expected to pinch-hit the next time the Browns loaded the bases. He was certain he could draw another walk and "drive in" a St. Louis run. He also informed the press he would like to bat against two of the AL's formidable fireballers—Bob Feller and Dizzy Trout. It was probably a good thing he never got the chance to face the latter. Trout, a battle-hardened veteran member of the Tigers' pitching staff, was more than annoyed by Veeck's outrageous stunt. Trout told Cain he would have plunked Gaedel "right between the eyes"[12] had he been on the mound.

Despite Gaedel's intentions to be MLB's ultimate role player, AL president Will Harridge, normally a mild-mannered and affable gentleman, was uncharacteristically furious about what had happened at Sportsman's Park. He swiftly nixed Gaedel's plans. Fearful the likes of Gaedel would hurt baseball's integrity, Harridge barred midgets from the sport. "There will be no more of that, boys,"[13] he sternly stated. The humorless Harridge also tried to have Gaedel's plate appearance expunged from the record books, but even an AL president did not possess the authority to erase history.

Although he did not like Harridge's decision about midgets, Veeck expected it. He told reporters he was considering asking the league to conduct an investigation to determine whether Phil Rizzuto of the New York Yankees, the AL MVP for 1950, was a short ballplayer or a tall midget. Rizzuto's height was listed in the Yankees' media guide, perhaps generously, as 5'6".

Gaedel was genuinely flummoxed by Harridge's opposition to his playing professional baseball. "Where does Harridge get that stuff?" he asked. "What did I do? I didn't talk to no gamblers. There ain't nothing in the rules about my size."[14] As a souvenir of his brief MLB career, Gaedel kept a copy of the game's box score that showed that he had batted for Frank Saucier in the first inning and had drawn a base on balls. Gaedel is one of just five players to walk in their only MLB plate appearances and never play defensively. His uniform is one of the historic artifacts on display at the National Baseball Hall of Fame in Cooperstown, NY. According to Gaedel's SABR biography, Gaedel pinch-hit in an amateur game in Sycamore, IL, on September 6, 1951. He took two called strikes and whiffed on a third pitch. He reportedly cussed a blue streak at the plate umpire.

The Sporting News, in stark contrast to Harridge, was thoroughly enamored of the shenanigans at Sportsman's Park. It allotted Veeck's prank a full page of coverage in its August 29 edition, which included a substantial biography of Gaedel. Ruefully, baseball's esteemed weekly newspaper reported that Harridge's decision would also prohibit an MLB club from using a giant in a future game. How an exceptionally tall player might create an unfair advantage for a baseball team was not explained by *TSN*.

For a time Gaedel did well exploiting his celebrity status. He was paid $17,000 for making two television appearances, including one cameo spot on Ed Sullivan's popular *Toast of the Town* variety program. Gaedel did, however, run afoul of the law in Ohio when, in a fit of rage, he engaged in an obscenity-laced tirade against a Cincinnati policeman who refused to believe he had once played major league baseball. In 1961 Veeck, by then the owner of the Chicago White Sox, hired Gaedel once again for a special project: He worked as a guest vendor on Opening Day. It was Veeck's cheeky way of responding to mild criticism that the regular hawkers of snacks and souvenirs at Comiskey Park sometimes blocked the spectators' views of the ballgame.

The key figures in Veeck's famous farce are all gone. Gaedel, Harridge, Hurley, Swift, and Veeck all died long ago. Even the St. Louis Browns are history, having relocated to Baltimore in 1954 where they became the Orioles. They have enjoyed considerably more success in Maryland than they ever did in Missouri. Frank Saucier, the man for whom Gaedel batted, was alive at the end of 2014 at age 88. According to the St. Louis Browns Fan Club website, Saucier was one of 22 ex-Browns still living as of February 2015. Connie Berry, Detroit's shortstop who turned 93 in January 2015, is the only remaining Tiger to have played in the Eddie Gaedel game. He went 0-for-4 at the plate and committed an error.

Bob Cain lived until 1997. Pitching to Gaedel was the lone noteworthy incident in an otherwise unspectacular five-year MLB career. For years, Cain's personalized Christmas cards featured the famous Bob Broeg photo of Gaedel at bat. The inscribed message said, "Hope your target in the future is better than mine was in 1951."[15] "I never saw Eddie after I pitched to him," Cain said, "but a few years later [my wife and I] heard that he had died. We went to his funeral. [We] both thought, well, since I'd pitched to him, it'd be no more than right to go. It really surprised me that no one else from baseball went to the funeral."[16]

MLB's tiniest player died in his hometown of Chicago on June 18, 1961, at the young age of 36, from injuries he sustained in a mugging. The perpetrator of the crime was never found. (Imagine—mugging a midget!) According to one website that specializes in baseball memorabilia, Gaedel's autograph is more desirable and valuable than Babe Ruth's because of its scarcity. Despite being deceased for more than half a century, Gaedel was in the news as recently as 2011. In June of that year his grand-nephew, Kyle Gaedele, was selected by the San Diego Padres in the MLB draft. Gaedele is listed as 6'3" tall. He was playing AA baseball in 2014. According to an interview Kyle gave in 2013, his family possesses the bat his late relative dared not swing on August 19, 1951.

Delsing played ten MLB seasons, but, like Cain, he was mostly remembered as a peripheral figure in Bill Veeck's timeless stunt and the answer to a related trivia question. Delsing once cheerfully told a reporter, "A lot of players have hit 50 home runs [in a season], but I'm the only guy who ever ran for a midget!"[17]

In 1999 *The Sporting News* deemed Eddie Gaedel's pinch-hitting appearance to be the number one "unusual and unforgettable moment" in MLB history. Really, how could it not be?

Detroit 6 at St. Louis 2

Game played on Sunday, August 19, 1951, at Sportsman's Park III

Detroit Tigers	ab	r	h	rbi	St. Louis Browns	ab	r	h	rbi
Priddy 2b	5	1	1	1	Saucier rf	0	0	0	0
Kryhoski 1b	4	1	1	0	Gaedel ph	0	0	0	0
Kell 3b	4	1	3	0	Delsing pr, cf	3	0	1	0
Wertz rf	2	0	0	0	Young 2b	4	0	1	0
Keller rf	2	0	1	2	Mapes cf, rf	5	0	2	0
Mullin cf	5	1	3	1	Lollar c	5	1	0	0
Souchock lf	4	0	1	1	Wood lf	3	0	2	1
Swift c	4	0	1	0	Arft 1b	4	0	0	0
Lipon pr	0	1	0	0	Marsh 3b	4	1	1	0
Ginsberg c	0	0	0	0	Jennings ss	4	0	0	0
Berry ss	4	0	0	0	Pillette p	2	0	0	0
Cain p	2	1	0	0	Suchecki p	0	0	0	0

Detroit Tigers	ab	r	h	rbi		St. Louis Browns	ab	r	h	rbi
Trout p	0	0	0	0		Maguire ph	1	0	0	0
Totals	36	6	11	5		Totals	35	2	7	1

Detroit   000 101 310—6 11 3
St. Louis   000 002 000—2 7 1

Detroit Tigers	IP	H	R	ER	BB	SO
Cain W(10–9)	8.1	7	2	0	5	1
Trout	0.2	0	0	0	0	1
Totals	9.0	7	2	0	5	2

St. Louis Browns	IP	H	R	ER	BB	SO
Pillette L(5–13)	6.2	9	5	5	4	3
Suchecki	2.1	2	1	0	0	0
Totals	9.0	11	6	5	4	3

E–Kell 2 (17), Berry (9), Young (17). DP–Detroit 1. Kell-Kryhoski. PB–Lollar (6). 2B–Detroit Mullin 2 (11), St. Louis Delsing (15); Wood (14); Marsh (12). HR–Detroit Priddy (7, 6th inning off Pillette 0 on). SH–Keller (1); Cain (2). CS–Souchock (2). U–Eddie Hurley, Art Passarella, Joe Paparella.

October 3, 1951

Site: Polo Grounds V, New York

Teams: Brooklyn Dodgers vs. New York Giants

Significance: The Shot Heard Round the World

Impact: It is the "moment" by which all other baseball moments are measured

> "The Dodgers went to eight games ahead with a lead of ten in the losing column and only 37 to play. That meant the Dodgers were safe unless they suffered ten more losses than New York in the meager remaining schedule."—an excerpt from the August 29, 1951, edition of *The Sporting News* after the Brooklyn Dodgers took two games from the St. Louis Cardinals.

> "It was likely the most dramatic and shocking event in American sports and has since taken on the transcendent character of Pearl Harbor and the Kennedy assassination."—journalist George W. Hunt

> "Everybody knows where he or she was when Bobby [Thomson] hit the home run. I was in Boston, watching on television at my mother-in-law's house…. My wife walked through the room, and I said, 'Wait a minute. You might see something you wouldn't want to miss.' And she walked out of the room, and she missed it."—Roger Angell

The most dramatic moment in the history of MLB—and perhaps all of American sports—occurred at the Polo Grounds in Manhattan on Wednesday, October 3, 1951. The stunning, joyous, shocking, gut-wrenching, jaw-dropping, heartbreaking events on that overcast afternoon made it the most memorable game in the glorious history of the sport. It also forever linked two opponents: Bobby Thomson and Ralph Branca.

To appreciate the importance of this one game, one must understand the times. In 1951, the National League was a cozy, eight-team outfit, just as it had been since 1900. Each team played every other team 22 times over the course of a 154-game season, 11 times at home and 11 times on the road. Rivalries flourished. None, however, was more intense than the feud between the Brooklyn Dodgers and the New York Giants.

Because the two clubs' ballparks were just a nickel subway ride apart, geography dictated that passionate Dodgers and Giants fans lived and worked close together. Both groups felt a connection with their teams that went well beyond a simple rooting interest. It was, Heywood Hale Broun eloquently wrote, "a world where baseball teams were the center of a love beyond the reach of intellect, and where baseball players were worshipped or hated with a fever that made bubbles in our blood."[1]

For the first 40 years of the 20th century, the Giants were a powerhouse while the Dodgers rarely finished in the top half of the NL. After the Second World War, the two teams' fortunes dramatically reversed. Suddenly the Dodgers were perennial contenders while the Giants were reduced to also-ran status.

Brooklyn had lost the 1950 pennant to the Phillies in excruciating fashion on the last day of the season, so redemption was the order of business the following year. The 1951 season was supposed to be a cakewalk for Brooklyn—and through the middle of August it was. The Dodgers amassed a huge, 13½-game lead over the Giants. The pennant seemed a certainty until the Giants suddenly caught fire and won 38 of 44 games. Never before had such a daunting lead in a major league title chase been whittled away. When the season ended, both teams were atop the NL standings with identical 96–58 records. A best-of-three playoff series would determine which club would go to the World Series.

New York's Bobby Thomson hit a key homer as the Giants won the first game, 3–1. Clem Labine threw a shutout for the Dodgers as Brooklyn easily took the second game, 10–0. Everything now rode on the decisive third game at the Polo Grounds on October 3.

In the top of the first inning, the Dodgers parlayed two walks and a Jackie Robinson single to score the first run. In the bottom of the second inning, with Whitey Lockman on first base, Bobby Thomson attempted to stretch a single into a double only to discover that Lockman had stopped at second. Thomson put on the breaks but was tagged out in the ensuing rundown. Disgusted, he hoped for a chance at personal redemption. The score remained 1–0 for Brooklyn until the bottom of the seventh, when Thomson's sacrifice fly scored Monte Irvin.

The 1–1 tie did not last very long. Brooklyn collected four singles and a walk to score three runs in the top of the eighth inning to assume a 4–1 lead. There was no further scoring until the dramatic bottom of the ninth. Dodgers fans could taste the NL pennant. The Polo Grounds' P.A. announcer had apparently conceded defeat. He informed reporters over the stadium loudspeaker to pick up their World Series credentials in the *visitors'* clubhouse at the conclusion of the game.

Dodgers starter Don Newcombe was still in the game but was tired, having pitched 271⅔ innings in 1951. "You pitch until your arm falls off!"[2] Jackie Robinson bluntly told him in the dugout.

Alvin Dark led off the home half of the ninth with a single. Despite having a three-run lead, Dodgers first baseman Gil Hodges curiously positioned himself close to the bag to keep Dark from taking a long lead. Don Mueller, an excellent placement hitter, saw the large gap between Hodges and second baseman Robinson and stroked a single that just bounded past Hodges' grasp and into right field. Had Hodges been playing in his normal infield spot, it may have been a double-play grounder. Instead it was a key single that advanced Dark to third base.

After Monte Irvin popped out, Whitey Lockman doubled, scoring Dark and sending Mueller to third. Mueller damaged some ligaments in his ankle sliding awkwardly into the bag and was replaced by pinch-runner Clint Hartung. The score was now 4–2. Bobby

Thomson was the next Giants batter. On deck was a promising 20-year-old, promoted in May from the minor league Minneapolis Millers, named Willie Mays, who would be named NL Rookie of the Year. Mays had batted just .103 in the previous eight games, so Giants manager Leo Durocher was mildly surprised when the Dodgers elected to pitch to Thomson instead of intentionally walking him to get to the struggling rookie. "I'm glad they didn't [walk Thomson]," Mays later admitted. "I didn't want the pennant hanging on my shoulders."[3]

Sensing Newcome was physically spent, Dodgers manager Chuck Dressen summoned Ralph Branca from the bullpen. It was an odd choice because Thomson had always hit Branca well. In fact, Thomson's homer in the first playoff game had been at Branca's expense.

Thomson took Branca's first offering. Plate umpire Lou Jorda called it a strike. Here is Giants radio broadcaster Russ Hodges' famous description of Branca's next pitch:

Branca throws. There's a long fly. It's gonna be, I believe…. The Giants win the pennant! The Giants win the pennant! The Giants win the pennant! The Giants win the pennant! Bobby Thomson hits into the lower deck of the left field stands! The Giants win the pennant! They're going crazy! They're going crazy!

Hodges was so delirious with joy that he forgot to mark Thomson's home run on his personal scorecard. It is displayed among the artifacts of the National Baseball Hall of Fame without showing any result for Thomson's ninth-inning at-bat.

The injured Mueller did not get to witness the historic clout. He was lying in pain on a table in the Giants' clubhouse when he heard the crowd erupt. Years later he told author Ray Robinson, "I couldn't be certain that it wasn't something good for the Dodgers because there were plenty of Brooklyn fans in that park. There was no radio in the clubhouse. But I knew pretty quickly what had happened once the players got back to the clubhouse and started to pour champagne over my injured ankle."[4] Mueller's injury kept him out of the World Series versus the New York Yankees that began the very next afternoon. The Giants, still riding on the momentum from the dramatic victory the day before, won the opener at Yankee Stadium, 5–1, but lost the World Series in six games.

Thomson, of course, became the toast of Giants fans everywhere for his pennant-winning homer (dubbed "The Shot Heard Round the World" by the fawning, incredulous newspaper men). He enjoyed the fame of his shining moment in the spotlight until his death at age 86 in 2010. The whereabouts of the home run ball is unknown, although an excellent 2009 book, Brian Biegel's *Miracle Ball*, presents a compelling theory on what might have happened to it. Collectors estimate its value at $1 million if it ever surfaces and can be positively certified as the Bobby Thomson home run ball—a highly unlikely scenario after all these decades have passed.

A few Dodgers graciously ventured into the joyful mayhem of the Giants' clubhouse to congratulate the victors. A teary-eyed Duke Snider was one. Jackie Robinson was another. Robinson magnanimously told New York coach Bill Rigney that the Dodgers hadn't lost the pennant—the Giants had won it. Then he left. Meanwhile Ralph Branca was absolutely crestfallen. He remained in the visitors' clubhouse for hours. He eventually sought the counsel of a priest to explain why fate had treated him so cruelly.

In 2014, the 88-year-old Branca said in an interview with MLB.com, "I was a good pitcher, but I was only known for throwing Thomson that home-run pitch. That gave me notoriety. People say I became famous, but I say I became infamous."[5]

Esteemed baseball writer Red Smith may have summed up the moment the best in beginning his report on the historic game: "Now it is done. Now the story ends. And there is no way to tell it. The art of fiction is dead. Reality has strangled invention. Only the utterly impossible, the inexplicably fantastic, can ever be plausible again."[6]

Branca and Thomson became historically inseparable. Together they appeared on Ed Sullivan's *Toast of the Town* program, where each man sang "Because of You" to a cardboard cut-out of the other. For whatever it is worth, Branca cannot be accused of being a poor sport—although he has lingering bitterness about the Giants' sophisticated sign-stealing system at the Polo Grounds that came to light years later.

While Russ Hodges' call of Thomson's homer became an all-time classic, few fans recall what Dodgers announcer Red Barber said to conclude his broadcast and console Brooklyn's stunned fans: "Ladies and gentlemen, 311 Americans were killed this week in Korea. Put this game in perspective."[7]

Brooklyn 4 at New York 5

Game played on Wednesday, October 3, 1951, at Polo Grounds V

Brooklyn Dodgers	ab	r	h	rbi		New York Giants	ab	r	h	rbi
Furillo rf	5	0	0	0		Stanky 2b	4	0	0	0
Reese ss	4	2	1	0		Dark ss	4	1	1	0
Snider cf	3	1	2	0		Mueller rf	4	0	1	0
Robinson 2b	2	1	1	1		Hartung pr	0	1	0	0
Pafko lf	4	0	1	1		Irvin lf	4	1	1	0
Hodges 1b	4	0	0	0		Lockman 1b	3	1	2	1
Cox 3b	4	0	2	1		Thomson 3b	4	1	3	4
Walker c	4	0	1	0		Mays cf	3	0	0	0
Newcombe p	4	0	0	0		Westrum c	0	0	0	0
Branca p	0	0	0	0		Rigney ph	1	0	0	0
Totals	34	4	8	3		Noble c	0	0	0	0
						Maglie p	2	0	0	0
						Thompson ph	1	0	0	0
						Jansen p	0	0	0	0
						Totals	30	5	8	5

Brooklyn	100 000 030—4 8 0
New York	000 000 104—5 8 0

Brooklyn Dodgers	IP	H	R	ER	BB	SO
Newcombe	8.1	7	4	4	2	2
Branca L(13–12)	0.0	1	1	1	0	0
Totals	8.1	8	5	5	2	2

New York Giants	IP	H	R	ER	BB	SO
Maglie	8.0	8	4	4	4	6
Jansen W(23–11)	1.0	0	0	0	0	0
Totals	9.0	8	4	4	4	6

E–None. DP–Brooklyn 2. Cox-Robinson-Hodges, Reese-Robinson-Hodges. 2B–New York Thomson (27, off Newcombe); Irvin (19, off Newcombe); Lockman (27, off Newcombe). HR–New York Thomson (32, 9th inning off Branca 2 on 1 out). IBB–Robinson (6, by Maglie); Westrum (15, by Newcombe). SH–Lockman (6, off Newcombe). CS–Snider (10, 2nd base by Maglie/Westrum). U-HP–Lou Jorda, 1B–Jocko Conlan, 2B–Bill Stewart, 3B–Larry Goetz. T–2:28. A–34,320.

April 14, 1953

Site: County Stadium, Milwaukee

Teams: St. Louis Cardinals vs. Milwaukee Braves

Significance: First Milwaukee Braves Home Game

Impact: The overwhelming financial success of the Braves' move from Boston to Milwaukee encourages other MLB owners to seek greener pastures

> "The first severing of ties occurred when the Boston Braves moved to Milwaukee in 1953. Since the Braves had drawn fewer than 300,000 customers in 1952, and since they had always seemed like strangers in what was essentially a Red Sox town, the move made sense, especially so when the Braves nearly septupled their attendance in their first year in Milwaukee."—Donald Honig in *Baseball America*

> "Baseball hysteria still has a firm grip on folks here. An enthusiastic turnout of 34,357 paid rooters rocked the stands and the temporary bleachers of the new Milwaukee County Stadium, April 14, when the Braves rewarded the townspeople with a 3–2 victory over the Cardinals. It was Milwaukee's first National League game since 1878 and its first big-time contest since the American League moved the city's franchise to St. Louis after the 1901 season."—*The Sporting News*, April 22, 1953

During the half-century from the start of the 1903 season to the end of the 1952 campaign, MLB was a quaint, compact institution that witnessed no franchise shifts, no expansion to new markets, and no contraction of its existing teams. Fans of the grand old game quietly saw such stability as reassuring. There would always be eight teams in each major league, located in the same stately ball parks that had become familiar features on the American landscape.

Times were changing in America, though. The postwar prosperity of the 1950s created larger families and new growth in suburbia. Automobiles were now a basic commodity in the typical American household. Better municipal roads and interstate highways meant many dwellers in major urban areas could now live comfortably in homes that had back yards and plenty of living space. Urban decay was starting to set in on many of the country's great metropolises—and MLB suffered because of it. The St. Louis Browns, Philadelphia Athletics, and Boston Braves struggled to survive. All three had clearly become the less fashionable of two MLB franchises in their respective cities.

Things were especially grim in Boston, where the Braves, a team that had represented the Hub continuously in the NL since 1876, were playing in front of vast stretches of empty seats at charmless Braves Field. Although the Braves won the 1948 NL pennant, their success did not secure affection among Boston's sporting public. In the first years of the 1950s, attendance at Braves Field dangerously dropped by nearly 50 percent each year. In 1950 the Braves had finished fourth and drawn more than 944,000 spectators. Team executives blamed the drop from more than one million in 1949 on excessive television coverage of home games. The following year the equally competitive fourth-places Braves of 1951 could not attract even 500,000 fans. By 1952 the Braves were a dismal outfit. They finished seventh in the NL with just 64 wins and attracted just 281,278 paying customers all season. Things could not continue apace. By comparison, the Boston Red Sox drew more than 1.1 million fans to Fenway Park in 1952.

As the 1952 season wound down, the Braves' 49-year-old owner, Lou Perini, who had become a millionaire in the construction business, declared he anticipated his club would absorb an enormous net loss of about half a million dollars for the season. Perini had owned the NL club since 1945 and had experienced both good and bad times. The good times were becoming a distant memory. As a Bostonian and a traditionalist, Perini said he wished to keep the Braves in Boston because of the team's long history there, but he was "not going to be stubborn about it. We are going to [experience] the greatest financial loss in the history of baseball [in 1952], and if it becomes necessary at a future time and the proper opportunity arose [to transfer the franchise elsewhere], we'd be silly if we didn't consider it."[1]

The 8,822 blasé people who were scattered around Braves Field on Sunday, September 21, 1952—a far cry from the 40,000 excited fans who had attended the first contest at the spacious ballpark on August 18, 1915—had absolutely no idea they were attending the last Boston Braves home game. The visiting Brooklyn Dodgers scored six runs in the top of the eighth inning to win, 8–2. (Joe Black threw a complete game for the victorious visitors. On his final pitch, Walker Cooper flied out to Andy Pafko in left field. Earlier in the game, Brooklyn's Roy Campanella hit the final home run at Braves Field. Jackie Robinson rapped out the final hit.) It was the largest turnout for a day game at Braves Field in 1952. *The New York Times* reported that Brooklyn fans made up a significant percentage of the patrons.

Exactly a week later, the Braves played their final game as a Boston entity at Ebbets Field, where they battled the Dodgers to a 12-inning tie. It was an odd finale, to say the least. In the middle of the tenth inning, plate umpire Al Barlick left the game so he could catch a train to take him to his winter home in Illinois. First-base umpire Tom Gorman replaced Barlick behind the dish and amused the Brooklyn crowd of 9,453 by comically mimicking Barlick's distinctive and exaggerated way of calling strikes. Lew Burdette, the last man to throw a pitch for the Boston Braves, apparently did not have his head in the game. With two out in the bottom of the 12th inning, Brooklyn had a runner, Bobby Morgan, on second base. Burdette fielded Tommy Holmes' ground ball and threw it to third base rather than make the routine toss to first base—presumably because he had lost track of the number of outs. Morgan was nevertheless retired in a rundown to end the inning. With the game still deadlocked 5–5, both teams agreed to terminate the meaningless contest. *The Sporting News* said the game ended because of darkness even though Ebbets Field had lights. However, Retrosheet's play-by-play notes bluntly say, "Game called due to lack of interest," which also aptly described the state of the Braves' existence in Boston at that point. The Dodgers were heading to an appointment in the World Series with the New York Yankees on October 1. In contrast the Braves, who had lost ten of their final 12 games, were quietly heading to the history books after 77 years of nobly representing Boston in the NL.

The October 8 edition of *The Sporting News* hinted at what drastic measures might be coming:

> The staggering losses suffered by the Boston Braves and the Pittsburgh Pirates during the season just closed dramatized a situation to which no owner can be indifferent. According to unofficial estimates, the deficits of the clubs … each ran well over $500,000. No businessman in his right mind, regardless of his wealth, would continue for any length of time to swim against such a flood-tide of red ink.

That time and opportunity Perini had alluded to came faster than almost anyone truly anticipated. On March 13, 1953, just a month before the new NL season was to begin, Perini made a startling announcement: Pending the formal approval of the other NL owners, the Braves would be moving to Milwaukee, the city where they presently operated their top farm club. Five days later, permission was granted for the team's relocation. The Braves' minor league team was subsequently shifted to Toledo.

Sports journalist Dan Daniel called the stunning move "an abrupt break with tradition."[2] It was indeed. The Boston Braves were a historic franchise. They had continually operated in the NL since the league's inaugural 1876 season. They had played in and won the first-ever NL game on April 22, 1876. They had also been a member of the old National

It may have lacked charm, but Braves Field was much larger than Fenway Park in terms of seating capacity, so the Red Sox chose to play their home games there during the 1916 World Series when this photograph was taken. In the 1952 season, fewer than 282,000 fans passed through the ballpark's turnstiles, creating the impetus for the Boston Braves to relocate to Milwaukee (Library of Congress, George Grantham Bain Collection).

Association from 1871 to 1875. All told the Boston franchise—the team of King Kelly, Hugh Duffy, Rabbit Maranville and Warren Spahn—had compiled an overall record of 5,118 wins and 5,598 losses. They had famously won the 1914 World Series in what was arguably MLB's greatest upset. Babe Ruth had concluded his illustrious career in a Boston Braves uniform (albeit it was just for 28 games). The longest game in MLB history—a titanic, 26-inning, 1–1 tie between Boston and Brooklyn on May 1, 1920—had been played at Braves Field.

Moreover, the club's sudden move to Milwaukee was the first franchise shift in MLB in recent memory. The last one had occurred exactly 50 years earlier when the AL's Baltimore Orioles uprooted after the 1902 season and moved to New York, where the team would eventually be called the Yankees. For the first time in two generations, baseball fans were reminded that MLB was first and foremost a business and that sentiment alone could not pay the bills. In the March 25 edition of *The Sporting News*—which featured a large cartoon of a native American with five foaming mugs of beer before him—Boston correspondent Lester Smith succinctly explained why the surprise move had occurred:

> There is room for only one major league team in the Hub. That's the simple reason for the removal of the Braves to Milwaukee.
> For a long time Lou Perini and his associates refused to recognize this fact. Even after last year's disastrous results the Braves' boss was not willing to concede that Boston had become an American League city. He magnanimously assumed the blame for the poor showing "because the owners failed to field a team justifying the support of the Boston fans."
> Perini was willing to wait another year before concluding that he was wrong. He thought the team that

would represent the Braves in 1953 would improve the box office take. But advance ticket sales failed to indicate such a trend was in the works.

The Braves last year had the unenviable distinction of losing more money in one season than any other team in the history of baseball, with the loss estimated at around $600,000. This deficit, brought on by a collapse in attendance, cause Perini to consider leaving Boston. Even a man with his financial means cannot be expected to absorb such losses for long.

A new stadium suitable for MLB was already under construction in Milwaukee, though some temporary bleachers would have to suffice in some areas of the ballpark for the Braves' first home stand. The city had expected to be the new digs for the St. Louis Browns. However, the AL vetoed the team's proposed move there, largely because five of the AL owners strongly disliked the flamboyant Browns' owner, Bill Veeck, and would do anything to thwart whatever plans he had for his team—good, bad, or otherwise. As for Perini, he remained connected with his old stomping grounds even after moving his club to Wisconsin. In fact, Perini maintained a home in Boston until shortly before his death at age 68 in April 1972. Knowing full well how dismally the Braves had been supported in Boston in their last two seasons there, few locals had qualms with Perini's business decision to uproot the longtime NL club.

Predictably, Milwaukee embraced the displaced Braves with great passion. Having an MLB team gave the city a new, loftier status. Some 2,000 excited fans greeted the Braves as conquering heroes at Milwaukee's airport after they had opened the 1953 season with a 2–0 victory in Cincinnati. "We can't let these people down," commented an impressed and thoroughly surprised Perini, obviously unused to his club being such an attraction in recent years.

Fans who attended the Milwaukee Braves' first home opener on Tuesday, April 14, 1953, were treated to an excellently played contest. National League president Warren Giles was among the huge crowd. He declared the turnout to be wonderful. Warren Spahn, who was quickly embraced as a local fan favorite, tossed a ten-inning complete game for the home team. Bill Bruton's home run in the bottom of the tenth inning off St. Louis Cardinals pitcher Gerry Staley—who had also lasted the distance—broke a 2–2 tie to send the crowd home happy. The outcome could not have been scripted better. The Milwaukee Braves were away to a tremendous start.

The Sporting News reported an astonishing statistic: The paid attendance for Opening Day in Milwaukee of 34,357 exceeded any *series* total the Boston Braves had drawn in 1952 by 65 percent, never mind the number of fans for a single contest! From a business standpoint, the Braves' move from Boston had already been a spectacular success after just one game.

By the end of the 1953 season, the Braves had won 92 games, one more than the championship Braves of 1948 had won. The Brooklyn Dodgers had won 105 games to take the NL pennant, but the Braves, however, had soundly defeated the Dodgers in what was becoming the most important statistic to MLB owners: tickets sold. The Braves drew precisely 1,826,397 fans to County Stadium to lead all of MLB in attendance—and set an all-time turnstile record for NL clubs—surpassing the 1,807,526 fans the Dodgers had drawn in Jackie Robinson's rookie season of 1947. Even the all-powerful and prosperous New York Yankees were 300,000 fans in arrears of the nouveau-riche Braves in 1953.

At the end of the season a wholly satisfied Perini told *The Sporting News,* "The baseball fans of the East and other sections of the country do not exhibit the grand support that I have noticed in Milwaukee and at other places in this part of the country. It is none of my business what any other club owner does with his team, but I would suggest that if any club is about to be moved from its present location, the Midwest is the place to locate it."

It was little wonder that other MLB teams, struggling mightily to balance the books, began earnestly to search for greener pastures elsewhere. Because of the overnight success of the Milwaukee Braves, the geography of MLB would undergo numerous and profound changes in the decade that followed.

St. Louis 2 at Milwaukee 3

Game played on Tuesday, April 14, 1953, at County Stadium

St. Louis Cardinals	ab	r	h	rbi	Milwaukee Braves	ab	r	h	rbi
Hemus ss	3	0	0	0	Bruton cf	5	2	3	1
Schoendienst 2b	4	0	0	0	Logan ss	2	0	0	0
Musial lf, cf	5	0	0	0	Mathews 3b	3	0	0	0
Bilko 1b	4	0	0	0	Gordon lf	4	0	1	1
Slaughter rf	3	1	0	0	Pafko rf	4	0	0	0
Jablonski 3b	4	0	2	1	Adcock 1b	3	1	1	0
Haddix pr	0	1	0	0	Crandall c	3	0	1	0
Johnson 3b	0	0	0	0	Dittmer 2b	4	0	0	0
Repulski cf	3	0	1	0	Spahn p	4	0	0	0
Lowrey ph, lf	1	0	1	1					
Rice c	3	0	1	0					
Benson pr	0	0	0	0					
Fusselman c	1	0	0	0					
Staley p	4	0	1	0					
Totals	35	2	6	2	Totals	32	3	6	2

St. Louis	000 010 001 0—2 6 1
Milwaukee	010 000 010 1—3 6 2

St. Louis Cardinals	IP	H	R	ER	BB	SO
Staley L(0–1)	9.1	6	3	2	2	6
Totals	9.1	6	3	2	2	6

Milwaukee Braves	IP	H	R	ER	BB	SO
Spahn W(1–0)	10.0	6	2	2	3	2
Totals	10.0	6	2	2	3	2

E–Jablonski (1), Dittmer (2), Spahn (1). DP–Milwaukee 2. Gordon-Mathews, Logan-Mathews-Dittmer. 2B–St. Louis D. Rice (1, off Spahn); Lowrey (1, off Spahn). 3B–Milwaukee Bruton (1, off Staley). HR–Milwaukee Bruton (1, 10th inning off Staley 0 on 1 out). SH–Schoendienst (1, off Spahn); Crandall (1, off Staley); Logan (1, off Staley). HBP–Logan (1, by Staley). U-HP–Jocko Conlan, 1B–Lon Warneke, 2B–Augie Donatelli, 3B–Tom Gorman. T–2:29. A–34,357.

September 24, 1957

Site: Ebbets Field, Brooklyn

Teams: Pittsburgh Pirates vs. Brooklyn Dodgers

Significance: Last Game at Ebbets Field

Impact: The most heart-wrenching franchise shift in sports history heralds the start of west-coast baseball

"Memories turned homeless."—narrator Donald Sutherland describing the demolition of Ebbets Field in Baseball's Hall of Fame.

"There is no reason why Los Angeles fans have to wait for a defunct club in order to bring the majors [there]. With cash in hand, enterprising citizens could approach any going club, buy it, and move it…"—New York Yankees co-owner Del Webb, quoted in the February 9, 1955, edition of *The Sporting News*

"Baseball is a game dominated by vital ghosts; it's a fraternity, like no other we have of the active and the no longer so, the living and the dead."—Richard Gilman

On the night of Tuesday, September 24, 1957, Tex Rickards, the longtime public-address announcer at Brooklyn's Ebbets Field, declared that the attendance for the season at the historic ballpark was 1,026,158. "This is the thirteenth straight year over a million," he noted, "and the only team to leave after doing it." Ballpark organist Gladys Gooding, another Ebbets Field fixture, was having trouble dealing with the finality associated with that night's Pirates-Dodgers game. She had locked herself in the ballpark's organ loft with her sheet music and a bottle of liquor, and was going through a repertoire of appropriately melancholy tunes she had specifically selected for her last assignment at the historic old ballyard. Among them were "My Buddy, Am I Blue?," "Don't Ask Me Why I'm Leaving," "What Can I Say After I Say I'm Sorry?," and "After You've Gone." When the final out was made, the upbeat refrains of "California, Here I Come" drifted across the largely empty stadium. As the tarpaulin was being placed across the infield, Gooding concluded her medley with "May the Good Lord Bless and Keep You" and the wholly appropriate "Auld Lang Syne."

The surprisingly small turnout of nostalgic fans who decided to come to the final MLB game ever played at Ebbets Field was there to witness baseball's version of a funeral. A reporter from the *San Francisco Examiner*, with the strangely apt name of Curly Grieve, had made his way east to cover the goings-on. Five days later Grieve would report on the New York Giants' last game at the Polo Grounds too. He was a glutton for punishment.

"The death of a ballclub in a city is a sorry spectacle," Grieve wrote in *The Sporting News*, "and don't mistake it. Only a small crowd of 6,702 showed up to bury the Dodgers, tabbed for Los Angeles." Grieve continued, "Only a year ago—give or take a week—those same stands held raving maniacs who screamed … at the hated Yankees. And as the Dodgers swept two World Series games in succession, the ancient, bilious blue edifice soon to be razed really rocked and rolled."

Just a few years earlier, the idea of the Dodgers leaving Brooklyn would have been met with utter incredulity. The Dodgers' famous victory in the 1955 World Series seemed to cement the team in Brooklyn forever. Reporting the celebrations that followed the Series, John Drebinger of the *New York Times* stated, "Far into the night rang shouts of revelry in Flatbush. Brooklyn at long last has won the World Series and now let someone suggest moving the Dodgers elsewhere."

It was an optimistic decree, but not an accurate one. The Dodgers' long-term future in Brooklyn was shaky. Certainly Ebbets Field, which had first opened its doors in 1913, had not aged especially well by 1957. Some folks said the ballpark was run-down. Others, less tactfully, called it dilapidated. It was undeniably situated in a decaying neighborhood with limited parking. (There were only about 700 spaces reasonably close to the ballpark.) Its seating capacity could not be expanded. But its occupants were still the powerful and famous Brooklyn Dodgers, perennial NL pennant contenders since 1941, and one of the truly elite teams in MLB. The pitiful St. Louis Browns, the unfashionable Philadelphia Athletics, and the underachieving Boston Braves had all been drawing sparse crowds to their home games, so their recent departures from their ancestral homes was at least understandable from the standpoint of survival economics.

But these were the mighty Dodgers: Reese, Hodges, Snider, Robinson, Furillo and Campanella. They were the World Series champs from just two seasons previous. Yes, Ebbets Field's attendance had peaked during the historic 1947 season and had declined since that time. The demographics of Brooklyn had changed in the decade since Jackie Robinson's debut. With the *Brooklyn Eagle* ceasing publication in January 1955, there was no longer a daily newspaper that uniquely served and united the borough. One of Brooklyn's largest employers, the Naval Yard, had dramatically slashed jobs. The trolley car service that had once dominated the borough's streets was discontinued. Many of the Dodgers' longtime fans had moved to suburbia and were no longer regular attendees at the ballpark. Instead they listened to their team's exploits on the vast Dodgers radio network that boasted 19 stations and extended into Connecticut, Massachusetts and Pennsylvania—or they tuned into the home games on free TV. Even with smaller attendance the team was still turning a profit—and they were the Dodgers. They were the MLB team at the forefront of integrating the National Pastime. They had made baseball history as well as American social history. Something was horribly wrong if the famous Brooklyn Dodgers were being uprooted and moved 3,000 miles away. To MLB fans at the time, California seemed as distant a location as Jupiter to relocate a team.

Specifically what went wrong in Brooklyn was a clash of wills and priorities between Dodgers owner Walter O'Malley and a headstrong, unelected New York City bureaucrat named Robert Moses. O'Malley had acquired control of the Dodgers in 1950. Moses, who held the position of New York City Construction Co-Coordinator, was a celebrated urban planner—and perhaps the most powerful person in New York City because he had the legal power to condemn property and re-assign it for the benefit of the public virtually at his whim.

As early as 1952, O'Malley began writing letters to Moses in which he asked for certain abandoned properties to be condemned under the city's bylaws so the Dodgers could build a new, more modern park in downtown Brooklyn at the intersection of Atlantic and Flatbush Avenue, a location easily accessed by public transportation. O'Malley, a forward-thinking businessman, envisioned a spectacular 50,000-seat stadium with a retractable roof—something that MLB would not see until the late 1980s. Moses, who believed that the automobile would soon usurp public transportation, steadfastly said no. If the Dodgers wanted a new ballpark, Moses would provide land in Queens near the site where the 1939 World's Fair had been staged. This option was absolutely out of the question as far as O'Malley was concerned. He insisted the Dodgers would cease to be the Brooklyn Dodgers if they had a home stadium in another New York City borough or somewhere else far beyond. "Whether it's five miles or 5,000 miles, they will not be the Brooklyn Dodgers,"[1] he declared. If the team had to move out of Brooklyn, the untapped California market was a more attractive alternative. Moses bluntly told O'Malley that if the Queens solution was not to his liking, he was free to build a new stadium anywhere he pleased, as long as he financed it with his own money.

Michael D'Antonio, the author of a history book on the Dodgers franchise titled *Forever Blue*, wrote in *Sports Illustrated* that O'Malley would have kept the team in Brooklyn but for the obstacles put in place by Moses and other New York politicians. "[O'Malley] had wanted to build the iconic ballpark in Brooklyn," says D'Antonio. "Instead, he was maneuvered into the role of baseball's Benedict Arnold. How this occurred is a case study in the power of the most imperious bureaucrat in the history of urban America: Robert Moses."[2]

Dave Anderson of the *New York Times* disagreed, placing the entire blame firmly on O'Malley. He asserted that O'Malley made demands that he knew Moses could not accept so that he could shift blame to the bureaucrat when the team inevitably uprooted from Brooklyn. "Please remember that Robert Moses didn't move the Dodgers," Anderson wrote. "Walter O'Malley did."[3]

All the while the city of Los Angeles was indeed wooing the Dodgers. Preliminary discussions about moving the club to southern California had begun in 1953. The West Coast had movie studios and gorgeous weather, but it did not yet have MLB. Minor league teams had flourished there for more than 50 years, but it was certainly not the same as having big-league teams. An MLB team meant status to a city. Accordingly, Los Angeles was prepared to present O'Malley with an offer he could not refuse.

In 1956 O'Malley began paying a different kind of hardball with New York City. He announced that the Dodgers would play seven of their 77 home games in both 1956 and 1957 at Roosevelt Stadium in Jersey City, NJ, a venue that had even fewer seats than the 32,000 at Ebbets Field. While O'Malley described it as "part of our effort to spread Dodger baseball,"[4] cynics claimed these games were the first westward movement in the team's eventual relocation to California. By the mid–1950s, significant improvements in air travel had made California a viable location for MLB clubs. A trip from New York to Los Angeles could be made in about 4½ hours—about half the time it took with a propeller-driven aircraft. Rail travel was considerably slower, of course. When the Dodgers purchased a 44-passenger airplane in January 1957—they were the first MLB club to do so—the writing was clearly on the wall for all those who wanted to see it.

To make relocation to the West Coast truly viable, a second team had to move there as well. It made no sense logistically to have just one NL team located 1,600 miles west of its closest neighbor, the St. Louis Cardinals. The New York Giants were the best candidates. The team that once was the pride of Gotham—and had been a fixture in the city since 1883—had become steadily unfashionable since the late 1930s. In 1957 they were last in NL attendance, failing to draw even 700,000 fans to the Polo Grounds. Only six radio stations carried Giants baseball broadcasts in their final season in New York. Even in 1954, when the Giants won the World Series and had the incomparable Willie Mays patrolling center field, their home attendance had been just slightly above 1.15 million. They never again drew a million fans to the Polo Grounds. "People have moved out of the city," Giants owner Horace Stoneham said in May 1957, describing his team's plight. "You used to be able … to go out and get a crowd from within walking distance of the park and fill the stands. You can't do that anymore."[5] Personal safety was also becoming a major concern. "People at the ballpark got mugged,"[6] noted future Giants broadcaster Lon Simmons.

Urban decay and general indifference to the historic team were undeniably making any sort of move more and more appealing to the Giants. MLB commissioner Ford Frick agreed. Reminiscing about the Giants' final years at the Polo Grounds, he wrote,

> The famous old park had deteriorated. Transportation facilities, once adequate, no longer met the demands of a growing population. Ninety percent of the available parking space, never adequate, had been taken over for public projects—the center-field area by a highway and a public school; the left-field area by high-rise,

low-income apartments. Even more critical, the whole neighborhood had become so run-down that fans were afraid to walk even a block or two to see a night game, and equally reluctant to park their cars in the area, for fear of robbery, or mugging, or even worse. To cap it all, Stoneham was given official notice that his lease, about to expire, would not be renewed. The park was to be razed, and the land taken over for public housing.[7]

In 1957 the federal government established the Celler Committee to examine MLB's exemption from antitrust laws. It was somewhat off-topic, but both O'Malley and Stoneham used the occasion to testify about how their businesses were now suffering as their ballparks' respective neighborhoods declined. "Look what's happening [to Brooklyn]," O'Malley said. "We've lost our last newspaper. We're losing our department stores, and there hasn't been a hotel or theater built there since 1929."[8] What was implied but not openly blamed was that the complexion of Brooklyn was changing. One Brooklynite laid the cards on the table when interviewed for Peter Golenbock's book *Bums: An Oral History of the Brooklyn Dodgers*. "The white families were moving out of Brooklyn," he said matter-of-factly, "and they were the backbone of Ebbets Field."[9]

Stoneham testified too and hinted that the same problem was affecting his business. The Washington Heights section of upper Manhattan, where the Polo Grounds was located, was no longer safe. "Our current location is such that it is impossible for us to operate profitably,"[10] Stoneham told the committee. In July 2009 a Giants supporter, using the internet name Bitter Fan, recalled in a post on the Baseball Fever blog, "Inner city parks did not tend to be well policed in those days," he noted. "Urban blight came very quickly, quicker than the police anticipated. You'd get a lot of kids who wanted to watch your car for a dollar, and if you didn't pay up, you might have a flat tire or a broken window when you came back. The building of the Polo Grounds Towers [a low-income housing development] next door … contributed to the feeling the Polo Grounds was an unsafe place to watch a ballgame." On July 4, 1950, a 53-year-old fan named Barney Doyle was killed in his seat at the Polo Grounds by a stray bullet fired indiscriminately from one of the nearby housing projects. A photo of Doyle's lifeless body sprawled over his seat appeared prominently in the next day's *New York Daily News*. It was not exactly a ringing endorsement for fans to flock to the Polo Grounds. The neighborhood was indeed changing in the postwar years—and not for the better.

The Giants initially fancied relocating to Minneapolis, where their top farm team, the Millers, played in a modern ballpark that was said to be better than all but two MLB grounds. However O'Malley easily convinced Stoneham to move his outfit to California too. The two clubs' long and bitter rivalry that dated to the 1890s could thus continue uninterrupted—at the other end of the continent. (What used to be a short commute between the rivals' respective ballparks would now, however, be a daunting 382-mile jaunt.) At a meeting of NL owners in Chicago on May 28, 1957, the Giants and Dodgers were unanimously given permission to relocate to the West Coast if they so chose—with the stipulation that both teams had to go, not just one of them. The two teams' collective decision about moving was not quite official yet, but it was plainly going to happen. In the June 5 edition of *The Sporting News*, Chicago correspondent Edgar Munzel described the excited atmosphere of the owners' meeting: "Approval of the National League magnates for the western move was so whole-heartedly enthusiastic that, if it had been a political convention, the session would have erupted into a huge parade with the band playing 'California, Here I Come.'"

Not yet conceding that the 1957 season would be the Dodgers' last campaign in

Brooklyn, O'Malley told Joseph M. Sheehan of the *New York Times*, "In fairness, all I can say now is that this action opens the door for exploration of further possibilities."[11] Similarly Stoneham said his ball club "would explore the possibilities [of moving westward] more thoroughly."[12] Sheehan noted in his story about the meeting, "While listening with an attentive ear to the blandishments of Los Angeles, the Dodger president still is on record as hoping that the long-stalled campaign to build a new, downtown Brooklyn stadium for the Dodgers will get off the ground."[13] Sheehan even desperately suggested that if the Giants and Dodgers left town, the Cincinnati Reds (called the Redlegs at the time) might consider moving to New York City because Crosley Field was even smaller and as "equally obsolete" as either the Polo Grounds or Ebbets Field.

When asked about taking his storied National League team away from the youngsters of New York, Stoneham coldly remarked, "The kids? I feel badly for the kids; I've seen lots of them at the Polo Grounds. But I haven't seen many of their fathers lately."[14] On the other hand, San Franciscans were as tickled to get the transplanted Giants as Angelinos were to adopt the Dodgers.

The Giants made their formal announcement first—which was a bit of a stunner because it was not seen to be quite as inevitable as the Dodgers leaving New York City. In the July 31 edition of *The Sporting News*, correspondent Joe King mourned the end of the Giants' tenure at the Polo Grounds, but he fully understood the financial realities of the situation. "The celebrated old grounds no longer is a prize," he wrote, "as it was when the elevated steam railroad, and later the marvel of rapid transit, the subway, brought eager fans to the park. It is obsolete, a relic in the age of the gas engine and PARKING, PARKING, PARKING! There is no parking in the narrow shelf which the Polo Grounds holds on the Harlem shore, between the river's edge and Coogan's bluff." Exposing more than a little personal bias not certainly shared by Dodgers rooters, King further declared, "John McGraw's team will wander, but McGraw's park will remain the queen of memories. No other can match its history."

On Sunday, September 8, 1957, the New York Giants defeated the Brooklyn Dodgers, 3–2, at the Polo Grounds to salvage one victory in a three-game series. Curt Barclay outdueled Don Drysdale for the win before 22,376 fans. It was a milestone contest: It was the last game the two storied teams ever played against each other on the East Coast. New York had won 650 games in the rivalry to Brooklyn's 606. The Giants had won 51.75 percent of the teams' head-to-head battles, mathematically proving what their fans already knew: The spirited competition had been remarkably close since their first game on May 3, 1890, a tilt Brooklyn won, 7–3.

Exactly three weeks later, at the Giants' final home game on Sunday, September 29, slightly more than 11,000 fans showed up at the Polo Grounds on an overcast afternoon for what was optimistically billed in the newspapers as the team's "farewell party" after 75 seasons of representing New York City in the NL. Most spectators were not in a jovial mood, however. A pregame ceremony featured Giants manager Bill Rigney presenting a bouquet of roses to Blanche McGraw (John McGraw's 74-year-old widow), who was referred to as "the First Lady of the Polo Grounds," a surprise appearance by 86-year-old Jack Doyle, who had managed the team way back in 1895, and the touching return of 81-year-old George Levy, who brought along the simple megaphone he had quaintly used to announce the lineups in the distant past. They were feted alongside a terrific array of star players from the home team's glorious yesteryears. Carl Hubbell, Rosy Ryan, Rube Marquard, Billy Jurges, Moose McCormick, Larry Doyle, Monte Irvin and a dozen others were on hand to take one final bow at their old digs. Bobby Thomson and Whitey Lockman, two heroes from the famous 1951 NL championship team, had been reacquired by the Giants in trades. Rigney put both of them in the starting lineup for old-time's sake. The thick layer of nostalgia did not make the impending death of the famous New York Giants any easier to swallow. Journalist Roger Angell, a passionate Giants fan, made a point of attending the last contest at the Polo Grounds. "I didn't feel anything," he would later write. "Nothing at all. I guess I just couldn't believe it. But it's true, all right. The flags are down, the lights in the temple are out, and the Harlem River flows lonely to the seas."[15]

Stoneham smartly chose not to be at the Polo Grounds for the final game and thus missed the spectacle of seeing himself hanged in effigy. He also missed witnessing the Pittsburgh Pirates thump the home team on Bob Friend's 9–1 complete game and hearing the patrons sing this lovely, heartfelt tribute to him after 1954 World Series hero Dusty Rhodes grounded out to Pittsburgh shortstop Dick Groat to end the game at 4:35 p.m.:

> *We want Stoneham!*
> *We want Stoneham!*
> *We want Stoneham—*
> *With a rope around his neck!*

The fans stormed the field in search of Polo Grounds souvenirs. Giants historian Noel Hynd likened the surreal scene to "a carcass being picked." Bases were ripped from their moorings. Dirt from the pitcher's mound was scooped into bags. Nothing was sacred. The Eddie Grant Memorial—a 100-pound bronze plaque honoring a former Giant who was killed in the waning days of the First World War—was ripped from its place on a five-foot-tall marble slab in deep center field and not seen again for 42 years. (Even though reporter Milton Bracker declared in the following day's *New York Times*, "the plaque was subsequently retrieved from three youths by the police," it vanished from the public's eye. In 1999 it was found in the attic of the former home of Gaetano Bucca, a police officer whose 1957 beat included the Polo Grounds.) After the looting subsided, the fans' wrath turned on the entire home team. According to the next day's *New York Times*, another ditty, sung to the tune of "The Farmer in the Dell," wafted through the emptying ballpark:

> *We hate to see you go!*
> *We hate to see you go!*
> *We hope to hell you never come back!*
> *We hate to see you go!*

Garry Schumacher, a former baseball journalist who worked as the Giants' public relations man, wryly commented, "If all the people who will claim in the future that they were here today had actually turned out, we wouldn't have to be moving in the first place."[16] Blanche McGraw was among the last fans to leave the old ball yard. The gates were padlocked shortly after her departure. As she was escorted to the car that would take her to her Pelham home, she ruefully said, "It would have broken John's heart."[17] The Giants finished a distant sixth in the NL standings in 1957, 26 games in arrears of the front-running Milwaukee Braves.

Five days earlier, it was the third-place Dodgers who played their final home game in Brooklyn. It was meaningless as far as the NL standings were concerned. The Dodgers had been eliminated from the pennant race on September 20. Unlike the Giants, though, the Dodgers went out as winners in their farewell appearance before their hometown fans. They won 2–0 against the Pirates in a subdued affair that lasted just 123 minutes.

Fittingly, that was the identical score by which the Dodgers had won Game Seven of the 1955 World Series. "Ebbets Field had become a desolate and unhappy place,"[18] wrote Michael D'Antonio. Duke Snider recalled, perhaps metaphorically, "It was dark that night at the ballpark. The lights didn't seem as bright as usual."[19] Jim Gilliam and Gino Cimoli scored the final runs at Ebbets Field. Gil Hodges drove in the final run in the third inning. In the home half of the eighth inning, Hodges also became the last Dodger to step into the batter's box. He was struck out by Pirates relief specialist Roy Face. Pittsburgh's first baseman, Dee Fondy, a one-time Brooklyn prospect, was the last man to come to bat; he grounded out to shortstop Don Zimmer. (When Fondy died in 1999, his obituary mentioned his esoteric claim to fame.) Danny McDevitt pitched a five-hit, complete-game shutout for the victors. All the Pirates hits were singles. After the final out was made, many of the Dodgers lingered near their dugout to sign autographs for the teary-eyed faithful before disappearing forever. There was none of the brazen souvenir-seeking that had occurred at the Polo Grounds. All the while the Ebbets Field grounds crew pointlessly raked the infield and pulled the tarp over the pitcher's mound in preparation for the next game that would never come. Ebbets Field had hosted more than 3,400 NL games over 45 MLB seasons. The Brooklyn Dodgers ended their 68th season on the road in Philadelphia with a 2–1 loss to the Phillies on the same day the Giants bid adieu to the Polo Grounds. A promising young left-handed fireballer with a streak of wildness named Sandy Koufax threw the last pitch in Brooklyn Dodgers history.

"After the 1957 season," baseball historian Michael Coffey wrote, "the Giants and the Dodgers left New York to the Yankees. They took with them a marvelous Willie Mays, an undiscovered Sandy Koufax, Vin Scully, Russ Hodges, an admirable past, and the future of baseball."[20] The 2007 HBO documentary *The Ghosts of Flatbush* put it even more romantically: "The Brooklyn Dodgers live on as the ghosts of baseball when it was perfect."

Brooklyn's loss, of course, was Los Angeles' gain. The Dodgers (and O'Malley specifically) were feted as heroic pioneers for bringing MLB to the West Coast. By Opening Day of 1962, the Dodgers had the most picturesque ballpark in the majors, erected on free land in Chavez Ravine that the city of Los Angeles was glad to finally have put to good use. The first game at Dodger Stadium was probably the greatest moment in Walter O'Malley's life. Surely both San Francisco and Los Angeles deserved to have MLB teams— but not at the expense of Brooklyn.

To this day, nearly six decades after the sad departure of Newk, Duke, Pee Wee and the rest of the Dodgers, Walter O'Malley remains a reviled figure in Flatbush. One commonly told wisecrack in Brooklyn says it all: If you were locked in a room with Adolf Hitler, Josef Stalin and Walter O'Malley, and you had a gun with only two bullets, whom would you shoot? Every Brooklynite knows the correct answer: You'd shoot O'Malley— twice.

Pittsburgh 0 at Brooklyn 2

Game played on Tuesday, September 24, 1957, at Ebbets Field

Pittsburgh Pirates	ab	r	h	rbi	Brooklyn Dodgers	ab	r	h	rbi
Baker 3b	4	0	0	0	Gilliam 2b	3	1	0	0
Mejias rf	4	0	0	0	Cimoli cf	4	1	1	0
Groat ss	3	0	1	0	Valo rf	4	0	1	1

Pittsburgh Pirates	ab	r	h	rbi
Skinner lf	4	0	1	0
Fondy 1b	4	0	0	0
Mazeroski 2b	3	0	1	0
Clemente cf	3	0	1	0
Peterson c	3	0	1	0
Daniels p	2	0	0	0
Freese ph	1	0	0	0
Face p	0	0	0	0
Totals	31	0	5	0

Brooklyn Dodgers	ab	r	h	rbi
Hodges 3b,1b	4	0	1	1
Amoros lf	3	0	0	0
Gentile 1b	2	0	0	0
Reese 3b	1	0	0	0
Campanella c	2	0	0	0
Pignatano c	1	0	0	0
Zimmer ss	2	0	2	0
McDevitt p	1	0	0	0
Totals	27	2	5	2

Pittsburgh	000 000 000—0	5 1
Brooklyn	101 000 00x—2	5 1

Pittsburgh Pirates	IP	H	R	ER	BB	SO
Daniels L (0–1)	7.0	5	2	1	3	2
Face	1.0	0	0	0	0	2
Totals	8.0	5	2	1	3	4

Brooklyn Dodgers	IP	H	R	ER	BB	SO
McDevitt W (7–4)	9.0	5	0	0	1	9
Totals	9.0	5	0	0	1	9

E–Daniels (1), Reese (19). DP–Pittsburgh 1. Mazeroski-Groat-Fondy, Brooklyn 2. Hodges-Gilliam-Gentile, Zimmer-Hodges. 2B–Brooklyn Valo (10, off Daniels); Zimmer (9, off Daniels). SH–McDevitt (4, off Daniels). U-HP–Augie Donatelli, 1B–Vic Delmore, 2B–Vinnie Smith, 3B–Jocko Conlan. T–2:03. A–6,702.

October 1, 1961

Site: Yankee Stadium I

Teams: Boston Red Sox vs. New York Yankees

Significance: Roger Maris's 61st Home Run

Impact: The longer 162-game schedule creates the great "asterisk debate" that lingers to this day

> "All it brought me was headaches."—Roger Maris, on his quest to break Babe Ruth's touchstone record of 60 homers in a season, as quoted in *Baseball America*

> "Baseball fans love numbers. They love to swirl them around their mouths like Bordeaux wine."—Pat Conroy

> "Baseball statistics are like a girl in a bikini. They show a lot, but not everything."—Toby Harrah

> "In a peculiar attempt to stem the tide of numerical unmeaning, then Major League Baseball Commissioner Ford Frick conducted a one-man witch-trial against [Roger] Maris that culminated in the public tattooing of an asterisk to the new record—a punctuation mark intended, I assume, to serve the same general purpose of Hester Prynne's scarlet A."—writer James Duncan from his novel *The Brothers K*

> "There was no doubt that Roger had an unfair advantage because of those extra eight games. But eight did not seem like so many; if the season had been lengthened to, say 175 games, there would have been no debate. But debate there was, as intense as any ever in baseball."—Donald Honig, *Baseball America*

To say that all MLB seasons are equal is folly. Over the 14 decades of top-level professional baseball that have been played, the lengths of schedules have varied enormously.

During the National League's formative seasons, each member club routinely played fewer than 100 games. In the NL's first season, 1876, each team played the other seven teams ten times apiece for a 70-game schedule. (At least they were supposed to play 70 games; only the Boston Red Caps managed the feat.) By 1880 the NL schedule had increased to 84 games per team. By 1895 it had increased dramatically to 132 games per NL club to accommodate the expanded 12-team league. Even when the NL contracted to eight teams at the beginning of the 20th century the schedule increased to 140 games per team to satisfy the public's demand for even more baseball. By 1904 both the American League and National League were playing 154-game schedules. The eight teams in each league were slotted to play the other seven clubs 22 times per season: 11 games at home and 11 on the road. It would stay that way for more than half a century.

The fluctuating length of schedules in MLB's first 30 years did not cause much concern to anyone who was interested in making comparisons from one season to the next, largely because few fans were doing so. At the time, one-season baseball records were not the cherished, touchstone numbers they are today. If a new mark for stolen bases, hits, doubles or even home runs was set for a single season, it did not garner much fanfare. The stability of the 16-team, two-league big leagues, however, created the pleasant byproduct of easy comparisons for one-season accomplishments. Ty Cobb's 1907 season, for example, could be reasonably compared with some other MLB player in 1957. Thus baseball fans' insatiable appetite for statistics can be readily understood. No other sport provides its fans with such an evenly distributed smorgasbord of data. Any development that might skew the symmetry of the sport's numbers would understandably be met with a certain level of hostility.

In 1961 the AL embraced expansion. Two new teams were added to the circuit, making the AL a ten-team loop. The unfashionable and generally unloved Washington Senators were permitted to move to Minneapolis, where they became more profitable as the Minnesota Twins. A new version of the Senators took root in D.C., while across the continent the Los Angeles Angels franchise was established. Increasing the AL to ten teams presented a problem: Elementary school arithmetic dictated that the traditional 154-game slate could not be maintained along with a balanced schedule. Instead of an eight-team league in which each club played the other seven teams 22 times, the AL's new schedule for 1961 would have each team facing the other nine clubs 18 times apiece. Nine times 18 equals 162. That meant eight extra games per team appeared on the AL's schedule, an increase of 5.2 percent over 1960. (The NL, which stayed an eight-team outfit in 1961, retained its 154-game schedule. In 1962 the NL accepted two expansion teams—the New York Mets and Houston Colt .45s—and similarly adopted a balanced, 162-game schedule.) For one season—and one season only—the two major leagues operated with different schedule lengths. Few people thought it would present any type of problem. The biggest impact, feared Frederick G. Lieb of *The Sporting News*, was that the AL's pennant contenders would steamroll the weak new expansion teams. Nevertheless, *TSN* was optimistic that "[the] 1961 campaign ... promises to be historic and highly fruitful." Yes, it was.

For the New York Yankees, winners of all but two AL pennants since 1947, the 1961 season was one of change at the top. Long-time manager Casey Stengel was dismissed after the club's surprising World Series loss to the underdog Pittsburgh Pirates the previous autumn. All Stengel had done since taking the reins of the Yankees in 1949 was win ten pennants and eight World Series in his 12 years as the club's colorful manager. Stengel's advancing age was cited as the reason for his dismissal. "I'll never make the mistake of being 70 years old again,"[1] humorously quipped the out-of-work Stengel.

The new man in charge of the Yankees was Ralph Houk. Houk, 41, had been a coach on Casey Stengel's staff and at one time had managed the Yankees' top farm team. Frequently seen as Stengel's heir apparent, Houk had the good fortune to step into the leadership role of a Yankees team that had very few weaknesses and was fully expected to repeat as AL champions in 1961. Although Houk could be hot-tempered at times—he was ejected 47 times from MLB games, the exact same number as Billy Martin's managerial total—he was considered a "players' manager" because he would seldom scold or humiliate one of his charges in front of his teammates. Houk's nickname was "the Major" because he had risen to that rank as a Marine combat veteran in the European Theater of the Second World War, where he had earned numerous citations.

Houk's greatest offensive weapon was his famous center fielder. Mickey Mantle, not quite 30 years old, was a beloved national institution. A feared switch-hitter, Mantle had won the AL Triple Crown in 1956. It was thought by some baseball writers that the watered-down pitching staffs that expansion had brought to the AL in 1961 might provide Mantle with a decent shot at some truly phenomenal power-hitting stats. Baseball-Almanac.com notes, "If anyone [was to do it] Mantle was scheduled to be the one to take over the spot on the all-time homer list. 'Mick' was loved by the fans and the press." In a 1996 ESPN feature on the 1961 home run chase, Keith Olbermann declared, "Some fans thought Mantle was the rightful heir to Ruth; others thought no one was."

On Opening Day at Yankee Stadium, however, the Yankees lost, 6–0, to the lowly Minnesota Twins before a shockingly small crowd of 14,607 on a cold and cloudy day. Minnesota's Pedro Ramos allowed only three hits—all singles—to the New Yorkers as Whitey Ford lost a rare home opener. The defeat was an aberration. The Yankees won their next five games and never looked back. Moreover, they would lose only 16 of their 81 home games in 1961 and would set some staggering offensive records before the season ended.

Mantle's teammate, outfielder Roger Maris, had a high pedigree himself, but was nowhere near as popular as Mantle. (No other Yankee was, of course.) Maris had played for both Cleveland and Kansas City before coming to New York in a trade following the 1959 season. It was a good fit, at least on the ball field. Maris, a left-handed slugger, hit 39 home runs in his first season as a Yankee. He led the AL in slugging percentage, RBI, and extra-base hits. When the 1960 season ended Maris was rightfully named the league's MVP. Maris and Mantle both possessed powerful batting strokes but had distinctly different personalities. While Mantle reveled in being a celebrity in New York City, the introverted Maris preferred solitude. Accordingly, Maris was perceived by fans and reporters as somewhat standoffish and sullen. Nevertheless, the two became great friends. In fact, they shared a home during the tumultuous 1961 season.

It took 11 games before Roger Maris hit his first home run of 1961. After 28 games he had just three. Then the homers started to come more frequently. By July 5 Maris had 32. By the end of July, Maris had whacked 40 home runs—a faster pace than Babe Ruth had hit them in 1927, when he set the seemingly untouchable MLB mark of 60 in a season. Four of Maris' clouts came in a doubleheader versus Chicago on July 25 off four different White Sox pitchers. All of a sudden, the extra eight games on the AL slate were significant. What if Maris eclipsed Ruth's magical mark somewhere between game 155 and the end of the season? Would it still be a new record? *The Sporting News* had no qualms about denying Maris the new record if circumstances merited it. In its July 26 edition, the weekly publication noted, "Because it is obviously unfair to subject 154-game records to feats achieved in the expanded 162-game schedule, while at the same time being unjust to bar athletes from beating the glittering performances of the past, Commissioner Ford Frick did the game a distinct service on July 17 when he announced that all shots at Ruth's mark would be judged on the 154-game basis."

Remarkably, Maris was not alone in pursuing Ruth's record. Teammate and house-mate Mickey Mantle was nearly keeping apace. When July ended, Mantle had 39 home runs. The home run derby between the two teammates became far more compelling than anything else occurring in baseball that season. As a team, the Yankees were breaking all existing home-run records. In an eight-game span from June 24–July 2 they hit 20 homers—a remarkable sum until one considers it was one homer shy of the 21 home runs they had accrued in another eight-game stretch earlier in 1961. In their first ten games versus Boston alone, New York hit 22 home runs. Long balls flying skyward off Yankees bats were good for business throughout the entire AL. After 45 road games, the Yankees had drawn more than one million fans at opposition ballparks. Customers want-ing to see a blast by either Maris or Mantle had gotten their wish an impressive 31 times.

Suddenly, the thought of Ruth's "unbreakable record" of 60 home runs in a season indeed being broken did not seem so far-fetched. On July 17, when Maris had 35 home runs and Mantle had 32—both well ahead of Ruth's 1927 pace—Commissioner Frick issued the aforementioned edict about the single-season home run record potentially falling in the elongated season. Any record set in the first 154 games would be a new record without any baggage attached to it. However, if it were attained in any games beyond the 154th game, "a distinctive mark" would denote it had been set in a longer season. Thus Ford Frick's infamous asterisk was foisted upon the baseball world. The asterisk is something of an urban myth. It was suggested by New York sportswriter Dick Young during a question-and-answer session he and other newsmen had with Frick. Frick never said there would be an asterisk attached to any seasonal record set beyond the 154th game—only that two records would be listed to make an allowance for the dif-ferent schedule lengths. Largely forgotten was that there was no official record book pub-lished by MLB at that time. Various statisticians and publications kept track of MLB milestones but they were all independent of the Commissioner's Office.

Almost a quarter of a century later, in Maris' obituary, the *New York Times* offered this explanation of Frick's ruling: "The commissioner of baseball ... apparently reflected the traditionalist view of many fans that the Olympian feats of Babe Ruth must be defended against long seasons, short fences and newly arrived sluggers—even one who eventually played in seven World Series and hit 275 home runs in 12 seasons in the big leagues."

Frick had been MLB's commissioner since 1951 and had not attracted a whole lot of attention doing his job until the summer of 1961. Some people questioned Frick's motives and neutrality in the "asterisk" controversy—with good reason. A former sports journalist for the Hearst newspaper chain, Frick had ghost-written numerous articles for Babe Ruth during the Bambino's heyday. The scribe and the world's most famous ballplayer became good friends. When Ruth was on his deathbed in the summer of 1948, dying of throat cancer, Frick was among the last non-family members who saw him alive.

Frick's decision may have been clear and logical to *The Sporting News*, but others were more inclined to consider a season to be a season—the extra eight games in 1961 be damned. Not even AL president Joe Cronin agreed with Frick's verdict. "I do not wish to become involved in a dispute with Ford," Cronin told *The Sporting News*, "but I can see no logic in the ruling that if Ruth's record is to be topped, it must be excelled inside 154 decisions. After all, the Babe hit his 60 [home runs] in 1927 in 151 games. Therefore, if you want to be technical, you could say that Maris and Mantle have to do it in 151 [games]. I certainly respect the Commissioner's feelings about the matter, but so far as I am concerned, it will be a new official record if either or both do it in 162 games."

"I don't care what Mr. Cronin says," Frick responded gruffly. "There will be two records if it happens in 162 [games]. One will say, 'Most home runs in a season, 154 games: Ruth, 60.' The other will say, 'Most home runs in a season, 162 games.'"

In 1962 the NL accepted two expansion teams—the New York Mets and Houston Colts—and similarly adopted a balanced 162-game schedule. Frick believed that the 162-game AL schedule would be a very temporary measure. He envisioned another round of expansion with both major leagues having 12 teams apiece. This would enable both leagues to revert back to a balanced 154-game slate with each team playing the other 11 clubs in its league 14 times. Be that as it may, for one season—and one season only—the two major leagues operated with different schedule lengths.

The debate extended beyond just raw numbers. Fans liked to point out that Ruth played in only day games—which could be a help or a hindrance—against only white players, and only had to travel within a small geographical area. Maris was playing at night and during the day, enduring cross-country flights, and batting against pitching staffs whose talent was clearly watered down by the AL's expansion but were racially integrated. (The home run rule was different in Ruth's era too: A fair ball that bounded over a fence was a home run until 1931; in Maris' era it was a ground-rule double. It was a moot point, though; Ruth had no "bounce" home runs in 1927. Often forgotten is that Maris and Mantle each had a home run nullified in the same game—July 17 in Baltimore—because the game was rained out before it became official. Ruth had no such misfortune.) Ruth and Maris both had one enormous advantage in common—each had a feared slugger batting behind him. Maris had Mantle. Ruth had Lou Gehrig. Maris was not intentionally walked a single time in 1961. That telling statistic was not kept in 1927, but it is quite likely that no pitcher deliberately gave Ruth a free pass in 1927 in order to face Gehrig. Ruth had actually broken the home run record four times. The first occurred in 1919 when he was still a member of the Boston Red Sox. That year the Bambino smacked 29 home runs in 138 games. The old record of 27 homers in a single season, set by Ned Williamson in 1884, occurred in just 113 games. "No one was running for an asterisk then," noted ESPN's Keith Olbermann years later.

Cynical fans suspected that the rash of home runs was the result of a conspiracy: They suspected that AL baseballs were livelier in 1961 than they had been in the past, a charge strenuously denied by Edwin L. Parker, the president of A. G. Spalding and Bros., who claimed in a press conference that his company had been manufacturing baseballs for MLB the same way—with the exception of the war years "when proper yarn and rubber were not available"—since the 1920s. Yes, the two-pronged assault on MLB's single-season home-run record had so captivated America that a sporting goods magnate was compelled to hold a press conference. Old-timers were skeptical, though. Former MLB manager, 75-year-old Bill McKechnie—who was the player/manager of the 1915 Newark Peppers of the Federal League—opined in *The Sporting News*, "Despite statements to the contrary, the 1961 ball is livelier than I've ever seen it. I see ordinary batters—even pitchers—hit the ball into the stands, even to the opposite field."

The debate about livelier baseballs aside, the pursuit of Ruth and history continued unabated. Fans in New York and elsewhere generally supported the more popular Mantle, somehow concluding that Maris was not a true Yankee since he had played on two other AL teams earlier in his career and was in only his second season with New York. Maris started receiving hate mail. Years later Tim McCarver, Maris' teammate on the St. Louis Cardinals, remembered, "He used to tell me about all the hate letters that he'd receive from those who revered Ruth. Because another guy was trying to break his record it was almost like [Maris] was desecrating an icon."[2] The weight of history and notoriety obviously took its toll: Maris' hair started to fall out in clumps.

As Maris and Mantle—collectively dubbed the "M&M Twins" by the sporting press—continued their assault on Ruth's record, it became the baseball topic on everyone's mind. Fans and players chose favorites and weighed the odds that one or both might surpass 60 homers. Rocky Colavito, whose Detroit Tigers were giving the Yankees some unexpected competition for the AL pennant, did not like either man's chances of topping the late Babe. "Several guys in our league are capable of it," he told *The Sporting News*, "but I don't think Ruth's record will be broken. Switching from day ball to night ball and back again is rough. Ruth didn't have to do that."

Old-timers chimed in with their two cents' worth too, usually in support of the Babe. Rogers Hornsby, arguably the greatest batter in National League history, said he didn't want to see Ruth's record beaten by a .270 hitter. (Maris batted .269 in 1961. Ruth batted .356 the year he swatted 60 homers.) "Maris has no right to break Ruth's record,"[3] Hornsby tersely concluded. Strangely, Maris became a villain. He became increasingly short-tempered with the hordes of reporters who kept asking him the same questions over and over. Keith Olbermann likened the media to "white blood cells going for a germ." There were no organized post-game press conferences in 1961. Following some games Maris would be answering questions in the Yankees clubhouse for nearly four hours until every reporter had left the premises with the raw material for his story. The intense scrutiny on Maris took its toll. "I was born surly," Maris acknowledged. "Even the Yankee clubhouse attendants think I'm tough to live with. I guess they're right; I'm miffed most of the time."[4] Years later Maris lamented, "I think the only privacy I had was when the game was going on."[5]

Manager Houk did his best to defend Maris and his occasional moodiness. "Roger answers a thousand questions a day from newspapermen, broadcasters, magazine writers, and others," the Yankees' manager told *The Sporting News* that summer. "Generally the questions run to a pattern, but there are a few smart alecks who have put words in his mouth and who give a misleading twist to what he says. That bothers him."

When he did comment on his attempt to surpass Ruth's record, Maris' replies could be amusing, thoughtful, angry—or any combination thereof. "I'm not trying to be Babe Ruth," he noted. "I'm just trying to hit 61 home runs and be Roger Maris."[6] On another occasion Maris facetiously asked which 154 games should count in the record chase—the first 154, the middle 154, or the last 154?

In the September 6 edition of *The Sporting News*, Joe King noted that the ordeal was negatively affecting both Mantle and Maris.

> Whatever sort of pressure the thumb screw might be grinding down on the nerves of the two sluggers, they surely were tired in what [manager] Houk referred to as a mental more than physical fatigue.

In addition to the normal attrition of the stretch, plus the five a.m. arrivals after night getaways in this fantastic schedule, the M&M combo was subjected to a ceaseless chase by autograph hounds, friends, and friends of friends wherever they went.

In Kansas City, the [Yankees'] hotel was jammed with sightseers, and there were many autograph-hunting elders among the kids. A writer there put the address of the Maris clan in suburban Raytown in the paper. Roger said, "When we got up that morning our street looked like the Los Angeles freeway."

Although Mantle and Maris were both ahead of Ruth's pace in mid–July, Ruth had saved his strongest home run months for the end of the 1927 season. Beset with a gimpy leg, Mantle would fade and fall off Ruth's pace, finishing with a mere 54 home runs—the highest total of his spectacular career. Mantle would never again hit as many as 40 in a year. Maris fell behind the ghost of Ruth too, but kept within striking distance. A productive series in Detroit, in which he hit his 57th and 58th home runs, gave Maris a fighting chance to beat the deadline established by Frick. Maris needed to connect for two home runs on Tuesday, September 20, in Baltimore on a windy and drizzly evening to equal the Babe. He got one. Having "failed" with 59 home runs in Frick's allotted time, Maris took a day off to escape from the pressure. Six days after Maris' 59th home run, he connected for number 60 at home versus Baltimore's Jack Fisher.

The record—tainted or not—came on the final day of the season, Sunday, October 1, versus Boston at Yankee Stadium. A sizable percentage of the 23,154 fans who were in attendance opted to buy seats in the right field bleachers in hopes of catching a historic souvenir. The game was meaningless as far as the standings, the Yankees having long since clinched the AL pennant. In the first inning, Maris flied out to rookie left fielder Carl Yastrzemski. His next at-bat came in the fourth inning. Maris got ahead in the count, 2–0, as 24-year-old, right-handed Boston rookie Tracy Stallard pitched to him cautiously. "Stallard's next pitch was a fastball that appeared to be waist high and right down the middle," declared John Drebinger of the *New York Times*. "In a flash, Roger's rhythmic swing, long the envy of left-handed pull hitters, connected with the ball." The solo home run was the only score in the game. Phil Rizzuto's radio call of the historic moment has been heard countless times:

Here's the windup. Fastball hit deep to right! This could be it! Way back there! Holy cow, he did it! Sixty-one for Roger Maris! Look at 'em fight for that ball out there! Holy cow—what a shot! Another standing ovation for Roger Maris. Sixty-one home runs! And they're still fighting for that ball out there. People are climbing over each other's backs. One of the greatest sights I've ever seen here at Yankee Stadium!

Years later, Stallard, who compiled a mediocre 30–57 career pitching record for three MLB teams, noted, "I'm glad [Maris] did it off me. Otherwise, I would never have been thought of again. That was about all I did, and I've had a good time with it."[7] (That's not exactly true. Stallard was on the wrong end of another historic feat: He was the losing pitcher for the woeful New York Mets when Jim Bunning of the Philadelphia Phillies threw a perfect game against them on June 21, 1964. It was the first perfect game tossed by an NL pitcher in the 20th century. It was also one of 20 losses Stallard was tagged with in 1964.) In John Drebinger's *New York Times* report, the scribe agreed that Stallard had earned a quirky place in baseball history. He wrote in his coverage of the game, "Stallard's name, perhaps, will in time gain as much renown as that of Tom Zachary, who delivered the pitch that Ruth slammed into the Stadium's right-field bleacher for number 60 on the next to last day of the 1927 season."

As for the home-run ball, a teenager from Coney Island named Sal Durante snagged Maris' 61st dinger with a bobble-free, one-handed grab—and tenaciously guarded the ball from numerous other patrons who tried to rip it from his hands. Security personnel eventually arrived to rescue Durante and take him and the baseball to the Yankees' clubhouse, where he met with Maris (and reporters, of course) after the game. Durante tried to give Maris the ball with no strings attached but the slugger graciously declined the prized souvenir. Durante eventually sold the ball to Sam Gordon, a New York City restaurateur, for $5,000. That was the equivalent of more than 83 weeks' salary based on what the 19-year-old was earning at the time as a truck driver. Gordon's standing offer for the baseball was well known. In fact, Red Barber's seldom heard call of Maris' 61st home run on WPIX-TV disappointingly gives more importance to the value of the home run ball than to Maris' feat. Half a century later, the 69-year-old Durante said it was the only baseball he ever caught at an MLB ballpark, although he claimed that he had one slip out of his grasp at a game he attended at Ebbets Field as a child.

An analysis of what Maris achieved in 1961 puts him in a favorable light compared to what Ruth did 34 years before. Thirty-six pitchers who surrendered homers to Maris won at least ten games in 1961. This could only be said of 33 of Ruth's adversaries. On average the pitchers Maris encountered had more MLB experience and were pitching in larger ballparks than those who faced Ruth in 1927. Maris was named AL MVP for 1961, his second consecutive honor. Shortly after the season ended, both Mantle and Maris appeared as special guests on Perry Como's television program. Maris was asked by the host if he had any advice for rookies. Maris gave a pithy reply that was probably scripted: "Don't hit 62."

In 1962 Maris' home-run output dwindled to a more human-like 33. The figure was not too shabby at all—good enough to tie Maris for fifth-best in the AL—but he was criticized by the New York media for not approaching the mammoth total he had hit the year before. Maris happily left the Yankees after the 1966 season after enduring years of pointless booing and hostility. He found MLB life much more tolerable as a member of the St. Louis Cardinals, where he won pennants in his two seasons there. Maris had an outstanding World Series in 1967 in which he batted .385. Maris walked away from baseball after the 1968 season and contentedly ran a beer distributorship in Florida. In his 12 MLB seasons from 1957 through 1968, only nine other players hit more home runs than Maris did—and only 12 produced higher RBI totals. Both are impressive totals, made even more significant by the frequent injuries that greatly restricted Maris' playing time. Only four times in his career did Maris have 500 or more at-bats in a season. Feeling that he had been abused and mistreated by the Yankees, Maris routinely declined invitations to appear at Old-Timers' Games and other special events at Yankee Stadium until Opening Day 1978. On that occasion, Maris was greeted with such a warm ovation that he completely changed his attitude about making public appearances for his old team. He never turned down any invitation afterward.

Roger Maris died of cancer at the young age of 51 on December 14, 1985. (He did live long enough to see the Yankees retire his number 9 in July 1984.) Despite adverse wintry weather, many of Maris' former teammates descended upon Fargo, ND, for the home run champion's funeral to pay their last respects to a fine and beloved colleague. They unanimously thought he had been treated badly by history. Tracy Stallard attended the rites. Mickey Mantle wept when he tried to tell a TV reporter what a great person Maris was. Maris' diamond-shaped headstone in Fargo's Holy Cross Cemetery bears an engraving of him swinging a bat. The bat separates the inseparable: the figure *61* from the year '*61*.

In 1991 MLB Commissioner Fay Vincent formally announced that the asterisk accompanying the single-season home run record would be expunged from MLB's record book; Maris' record would finally stand alone without any special designation that might detract from its legitimacy. That was quite a remarkable statement considering the asterisk had never actually existed in the first place.

Boston 0 at New York 1

Game played on Sunday, October 1, 1961, at Yankee Stadium

Boston Red Sox	ab	r	h	rbi	New York Yankees	ab	r	h	rbi
Schilling 2b	4	0	1	0	Richardson 2b	4	0	0	0
Geiger cf	4	0	0	0	Kubek ss	4	0	2	0
Yastrzemski lf	4	0	1	0	Maris cf	4	1	1	1
Malzone 3b	4	0	0	0	Berra lf	2	0	0	0
Clinton rf	4	0	0	0	Lopez lf, rf	1	0	0	0
Runnels 1b	3	0	0	0	Blanchard rf, c	3	0	0	0
Gile 1b	0	0	0	0	Howard c	2	0	0	0
Nixon c	3	0	2	0	Reed lf	1	0	1	0
Green ss	2	0	0	0	Skowron 1b	2	0	0	0
Stallard p	1	0	0	0	Hale 1b	1	0	1	0
Jensen ph	1	0	0	0	Boyer 3b	2	0	0	0
Nichols p	0	0	0	0	Stafford p	2	0	0	0
					Reniff p	0	0	0	0
					Tresh ph	1	0	0	0
					Arroyo p	0	0	0	0
Totals	30	0	4	0	Totals	29	1	5	1

Boston   000 000 000—0 4 0
New York   000 100 00x—1 5 0

Boston Red Sox	IP	H	R	ER	BB	SO
Stallard L (2–7)	7.0	5	1	1	1	5
Nichols	1.0	0	0	0	0	0
Totals	8.0	5	1	1	1	5

New York Yankees	IP	H	R	ER	BB	SO
Stafford W (14–9)	6.0	3	0	0	1	7
Reniff	1.0	0	0	0	0	1
Arroyo SV (29)	2.0	1	0	0	0	1
Totals	9.0	4	0	0	1	9

E–None. PB–Nixon (11). 3B–Boston Nixon (2, off Stafford). HR–New York Maris (61, 4th inning off Stallard 0 on, 1 out). SH–Stallard (4, off Stafford). SB–Geiger (16, 2nd base off Stafford/ Howard). WP–Stallard (3). U-HP–Bill Kinnamon, 1B–Red Flaherty, 2B–Jim Honochick, 3B–Al Salerno. T–1:57. A–23,154.

April 12, 1965

Site: Houston Astrodome

Teams: Philadelphia Phillies vs. Houston Astros

Significance: First Regular-Season MLB Indoor Game

Impact: For the first time adverse weather could not impact an MLB game; beginning of artificial turf replacing natural grass at MLB ballparks

"I don't know; I've never smoked AstroTurf."—Tug McGraw, on whether he preferred grass or artificial turf

"If a horse can't eat it, I don't want to play on it."—Dick Allen's opinion on artificial turf

"Everybody had his own enthusiastic slant on the Astrodome. All players, particularly the older ones, would find it more enjoyable and less tiring to work in air-conditioned comfort under the Houston dome. Women spectators certainly liked the climate. They were dolled up in their Neiman-Marcus finest, without a worry about rain or the harrowing effect of wind on the hairdo. For a comparison, in other cities, the gals sometimes huddle under umbrellas and in rain gear when the weather threatens, and there can be gusty little twisters of peanut shells and debris to shower over them."—Joe King, in the April 24, 1965, edition of *The Sporting News*

"It's easy to rave over the Astrodome, but it is probably not possible to overrate its significance for the future of sports. The Astrodome immediately projects sports onto the level of show business as a competitor with great power with other forms of entertainment for the luxury dollar."—Joe King, in the April 24, 1965, edition of *The Sporting News*

"The [Houston] Astros are pioneers who may have elevated baseball to a hitherto undreamed of prestige." That was the bold declaration made by *The Sporting News'* correspondent Joe King after he witnessed the first few MLB games ever played in an indoor environment.

To baseball fans, players, and writers in Houston, the new domed stadium must have seemed like a futuristic godsend when it opened in the spring of 1965. After all, attending MLB games in Houston for the first three years the city had a National League franchise was often a miserable experience. The Houston Colt .45s had joined the National League with the New York Mets in 1962, increasing the circuit from eight to ten teams. The American League had done so a year earlier with the addition of the Los Angeles Angels and a new version of the Washington Senators after the old Senators uprooted to Minnesota after 60 seasons in the District of Columbia and became the Twins.

When the city was awarded an NL franchise in 1960, Houston had no viable stadium to host top-flight baseball. A domed stadium was planned from the outset, but its overall planning and construction would take years. In the meantime, a temporary outdoor venue would have to be built. Colt Stadium was the Houston club's home park for 1962, 1963, and 1964. The temporary, one-tier ballpark could accommodate 33,000 patrons. Replete with multi-colored seats, it was a garish-looking place. Neither fans nor players held any fondness for the venue. Rusty Staub, who joined the Colts as a 19-year-old in 1963 and played 23 seasons in MLB, said, "I don't care what ballpark they ever talk about as being the hottest place on the face of the Earth, Colt Stadium was it."[1] Staub was hardly alone in condemning the place. Consider this thoroughly unflattering description of the ballpark in *The Baseball Hall of Shame*:

There was one good thing to be said about the first home of the expansion team Colt 45s (later to be renamed the Astros): It didn't last very long. If it had, it might have been the end of Houston baseball for a very basic reason. Neither the players nor the fans could have long survived its tortures—unbearable heat, poor lighting, and, worst of all, mosquitoes.

Colt Stadium's singular claim to fame is that it was the only park in history where the concession stands sold more mosquito repellent than beer. Women spectators didn't wear perfume, they wore Off! Everything is always bigger in Texas, and that includes mosquitoes, gnats and horseflies. In fact, the term "infield fly" took on a whole new meaning in Houston.

Fans foolish enough to attend a game sweltered and steamed in the oppressive heat. That simmering humidity coming off the nearby smelly swamp sent 100 spectators to the first-aid station during one Sunday afternoon doubleheader.

Determined to keep their hold on their swampland, the swarms of twin-engine mosquitoes and bugs gave the visiting ballplayers more competition than the Colt 45s. Players also risked career-ending injuries during night games because the park was so dimly lighted. When he was a Met in 1962, Richie Ashburn complained, "If they're going to play night ball there, at least they should put in lights."

The attendance for the first MLB series ever played in Houston was telling. Opening Day at Colt Stadium on April 10, 1962, drew about 25,000 fans who saw the Colt .45s handily beat the Chicago Cubs 11–2 on club owner Roy Hofheinz's 50th birthday. The next day's game drew approximately 20,000 customers. The following day the attendance dipped below 8,000. Obviously, the plentiful shortcomings of Colt Stadium made Houston the best candidate to have something utterly revolutionary in sports: an indoor stadium sizable enough to host professional baseball. Attendance at Colt Stadium was 924,446 in 1962, an average of about 11,000 fans per game. The next two seasons Houston home attendance dropped to under 9,000 spectators per game. The expansion Colt .45s were not pennant contenders yet, but they did not attract even 750,000 fans in either 1963 or 1964, when NL teams averaged about 1.2 million paying customers per season (with the Colt .45s' poor numbers factored into the calculation). Most everyone blamed the unfriendly confines of Colt Stadium for the team's disappointing fan support. However, the dwindling number of fans who did attend games could easily see what lay in store in the near future; within eyeshot, beyond the seats on the first-base side, the wondrous new Houston Astrodome was under construction.

To no one's great sadness, the Colt .45s played their last game at the detestable ballpark on September 27, 1964. The home team beat the visiting Los Angeles Dodgers, 1–0, in 12 innings. Jimmy Wynn was the last man to bat at Colt Stadium, driving in Rusty Staub with the game's only run. The typically low attendance was 6,246. Few tears were shed as the fans exited Colt Stadium for the final time. After the Astrodome opened its doors in 1965, abandoned Colt Stadium remained standing for five years. Since it was situated so close to the team's new home, during that time it served as something akin to a storage yard for the newly christened Astros. Somewhat comically, team owner Roy Hofheinz (who was Houston's mayor from 1953 to 1955) tried to make Colt Stadium disappear from the city's landscape. He had the old ballpark painted a dull gray so it would not stand out in wide-angle aerial photos of the Astrodome. In the late 1960s, Colt Stadium was sold to a minor league team south of the border for $100,000. The ballpark was disassembled and moved to Torreon, Mexico. Later the stadium was moved once again, this time to Tampico, Mexico, where it still sits today as part of a public playground.

A covered stadium in Houston was part of the plan since day one. The NL only granted Houston a franchise on the condition that the group led by Hofheinz would build a covered facility suitable for baseball. Minor league games played in Houston were often contested in temperatures that hovered close to 100 degrees Fahrenheit combined with oppressive humidity. Hofheinz later claimed he was inspired to build an indoor sports facility after he toured Rome. He learned that the ancient Colosseum was equipped with gigantic velaria—similar to modern-day awnings—to shield patrons from the scorching sun. Hofheinz figured if the Romans could have something close to a covered stadium 2,000 years ago, so could Houston.

"I knew that with our heat, humidity, and rain that the best chance for success was in the direction of a weather-proof, all-purpose stadium," Hofheinz said. "We had to have a stadium that would be a spectator's paradise, but also one that could be used for events other than sports."[2] Construction on the Astrodome began on January 3, 1962—

three months before the Colt .45s played their first outdoor home game and within eye-shot of what would be their new home sometime in 1965.

Originally and officially called the Harris County Domed Stadium when it first opened its doors to the curious public, the Astrodome was designed by architects Hermon Lloyd & W. B. Morgan, and Wilson, Morris, Crain and Anderson. Structural engineering and design were performed by Walter P. Moore Engineers and Consultants. The actual construction of the Astrodome was done by H. A. Lott, Inc. The stadium's marvelous air conditioning system was designed by Houston mechanical engineers Israel A. Naman and Jack Boyd Buckley. Because of Houston's importance to America's burgeoning space program, the indoor stadium was dubbed the Astrodome and the city's NL club was renamed the Astros in 1965.

Standing an impressive 18 stories tall, the Astrodome encompasses 9.5 acres of land. Its dome is 710 feet in diameter, while the ceiling is 208 feet above the diamond. Many people do not realize the Astrodome's playing surface is fully 25 feet below street level. The Astrodome was completed in November 1964, six months ahead of schedule, even though many significant engineering changes were required during its construction period. Most note-worthy was a modest flattening of the supposed "hemispherical roof" to cope with structural problems and soil issues that were best understood by architects but scarcely fathomable to laymen. Like other indoor stadiums that followed it in the next two decades, the nearly circular Astrodome was designed as a multi-purpose stadium mainly to facilitate two major sports. Accordingly, it has movable lower seating areas to adapt to baseball or football configurations. Originally more than 42,000 baseball fans could be accommodated in comfort. (Not one to miss out on a golden opportunity, Hofheinz had a luxurious apartment specially built for himself within the Astrodome.) Houston's oppressive heat and humidity—and the nuisance of persistent mosquitoes—would bother patrons no more when the 1965 MLB season began. Hofheinz was also hopeful that the indoor venue would attract great quantities of female customers. "Women will go to the ball game now because there will be no wind to whip their hairdos, no rain to ruin their dresses and no sun to turn them red," Hofheinz told the *Houston Chronicle*. "The Astrodome will get a promenade of the best-gowned, best-looking and most influential women ever collected."[3]

People began referring to the Astrodome, with some justification, as "The Eighth Wonder of the World," but baseball fans were understandably skeptical about this revolutionary new playing ground. Could high-caliber baseball really be played indoors? To test what effects the enclosed air-conditioned environment might have on the delivery of breaking balls, on February 7, 1965, the ageless Satchel Paige, clad in a full Astros uniform, threw the first pitches at the Astrodome simply to test the place. He labeled the stadium a "pitcher's paradise."[4] Paige opined that the lack of any wind allowed for off-speed pitches to maneuver more easily than in an outdoor setting.

On April 9, 1965, a sold-out crowd of 47,879—more than 5,000 above the official capacity for baseball at the time—turned out for an exhibition game between the newly renamed Houston Astros and the visiting New York Yankees. The two teams purposely represented a contrasting combination of old baseball tradition with the space-age future. Texas governor John Connally and Houston mayor Louie Welch were both on hand for the opening ceremonies. Connally dutifully tossed out the ceremonial first ball for the first MLB game ever played in an indoor facility. Turk Farrell of the Astros threw the first pitch. Mickey Mantle recorded both the first hit (a single) and the first home run in the Astrodome. The Astros beat the Yankees that night by a 2–1 score.

The opening of the Houston Astrodome in 1965 introduced indoor baseball to MLB. Prior to 1965, Houston's baseball fans had to endure brutal heat and ravenous mosquitoes at Colt Stadium. Now antiquated and in disuse, the Astrodome was the first truly modern, multi-purpose sports facility (National Baseball Hall of Fame Library, Cooperstown, New York).

President Lyndon Baines Johnson and his wife Lady Bird were in attendance too— but they were a trifle late in getting to the game. During the second inning the chief executive dropped in to pay his respects to both the national game and to Astros president Roy Hofheinz. (Hofheinz, a longtime friend, had been a campaign manager for Johnson back in the 1940s.) LBJ and Lady Bird watched the ballgame from Hofheinz's private box, situated high in right field just to the right of the giant scoreboard. It was reported that the president snacked on hors d'oeuvres, chicken, and ice cream while he watched the action. "Roy, I want to congratulate you; it shows so much imagination,"[5] LBJ was heard to say. President Johnson's visit was the first of many similar pilgrimages made by dignitaries who wanted to see and experience a sporting event at the Astrodome. The Yankees played three pre-season games in Houston before ironically venturing to the unpleasant, frigid conditions of Minnesota's Metropolitan Stadium to conclude their 1965 exhibition schedule.

The first NL team to play in the Astrodome would be the Philadelphia Phillies when the regular season began on Monday, April 12. The visitors won, 2–0. Left-hander Chris Short threw a nifty four-hit shutout and whiffed 11 Astros for the victors in a game that took two hours and 34 minutes to play—surprisingly long for a low-scoring contest in that era. Dick Allen's two-run homer in the top of the third inning accounted for all the offense in the game. Despite the home team losing the first meaningful indoor baseball game ever played, the debut of the Astrodome had been a rousing success. By the end of the 1965 season the Astros had nearly tripled their attendance from 1964, exceeding 2.1 million paid admissions. (Obviously the novelty of the Astrodome was the major attraction as the Astros floundered to a ninth-place finish in the ten-team NL. The club's record attendance of 1965 would not be topped until the 1980 season, when the Astros won the NL West championship.)

There were still a few bugs that needed to be worked out with the sparkling new facility, however. The playing surface of the Astrodome presented a unique problem. Originally, the stadium's surface was a special strain of Bermuda grass that had been specifically bred for indoor use. It may have worked in a football-only facility. However, the Astrodome's ceiling contained numerous semi-transparent panes made of Lucite. Ballplayers—outfielders in particular—quickly complained that glare coming off the panes made it more than challenging for them to track fly balls. To solve the problem, two sections of panes were painted white. Within a few months, though, the Bermuda grass died from a lack of sunlight. Cosmetics were applied. For most of the 1965 season, the Astros played on green-painted dirt and dead grass—hardly ideal conditions. The clear ceiling panels also added a problem when combined with the natural grass. The grass tended to hold moisture and then suddenly release it, often resulting in the curious occurrence of rain falling within the enclosed structure! There were several instances when games had to be delayed while the grounds crew cleaned up the damp playing surface.

The solution was to install artificial grass on the Astrodome's floor. Its technical name was ChemGrass—which soon became known colloquially as AstroTurf. Because the available supply of AstroTurf was limited, only a restricted amount was available at the start of the 1966 season. There was not enough for the entire outfield of the Astrodome, so the first phase of its installation covered only the traditional grass portion of the infield and foul territory. The cost of the carpet that would dramatically change both baseball and football stadia for years to come was $2 per square foot. It was installed on the Astrodome's floor in time to test it during a series of exhibition games against the Los Angeles Dodgers in March 1966. Infielders overwhelmingly liked the true hops the turf provided them but some were quick to complain that the ball got to them noticeably faster than on traditional grass infields.

The Astrodome was also the first MLB ballpark to feature a modern scoreboard with an ancient ancestor of today's high-definition video screens. All Astros home runs were greeted with fireworks, animated pistol-firing cowboys, and general merriment. The graphics seem simple and antiquated now, but they were stunning to baseball fans in the 1960s.

The outfield at the Astrodome remained mere painted dirt until the 1966 All-Star Game. During a long road trip, the club had the outfield covered with the new turf. It debuted in a July 19 game with the Phillies. In keeping with the futuristic theme the Astrodome inspired, the groundskeepers wore spacesuits between innings as they tidied the turf with vacuum cleaners. Outfielders quickly learned the perils of diving for a batted ball on AstroTurf and missing it: On any other diamond, natural grass would deaden the ball's roll and generally keep it nearby; on turf it skidded away and seemingly rolled forever. Curiously, the Astrodome was not the first ballpark to have "cutout" dirt sliding areas amid a turf infield. When the Cincinnati Reds moved from Crosley Field to Riverfront Stadium in June 1970, their new home featured a turf outfield and a largely turf infield. Only the immediate area around the bases was dirt. The lower maintenance costs of artificial turf compared to grass was the primary factor for the design. Within a short time every MLB park with turf mimicked Riverfront's setup—including the Astrodome. The lamentable age of the "cookie-cutter stadium" had arrived in the NL.

Times and tastes change, though. By the early 1990s, the trend in MLB began to shift towards single-purpose "retro" ballparks—new stadiums having an old-time feel to them. It began with Oriole Park at Camden Yards in Baltimore in 1992. Jacobs Field in Cleveland soon followed. Nostalgia was now all the rage, and sterile domes that shut out the summer sunshine did not fit the bill. The Astrodome slowly fell out of favor with the public and descended into various stages of disrepair. A pre-season NFL game in August 1995 was postponed because the playing surface was no longer up to league standards. Finding the Astrodome to be inadequate for a modern NFL team, the Houston Oilers abruptly uprooted and moved to greener pastures—and a considerably bigger outdoor stadium—in Tennessee in 1996. The Astros threatened to leave town too unless a newer and more fashionable baseball park was built for them. Accordingly, the Astros played their final home game in the Astrodome on October 9, 1999. It was a 7–5 National League Division Series loss to the Atlanta Braves that eliminated Houston from the post-season. Enron Field—which combined an old-style ballpark with a retractable roof—became the team's new downtown home in 2000. Since 2003 Enron Field has been known as Minute Maid Park.

Half a century after its gala opening, the "Eighth Wonder of the World" now sits empty and apparently unwanted. Various initiatives to convert the Astrodome to a movie studio, a convention center, and a luxury hotel have gotten nowhere. Even plans to demolish it have been scuttled due to fears of environmental damage. The Astrodome finds itself in a peculiar state of limbo because all renovation plans must deal with the problem of uncorrected municipal occupancy code violations that have shuttered the facility for the foreseeable future. Thus the Astrodome cannot be safely used, nor can it be safely demolished. In 2013, the National Trust for Historic Preservation included the Astrodome on its list of 11 most endangered historic places. The following year, it was formally listed on the National Register of Historic Places. Whatever its future might hold, the Houston Astrodome will always have a unique place in baseball history as the stadium that changed the game by ushering in the future.

Philadelphia 2 at Houston 0

Game played on Monday, April 12, 1965, at Astrodome

Philadelphia Phillies	ab	r	h	rbi	Houston Astros	ab	r	h	rbi
Taylor 2b	5	0	2	0	Lillis ss	4	0	0	0
Allen 3b	4	1	2	2	Morgan 2b	3	0	2	0
Callison rf	4	0	1	0	Wynn cf	4	0	0	0
Covington lf	3	0	0	0	Bond 1b	4	0	0	0
Herrnstein lf	0	0	0	0	Aspromonte 3b	4	0	1	0
Gonzalez cf	4	0	2	0	Beauchamp lf	3	0	0	0
Stuart 1b	3	0	1	0	Gaines rf	3	0	0	0
Wine pr, ss	0	0	0	0	Bateman c	2	0	1	0
Dalrymple c	4	0	0	0	Bruce p	2	0	0	0
Amaro ss,1b	3	1	1	0	White ph	1	0	0	0
Short p	3	0	1	0	Woodeshick p	0	0	0	0
Totals	33	2	10	2	Totals	30	0	4	0

| Philadelphia | 002 000 000—2 10 1 |
| Houston | 000 000 000—0 4 0 |

Philadelphia Phillies	IP	H	R	ER	BB	SO
Short W (1–0)	9.0	4	0	0	3	11
Totals	9.0	4	0	0	3	11
Houston Astros	IP	H	R	ER	BB	SO
Bruce L (0–1)	7.0	9	2	2	1	5
Woodeshick	2.0	1	0	0	1	1
Totals	9.0	10	2	2	2	6

E–Allen (1). DP–Philadelphia 1, Houston 2. 2B–Philadelphia Taylor (1, off Bruce), Houston Morgan (1, off Short). HR–Philadelphia Allen (1, 3rd inning off Bruce 1 on, 2 out). SH–Short (1, off Bruce); Herrnstein (1, off Woodeshick); Bateman (1, off Short). IBB–Amaro (1, by Bruce); Stuart (1, by Woodeshick). IBB–Bruce (1, Amaro); Woodeshick (1, Stuart). U–HP–Al Barlick, 1B–Augie Donatelli, 2B–Stan Landes, 3B–Mel Steiner. T–2:34. A–42,652.

April 14, 1969

Site: Parc Jarry (Jarry Park), Montreal

Teams: St. Louis Cardinals vs. Montreal Expos

Significance: First MLB Game in Canada

Impact: Established the viability of having MLB franchises located beyond America's borders

> "You know something special is happening when fans bypass exits, parking lots and taverns to head straight for the advance ticket widows and beg for more. That was the scene here on April 14 when they lined up to buy more ducats seconds after the Expos had brought big league baseball to Montreal by edging the Cardinals 8–7, in a scene that would make Frank Merriwell blush. Employing the rousing fireworks and nail-biting fumbling that had typified their every game, the Expos let it all hang out for a mob of 29,184 enraptured customers who came to cheer at Jarry Park. They left wanting more."—*The Sporting News*, April 26, 1969

The city of Montreal has a long and storied baseball history. Minor league teams known as the Royals played in the Canadian city from 1896–1917 and again from 1928–1960. The latter, holding membership in the International League, is likely best known to baseball fans today as being one of the Brooklyn/Los Angeles Dodgers' AAA affiliates from 1939–1960.

Most famously, Jackie Robinson played for the 1946 incarnation of the Royals, a team that won the Little World Series that year. Robinson was beloved by Montrealers; at the end of the 1946 season Robinson was chased to his train by a cheering mob of well-wishers. Sam Matlin of the *Pittsburgh Courier* famously wrote, "It was probably the only day in history that a black man ran from a white mob with love instead of lynching on its mind."

When the Dodgers decided to shutter the Montreal Royals in 1960 as the franchise felt it no longer required three AAA affiliates, both Montreal mayor Jean Drapeau and Gerry Snyder (vice-chair of Montreal's executive committee) worked to bring baseball back to Montreal—preferably Major League Baseball.

In 1962, Moscow backed out of hosting a World's Fair. Montreal (which had placed second in the original balloting in 1960) was permitted to bid again and was awarded the 1967 exposition, dubbed Expo '67. Although many members of Drapeau's original Expo committee resigned in 1963 after a computer simulation determined that it would be impossible to execute Drapeau's Expo plans in time for 1967, the exposition opened on time and (as of 2015) is still the fourth-best-attended World Exposition. Montreal had cemented its status as a world-class city and could set its sights on other ventures. Major League Baseball took notice.

In 1967 the American League was having some issues of its own. The league's hand was forced on the expansion front by Charlie O. Finley's decision to move the Kansas City Athletics to Oakland. In response, Missouri senator Stuart Symington threatened legislation that would challenge baseball's antitrust exemption and its reserve clause. To appease Symington, AL president Joe Cronin announced in December 1967 that the AL would expand in 1969 to 12 teams, placing expansion franchises in Kansas City and Seattle. The National League elected to follow suit, and at MLB's meetings that same month in Mexico City, Montreal sent Snyder and Drapeau to pitch their city to the NL owners.

One thing that worked heavily in Montreal's favor was that the chair of the NL's expansion committee was Dodgers owner Walter O'Malley. It could still be said that O'Malley had retained a bit of a soft spot for Montreal from the days of the Royals.

Nevertheless, most baseball insiders were expecting San Diego and Buffalo to be the most likely expansion candidates for the National League in 1969. Thus when O'Malley announced Montreal as the 12th NL city on May 27, 1968, it came as quite a surprise.

In Drapeau's hallmark style of "act first, then figure out the details later," the city had its desired MLB team but no stadium to play in and a hastily assembled ownership group. Nearly from the get-go, the team's ownership consortium began to fracture. Robert Irsay—who became better known in professional sports for buying the National Football League's Los Angeles Rams, trading franchises with the Baltimore Colts, then moving those Colts to Indianapolis—abruptly backed out. Jean Louis Levesque (originally set to become the chairman of the ownership group) also withdrew. Charles Bronfman of Seagram's distillery fame ended up becoming the face of the team's ownership group after being convinced by Drapeau at the ultimate last minute to stay on. He was promised, somewhat optimistically, a domed stadium.

In the *Montreal Gazette* the day after the announcement, Frank J. Shaughnessy (who was elected International League president in 1937 and served for 24 seasons) said, "You've got to give the people a good ball park"—a quote eerily prescient considering the unnamed team's future troubles.

The *Gazette* seemed confident that the new franchise would play at the recently opened Autostade (the home stadium of the Canadian Football League's Montreal Alouettes at the time) and that a new baseball park would open within a few years. Curiously the *Gazette* itself was contradictory as to a timeline. The front page of that same May 28, 1968, *Gazette* said a domed stadium would open in 1971, whereas a headline in the sports section gave 1972 as the debut date.

Meanwhile the stadium seemed to have as many issues as the ownership group. In what retrospectively seemed to be the only expenditure the free-spending city of Montreal balked at between 1963 and 1976, the city felt that putting a dome on the Autostade was too expensive. Additionally, the Alouettes demanded too much rent from the baseball franchise, ultimately scuppering the Autostade plan. The team eventually selected Jarry Park, which at the time was a 3,000-seat stadium. Somehow Drapeau convinced NL President Warren Giles to accept the tiny Jarry Park site as the location for the inaugural MLB stadium in Montreal. Harking back towards the spectacular success of 1967's World's Fair, the franchise was named the Expos.

MLB Deputy Commissioner John McHale, Sr., was hired as the team's President; McHale then hired Jim Fanning as the team's first general manager. Fanning had actually served as McHale's assistant when McHale was GM of the Milwaukee/Atlanta Braves. Former Phillies manager Gene Mauch was named the club's first field boss.

Going into the expansion draft after the 1968 season, McHale and Fanning decided that the best course of action was to try to draft players they felt had market value and perhaps could be packaged together in trades down the road. That strategy seemed to work perfectly. On January 22, 1969, the Expos traded Jesus Alou and Donn Clendenon to Houston to obtain Rusty Staub. There was only one problem: Clendenon refused to report to Houston (choosing instead to retire) and Houston wanted the deal undone.

As author Jonah Keri chronicled in his 2014 retrospective of the club *Up, Up, & Away*, the Expos at spring training that year managed to get Staub to pose for a picture—in a Montreal uniform—along with first-year MLB Commissioner Bowie Kuhn. Houston owner Roy Hofheinz was beyond incensed. In order to make the deal official, Clendenon (who by that point was working as a pen salesman in Atlanta) had to be lured out of retirement to play in Montreal. The Expos then had to send Jack Billingham, Skip Guinn, and $100,000—along with Alou—to Houston in order to ensure that Staub became an Expo. (Kuhn was saved from losing a great deal of face due to the orchestrated publicity stunt.)

Opening Day for the Expos saw the team play the New York Mets at Shea Stadium. The Canadian team's first home run came from an unlikely source. Relief pitcher Dan McGinn—left in to bat by Mauch against Tom Seaver—hammered a mistake by the future Hall of Famer over the right-center-field fence. The Expos held an 11–6 lead going into the bottom of the ninth inning. Lacking bullpen strength, they allowed the Mets to score four runs before holding on for a nail-biting 11–10 win—with the Mets' potential winning run stranded on base. Amazingly, the Mets would end up as World Series champions in 1969 after their inauspicious Opening Day loss to the expansion Montrealers.

After six games, the 2–4 Expos came to Montreal for their history-making home opener on Monday, April 14, against the defending NL champion St. Louis Cardinals. Montreal's 1968–1969 winter had been immensely cold and long with temperatures averaging -4 degrees Fahrenheit all season. The city's last snowfall that spring had occurred on April 2, less than two weeks before Opening Day. Nevertheless Parc Jarry (as the Francophones called it) was deemed ready for baseball despite a mid–February *Associated Press* article that described the Expos' home field as a "snow-covered expanse that resembles a disaster area more than a future diamond."

In the days before April 15, the thawing frost rendered much of the field a soggy morass. Many people felt that Jarry Park's conditions were unsuitable for professional baseball. (Curt Flood of the Cardinals was the biggest critic, telling the *Montreal Gazette* hyper-dramatically, "I pray I don't get killed out there tomorrow.")[1] The Expos players tactfully refrained for the most part from making comments about the stadium's conditions. Maury Wills diplomatically said, "It wouldn't be baseball if the players didn't complain," and "half the time they don't mean it." Rusty Staub—who was an accredited expert in poor playing conditions after two seasons at dreadful Colt Stadium in Houston— declared Jarry to be "my kind of park." Be that as it may, Wills—who had set the modern-day, single-season stolen base record with 104 in 1962—chose not to attempt any steals during Jarry Park's first game, with good reason: traversing the basepaths, as the *Gazette*'s Ted Blackman put it, "was like running on a hunk of Gouda cheese."[2]

Pomp and circumstance in Montreal surrounded the home opener—the first MLB game ever contested outside of the United States. McGinn commented on the hoopla: "You thought you were at an inauguration." It had been nine springs since there had been a pro baseball game in Montreal, and the organizers were a little rusty: Jarry Park's gates were late opening and the pre-game ceremony began 24 minutes behind schedule. Some things never change, though; the presence of Jean-Jacques Bertrand (the premier of Quebec) was greeted by more boos than polite applause by the sellout crowd. More than 200 reporters were on hand at Jarry Park to cover the festivities. Ed McAuley, writing in the *Gazette*, chronicled the peripheral goings-on in an amusing journal-like fashion for his readers. Some examples:

> 1:42 p.m.: Section 4 usherette in blue with the miniskirt getting a big play from the late arriving crowd. But she's all business and everyone is seated.
> 1:43 p.m.: First pass made at usherette in blue with the miniskirt.
> 3:07 p.m.: Expo director Syd Maislin lights up third cigar of afternoon, without putting out second.
> 3:34 p.m.: Baseball Commissioner Bowie Kuhn enters press box to greet fourth estate, uses word 'exciting' twice in describing Montreal home opener. Commissioner not in midseason form, as he wishes there was elevator up to press box.

Larry Jaster and Lou Brock made history by being the first hurler and batter respectively in an MLB game outside of the United States; Brock lined out to Gary Sutherland at second base. Mack Jones became an instant hero in Montreal with a three-run homer off visiting starter Nelson Briles in the bottom of the first inning. Jones added a two-run triple in the bottom of the second. Jaster contributed an RBI single of his own in the third inning to increase the Expos' advantage to 6–0.

The top of the fourth was not kind to the Expos. Five Expos errors and a Jaster balk were committed in the inning and Dal Maxvill—who had a lifetime batting average of .217 and just six home runs in nearly 4,000 plate appearances—sent a Jaster offering over the right-center-field fence for a grand slam. After a Vada Pinson RBI single and a second home run to right center—this one off the bat of Joe Torre—Jaster was relieved for McGinn.

Gary Waslewski's wild pitch brought in Wills to re-tie the game at 7–7 in the bottom of the fourth. Following that scoring play, the pitching miraculously seemed to take over with Waslewski and McGinn trading zeros until Mauch—once again—chose to let his relief pitcher bat in the bottom of the seventh with Coco Laboy on second base. The gamble paid off as McGinn delivered his second clutch hit in the span of a week (out of only five hits all season) with a single to left field, plating Laboy with what proved to be the winning run in a thrilling, 8–7 Expos win. The home fans exited Jarry Park happy but not before hundreds of Expos supporters went straight to the club's box office, clamoring for tickets to future home games.

While the 1969 Expos managed to win both their first game and their home opener, they won just 50 other games that first season and finished tied with the San Diego Padres for the worst record in the National League at 52–110 in the first year of divisional MLB play. The Expos were also the first expansion team to draw more than a million fans during their inaugural season. Montreal and its Expos had made it abundantly clear that MLB could thrive beyond the American borders.

St. Louis 7 at Montreal 8

Game played on Monday, April 14, 1969, at Parc Jarry

St. Louis Cardinals	ab	r	h	rbi	Montreal Expos	ab	r	h	rbi
Brock lf	5	0	0	0	Bosch cf	5	1	2	0
Flood cf	5	1	4	0	Wills ss	5	2	1	0
Pinson rf	5	1	1	1	Staub rf	4	2	2	0
Torre 1b	5	1	2	2	Jones lf	4	1	2	5
Shannon 3b	5	1	0	0	Bailey 1b	4	0	1	0
McCarver c	5	1	1	0	Bateman c	2	0	0	0
Javier 2b	4	1	2	0	Laboy 3b	3	2	1	0
Maxvill ss	4	1	2	4	Sutherland 2b	4	0	0	0
Briles p	2	0	0	0	Jaster p	2	0	1	1
Waslewski p	1	0	0	0	McGinn p	2	0	1	1
Gagliano ph	0	0	0	0					
Hoerner p	0	0	0	0					
Totals	41	7	12	7	Totals	35	8	11	7

St. Louis   **000 700 000—7 12 0**
Montreal   **321 100 10x—8 11 5**

St. Louis Cardinals	IP	H	R	ER	BB	SO
Briles	3.0	9	7	7	3	3
Waslewski L (0–1)	4.0	2	1	1	2	5
Hoerner	1.0	0	0	0	0	1
Totals	8.0	11	8	8	5	9

Montreal Expos	IP	H	R	ER	BB	SO
Jaster	3.2	9	7	2	0	1
McGinn W (1–0)	5.1	3	0	0	1	0
Totals	9.0	12	7	2	1	1

E–Bosch (1), Wills (1), Bailey (2), Bateman (3), Jaster (1). 2B–St. Louis Flood (4, off Jaster); Torre (2, off McGinn), Montreal Bailey (3, off Briles); Staub (3, off Briles); Laboy (5, off Waslewski). 3B–Montreal Jones (1, off Briles). HR–St. Louis Maxvill (1, 4th inning off Jaster 3 on, 0 out); Torre (2, 4th inning off Jaster 1 on, 2 out), Montreal Jones (2, 1st inning off Briles 2 on, 1 out). IBB–Jones (1, by Waslewski); Bateman (1, by Waslewski). WP–Waslewski (1). BK–Jaster (1). IBB–Waslewski 2 (2, Jones, Bateman). U-HP–Mel Steiner, 1B–Bob Engel, 2B–Dick Stello, 3B–Augie Donatelli. T–2:16. A–29,184.

October 13, 1971

Site: Three Rivers Stadium, Pittsburgh

Teams: Baltimore Orioles vs. Pittsburgh Pirates

Significance: First World Series Night Game

Impact: Heralded the end exclusively of daytime World Series games

> "Fittingly, the game contained many of the ingredients for diamond drama because it was, after all, the first [World] Series game played at night … after 397 day games … and was witnessed by an estimated 61,000,000 [viewers] on national television and by a record Pittsburgh baseball crowd of 51,378."—*The Sporting News*, October 30, 1971

"Nowadays, the idea of a World Series day game is as outdated and antiquated as, well, as either the Pirates or Orioles winning the pennant."—baseball writer Chris Jaffe, commenting in 2011 on the 40th anniversary of the first World Series night game

"Do you believe the Pirates had a hand in starting that crap? The World Series in the day was part of our autumn as kids. [It was] part of October. It was running home from school to watch it. They're always trying to market the game to kids, but that night, they started stealing the game from kids."—Steve Blass, winning pitcher of Game Seven of the 1971 World Series

For generations of fans, the World Series meant championship baseball in the cool October afternoon. Rituals were developed. Transistor radios were smuggled into schools. Some open-minded teachers simply allowed the TV and radio broadcasts into their class-rooms. Office workers took long lunches or put in half-days so they could follow the action. It was more than a quaint custom. Day games were both the norm and the rule. Although baseball under the lights had been a reality in MLB since 1935, remarkably it was not until 1971 that the first WS game was scheduled for a nighttime start. (As early as 1949, there were instances where stadium floodlights had been turned on during World Series games as dusk approached.) But this game would be different. That historic first WS night game took place at Pittsburgh's Three Rivers Stadium on Wednesday, October 13, 1971, and drew an enormous television audience. From that point onward World Series day games were doomed to extinction. Nostalgic folks would say the day games were *sadly* doomed to extinction.

The real question is why did it take so long for MLB to schedule its showcase event in front of a prime-time TV audience? The simple answer is that tradition is deeply entrenched in baseball. For years the afternoon starts did not affect the TV ratings at all. They were steadily terrific. Since the Fall Classic was annually a ratings bonanza for NBC, they were more than happy to continue to carry on with the quaint custom of playing World Series games in the daytime and leave their beloved and lucrative prime-time pro-gramming untouched. Toward the end of the 1960s, though, television ratings dipped slightly. Undoubtedly someone at MLB noticed that ABC was garnering unexpected huge ratings with Monday Night Football and figured the World Series ought to be able to do at least as well as regular-season NFL games during prime time. Thus, in 1971—some 36 years after it was proven that quality baseball could be played at night—as an experiment NBC slated Game Four of the 1971 World Series between the visiting Baltimore Orioles and the hometown Pittsburgh Pirates for a Wednesday night. It was a stunning change for generations of fans used to taking half-days off work to watch the games. The previous 397 World Series games had all started in the autumn sunshine—or at least daylight.

The premiere of World Series night baseball nearly happened two days earlier. Game Two, scheduled for Sunday, October 10, was rained out and postponed to what was sup-posed to be a travel day on Monday. The Orioles, fearful that many ticketholders to Sun-day's game would not be able to attend a hastily rescheduled Monday day game, asked Commissioner Bowie Kuhn for permission to play on Monday night. Kuhn was reputedly prepared to okay the idea, but the Pirates opposed it. Presumably the Pirates did not want to be usurped out of the honor of hosting the first World Series night game, or they did not want to play Game Three on a Tuesday afternoon in Pittsburgh after a night game in Baltimore on Monday—or a combination of the two. With no consensus, Kuhn ordered Game Two to be played at 1 p.m. on Monday. Interestingly, Game Two drew 53,239 spectators—ten more than had attended Game One on a brilliant Saturday after-noon.

"It seemed odd today to be standing around a hotel lobby in the afternoon waiting for a World Series game at night," said Curt Gowdy to his broadcast partner, Bob Prince, in the NBC-TV booth just before the national anthem was played. Joe Garagiola opened NBC's pregame show by noting, "Good evening—and what an evening this figures to be! Since 1935 when the very first major league night game was played in Cincinnati, night baseball has become an important part of the baseball scene. Since 1903 the World Series has become America's number-one sports event. Tonight—for the very first time—the two come together." Oddly, Three Rivers Stadium had been used in the afternoon by the NFL's Pittsburgh Steelers for a practice, but it was re-transformed into a baseball venue in ample time for the historic contest.

The truly milestone game was a beauty. Pittsburgh's Luke Walker's threw the first pitch under the lights to Paul Blair—and it was called a strike by plate umpire Ed Vargo. The ball was secured as a historic artifact and couriered to the Hall of Fame. Things went awry for Walker shortly thereafter. Baltimore rocked Walker for three consecutive singles by Blair, Mark Belanger, and Merv Rettenmund to begin the game. A passed ball and two sacrifice flies later, the AL champs were up, 3–0. Walker—who compiled a 10–8 record during the regular season—was pulled from the game by panicky Pittsburgh manager Danny Murtaugh. Incredibly, Baltimore's offense completely vanished after that point. The Orioles mustered only one more hit the rest of the game. Bruce Kison relieved Walker and stayed in the game through the seventh inning. He allowed one hit in 6⅓ innings— a second-inning double by Blair, who was stranded on base. (In a disastrous Game Two relief stint, Kison had faced two Orioles and had walked both of them—including pitcher Jim Palmer with the bases loaded.) On this night Kison issued no walks but he did hit three Orioles to set a World Series record for most hit batsmen in a game by a pitcher. None of the plunked Orioles came close to scoring. Twenty-eight years would go by before another pitcher would pick up a post-season win with at least six innings of relief work: Pedro Martinez in Game Five of the 1999 ALDS.

With the Pirates' bullpen stifling the Baltimore batters, Pittsburgh began clawing their way back into the game in the bottom of the first inning. Pat Dobson, one of four Orioles pitchers to win 20 games in 1971, was on the mound for Baltimore. A leadoff walk and doubles by Al Oliver and Willie Stargell got the Pirates two quick runs. In the bottom of the third inning, three singles tied the score. Pittsburgh seemingly had rallies building in every inning while Baltimore was struggling dearly to stay in the game. In the home half of the fifth inning, Pittsburgh loaded the bases with one out but failed to score. The following inning, Pittsburgh again had the bases loaded—this time with two out and fearsome Willie Stargell at the plate. Stargell grounded out to second baseman Davey Johnson to end the threat.

In the seventh inning, Pittsburgh finally got the go-ahead run they sought. Three singles and a rare error by center fielder Paul Blair (who dropped a fly ball) combined to give Pittsburgh a deserved 4–3 lead. That's how the game would end. Kison got the win for Pittsburgh. Dave Giusti notched a save. Eddie Watt, Baltimore's third pitcher of the game, was saddled with the loss. Pittsburgh's win leveled the World Series at two games apiece. The Pirates would eventually win the Series in seven games. The home team won every game except the final one.

Roberto Clemente quietly collected three hits for Pittsburgh—all singles. Clemente may have been deprived of a home run because of a strange and surprising omission from Three Rivers Stadium, a supposedly modern ballpark that was less than two years old. Right field umpire John Rice of the AL recalled the situation years later in an interview:

> The park didn't have any foul poles. You had the foul line on the field and then there was a fence with a yellow line on it and about an 18-inch gap and a wall with a yellow line on it and that was it. I remember before the first game there, when we were discussing the ground rules with the managers, [fellow AL umpire] Nestor Chylak complained about it. But what could you do?
>
> In the middle of the [first night] game, Roberto Clemente hits this wicked drive down the right-field line. It went into the stand right in the area where there was no foul pole. When you have to make a call like that, it's a killer-diller. I called it foul.
>
> Everybody told me afterward if there had been a foul pole it would have been a home run. The next year they put up a foul pole! [Authors' notes: Rice's debatable call hardly fazed the unflappable Clemente, who batted .341 in 1971: In that same at-bat Clemente lashed a base hit. Rice was somewhat mistaken about the absence of a foul pole. There was a metal pole, painted yellow, attached to the right-field bleachers on the wall behind the outfield fence. It was nothing like the tall, prominent foul poles that are now common at all MLB stadia, but it was there as a reference point. Bob Prince and Curt Gowdy, who were calling the game for NBC, agreed the video replay was inconclusive as to whether or not Clemente had been deprived of a home run.]

The next afternoon, Game Five reverted to its traditional daytime slot, likely setting a record for the shortest interval between two World Series games. The quick turnover time nearly resulted in the Orioles having nothing to wear. During NBC's telecast, Curt Gowdy informed viewers that a local laundry company did not return the visitors' lone set of road uniforms until after 11 a.m.—less than two hours before the first pitch.

The public's response to the experimental World Series night game was spectacular: a viewing audience in excess of 60 million people tuned in to watch two teams that did not have a particularly large national fan base. The record TV viewership did not affect the live crowd in Pittsburgh one iota; in fact, a new attendance record of 51,378 paid spectators passed through the turnstiles of Three Rivers Stadium. Advertisers took note of the demographics of those tuned in and saw that World Series viewership spanned all generations and both genders. Tradition was discarded quickly when big profits were at hand. The transition to primarily World Series night games was stunningly swift. During a pre-game interview with Tony Kubek, Commissioner Bowie Kuhn proudly announced that only the Saturday and Sunday games during the 1972 World Series would be played during the day. He maintained such a move served the best interest of the majority of baseball fans—including children and adults—because everyone could now watch a weekday World Series game in its entirety. (Indeed, in 1972—just one year later!—the final weekday World Series day game was played on a Friday afternoon in Oakland, and only because a rainout earlier in the series and a day game in Cincinnati on Saturday necessitated a daytime start.) Weekend World Series day games were the next custom to fall. A generation has passed without seeing a World Series day game on any day of the week. The last one occurred in 1987, when Game Six between the St. Louis Cardinals and Minnesota Twins started at 4:04 p.m. Eastern Time on a Saturday.

Fast-forward four decades from October 13, 1971: All World Series games are night games. The average length of a World Series game in 2011 was 3 hours and 31 minutes. TV audiences are only about one-fifth of what they were in their heyday. Late starts and longer games have prevented many youngsters in the Eastern and Central time zones from watching MLB's showcase event. The overwhelming competition from the vast array of cable and satellite channels has undoubtedly affected viewership too. The extra tiers of post-season games have also made night games uncomfortable for both fans and players. During the 2008 Phillies-Rays World Series, some players donned ski masks and ear flaps because of the frigid evening temperatures in Philadelphia. Players on both teams maintained that they could not feel their toes. Accordingly, many writers and notable ex-players are calling for the return of World Series day games.

Michael McCarthy of *USA Today* is a strong advocate of bringing back World Series baseball in the autumn sunshine. "Baseball has been losing a generation of kids and other fans who are in bed during the game's biggest moments," he wrote in a 2009 piece aptly titled "Time for World Series to See Light of Day Again." "There's no question a [World Series] day game would be a financial gamble. It could be a ratings bust because of the smaller daytime television audiences. In the best-case scenario a nostalgic, old-time day game could become a TV event for MLB and Fox … the way the NHL's outdoor Winter Classic has become for NBC."

In that same article, Cal Ripken, Jr., concurred. "For the beauty of the sport, I am an advocate. I do like the idea of playing times when kids can see [the World Series]. I certainly enjoyed it when I was a kid. I remembered they rolled TVs into schools so we could watch the Orioles when they were in the Series."

Ron Darling also pines for a return to at least one day game per World Series as a special event. "It would be such an anomaly that everyone would get on board. If the corporate partners are forward thinking, they'd want to be part of a historic event," Darling said. "At some point, you have to generate new viewership, new fans. These kids have so many things to watch these days that it's a step in the right direction to have kids and their dads and moms sit and watch a [World Series] game together. I think it would be unbelievable."

Richie Hebner, who played in three games in the 1971 WS and was the Pirates' third baseman in that inaugural night game, wants World Series day games to make a comeback too. "I can't stay up and watch a World Series game," admitted Hebner in a 2011 interview. "There are six freaking commercials between every half inning. I mean I'm no different than anybody else. It's too late. I think the playoffs are much more interesting. At least in the playoffs, you still get a couple of afternoon games. That to me is the best of baseball."[1]

Baltimore 3 at Pittsburgh 4

Game played on Wednesday, October 13, 1971, at Three Rivers Stadium

Baltimore Orioles	ab	r	h	rbi	Pittsburgh Pirates	ab	r	h	rbi
Blair cf	4	1	2	0	Cash 2b	4	1	1	0
Belanger ss	4	1	1	0	Hebner 3b	5	1	1	0
Rettenmund lf	4	1	1	0	Clemente rf	4	0	3	0
Robinson F. rf	2	0	0	0	Stargell lf	5	1	2	1
Robinson B. 3b	3	0	0	1	Oliver cf	4	0	2	2
Powell 1b	3	0	0	1	Robertson 1b	4	1	1	0
Johnson 2b	3	0	0	0	Sanguillen c	4	0	2	0
Etchebarren c	2	0	0	0	Hernandez ss	3	0	1	0
Dobson p	2	0	0	0	Davalillo ph	1	0	0	0
Jackson p	0	0	0	0	Giusti p	0	0	0	0
Shopay ph	1	0	0	0	Walker p	0	0	0	0
Watt p	0	0	0	0	Kison p	2	0	0	0
Richert p	0	0	0	0	May ph	1	0	1	1
					Alley pr, ss	0	0	0	0
Totals	28	3	4	2	Totals	37	4	14	4

Baltimore	300 000 000—3 4 1
Pittsburgh	201 000 10x—4 14 0

Baltimore Orioles	IP	H	R	ER	BB	SO
Dobson	5.1	10	3	3	3	4
Jackson	0.2	0	0	0	1	0
Watt L (0–1)	1.1	4	1	1	0	1
Richert	0.2	0	0	0	0	1
Totals	8.0	14	4	4	4	6
Pittsburgh Pirates	IP	H	R	ER	BB	SO
Walker	0.2	3	3	3	1	0
Kison W (1–0)	6.1	1	0	0	0	3
Giusti SV (1)	2.0	0	0	0	0	1
Totals	9.0	4	3	3	1	4

E–Blair (1). DP–Baltimore 1, Pittsburgh 1. PB–Sanguillen (1). 2B–Baltimore Blair (1, off Kison), Pittsburgh Stargell (1, off Dobson); Oliver (1, off Dobson). SF–B Robinson (1, off Walker); Powell (1, off Walker). HBP–Johnson (1, by Kison); F Robinson (1, by Kison); Etchebarren (1, by Kison). IBB–F Robinson (1, by Walker); Oliver (1, by Dobson). SB–Sanguillen (1, 2nd base off Dobson/Etchebarren); Hernandez (1, 2nd base off Dobson/Etchebarren). HBP–Kison 3 (3, Johnson, F Robinson, Etchebarren). IBB–Dobson (1, Oliver); Walker (1, F Robinson). U–Ed Vargo (NL), Jim Odom (AL), John Kibler (NL), Nestor Chylak (AL), John Rice (AL), Ed Sudol (NL). T–2:48. A–51,378.

April 6, 1973

Site: Fenway Park

Teams: New York Yankees vs. Boston Red Sox

Significance: Debut of the Designated Hitter

Impact: The AL and NL begin distinctly different styles of play because of the AL adopting the DH

> "The average fan comes to the park to see action, home runs. He doesn't come to see a one-, two-, three- or four-hit game. I can't think of anything more boring than to see a pitcher come up [to bat], when the average pitcher can't hit my grandmother. Let's have a permanent pinch-hitter for the pitcher."—Oakland A's owner Charlie O. Finley

> "The DH keeps the best hitters and the best pitchers in the game. One of the most frustrating things about NL games is when the staff ace gets removed for a pinch-hitter in the seventh inning with his team trailing 2–1. There's the argument that the DH takes managerial strategy out of the game, but I'd much rather see the players decide the game on the field."—Steve Gardner in *USA Today* (June 10, 1999)

> "Baseball is simply a better game without the DH."—broadcaster Bob Costas

> "The designated hitter rule is like letting someone else take Wilt Chamberlain's free throws."—Rick Wise

> "I screwed up the game of baseball. Baseball needed a jolt of offense for attendance, so they decided on the DH. I never thought it would last this long."—Ron Blomberg, the first-ever designated hitter in MLB, as quoted 30 years later in *The Journal News* (April 5, 2003)

Ron Blomberg had a largely undistinguished career in major league baseball. In the space of eight seasons and 1,333 at-bats, Blomberg hit 52 home runs and collected 224 RBI, the vast majority while wearing a New York Yankees uniform.

Despite this rather ordinary output, Blomberg became an important figure in his sport just by stepping into the batter's box one blustery afternoon at Boston's Fenway

Park. On Friday, April 6, 1973, Blomberg achieved his noteworthy niche in baseball history by being the first designated hitter in the major leagues.

"It's incredible," said Blomberg in a 1993 interview in *Yankees* magazine. "I was an answer in *Trivial Pursuit*. I was a question on *Jeopardy!*—and it all happened because I pulled my hamstring in spring training 20 years ago."[1]

Weak-hitting pitchers have been a scourge to MLB for at least 11 decades. For years *The Baseball Encyclopedia* did not list comprehensive offensive stats for pitchers—presumably because they were so universally bad that the editors assumed no one would want to check them out. There were exceptions to the stereotype of the weak-hitting MLB pitcher, of course. Walter Johnson was a fine hitter. Wes Ferrell slugged 38 career homers, nine of them in 1931 alone. Ned Garver, who had a .305 batting average in 1951, was known to bat sixth in the St. Louis Browns' lineup. Babe Ruth, of course, started his magnificent MLB career as a dominating left-handed pitcher. George Sisler and Sam Rice, both Hall of Famers, also began as a hurlers before finding greater fame and satisfaction in hitting baseballs rather than pitching them.

The concept of the designated hitter (a player inserted into the lineup solely to bat for the pitcher) was first discussed in baseball circles from the moment pitchers became impotent at the plate, but was never given serious consideration until the late 1960s, when pitching dominated the professional sport and stifled run scoring. In 1969, the AAA International League adopted the DH for one season as a means of generating greater offence. The desired effect was achieved as the league's overall batting average jumped from .251 to .268 and runs scored increased by an average of 42 per team. Nevertheless, the IL shelved its DH experiment after one year, much to the delight of baseball traditionalists who insisted that pitchers should have to take their turn at the plate just like everyone else. In a tongue-in-cheek article published in the April 5, 1969, edition of *The Sporting News*, Leonard Koppett predicted that by the time the bicentennial of professional baseball in 2069, there would be "three-platoon baseball" with MLB players all specializing in fielding, hitting or baserunning—but never a combination of any two separate skills. (Koppett also kiddingly predicted the pitcher's mound would be replaced by a deep ditch so that hurlers would be heaving the ball upwards toward home plate, thus guaranteeing lofty batting averages. He also foresaw MLB franchises being established in all parts of the world—such as the Peiping Toms and the Nigeria Africans.)

In 1972 the combined batting average for pitchers on AL rosters ranged from .100 to .150. With attendance stagnating or dwindling in various American League cities in the early 1970s—only three of the 12 AL teams drew more than one million fans in 1972—the AL decided to give the DH a try in 1973 on a three-year experimental basis to see if greater offense would sell more tickets. Of course the move was met with resistance from those who believed that the nature of the game would be radically changed and that managing an AL team would be less challenging than managing an NL team. In his April 14, 1973, column in *The Sporting News*, Leonard Koppett was dismissive of the volume of criticism coming from the mouths of baseball traditionalists. He thought the AL's adoption of the DH was creating much ado about nothing. He wrote,

The designated hitter is about to burst upon us in official American League play, so let's talk about what we can reasonably expect.

There are some things we cannot expect. We can't expect any huge, dramatic, revolutionary increase in scoring. We can't expect suddenly, magically an end to the American League's deep problems (compared to the National League). Nor should we expect any tragic, traumatic destruction of "baseball as we know it." It just isn't going to make all that much difference.

Koppett correctly surmised that most AL teams would likely have a platoon system in which they use a right-handed DH versus left-handed pitchers and vice versa. He wrongly predicted that since the DH was completely optional, a team might choose not to use it on days when they had a capable hitting pitcher on the mound. Koppett cited Bob Gibson of the St. Louis Cardinals, who had hit .194 in 1972, as an example of a pitcher who might be penciled into the batting order if he played in the AL. He also unknowingly described the Ron Blomberg situation perfectly: "In some [cases] it will be more complicated," Koppett noted. "It will involve players who might be affected with fatigue or minor injury, but who can go to bat."

On Opening Day, the earliest AL game was scheduled at Boston's Fenway Park, where the Red Sox would host the Yankees. Therefore either Boston's Orlando Cepeda or New York's Ron Blomberg would earn himself a quirky spot in MLB annals as the first DH at the top level of pro baseball. It all depended upon which one of them came to bat first.

Even as a child, Blomberg was a stereotypical candidate to become a future DH. As a nine-year-old in Atlanta he had taught himself to hit by picking berries from a bush, putting them in his mouth, spitting them up in the air, and hitting them with a stick. "There was nobody to hit berries to me," he joked, "so I didn't become a good fielder."[2] Indeed, Blomberg was once cut from a Little League team because his fielding was so dreadful. Undaunted, he came back the next day and made a different team based solely on his hitting prowess.

Yankees manager Ralph Houk figured on using either Felipe Alou or Johnny Callison as the team's DH when the 1973 season began, but Blomberg—a first baseman—pulled his right hamstring during spring training. "Ralph told me if it was cold in Boston on Opening Day he might put me into the lineup as DH to keep me from really hurting myself,"[3] Blomberg recalled.

Sure enough, the temperature in Boston at game time on April 6 was about 41 degrees Fahrenheit, but a persistent wind made it feel far colder. Blomberg was inserted as New York's DH in the number-six spot. He quickly became the focus of media members who wanted to know how it felt being a DH. "I don't know," said Blomberg, stating the obvious. "I've never done it before."[4] By the end of the 1973 season, Blomberg would be used to the new "position"; he would play more games for the Yankees as a DH than as a first baseman by a 56:41 ratio.

How the game progressed would determine whether Blomberg or Cepeda would be remembered in the history books as the first DH. Like Blomberg, Cepeda was slotted sixth in his team's batting order. After Boston pitcher Luis Tiant got the first two in the top of the first inning, Matty Alou hit what normally should have been an inning-ending fly ball. However, the deceptive wind played tricks with the ball, causing it to fall in front of Red Sox center fielder Reggie Smith for a double. Bobby Murcer and Graig Nettles both walked to load the bases.

Blomberg entered the batter's box as baseball's first DH at the major league level. "Why are you the designated hitter?" joked Red Sox catcher Carlton Fisk. "I thought the DH is supposed to be some guy who's 60 years old!"

"Sometimes I feel 60 years old,"[5] retorted the 24-year-old Blomberg, who also drew a base on balls to force in the first run of the DH era. Thus, the first plate appearance by a DH was not even an official at-bat.

Blomberg remembered being unsure about the DH's status once he reached first base. "I looked at the umpire [Don Denkinger] because I didn't know what to do. He told me to just do what I always do."[6] But old habits die hard. When the side was retired, Blomberg instinctively stayed on the field and waited for a teammate to bring him his first-baseman's mitt. Eventually coach Elston Howard realized Blomberg had no reason to be on the field and waved him to the Yankees' bench.

New York scored three runs in that first inning but eventually lost, 15–5, in a game where the Red Sox pounded out 20 hits off three ineffective New York hurlers. Tiant went the distance for the winners. Four Red Sox connected for at least three hits. Second baseman Doug Griffin—who would compile a .255 batting average in 1973—got four. Carlton Fisk wielded the most lethal Boston bat, smashing two homers and collecting six RBI. Ironically, the only Boston player in the starting nine who failed to get a hit was DH Orlando Cepeda, who went 0-for-6 with two strikeouts. Blomberg went 1-for-3, his lone hit a meager broken-bat single.

Yankees PR director Marty Appel realized that Blomberg, in a tiny way, had made baseball history. He randomly grabbed one of Blomberg's bats and shipped it to the Hall of Fame in Cooperstown. (The bat Blomberg shattered when he got his hit ended up discarded in a trash can.)

Blomberg is the first to admit his esoteric claim to fame does not merit his inclusion among the all-time greats of the sport. "People might have forgotten about me if I hadn't been the first DH," he said. "There aren't too many firsts in baseball, and I'm a first: The first DH. I went into the Hall of Fame through the back door. Who thought one at-bat could be so important?"[7]

More than four decades after Ron Blomberg achieved a footnote in the sport's history books, the designated hitter remains a part of American League baseball, although the passionate voices of the purists who wish it would disappear will never be silent on the issue. Blomberg still enjoys the notoriety that he achieved at Fenway Park on April 6, 1973. "How many guys who've been out of baseball for 35 years can say they're still part of the game? Every year I take my new campers [from the Ron Blomberg Baseball Camp in Milford, PA] to see the bat and the accolades. It's a wonderful feeling. It's great for my family, it's great for me, and it's great for the game of baseball."[8]

Although injuries prevented Blomberg from fully realizing his schoolboy reputation as "the Jewish Mickey Mantle," his unchallengeable and distinctive place in baseball history has provided him with a seemingly endless supply of peripheral income from speaking engagements and gigs on baseball-themed cruises. He even penned a book cleverly titled *Designated Hebrew: The Ron Blomberg Story.*

New York 5 at Boston 15

Game played on Friday, April 6, 1973, at Fenway Park

New York Yankees	ab	r	h	rbi	Boston Red Sox	ab	r	h	rbi
Clarke 2b	5	0	1	0	Harper lf	6	1	3	1
White lf	5	0	0	0	Aparicio ss	6	0	1	1
Alou M. rf	5	2	2	0	Yastrzemski 1b	4	2	2	2
Murcer cf	3	1	0	0	Smith cf	5	2	2	0
Nettles 3b	2	2	1	2	Miller pr, cf	0	0	0	0
Blomberg dh	3	0	1	1	Cepeda dh	6	0	0	0
Alou F. 1b	4	0	3	2	Petrocelli 3b	4	3	3	0
Munson c	3	0	0	0	Fisk c	4	4	3	6
Michael ss	4	0	0	0	Griffin 2b	5	2	4	2

New York Yankees	ab	r	h	rbi		Boston Red Sox	ab	r	h	rbi
Stottlemyre p	0	0	0	0		Evans rf	5	1	2	1
McDaniel p	0	0	0	0		Tiant p	0	0	0	0
Cox p	0	0	0	0						
Totals	34	5	8	5		Totals	45	15	20	13

New York 301 010 000—5 8 2
Boston 143 403 00x—15 20 0

New York Yankees	IP	H	R	ER	BB	SO
Stottlemyre L (0–1)	2.2	8	8	6	0	1
McDaniel	2.1	7	4	4	1	2
Cox 3.0	5	3	2	1	0	
Totals 8.0	20	15	12	2	3	

Boston Red Sox	IP	H	R	ER	BB	SO
Tiant W (1–0)	9.0	8	5	5	5	2
Totals 9.0	8	5	5	5	2	

E–Nettles (1), Michael (1). DP–Boston 1. 2B–New York M Alou 2 (2, off Tiant 2); F Alou (1, off Tiant), Boston Fisk (1, off Stottlemyre); Smith (1, off McDaniel); Evans (1, off McDaniel); Harper (1, off Cox). HR–New York Nettles (1, 3rd inning off Tiant 0 on, 2 out), Boston Yastrzemski (1, 1st inning off Stottlemyre 0 on, 2 out); Fisk 2 (2, 2nd inning off Stottlemyre 1 on, 1 out, 4th inning off McDaniel 3 on, 1 out). SF–Yastrzemski (1, off Cox). HBP–Fisk (1, by Cox); Smith (1, by Cox). IBB–Petrocelli (1, by McDaniel). CS–Clarke (1, 2nd base by Tiant/Fisk). SB–Griffin (1, 2nd base off Stottlemyre/Munson); Yastrzemski (1, 2nd base off Cox/Munson). HBP–Cox 2 (2, Fisk, Smith). IBB–McDaniel (1, Petrocelli). U-HP–Frank Umont, 1B–Don Denkinger, 2B–Merlyn Anthony, 3B–Bill Deegan. T–2:57. A–32,882.

April 8, 1974

Site: Atlanta-Fulton County Stadium

Teams: Los Angeles Dodgers vs. Atlanta Braves

Significance: Hank Aaron's 715th Career Home Run

Impact: One of MLB's "unbreakable records" falls; a black man captures MLBs most prestigious record

"What a marvelous moment for baseball! What a marvelous moment for Atlanta and the state of Georgia! A black man is getting a standing ovation in the Deep South for breaking the record of an all-time baseball idol."—Los Angeles Dodgers broadcaster Vin Scully

"Aaron's problem was that in a country that prefers its heroes to be soaked with drama, charisma, and dollops of controversy, he was a steady, unexciting performer who never lit up a footlight."—baseball historian Donald Honig

"It was terrible, terrible. Those were bad times for me."—Hank Aaron recalling the bagfuls of hate mail he received while pursuing Babe Ruth's career home run record.

The cover of the April 15, 1974, issue of *Sports Illustrated* was beautiful in its simplicity. It featured a smiling headshot of Hank Aaron of the Atlanta Braves a few minutes after he had smashed one of the most famous home runs in baseball history. The caption superimposed on the photo simply said, "715." Aaron was not identified; he did not need to be. The number 715 was not explained. Everyone who followed sports in North America even marginally already knew the number's significance—it was one more regular-season home run than the great Babe Ruth had hit during his illustrious 22-year MLB career.

The accompanying feature story about the momentous occasion when Henry "Hank" Aaron hit his 715th career home run was penned by Ron Fimrite, one of *SI's* best reporters. It was accurately titled, "End of the Glorious Ordeal." Indeed, what should have been fabulous experience for one of baseball's most overlooked stars instead was a prolonged descent into the dark abyss of senseless racism. "Henry Aaron's ordeal ended at 9:07 p.m. Monday, [April 8]," Fimrite wrote. "It ended in a carnival atmosphere that would have been more congenial to the man he surpassed as baseball's all-time home run champion. But it ended. And for that, as Aaron advised the 53,775 Atlanta fans who came to enshrine him in the game's pantheon, 'Thank God.'"

Hank Aaron was a quiet superstar. He broke into the Milwaukee Braves' lineup in 1954 after playing for the Indianapolis Clowns of the Negro League. (When he retired at the end of the 1976 season, Aaron held the distinction of being the last active MLB player to have played in segregated professional baseball.) Always a reliable and dangerous hitter, his career was a superb monument to steadiness, if not spectacular play. If Aaron's 755 home runs were expunged from his stats, he would still have more than 3,000 career hits.

As of the end of the 2014 MLB season, there had been 68 different occasions when a player had hit 50 or more home runs in a season. Aaron never achieved the feat. There were only six players who had attained that number when Aaron first played in the majors in 1954. Although he approached the magical 50-home run plateau frequently, Aaron never hit more than 47 homers in any single season. Four times Aaron finished a season with exactly 44 home runs. Despite also holding the MLB record for runs batted in for a career, none of Aaron's seasonal totals in that department ranks in history's top 100. "Aaron has labored for most of his 21-year career in shadows cast by more flamboyant superstars," wrote Fimrite, "and if he was enjoying his newfound celebrity, he wasn't showing it."

The *Washington Post* lauded Aaron's sustained yet anonymous excellence in an editorial on April 9, 1974: "Here is a person who is authentic, whose acclaim is based on the results of his self-confidence and not self-promotion, who has been faithful to his vocation whether noticed or not."

In his terrific book *Baseball America*, historian Donald Honig described Aaron this way:

> Aaron … covered the indignities of his black experience with a career-long smile and affability of disposition. Unseating Ruth as the game's most prolific striker of home runs probably caused him as much travail as satisfaction. Not only was he peppered with hate mail from offended racists (including death threats, bleak prophecies, and whatever other vituperation the anxiety-ridden were able to flush from themselves for the price of a postage stamp), but even the disinterested kept pointing out that it had taken him an extra 4,000 at-bats to pop 41 more homers than Ruth, and that therefore as a home-run king, he was really little more than a freak of longevity.

The racist hate mail that Aaron received by the bagful was staggering considering the year was 1974. MLB had been integrated in 1947. Every MLB team had had black players on its roster since the late 1950s. The Civil Rights movement had expunged the demeaning Jim Crow laws in Southern states. Yet in the spring of 1974 it was totally unacceptable and unthinkable to many American sports fans that a black man could ascend to the top of MLB's all-time home run chart. Consider this small sample of snippets from the correspondence that was entirely typical of Aaron's daily mail during the winter of 1973–1974:

- I hope lightning will strike you before next season.
- You black animal, I hope you never live long enough to hit more home runs than the great Babe Ruth.
- Everybody loved Babe Ruth. You will be the most hated man in this country if you break his career home run record.
- I hope you don't break the Babe's record. How do I tell my kids that a nigger did it?

Age did not seem to be an impediment to Aaron. As a 39-year-old in 1973, Aaron continued to hit as consistently as he had with the championship Milwaukee Braves 16 years before. Thus Aaron's march toward Ruth seemingly unassailable mark became inevitable. As the 1973 season wound down, excitement over Aaron's pursuit of Ruth's 714 homers occupied much of the sports pages. Aaron strangely became more of a celebrity in other teams' ballparks than he was at home. When Aaron hit his 711th career home run during a home date on September 17, 1973, there were only 1,362 fans at the Padres-Braves game scattered around vast Atlanta-Fulton County Stadium that Monday night. (True, the Braves were a sub-.500 team in 1973, languishing in fifth place in the NL West—and they would finish 22½ games in arrears of the divisional champion Cincinnati Reds—but the allure of watching someone chase one of MLB's touchstone numbers should have been far greater in Atlanta.) When the 1973 schedule reached its conclusion, the long-dead Ruth still led Aaron on MLB's all-time home run list by a 714–713 count. MLB kept the spotlight on Aaron as much as possible. He threw out two ceremonial first balls at the first game of the 1973 World Series in Oakland and was received warmly by the crowd. Aaron would have an entire off-season to think about the historic milestone— and the mail would keep pouring in. For both Aaron and those who wished to see Ruth continue as MLB's home run king, it truly was a winter of discontent.

As the 1974 season began, Aaron was more concerned about personal safety issues than baseball. Calvin Wardlow, an undercover Atlanta policeman, was given the full-time responsibility of ensuring Aaron's protection. Trying to look like a fan, Wardlow accompanied Aaron everywhere. He kept a snub-nose, .45 caliber handgun concealed in a binocular case. While trying to be as accessible to the media as possible, Aaron drew the line at riding in open convertibles. He feared being the target of a sniper.

The schedule had Atlanta opening the 1974 season in Cincinnati on Thursday, April 4. Typical of Aaron's aversion for providing any sort of sustained drama, he quickly tied Ruth with a home run on his very first swing of the season—a three-run shot off Jack Billingham. An eight-minute ceremony followed Aaron's record-tying shot. "I'm just thankful it's almost over," he said. The Reds won the first game of the NL season, 7–6, in 11 innings. With the Braves leading, 6–2, Aaron was pulled from the game after three at-bats by manager Eddie Mathews, a move which irked quite a few fans at Riverfront Stadium who wanted to see every possible Aaron plate appearance just in case it happened to be the historic one. "Without [Aaron]," wrote Furman Bisher in *The Sporting News*, "the Braves melted down to a puddle of painfully mortal bunglers."

There was no game scheduled for Friday. Mathews drew the ire of Cincinnati fans— and a stern warning from MLB commissioner Bowie Kuhn—for not playing Aaron at all in Saturday's game versus the Reds, a contest Cincinnati won, 7–5. It was obvious that

Mathews and the Braves' ownership preferred to see Aaron break Ruth's record at home before a huge crowd. Kuhn informed Mathews that he had an obligation to baseball fans everywhere to put his best lineup on the field, which obviously included Aaron in his usual spot in the Braves' outfield. Anything short of that, said the miffed Kuhn, could be construed as deliberately dumping a game. The Braves had one final game in Cincinnati on Sunday afternoon before their home opener the next night versus the Los Angeles Dodgers. Mathews reluctantly complied with Kuhn's edict, but only up to a point. Aaron played about two-thirds of the game before he was replaced by Rowland Office. Aaron went 0-for-3 in his three plate appearances before about 36,000 Cincinnati fans who had hoped to witness baseball history. The Braves won their first game of 1974 by a 5–3 score.

To accommodate coverage by NBC-TV, the Braves' home opener was switched to a night game. The gaudy pre-game ceremonies were a bit over the top by 1974 standards. Aaron was paraded onto the field accompanied by majorettes. Helium-filled balloons ascended to the sky when Aaron took his position in left field. Pearl Bailey was on hand to sing the national anthem. The Jonesboro High School Band and the Morris Brown College Choir provided musical accompaniment for the festivities. Atlanta mayor Maynard Jackson was in attendance, as were Sammy Davis, Jr., and Jimmy Carter (then the governor of Georgia). Conspicuous by his absence was Commissioner Kuhn. Inexplicably, he was in Cleveland. (The Indians weren't even in Cleveland that night; they were in New York playing the Yankees!) One homemade banner that hung near the left field fence said, in part, "Fooey on Bowie." In his coverage for *Sports Illustrated*, Ron Fimrite wrote, "If the Braves' management overdid it a bit with the balloons, the fireworks, the speeches, and the all-round hoopla, who is to quibble? There have not been many big baseball nights in this football-oriented community—and those few have been supplied by Aaron."

Los Angeles had an excellent team in 1974 and their best shot to win the NL pennant since the dominant days of Sandy Koufax and Don Drysdale in the 1960s. The Dodgers' starter on April 8 was the soon-to-be famous Al Downing, a 32-year-old, veteran left-hander, who said before the game he was not going to pitch to Aaron any differently than he would to any other batter. Downing had been in the majors since 1961. In 1971, his best season, he won 20 games for the Dodgers, but he was clearly on the downside of his career by 1974. He would pitch only one complete game all season for a team that would win the NL pennant. Downing's uniform number was 44—the same number that Aaron wore. Atlanta Braves radio announcer Milo Hamilton took it as an omen that the record-breaking home run would occur that night.

The Braves went down in order in the bottom of the first inning. Aaron was slotted in the cleanup position; thus, he would lead off the second inning. Aaron drew a walk, prompting a loud chorus of boos from the capacity crowd. Aaron came around to score to give the Braves a 1–0 lead, but Los Angeles scored three runs in the top of the third inning to move back in front, 3–1. Atlanta failed to score in the home half of the inning. Despite a strong start, Downing would not retire another Braves hitter.

In the bottom of the fourth inning, Darrell Evans led off for the Braves. Evans once said there was "no better feeling in the world than hitting a home run,"[1] but he settled for reaching first base on an error by Dodgers shortstop Bill Russell. It was one of six errors the Dodgers committed on the night. Aaron was the next batter. Here is Fimrite's description of what unfolded:

Downing's momentous mistake was a high fastball into Aaron's considerable strike zone. Aaron's whip of a bat lashed out at it and snapped it in a high arc toward the 385-foot sign in left center field. Dodger center fielder Jimmy Wynn and left fielder Bill Buckner gave futile chase, Buckner going all the way to the six-foot fence for it. But the ball dropped over the fence in the midst of a clutch of Braves' relief pitchers who scrambled out of the bullpen in pursuit. Buckner started to go over the fence after the ball himself, but gave up after he realized he was outnumbered. It was finally retrieved by reliever Tom House, who even as Aaron triumphantly rounded the bases, ran hysterically toward home plate holding the ball aloft. It was, after all, one more than Babe Ruth ever hit over a fence, and House is a man with a sense of history.

Here is how Milo Hamilton called the home run on the Braves' radio network:

Henry Aaron, in the second inning, walked and scored.... He's sittin' on 714.... Here's the pitch by Downing ... swinging ... there's a drive into left-center field ... that ball is gonna beeee ... outta here! It's gone! It's 715! There's a new home run champion of all time ... and it's Henry Aaron!

Stadium security conspicuously failed once the ball sailed over the fence. Two teenage males bolted from the stands near first base and ran unimpeded toward Aaron. Looking very much like younger versions of 1970s TV cops Starsky and Hutch, they caught up with the surprised Aaron as he passed second base. They were merely well-wishers who only wanted to pat MLB's new home run leader on the back, an image transmitted live by NBC-TV.

The trespassers were later identified as Britt Gaston and Cliff Courtenay, both 17. They were extremely lucky not to have been struck down by police bullets. Special law enforcement agents were prepared to shoot anyone who presented a threat to Aaron's safety. A split-second judgment call by a police sniper correctly categorized Gaston and Courtenay as harmless interlopers. (Imagine the uproar if the twosome had run onto the field with malevolent intentions and had succeeded!) Both teens tried to elude security personnel by running in separate directions, but they were apprehended in short order and placed under arrest. They were bailed out of jail at about 3:30 a.m. by Gaston's father, who was at the game. Charges against them were quickly dropped when they appeared in court on April 9. In the years since their few seconds of fame, Gaston and Courtenay were reintroduced to Aaron on two occasions. "It's wonderful to see them," Aaron graciously said before their reunion in 2010. "I often get asked, 'Whatever happened to those two guys?' It's nice to see them once again and know they're doing fine, doing well. The older you get, the more you think about it," Aaron added. "I'm just glad things worked out the way they did. It could have been a lot worse. They were having fun with it as kids. They didn't get beat up and all that. I think they spent two or three hours in jail. Other than that, it was a happy moment."[2] (Gaston died of cancer in 2011 at age 55. Courtenay was featured in *Sports Illustrated*'s annual "where are they now" issue in 2014. He is an optometrist who says he is mystified that his brief moment in the spotlight led to 40 years of fame.)

Upon reaching home plate, Aaron was engulfed in a vigorous bear hug by his mother, Estella. "I didn't know she could hug so hard,"[3] Aaron later said. Estella admitted afterward that her embrace was more protective than affectionate; she was shielding her son from possible gunfire from the stands. Her concern was valid. At Fisk University in Nashville, TN, Estella's granddaughter Gaile, an enrollee there, was under FBI protection after she received a kidnapping threat. She watched her father's historic moment on television.

The Braves scored two additional runs in the bottom of the fourth inning to assume a 5–3 lead that they would not relinquish. Atlanta won the game, 7–4. Downing did not retire any Braves in the bottom of the fourth inning. He was replaced on the mound by

Mike Marshall, who would set an MLB record in 1974 for relief appearances with 106. He was a key figure in the Dodgers' NL championship that season. Unlike his last two games in Cincinnati, Aaron played the full game but failed to get another hit in two more at-bats. Years later, at a testimonial dinner for Aaron, Downing joked that the fateful pitch was "a sinker that didn't sink."[4]

Aaron's record-smashing home run was the highlight of the year for the Atlanta Braves. They finished the 1974 season with an 88–74 record, good enough for third place in the NL West but 14 games behind the Dodgers, who won 102 games. The Braves did not draw a million fans to their home games in 1974. They averaged just 12,112 paying customers per game. The huge crowd that saw Aaron's historic clout on April 8 represented nearly 5.5 percent of the Braves' attendance for the entire year. (The night after Aaron's famous home run, just 10,648 customers bought tickets to see the Dodgers handily thump Atlanta, 9–2. Aaron sat out that game.) In 1975 the average attendance tumbled to just 6,642 patrons per game at Atlanta-Fulton County Stadium. Milo Hamilton, who made the memorable radio call of Aaron's famous homer, was fired at the end of the 1975 season for constantly and accurately commenting on the Braves' sorry home attendance stats. He got other announcing gigs in Chicago and Pittsburgh. He is best known, however, as the voice of the Houston Astros, where he spent 25 seasons calling games before his retirement in 2012. He won the Hall of Fame's Ford Frick Award in 1992. A street in Houston is named after him.

Aaron eventually added 40 more home runs to his career total, upping it to 755 before he hung up his spikes. His final MLB homer flew over the head of outfielder Bobby Bonds. Only in his last two seasons, when he was 41 and 42 years old, did Aaron's offensive numbers decline noticeably. Because Aaron's record fell to the unpopular Barry Bonds (Bobby's son) in the dubious era of performance-enhancing drugs, Aaron is still regarded as MLB's "true home run champion" by a great many fans. Aaron, now an octogenarian, prefers not to discuss the hate mail and racial tension leading up to his glorious, history-making moment on April 8, 1974.

To the surprise and disappointment of many fans, Aaron himself got into some hot water with racially charged comments of his own on the 40th anniversary of his home run off Al Downing in 2014. In an interview with Bob Nightengale of *USA Today*, Aaron was asked to comment on how race relations had changed in the United States since the troublesome days he had experienced back in 1973 and 1974. Aaron surprisingly remarked,

> We can talk about baseball. Talk about politics. Sure, this country has a black president. But when you look at a black president, President Obama is left with his foot stuck in the mud from all of the Republicans with the way he is treated. We have moved in the right direction, and there have been improvements, but we still have a long way to go in this country. The bigger difference is that back then they had hoods. Now they have neckties and starched shirts.[5]

Aaron's equating Barack Obama's duly elected political opponents with the Ku Klux Klan was polarizing. His comments angered many of his longtime white fans, who pointedly accused MLB—and the news media in general—of not treating racism with the same level of outrage and zeal when the ethnicities of the parties are reversed. A week after Nightengale's story appeared, *USA Today* reported that history was repeating itself: Aaron and the Atlanta Braves had received hundreds of angry emails, letters and telephone calls, many with racist overtones. Some baseball fans vowed to boycott the Braves if Aaron—the team's most famous alumnus by far—were not removed from the executive position he had held with the ball club since his retirement as a player in 1976. One outraged reader of New York's *Daily News* said in an online post that he had tossed his once-prized biography of Aaron into the trash can. Similarly, a Braves fan named David informed the team he was going to burn his copy. In an email to the team, another enraged fan named Edward felt compelled to conclude his correspondence with, "My old man instilled in my mind at a young age the only good nigger was a dead nigger."[6]

In the end, nothing came of Aaron's inflammatory remarks; he faced no punishment from the Braves or from MLB. (Commissioner Bud Selig is a longtime friend of Aaron's.) However, the controversy proved that four decades after Aaron's heroic chase of MLB's most sacred record amid a barrage of hate mail, Hammerin' Hank could still ignite racial outrage.

Los Angeles 4 at Atlanta 7

Game played on Monday, April 8, 1974, at Atlanta Stadium

Los Angeles Dodgers	ab	r	h	rbi		Atlanta Braves	ab	r	h	rbi
Lopes 2b	2	1	0	0		Garr rf, lf	3	0	0	1
Lacy ph,2b	1	0	0	0		Lum 1b	5	0	0	1
Buckner lf	3	0	1	0		Evans 3b	4	1	0	0
Wynn cf	4	0	1	2		Aaron lf	3	2	1	2
Ferguson c	4	0	0	0		Office cf	0	0	0	0
Crawford rf	4	1	1	0		Baker cf, rf	2	1	1	0
Cey 3b	4	0	1	1		Johnson 2b	3	1	1	0
Garvey 1b	4	1	1	0		Foster 2b	0	0	0	0
Russell ss	4	0	1	0		Correll c	4	1	0	0
Downing p	1	1	1	1		Robinson ss	0	0	0	0
Marshall p	1	0	0	0		Tepedino ph	0	0	0	1
Joshua ph	1	0	0	0		Perez ss	2	1	1	0
Hough p	0	0	0	0		Reed p	2	0	0	0
Mota ph	1	0	0	0		Oates ph	1	0	0	1
						Capra p	0	0	0	0
Totals	34	4	7	4		Totals	29	7	4	6

Los Angeles 003 001 000—4 7 6
Atlanta 010 402 00x—7 4 0

Los Angeles Dodgers	IP	H	R	ER	BB	SO
Downing L (0–1)	3.0	2	5	2	4	2
Marshall	3.0	2	2	1	1	1
Hough	2.0	0	0	0	2	1
Totals	8.0	4	7	3	7	4

Atlanta Braves	IP	H	R	ER	BB	SO
Reed W (1–0)	6.0	7	4	4	1	4
Capra SV (1)	3.0	0	0	0	1	6
Totals	9.0	7	4	4	2	10

E–Lopes (2), Buckner (1), Ferguson (1), Cey (1), Russell 2 (3). PB–Ferguson (1). 2B–Los Angeles Russell (1, off Reed); Wynn (2, off Reed), Atlanta Baker (1, off Downing). HR–Atlanta Aaron (2, 4th inning off Downing 1 on, 0 out). SH–Garr (1, off Marshall). SF–Garr (1, off Marshall). WP–Reed (1). U–HP–Satch Davidson, 1B–Frank Pulli, 2B–Ed Sudol, 3B–Lee Weyer. T–2:27. A–53,775.

April 9, 1974

Site: San Diego Stadium
Teams: Houston Astros vs. San Diego Padres

Significance: Debut of the San Diego Chicken

Impact: The debut of "fuzzy mascots" that take their comedic shticks onto the playing field

> "When I started, the game was played by nine tough competitors on grass, in graceful ballparks. But while I was trying to answer the daily Quiz-O-Gram on the exploding scoreboard, a revolution was taking place around me. By the time I finished, there were ten men on each side, the game was played indoors on plastic, and I had to spend half my time watching out for a man dressed in a chicken suit who kept trying to kiss me."—AL umpire Ron Luciano

> "A guy in a chicken suit can have such a catalytic effect on people. We, as a country, have the best sense of humor in the world. I'm waddling proof of that."—Ted Giannoulas

> "The Chicken is the most visible—and perhaps most risible—member of a subculture of professional mascots and bleacher creatures that has sprung up across the land."—*Sports Illustrated*, September 17, 1979

> "There are some things the world could do just fine without: War … famine … pestilence … baseball mascots. Who needs them? Fans go to the ballpark to watch a game, not some waddling, squawking Sesame Street–type mutant."—Bruce Nash and Allan Zullo in *The Baseball Hall of Shame*

The National Baseball Hall of Fame is a repository of historical goodies. With the price of admission one can see Ty Cobb's glove, Babe Ruth's bat, the cornerstones to both Shibe Park and Ebbets Field, and a ticket box from Forbes Field. Significantly, as one of its treasured artifacts, the Hall of Fame also displays a costume worn by Ted Giannoulas—better known to generations of baseball fans as the Chicken (a.k.a. the San Diego Chicken, the KGB Chicken, and the Famous Chicken). That is the ultimate testament to the importance that a 5'4" comedic performer has had on all levels of professional baseball for the past 40 years.

During the George W. Bush presidency, the Chief Executive invited Giannoulas to the White House. In the late 1970s Ted Turner supposedly tried to trade an Atlanta Braves catcher for him. When that ploy didn't work, Turner attempted to lure him away from San Diego as a free agent with a $100,000 salary. "I'll make you bigger than Mickey Mouse," Turner allegedly promised Giannoulas. He is not really a Hall of Famer, but who knows? Perhaps the honor is coming someday. "They've got a players' wing [in the Hall of Fame]," Giannoulas said in a 2009 interview with Gene Wojciechowski of ESPN.com. "They've got a broadcasters' wing. And I hope one day they'll have a chicken wing." At the time of the ESPN interview, Giannoulas had made more than 20,000 lifetime public appearances in his fowl garb, although only about 6,000 were at baseball parks.

Giannoulas is the classic American success story. He took advantage of a small opportunity that presented itself and used it to launch a unique and distinguished career, albeit an unusual one. It began in 1974. Giannoulas, 20, was studying journalism at San Diego State University. "A bunch of us from the radio communications class were sitting around trying to figure out how we could get a job for the spring holidays," he told *People* magazine in a 1978 interview. When local radio station KGB offered two weeks inside a chicken costume as a publicity stunt, he and his pals volunteered. Giannoulas got the job because, at 5'4", he was the only one of the group who could comfortably fit into the suit. His pay was a whopping $2 an hour. Giannoulas' assignment was to distribute candy Easter eggs to children at the city zoo. It did not take long before drudgery set in and he was on the verge of quitting. After two weeks, he suggested he should start showing up at San Diego Padres home games. KGB thought it was a good idea. Years later Giannoulas admitted he was simply looking for a way to get into MLB games for free.

The KGB Chicken, as Giannoulas' character was officially called, made its MLB debut at San Diego Stadium on Tuesday, April 9, 1974. It was the beginning of something big in North American sports culture. The Houston Astros were the visiting club. It was the Padres' home opener, and it was the day after Hank Aaron surpassed Babe Ruth on the all-time home run list. It was also the infamous day when the Padres' new owner, Ray Kroc, publicly lambasted his own team over the stadium's public-address system. "Ladies and gentlemen, I suffer with you. I've never seen such stupid baseball playing in all my life,"[1] Kroc announced for all and sundry to hear during the eighth inning of Houston's 9–5 win over the Padres, in a game which the home team surrendered 15 hits and committed three errors. Indeed, it was quite a historic day for San Diego's NL club—and it was abundantly clear that any sort of peripheral distraction would be welcome.

In all likelihood KGB was happy enough to get the simple publicity of a guy wearing a chicken suit with the station's call letters on a bib in front of 39,000 baseball fans. Giannoulas had bigger plans. "I saw the Chicken as a visual comedian,"[2] he recalled. Within a very short time Giannoulas was engaging in all sorts of amusing behavior with spectators. Nobody seemed to care that the fans were distracted from the action on the field. The 1974 Padres lost 102 games, so there was not much about the team for the fans to get excited about anyway.

In a 1979 *Sports Illustrated* feature article about the phenomenon of stadium characters and mascots, Bruce Newman described the transformation that was happening to Giannoulas:

> Rather than confining him to a narrow range of comedy, Giannoulas found that the Chicken costume liberated him. The Chicken, in fact, became his alter ego. He never took the suit off in public or allowed himself to be photographed without it on. "It would be great for my ego to be recognized out of the suit," he says, "but when I was growing up, I was fascinated with the Batman mystique and I wanted to create a character of my own. I didn't want people to think of the Chicken as a man in a costume. I don't want the person underneath to supersede the Chicken. I don't want them to say, 'Hi, Ted, how are you?' I want them to talk to the Chicken. There's no fear of rejection as the Chicken."[3]

Nobody had ever seen anything like it. MLB teams had occasionally employed "mascots," dating back to the late 19th century. Often they were just boys in miniature uniforms who travelled with the team and ran errands for the players. Hunchback mascots and simpletons seemed to be popular in the first three decades of the 20th century. The Brooklyn Dodgers hired renowned circus clown Emmett Kelly to entertain their fans during their last two seasons at Ebbets Field. Baseball had even had its own professional comedians such as Max Patkin and Nick Altrock, who would do baseball-related routines before the games. Having a diminutive chap in a chicken suit engaging in all sorts of hijinks was something absolutely out of the ordinary, though. The Padres fans immediately loved it. "It's quite a sound to hear a whole stadium laughing," Giannoulas told *People*. "If I can make 30,000 people laugh at one time, well, that's the bottom line. It's music to my ears."

Here's how *People* described the typical Giannoulas antics in a September 25, 1978, article titled "Looking for Chicken Delight? Just Order up Ted Giannoulas, Who's Sure Not to Lay an Egg":

> Down on the field the San Diego Padres are mounting a one-out rally in the second inning. The hometown fans, however, are staring toward the seats where somebody in a Day-Glo chicken suit has jumped to his feet. The bird-man struts, leads a cheer, then falls to his knees and clucks *Mammy*. While the crowd is still smiling, he vaults a railing and webfoots up the aisle toward a young woman 10 rows back. She knows what's coming and shrieks. In an instant her head disappears inside the giant yellow beak. The stadium

erupts. The Padres lose, incidentally, but no matter. The KGB Chicken is again the clear winner of the evening.

With Giannoulas keeping the crowds in stitches, Padres attendance shot up dramatically from the previous season. In 1973, the Padres—a team that lost 102 games and finished last in the NL West—drew just 611,826 spectators to San Diego Stadium. In 1974, the figure jumped more than 75 percent to 1,075,399. It was the first time in the six-year history of the club that attendance had surpassed one million fans. Because of the spectacular success of the KGB Chicken, Giannoulas was given more latitude to amuse the patrons. He was allowed to mingle with the players and go onto the field between innings. Even NL umpires—normally a conservative and stodgy lot—allowed the Chicken to engage them in his comedy routines. Purists were aghast, but the vast majority of fans approved. Bob Rubin of the *Miami Herald* praised Giannoulas, saying, "The Chicken may be the most gifted physical comic since Curly, Larry and Moe."[4]

The Sporting News ran several articles about the team in April and May 1974 that mentioned the significant boost in Padres' attendance, but the esteemed baseball publication made no mention of the KGB Chicken's role in San Diego's greatly improved turnstile count. Perhaps *TSN* did not want to acknowledge that the Giannoulas comedy act in the stands was far more appealing than the comedy act the Padres were putting on the field most nights. By 1978, a poll conducted by a regional magazine in San Diego indicated that fully 11 percent of ticket buyers for Padres' games were attending solely to see the KGB Chicken's routine; the ballgame itself was just secondary entertainment. The radio station was reaping the rewards of the publicity. KGB quickly ascended from the number-five position among San Diego's radio stations to the top spot. At one point the station organized a contest where a lucky winner got to go on a "dream date" with the KGB Chicken in full regalia. More than 4,000 entries were received. (The winner got dinner and tickets to the ballet with Ted in his Chicken garb.) Giannoulas had somehow become an entertainment superstar—at least at San Diego Stadium.

His success at consistently drawing crowds did not go unnoticed. Giannoulas began accepting invitations to appear elsewhere in the Chicken suit. He was sought after to come to trade shows, supermarket openings, and other San Diego-area sporting events. He was now travelling beyond the city limits to do his unique brand of comedy. KGB had no problem with Giannoulas earning a few extra bucks in their costume, as long as he continued to wear the bib with the station's call letters at every appearance. It did not matter that the locales where Giannoulas was strutting his feathers were often well outside the reach of KGB's broadcast signal—that was the stipulation, period. Giannoulas thought it was a stupid requirement and often discarded the KGB bib when he was far away from San Diego. It was the beginning of a rift that would terminate Giannoulas' relationship with the radio station and launch lawsuits aplenty.

Giannoulas was being paid an annual salary of $25,000 by KGB—an absolute bargain considering how much publicity he had given the radio station. Atlanta Braves owner Ted Turner offered to quadruple that figure if Giannoulas would leave San Diego for his team. The $100,000 salary would have placed Giannoulas' pay slightly above the $97,000 that the average MLB player earned during the 1978 season. Giannoulas and KGB were inundated with pleas from fans—especially children—who urged him to remain in San Diego. When KGB doubled his salary to $50,000, the Chicken opted to stay put in southern California. Turner was astounded that his offer was turned down. He told Giannoulas that he would have had his own office next to Hank Aaron's. Giannoulas' plucky sense of loyalty endeared him to his San Diego fans even more. When it was announced during a Padres game that Giannoulas would indeed remain in San Diego, the crowd and the Padres rejoiced. Several players spontaneously hoisted the Chicken onto their shoulders and triumphantly paraded him around the field as the crowd cheered wildly.

Things suddenly turned nasty between KGB and its most famous employee in May 1979. Giannoulas appeared at an NBA playoff game in Seattle minus the required bib bearing the KGB call letters. The game was shown on national television—and Giannoulas was promptly fired for his transgression. The people of San Diego were outraged. Threats of violence poured into the radio station from fans of the deposed Chicken. Employees had their tires slashed in the station's parking lot. KGB briefly hired a new man to don its suit at Padres games under the mistaken belief that one Chicken was as good as another. The ersatz fowl was mercilessly booed off the field in his debut at San Diego Stadium. "When people buy a bottle of wine, they buy it for its contents, not the bottle,"[5] Giannoulas cackled with satisfaction. It was later reported that KGB had its replacement chicken wear a bulletproof vest under his costume—just in case.

Meanwhile Giannoulas patented another similar chicken costume and made lucrative appearances elsewhere. KGB sued and, temporarily at least, got an injunction that prevented Giannoulas from billing himself as "The Chicken." The plucky Giannoulas hardly cared, realizing full well that people were going to refer to him as the Chicken regardless of what any legal ruling might be. Later in 1979 Giannoulas made a one-time deal with the Padres to return in exchange for a cut of the gate. More than 47,000 charged-up spectators were on hand for the Chicken's eagerly awaited return. Most came to see the elaborate pre-game ceremony where Giannoulas' version of the Chicken triumphantly emerged from an enormous egg. He received thunderous applause—and about $40,000 for a single night's work.

Of course Giannoulas' success spawned numerous other weird, fuzzy mascots throughout MLB and the entire North American sports landscape. (Giannoulas was flattered. "Elvis Presley has his imitators,"[6] he immodestly said.) Some were good; some were utterly forgettable. Generally considered the best of the bunch behind Giannoulas was Dave Raymond, who occupied the Phillie Phanatic costume from 1978 through 1993. Thus it was only natural for Giannoulas to appear at a Philadelphia Phillies home stand against the Padres for a Battle of the Mascots. Reported *SI*, "The show staged by the Chicken his first night in Veterans Stadium so overwhelmed the game itself that the next day's local papers buried reports of the action between the Phillies and Padres beneath an orgy of Chicken commentary."[7] Giannoulas, like any red-blooded male, saw an opportunity to get some personal time with Mary Sue Styles—the gorgeous, blonde sexpot who conspicuously served as a Phillies ball girl. "He got out there where Mary Sue was sitting in the outfield," Raymond told *SI* with a mixture of awe and incredulity. "While he was talking to her, he kept moving closer and closer to where she was sitting. Then all of a sudden he did some things that weren't too family-oriented."[8] Years later Raymond was a little bit more specific about what Giannoulas did: "He graphically humped her."[9] The displeased Styles was none too happy about what happened. "Anyone but a Chicken would have gotten arrested,"[10] she complained.

Giannoulas' Chicken has had some interesting experiences over the years. At the 1978 Holiday Bowl, oblivious security guards detained him as he tried to descend to the sidelines to do his shtick. Even though Brigham Young University was marching toward a crucial touchdown, the fans were more engrossed by the Chicken's troubles than the important action occurring on the gridiron. Another time Giannoulas was sued by the producers of the children's TV show *Barney & Friends* for beating up a Barney lookalike in one of his routines. Giannoulas won the case; the court ruled his performance was a form of satire duly protected by the First Amendment of the United States Constitution, although one has difficulty envisioning America's esteemed Founding Fathers worrying about the civil rights of a 64-inch man dressed in a chicken suit 200 years in the future.

By the early 1980s, the Chicken was recognizable enough to be a regular character on the kids' television program *The Baseball Bunch* and to have his own baseball card in the MLB Donruss sets of 1982, 1983 and 1984.

Say what you will about the bevy of odd and fuzzy creatures that Giannoulas inspired, Jack O'Connell, a one-time secretary-treasurer of the Baseball Writers' Association of America, believes they have earned a distinctive place in the annals of baseball. He asks with all sincerity, "Could you write a history of the game without mentioning these people?"[11]

Houston 9 at San Diego 5

Game played on Tuesday, April 9, 1974, at San Diego Stadium

Houston Astros	ab	r	h	rbi	San Diego Padres	ab	r	h	rbi
Gross rf, lf	5	3	3	0	Tolan rf	4	1	0	0
Metzger ss	3	0	0	0	Beckert 2b	5	0	3	0
Cedeno cf	5	3	3	4	Colbert lf	3	1	0	1
Watson lf,1b	4	0	1	2	McCovey 1b	4	1	1	0
May 1b	3	1	0	0	Grubb cf	4	0	0	0
Gallagher rf	1	0	1	0	Kendall c	4	1	1	0
Rader 3b	5	0	2	1	Thomas 3b	3	1	2	1
Edwards c	4	0	1	0	Hernandez ss	3	0	0	0
Helms 2b	4	1	2	1	Gaston ph	1	0	1	2
Milbourne 2b	1	0	0	0	Morales ss	0	0	0	0
Dierker p	3	1	2	0	Arlin p	0	0	0	0
Scherman p	1	0	0	0	Garcia p	0	0	0	0
					Troedson p	0	0	0	0
					Roberts ph	1	0	0	0
					McIntosh p	0	0	0	0
					Alou ph	1	0	0	0
					McAndrew p	0	0	0	0
					Hilton ph	1	0	0	0
					Corkins p	0	0	0	0
					Williams ph	1	0	0	0
					Romo p	0	0	0	0
Totals	39	9	15	8	Totals	34	5	8	4

Houston	330 010 020—9	15 2
San Diego	011 000 030—5	8 3

Houston Astros	IP	H	R	ER	BB	SO
Dierker W (1–0)	7.0	6	2	1	3	5
Scherman	2.0	2	3	0	1	3
Totals	9.0	8	5	1	4	8

San Diego Padres	IP	H	R	ER	BB	SO
Arlin L (0–1)	1.0	6	5	5	2	0
Garcia	0.1	2	1	1	0	0
Troedson	0.2	1	0	0	0	2
McIntosh	2.0	1	0	0	1	2
McAndrew	3.0	2	1	0	0	1

San Diego Padres	IP	H	R	ER	BB	SO
Corkins	1.0	3	2	1	0	0
Romo	1.0	0	0	0	0	1
Totals	9.0	15	9	7	3	6

E–Rader (2), Dierker (1), Beckert (3), McCovey (1), Thomas (2). DP–Houston 2, San Diego 1. PB–Edwards (1). 2B–Houston Cedeno (3, off Arlin); Rader (1, off Arlin); Edwards (1, off McAndrew), San Diego Gaston (1, off Scherman). SH–Dierker (1, off McAndrew); Metzger (1, off Corkins). SF–Watson (1, off Corkins); Colbert (1, off Dierker). IBB–Edwards (1, by Arlin). SB–Metzger (1, 2nd base off McAndrew/Kendall). WP–Dierker (1), Garcia (1). IBB–Arlin (1, Edwards). U–HP–Art Williams, 1B–Doug Harvey, 2B–Harry Wendelstedt, 3B–Nick Colosi. T–2:55. A–39,083.

October 21, 1975

Site: Fenway Park

Teams: Cincinnati Reds vs. Boston Red Sox

Significance: Game Six of the 1975 World Series

Impact: Ushered in a renaissance of baseball interest

"Carlton Fisk didn't run. He turned sideways and took three abbreviated hops down the first base line, wildly waving his arms at the ball like a kid in a Little League game, urging, willing, begging it to stay fair."—Mark Frost, *Game Six*

"The 1975 season gave baseball a galvanic moment that I believe changed much of the nation's attitude toward baseball. It seemed that we all stayed up all night long to see the conclusion [of Game Six of the World Series]. It's from that moment that I date the resurgence of interest in baseball that came to establish all sorts of new records in attendance and viewership."[1]—Daniel Okrent, editor of *The Sporting News*

"If we could all get younger, you know what I'd like? We'd play Game 6 and Game 7 all over again tomorrow … that would be the best doubleheader of all time."—Pete Rose

"A man does his profession proud and he represents it with class. That was the most important thing about our team in 1975, and that Boston team, the thing that made them both great, the thing that put so many of them in the Hall of Fame: They were all men."—Sparky Anderson

For many years, whenever WGBH, the public television affiliate in Boston, needed a fund-raising gimmick, the station replayed a classic program that never failed to inspire pledges: Game Six of the 1975 World Series, featuring the Cincinnati Reds and the Boston Red Sox. Forty years after October 21, 1975, the evening when the riveting contest unfolded at fabled Fenway Park, it is still widely regarded as the greatest baseball game ever played. It is certainly among the most famous.

Bob Ryan of *Sports Illustrated* called Game Six "a four-hour morality play highlighted by a final five innings that contained the type of sustained drama only baseball is capable of generating." In 1994, Roger Angell, the eloquent baseball writer for the *New Yorker* magazine, marveled at what transpired that night. "Game Six is still the greatest game ever played in the World Series," he said. "There's no doubt about it. All the way through it kept on astounding you."[2]

Daniel Okrent, editor of *The Sporting News*, likened the titanic struggle to a great work of literature. "That game was like a Russian novel: It had character development. It had history behind it. It had plot moving forward. It had twists near the end—and then the spectacular conclusion. The seventh game—which people underrate—was the exquisite literary denouement."[3]

Entering the 1975 World Series, the Reds and Red Sox had two things in common: Both teams were unquestionably the best in their respective leagues and both franchises had gone an extraordinarily long time without winning a World Series. The Reds, managed by Sparky Anderson, won the remarkable total of 108 games during the regular season and swept past the Pittsburgh Pirates in the NLCS, but they had not won a World Series since 1940. The Red Sox, who had also easily swept the three-time defending champion Oakland Athletics in the ALCS, had not tasted ultimate victory since 1918.

Both teams were loaded with superstars. Cincinnati had Pete Rose, Johnny Bench, Tony Perez, Joe Morgan, George Foster and Ken Griffey. Boston countered with Carl Yastrzemski, rookie phenom Fred Lynn, Luis Tiant, and Carlton Fisk. (Another Boston rookie sensation, outfielder Jim Rice, who batted .309 with 22 home runs, was unfortunately sidelined with a severe wrist injury he sustained on September 21 after being hit by Detroit's Vern Ruhle. Rice missed the entire post-season.)

Even without Game Six, the 1975 World Series had been terrific. The first five games had produced an array of heroes. Three of the five contests were decided by a single run. The Reds won the pivotal fifth game in Cincinnati to take a 3–2 lead in the Series. Both clubs headed to Boston for the sixth (and perhaps seventh) game, but rain postponed play for three consecutive days. Perfect autumn weather returned to New England on the night of Tuesday, October 21.

From the first out of the game (when left fielder Carl Yastrzemski robbed Pete Rose of a base hit with a sprawling catch) until the final pitch at 12:34 a.m., fans across North America were mesmerized by the scintillating play.

Fred Lynn—who won both the AL's Rookie of the Year and MVP honors—put Boston into a 3–0 lead with a first-inning homer into the right field seats off Reds starter Gary Nolan. Nolan lasted just two innings before being yanked. Sparky Anderson, known to the press and his pitching staff alike as "Captain Hook" for his impatience with struggling pitchers, ended up using a World Series–record eight pitchers throughout the course of the long, tense game. None of the eight lasted longer than two innings. On NBC's telecast Joe Garagiola commented, "Sparky is going to make the complete game obsolete."

Meanwhile, Boston's Cuban-born starting pitcher, Luis Tiant, and his quirky deliveries held the powerful Cincinnati offense scoreless for four innings. Tiant had extra reason for wanting to put on a good show. His parents had been given permission to travel from communist Cuba to see their son for the first time since 1961. They were in attendance for Game Six. They chose not to return to Cuba after the World Series ended.

The Reds finally came alive in the fifth inning with three runs to tie the score, the key blow being Ken Griffey's two-run triple. Two more Cincinnati runs in the seventh plus Cesar Geronimo's solo homer in the eighth gave the Reds a solid 6–3 lead. It probably wasn't necessary, but as the joyful Geronimo was greeted by his smiling teammates in the Reds' dugout, NBC's Tony Kubek reminded the large television audience that Sparky Anderson's crew was just six outs away from winning the World Series.

To the delight of the capacity crowd at Fenway Park, the Red Sox refused to die. In the bottom of the eighth, Lynn and Rico Petrocelli both reached base. With two out, Bernie Carbo, a former Red, pinch-hit for Boston relief pitcher Roger Moret. It initially looked like a bad move. After two swings Carbo appeared badly overmatched by Cincinnati's hard-throwing Rawly Eastwick. Everything changed on Eastwick's next pitch, when

Carbo blasted a long home run over the center field wall to tie the game. The Red Sox manager now looked like a genius. "Darrell Johnson has been falling out of trees all season and landing on his feet,"[4] quipped Bill Lee, who was not a big supporter of his manager in 1975. The score remained level at 6–6 for four more innings thanks to a couple of sparkling defensive plays.

The Red Sox looked poised to win the game in the bottom of the ninth. With the bases loaded and none out, Fred Lynn lofted a fly ball about 150 feet down the left field line. George Foster drifted under the ball and made the catch in the tiny patch of foul ground between the chalk line and the stands. Against orders, Denny Doyle, Boston's runner at third base, attempted to score. Doyle's boldness seemed justified, but Foster nailed him at the plate with a perfect throw. Catcher Johnny Bench deftly applied a sweeping tag and plate umpire Satch Davidson emphatically called Doyle out. After the game Doyle explained why he had tried to score. In the deafening clamor, Doyle had misheard Eddie Popowski, Boston's third base coach. Popowski was yelling, "No! No!" Doyle thought he was saying, "Go! Go!" Boston's promising inning ended with a goose egg when Rico Petrocelli grounded out.

In the top of the 11th inning, Cincinnati threatened. Ken Griffey was at first base with one out when Joe Morgan came to bat. Morgan, the NL MVP for 1975, turned on an inside pitch and hit a long drive off Dick Drago to deep right field. Author Mark Frost, whose *Game Six* is an excellent batter-by-batter account of the entire heart-stopping contest, described the miraculous play that unfolded next:

> [Dwight] Evans had played right field in Fenway for three years now, and this one looked like trouble from the jump. Normally whenever a left-hander hit an inside pitch this hard toward him, it turned over toward the line, hooking like an errant golf ball, and that's where Evans headed on instinct. But as Evans sprinted toward where his heightened senses told him this ball was going to land … he realized it wasn't breaking toward the line at all, it was heading straight for him; he'd taken the wrong path, and in another split second the ball would be behind him, over his head, right where the Reds' bullpen ended, 380 feet from home plate. Somehow, at full speed, even losing sight of the ball for a split second, Evans adjusted in a single step back toward center, threw his glove hand up behind his head, leapt into the air, and came down somehow in balance, with his left knee and hip bumping up against the lowered wall, and, to his infinite surprise and delight, the baseball stuck firmly in the webbing of his glove.
>
> The front row of fans and ushers in the right field bleachers jumped to their feet screaming, the first [people] in Fenway to realize he'd pulled off the impossible grab. Reds' pitcher Clay Kirby—their lone man now in their bullpen, less than ten feet from the play—flung his arms down in disgust.

Evans' throw to first base was well off line, but it did not matter. Griffey, who had already rounded second base, was easily doubled up at first base to end the inning. "That was the greatest catch I've ever seen," Sparky Anderson coolly remarked after the game. Mark Frost did not agree or disagree with Anderson, but instead opined, "No man before or since ever made a better one at a more important moment."

The nerve-wracking affair finished dramatically when Carlton Fisk led off the bottom of the 12th inning for Boston. Facing Pat Darcy, Cincinnati's eighth pitcher of the game, Fisk drove a low fastball toward the left field wall. It was long enough for a homer but appeared to be fading foul. Fisk attempted to will the ball fair with some exaggerated body English—and it worked. The ball clanged off the foul pole for a game-winning homer.

In the Red Sox radio booth, Ned Martin's call was as follows: "The one-oh delivery to Fisk. He swings. Long drive … left field! If it stays fair, it's gone! Home run! The Red Sox win! And the Series is tied, three games apiece!" Martin's broadcasting partner, Curt

Gowdy, added, "Carlton Fisk has hit a one-nothing pitch. They're jamming out on the field.… His teammates are waiting for him. And the Red Sox have sent the World Series into Game Seven with a dramatic 7–6 victory. What a game! This is one of the greatest World Series games of all time!"

Frost wrote, "Fisk's urging, ecstatic dance down the first base line [became] an instant classic that soon became one of the most enduring and iconic images in the history of televised sport." Fisk's famous reaction became a seminal moment in sports broadcasting too—purely by accident. Before that at-bat, baseball cameramen were generally instructed always to follow the ball. Reputedly, Fisk's joyous reaction was only recorded because NBC cameraman Lou Gerard, shooting from a peephole inside the Green Monster, had become momentarily transfixed by a large rat nearby. The rodent caused Gerard to lose sight of the home run ball for a split-second and he simply kept his camera focused on Fisk. It turned out to be a brilliant shot. That solitary play was perhaps the most important catalyst in getting camera operators to focus at least some of their attention on the players themselves.

Longtime Fenway Park organist John Kiley appropriately played Handel's "Hallelujah Chorus" as the Red Sox and their fans celebrated the hard-fought victory. The joyous crowd was in no hurry to disperse. When Fisk returned to the field for a post-game interview, many fans were still milling about the infield as Fenway Park security had long given up trying to control the peaceful celebrants. When Kiley saw Fisk emerge from the dugout, he played "For He's a Jolly Good Fellow"—and the crowd enthusiastically sang along, of course.

Through 1976, NBC's World Series coverage featured the participating teams' announcers working alongside the regular network crew on both radio and television. Dick Stockton, a Boston announcer scarcely known beyond New England before Game Six, was lucky enough to call Fisk's game-winning home run for NBC's enormous television audience. More than anything else, that one at-bat propelled him into national prominence and launched a distinguished sportscasting career. When the game ended, Stockton shook his head as he recalled the three-day rain delay that had interrupted the Series. "And to think," he marveled, "that yesterday people were saying let's just get this thing over with."

Having seen one of the greatest games in American sports history, the public was left wanting more of the same. Less than 24 hours later, some 75 million viewers tuned into NBC to watch Game Seven (won by the Reds on Joe Morgan's RBI single in the ninth inning, 4–3). At the time it was the greatest television audience for any sporting event in American history. Viewership even surpassed the Beatles' famous debut appearance on *The Ed Sullivan Show* 11 years earlier.[5]

After Game Six, the Reds, despite losing a heartbreaker, realized they had been part of history. "I don't think there's ever been a better game," insisted Sparky Anderson. Pete Rose echoed those sentiments over and over again to whomever would listen. He said it had been a privilege to participate in it.

It had also been an absolute privilege to watch.

Cincinnati 6 at Boston 7

Game played on Tuesday, October 21, 1975, at Fenway Park

Cincinnati Reds	ab	r	h	rbi	Boston Red Sox	ab	r	h	rbi
Rose 3b	5	1	2	0	Cooper 1b	5	0	0	0
Griffey rf	5	2	2	2	Drago p	0	0	0	0

Cincinnati Reds	ab	r	h	rbi
Morgan 2b	6	1	1	0
Bench c	6	0	1	1
Perez 1b	6	0	2	0
Foster lf	6	0	2	2
Concepcion ss	6	0	1	0
Geronimo cf	6	1	2	1
Nolan p	0	0	0	0
Chaney ph	1	0	0	0
Norman p	0	0	0	0
Billingham p	0	0	0	0
Armbrister ph	0	1	0	0
Carroll p	0	0	0	0
Crowley ph	1	0	1	0
Borbon p	1	0	0	0
Eastwick p	0	0	0	0
McEnaney p	0	0	0	0
Driessen ph	1	0	0	0
Darcy p	0	0	0	0
Totals	50	6	14	6

Boston Red Sox	ab	r	h	rbi
Miller ph	1	0	0	0
Wise p	0	0	0	0
Doyle 2b	5	0	1	0
Yastrzemski lf,1b	6	1	3	0
Fisk c	4	2	2	1
Lynn cf	4	2	2	3
Petrocelli 3b	4	1	0	0
Evans rf	5	0	1	0
Burleson ss	3	0	0	0
Tiant p	2	0	0	0
Moret p	0	0	0	0
Carbo ph, lf	2	1	1	3
Totals	41	7	10	7

Cincinnati 000 030 210 000—6 14 0
Boston 300 000 030 001—7 10 1

Cincinnati Reds	IP	H	R	ER	BB	SO
Nolan	2.0	3	3	3	0	2
Norman	0.2	1	0	0	2	0
Billingham	1.1	1	0	0	1	1
Carroll	1.0	1	0	0	0	0
Borbon	2.0	1	2	2	2	1
Eastwick	1.0	2	1	1	1	2
McEnaney	1.0	0	0	0	1	0
Darcy L (0–1)	2.0	1	1	1	0	1
Totals	11.0	10	7	7	7	7

Boston Red Sox	IP	H	R	ER	BB	SO
Tiant	7.0	11	6	6	2	5
Moret	1.0	0	0	0	0	0
Drago	3.0	1	0	0	0	1
Wise W (1–0)	1.0	2	0	0	0	1
Totals	12.0	14	6	6	2	7

E–Burleson (1). DP–Cincinnati 1, Boston 1. 2B–Cincinnati Foster (1, off Tiant), Boston Doyle (1, off Norman); Evans (1, off Billingham). 3B–Cincinnati Griffey (1, off Tiant). HR–Cincinnati Geronimo (2, 8th inning off Tiant 0 on, 0 out), Boston Lynn (1, 1st inning off Nolan 2 on, 2 out); Carbo (2, 8th inning off Eastwick 2 on, 2 out); Fisk (2, 12th inning off Darcy 0 on, 0 out). HBP–Rose (1, by Drago). SH–Tiant (1, off Billingham). IBB–Fisk 2 (2, by Norman, by McEnaney). SB–Concepcion (3, 2nd base off Drago/Fisk). HBP–Drago (1, Rose). IBB–Norman (1, Fisk); McEnaney (1, Fisk). U–Satch Davidson (NL), Art Frantz (AL), Nick Colosi (NL), Larry Barnett (AL), George Maloney (AL), Dick Stello (NL). T–4:01. A–35,205.

September 9, 1979

Site: Fenway Park, Boston
Teams: Baltimore Orioles vs. Boston Red Sox

Significance: Bob Montgomery's Final Game

Impact: Montgomery was the last MLB player permitted to bat without a protective helmet

> "I was what they call a 50/50 player. I didn't help you an awful lot, but I didn't hurt you either."—Bob Montgomery, summarizing his unspectacular ten-year MLB career as a backup catcher with the Boston Red Sox

> "It took the National Pastime more than a hundred years to realize that in a collision between a baseball and a human skull, the skull comes out the loser."—author Dan Gutman in *The Way Baseball Works*

It was the bottom of the ninth inning of Game Seven of the 1975 World Series. There was high drama aplenty. The visiting Cincinnati Reds had scored a run to assume a 4–3 lead in the top of the ninth inning. The hometown Boston Red Sox were down to their final three outs of the season to try to level or win the game. The first Red Sox batter, pinch-hitter Juan Beniquez, flied out to Ken Griffey in right field. The next batter was another pinch-hitter, Bob Montgomery, who was making his only post-season appearance of 1975. To the casual baseball fan watching that Wednesday night—and they were plentiful among the 75 million tuned into NBC's television broadcast—there was something just a little bit different about the 31-year-old from Nashville, TN, as he stepped into the right-handed hitter's batter's box in place of Denny Doyle in the tension-filled game.

It might have taken more than a quick glance to realize what separated Montgomery from all the other players in that famous World Series. Curt Gowdy, doing the commentary for NBC-TV, noted that Montgomery was a potential home run threat, and anecdotally, that he was a licensed pilot and a model-train enthusiast. But Gowdy made no mention of what made Montgomery truly stand out among his peers: *He was not wearing a batting helmet.* Much as MLB players had done for years, Montgomery wore a typical cloth Red Sox cap with a flimsy protective liner underneath it. It did not provide much in the way of protection to anything below the crown of his head. Montgomery did not last long at the plate. On the first pitch from Will McEnaney, he slapped a ground ball to Reds shortstop Dave Concepcion for the second out of the inning. Carl Yastrzemski ended the game shortly thereafter with a routine fly ball to Cesar Geronimo in center field. Game over. World Series over.

Despite the obvious dangers associated with baseballs hurtling through the air at high speeds towards hitters, batting helmets developed surprisingly late in the history of baseball. Early models of catcher's masks were first seen on baseball diamonds as far back as the 1870s. The best evidence points to an Ivy League catcher at Harvard University named James Tyng in 1876 being the first to don a mask. Masks and chest protectors were commonly in use by the 1890s. Shin guards were introduced in the first decade of the 20th century, but batters generally remained unprotected for decades.

Even after Cleveland's Ray Chapman was fatally beaned by a Carl Mays pitch in 1920, there was no sustained outcry to have players were any sort of protective helmet. Hockey and football players were mostly performing without helmets in 1920, so it was perfectly reasonable to think that baseball batters ought to do the same at all levels of the sport.

There had been some attempts early in the 20th century to introduce batting helmets. In 1905, inventor Frank Mogridge created the first crude protective head gear and was granted U.S. Patent No. 780899 for a device called a "head protector." This first attempt at a batting helmet was said to look like an "inflatable boxing glove that wrapped around the hitter's head." Said Mogridge optimistically, "The use of my invention will not only insure the batter against injury to the head from being struck by the ball, but will give the batter confidence and prevent him from being intimidated by the pitcher."[1] After future Hall of Fame catcher Roger Bresnahan was struck in the head with a pitch, he developed a leather batting helmet in 1908 which he began using for a time. (Like Mogridge's device, Bresnahan's "helmet" is better described as a protective set of earmuffs. Neither protected the batter's head; it was designed to protect the ear and temple region.) In 1908, Freddie Parent wore a head protector of some sort, and Frank Chance did the same thing in 1913, though Chance's headgear was described as "little more than a sponge wrapped in a bandage." That same year, Joe Bosk began to wear a protector after being severely injured when he was struck in the head by a pitch in 1911. The first known case of a manager issuing head protectors to his players on a large scale was Phillies manager Pat Moran, who gave cork-cushioned hats to his players in 1917. None of the devices ever caught on with professional players.

On May 25, 1937, a truly frightful incident involving future Hall of Fame catcher Mickey Cochrane graphically showed the need for some sort of effective head protection for MLB batters. Cochrane, the player-manager of the Detroit Tigers, was hit in the head in the fifth inning by a rising 3–1 pitch from the Yankees' Irving "Bump" Hadley at Yankee Stadium. The pitch fractured Cochrane's skull in three parts, abruptly ending his terrific 13-year career as a player. Somewhat suspiciously, Cochrane had homered off Hadley in his previous at-bat. "He just lay there and quivered," recalled teammate Elden Auker, who helped carry Cochrane off the field. "I thought for sure he was going to die."[2]

For a while Cochrane did linger between life and death. (One inaccurate report that was quickly quashed said he had died.) In *The Sporting News*, Detroit correspondent Sam Greene reported, "Alarm spread through the ranks of baseball followers everywhere." Cochrane maintained the incident had wholly been an accident and said he had simply lost sight of the baseball. Hadley, who had no reputation whatsoever as a beanball pitcher, was among the first people to visit Cochrane at St. Elizabeth's Hospital in New York City. Cochrane was asked a month later if he believed there ought to be a rule making batting helmets mandatory at the MLB level. He replied, "Absolutely. A thrown ball even in the hands of a careful, sporting pitcher can perform weird trips … and a hitter is liable to be struck at any time." (Hadley could never shake the unfortunate association with Mickey Cochrane. When he died of a heart ailment in 1963, the *Associated Press* noted in the first paragraph of Hadley's obituary that he was the pitcher who had beaned the famous catcher.) Even though they were not involved in the Cochrane incident, a week later the Philadelphia Athletics began to wear polo-style helmets during batting practice but never actually in a game.

Scary scenes involving the Brooklyn Dodgers in the 1940s rekindled interest in batting helmets. The first such incident befell promising rookie shortstop Pee Wee Reese on Saturday, June 1, 1940, in Chicago. Cubs pitcher Jake Mooty tossed Reese a high, inside pitch. Reese was temporarily blinded by the white-shirted fans in Wrigley Field's center-field bleachers … and he froze. Mooty's pitch hit Reese squarely in the head. Reese was transported to the Illinois Masonic Hospital, where he remained under observation for two and a half weeks with what *The Sporting News* described as "a bad concussion." Upon his return to the Dodgers' lineup on June 21, Reese showed no ill effects of the beaning. He promptly singled, doubled, and tripled.

Beanballs continued to plague the Dodgers the following summer—even though they had provided protective cap liners to their Brooklyn players and to the players in the Dodgers' minor league clubs to wear if they wished to do so. In the first game of a Sunday doubleheader at Ebbets Field on August 10, Dick Errickson of the Boston Braves hit three Dodgers batters in three wild innings of relief pitching in which he allowed ten runs. Joe Medwick was struck in the head by one of Errickson's wayward offerings and was so shaken up he had to leave the game. Medwick was in no shape to play the second game either. (Nevertheless, Medwick's injury was so commonplace it did not merit any special mention by Brooklyn correspondent Tommy Holmes in his weekly report on the Dodgers in the August 14 issue of *The Sporting News*. In that same edition, though, *TSN* reported the death of Hall of Famer Cap Anson's 13-year-old grandson, who had succumbed to undisclosed injuries he had received during a sandlot football game.)

Larry MacPhail, the Dodgers' general manager, was seriously dismayed by the head injury sustained by Medwick, the 1937 Triple Crown winner. After the Medwick incident, MacPhail ordered the entire Dodgers team to wear protective headgear while batting; it was no longer optional. Those helmets were roughly based on the type that jockeys wore and were much like a normal baseball cap with the addition of a hard liner inside. Calling it the "Brooklyn Safety Cap," the Dodgers offered it to every MLB club but received only scant interest. MacPhail's order to his own players was rescinded after a short time because most of the Dodgers complained about the distracting and uncomfortable feel of the headgear. With the 1941 NL pennant in sight, the Dodgers wanted to retain their focus. Personal safety took a back seat as the helmets were permanently shelved. The Dodgers players opted to rely on their reflexes and take their chances just as generations of ballplayers had done before them. They did win the NL pennant in 1941—their first since 1920.

In 1971, Major League Baseball made batting helmets mandatory, although veterans were permitted to wear cloth caps with liners under a "grandfather clause" attached to the rule. Notable abstainers included Norm Cash, Tony Taylor … and Bob Montgomery. Montgomery had debuted in MLB on September 6, 1970, and had just 22 MLB games under his belt. Nevertheless, he was still considered a "veteran" for the purposes of the exemption to the mandatory helmet rule because he had started his MLB career prior to 1971.

For enhanced safety, starting in the 1983 season, MLB players were required to wear batting helmets with flaps extending down from the crown to cover the ear closest to the pitcher. This "flap" innovation began in the early 1960s as two teammates on the Minnesota Twins—Earl Battey and Tony Oliva—improvised flaps on their personal helmets. The first man to wear a helmet with a flap that was actually molded to the helmet as part of the factory construction was Tony Gonzalez of the Philadelphia Phillies in 1964. Players who had previously worn flapless helmets prior to 1983 were allowed to continue doing so, again thanks to a grandfather clause in the rule. Tim Raines, Sr., was the last player to wear a flapless helmet in an MLB game.

In 2013, MLB introduced a new model of helmet manufactured by Rawlings. It was specifically designed to absorb a greater shock than any previous batting helmet had. Called the S100 Pro Comp, it was shown in laboratory tests to be able to withstand the impact of a 100-miles-per-hour fastball. (Previous models were only tested to a mere 68 mph.) Constructed of aerospace-grade carbon fiber composite, it was made mandatory throughout MLB as a provision of the 2011 Collective Bargaining Agreement.

Of course players are absolutely allowed to wear helmets that offer more protection than the standard design. Over the years a handful of MLB batters have worn helmets featuring cheek protectors, often after having suffered facial injuries. Gary Roenicke and Ellis Valentine are two examples. Safety advocates have often encouraged youth leagues to adopt helmets with a full facemask, much like those used by cricket batsmen, but the response has generally been tepid. Safety be damned: Baseball players just do not wear masks while batting.

It was left to Bob Montgomery to be the last of the brave (or foolhardy), helmetless MLB batters. His inauspicious ten-season career came to a close at Fenway Park on Sunday, September 9, 1979. Entering the game as a substitute after pinch-hitter Jim Dwyer batted for starting Boston catcher Gary Allenson, Montgomery managed a base hit in two at-bats. He also tallied a meaningless run as the Red Sox absorbed a 16–4 thumping at the hands of the visiting Baltimore Orioles, who won the AL pennant that season. Montgomery was unaware at the time it was his MLB swansong, but he did not appear in any further games during the final month of the 1979 season, despite accruing a respectable, career-high .349 batting average in 86 at-bats. Montgomery attended spring training in 1980 but the 36-year-old was handed his walking papers by the only MLB team he had ever played for. The Red Sox had decided their aging backup catcher was no longer part of their plans.

Soon afterwards, Montgomery embarked on a new career away from the diamond— but not too far away. He stayed in baseball as a Red Sox broadcaster, a position he held until 1995. During broadcasts Montgomery was known to comically disparage his own baseball-playing abilities. Herb Crehan, the author of *Red Sox Heroes of Yesteryear*, disagreed with Montgomery's claims of extreme mediocrity. Crehan concluded his profile of MLB's last helmetless batter with high praise, stating that Montgomery was "probably the premier backup catcher in the major leagues throughout the seventies."

Baltimore 16 at Boston 4

Game played on Sunday, September 9, 1979, at Fenway Park

Baltimore Orioles	ab	r	h	rbi	Boston Red Sox	ab	r	h	rbi
Bumbry cf	4	3	2	1	Remy 2b	2	0	0	0
Dauer 2b	5	3	2	1	Papi 2b	1	1	0	0
Singleton lf	5	1	2	1	Burleson ss	3	0	1	1
Corey rf	0	0	0	0	Lynn cf	4	0	1	2
Murray 1b	5	1	1	1	Rice lf	4	1	2	1
DeCinces 3b	6	2	2	1	Yastrzemski 1b	4	0	1	0
Crowley dh	4	2	3	2	Fisk dh	4	0	0	0
Roenicke rf, lf	4	2	2	4	Hobson 3b	3	0	0	0
Dempsey c	5	1	1	4	Evans rf	3	1	1	0
Belanger ss	5	1	1	0	Allenson c	0	0	0	0
Stone p	0	0	0	0	Dwyer ph	1	0	0	0
Stoddard p	0	0	0	0	Montgomery c	2	1	1	0
					Torrez p	0	0	0	0
					Ripley p	0	0	0	0
					Finch p	0	0	0	0
					Remmerswaal p	0	0	0	0
Totals	43	16	16	15	Totals	31	4	7	4

Baltimore	020 056 012—16 16 1	
Boston	000 100 300—4 7 4	

Baltimore Orioles	IP	H	R	ER	BB	SO
Stone W (10–7)	6.1	4	4	4	5	4

Baltimore Orioles	IP	H	R	ER	BB	SO
Stoddard	2.2	3	0	0	1	0
Totals	9.0	7	4	4	6	4

Boston Red Sox	IP	H	R	ER	BB	SO
Torrez L (14–11)	4.0	6	6	6	3	2
Ripley	1.2	4	4	3	1	0
Finch	1.1	4	4	4	2	1
Remmerswaal	2.0	2	2	2	1	2
Totals	9.0	16	16	15	7	5

E–Dauer (14), Burleson (15), Lynn 2 (4), Hobson (23). DP–Baltimore 4, Boston 1. PB–Allenson (10). 2B–Baltimore Bumbry (25, off Torrez); Crowley (5, off Ripley); DeCinces (22, off Ripley); Murray (27, off Remmerswaal), Boston Rice (33, off Stone). HR–Baltimore Roenicke (25, 2nd inning off Torrez 1 on, 1 out); Bumbry (5, 6th inning off Ripley 0 on, 0 out); Dempsey (6, 6th inning off Finch 3 on, 2 out), Boston Rice (36, 4th inning off Stone 0 on, 1 out). HBP–Bumbry (3, by Remmerswaal). IBB–Murray (9, by Ripley); Crowley (2, by Finch). SB–Bumbry (30, 2nd base off Torrez/Allenson). WP–Stone (3). HBP–Remmerswaal (1, Bumbry). IBB–Ripley (3, Murray); Finch (3, Crowley). U-HP–Al Clark, 1B–Durwood Merrill, 2B–Dallas Parks, 3B–Dave Phillips. T–2:55. A–34,419.

October 26, 1985

Site: Royals Stadium, Kansas City

Teams: St. Louis Cardinals vs. Kansas City Royals

Significance: Game Six of the 1985 World Series

Impact: The movement begins for umpires to use video review to get calls right

> "Orta, leading off, swings and hits it to the right side, and the pitcher has to cover he is.... SAFE! SAFE! SAFE! And we'll have an argument!" –broadcaster Jack Buck's call of the infamous play on CBS radio

> "An umpire in the 1985 World Series named Don Denkinger made a bad call. His family still maintains the effect the call had on him led to his early death at age 51."—"Hockey Night in Canada" analyst Elliotte Friedman, arguing the merits of video review in hockey and other sports on April 20, 2014 ... and wrongly asserting that Don Denkinger was dead (he wasn't) and that his infamous missed call in the 1985 WS had led him to an early grave (it hadn't).

Donald Anton Denkinger umpired for 30 seasons in the American League, from 1969–1998. He worked in excess of 4,000 MLB games including six American League Championship Series, four World Series and three All-Star Games—a superb officiating career by any measure. Despite his glowing resume, Denkinger is most widely remembered for one glaring mistake—arguably the most ill-timed bad call in MLB history. Baseball fans who are old enough to remember it will never forget it.

The date was October 26, 1985. The site was Royals Stadium in Kansas City. It was Game Six of the 1985 World Series. The Fall Classic that year was an all-Missouri affair with the St. Louis Cardinals facing the Kansas City Royals. The Cardinals led the Series three games to two and held a tenuous 1–0 lead in what could be the deciding game. St. Louis had broken a 0–0 deadlock in the eighth inning when seldom-used backup catcher Brian Harper entered the game as a pinch-hitter. He delivered an RBI single off Charlie Leibrandt to score teammate Terry Pendleton. Danny Cox had shut out the Royals through seven innings. Harper had batted for Cox, so the starting pitcher's evening was done. Ken Dayley replaced Cox on the mound and shut out the Royals in the home half of the eighth inning. The Cardinals did not add to their lead in the top of the ninth inning. To win the 1985 World Series, all St. Louis had to do was maintain their one-run edge for another three outs. Cardinals closer Todd Worrell was summoned by manager Whitey Herzog to close the deal.

Royals manager Dick Howser made the next strategic move: Thirty-four-year-old Jorge Orta, a pinch-hitter, was sent up as the first batter in the bottom of the ninth. Orta hit a slow bounding ball. St. Louis first baseman Jack Clark moved to his right and fielded it in front of second baseman Tommy Herr. Worrell recognized the situation and knew he had to hustle to cover first base. Orta had decent foot speed, so it was going to be a close play. Clark fielded the ball and tossed it to Worrell, who was exactly where he was supposed to be. Most observers thought Orta was out. First-base umpire Don Denkinger did not. He emphatically called Orta safe.

Whitey Herzog and most of the Cardinals' infielders angrily surrounded Denkinger near first base. They had a justifiable beef; television replays confirmed that Orta was out by at least half a step. "Looks like he's out," noted ABC's Jim Palmer. "Oh, I don't think there's any doubt about it," replied Palmer's World Series broadcasting partner, Al Michaels. Jack Buck, the longtime voice of the St. Louis Cardinals, was calling the World Series for CBS Radio. He was incredulous. "He [Worrell] had the base and he had the ball, man! What else is there? That's the rule isn't it?" As had happened innumerable times in past baseball games at ballparks big and small, the call stood—erroneous as it was. Television replays could not be consulted. The Cardinals proceeded to self-destruct.

Steve Balboni was the next batter. Although a sacrifice bunt seemed like the best strategy given the circumstances, Balboni was a power hitter. He swung at Worrell's first offering and popped it up between first base and home plate near the Royals' dugout. There was a miscommunication between St. Louis catcher Darrell Porter and first base-man Clark. Clark, who had spent most of his career as an outfielder, looked lost on the play. The ball fell harmlessly to the stadium's green turf. Given a second life, Balboni slapped an 0–2 pitch into left field for a single. Orta advanced to second base. The sellout crowd was in a frenzy.

Onix Concepcion entered the game as a pinch-runner for the slow-footed Balboni. The next batter, Jim Sundberg, also tried to lay down a bunt—actually three bunts. The first one was fouled to the backstop. The second attempt rolled just foul along the first-base line. With the count 2–2, Sundberg bunted a low pitch that was fielded by Worrell in front of the mound. Worrell opted to get the lead runner and threw to third base to retire Orta on a force out. Another pinch-hitter, Hal McRae, came to bat. With the count 1–0, Porter was expecting Worrell to throw a fastball. Instead, it was an offspeed pitch—and it crossed him up. The ball deflected off Porter's mitt and rolled a few yards to his right. The passed ball moved the two Royals' runners into scoring position. McRae was intentionally walked to set up force plays at every base. Dick Howser sent John Wathan to first base to run for McRae. Remembering that some critics had said the first five games of the Fall Classic had lacked drama, Al Michaels sarcastically quipped, "This is some boring World Series, isn't it?"

Kansas City radio broadcaster Denny Mathews wished and prophesized at the same time. "Yes, there are more important things on this Earth than sports, I guess," he said, "but I daresay tonight, nothing can bring more joy to Kansas City than a little single into right field to get this thing to game seven. This improbable little team, doing improbable little things, now has pushed this thing to the brink."

The Royals' third pinch-hitter of the inning was Dane Iorg, who had batted just .223 in 1985. Iorg had been on the 1982 Cardinals team that had won the World Series. The Cardinals kept their defense at double-play depth. In a post-game TV interview with Reggie Jackson, Iorg said, "I'll tell you exactly what was going through my mind: How many kids dream of getting to hit in that situation? I've dreamed about that all my life."

On a 1–0 fastball, Iorg dramatically looped a single into right field. Concepcion scored easily. Right fielder Andy Van Slyke, an outfielder with a strong arm, fielded the ball on one hop and unloaded an accurate throw to home plate, but Sundberg's excellent head-first slide eluded Porter's tag for the game-winning run. (Porter was criticized by some observers for being too far in front of home plate to receive the throw and apply the tag.) Instead of the 1985 World Series being over, it was now headed for a seventh game. Although there had been numerous gaffes in the bottom of the ninth inning by the Cardinals, predictably umpire Denkinger became the center of attention in the sports world.

Cardinals manager Whitey Herzog was quick to pin the loss on Denkinger's mistake. In an obscenity-laced tirade, Herzog said the blown call on Orta had irretrievably shifted the momentum of the game. Realizing how the umpires rotated positions, Herzog ruefully declared, "Now we've got him behind the plate tomorrow." After a pause, the surly Herzog added, "Maybe we shouldn't even show up tomorrow. Maybe we won't."[1]

Others were quick to point out that St. Louis had benefitted from a bad call at second base in the fourth inning when Royals runner Frank White was wrongly called out on an attempted steal. Few Cards fans were buying it, though. The *St. Louis Post-Dispatch* began referring to Denkinger as "Jesse James." Two St. Louis radio deejays broadcast Denkinger's telephone number and home address in Iowa—and encouraged their listeners to harass his family. Jack Clark, who escaped being a goat because Denkinger was a more convenient scapegoat, said afterwards. "Those umpires were in over their heads. We got burned on a call that cost us the Series. It's understandable if we were moody."[2]

Curry Kirkpatrick of *Sports Illustrated* begged to differ. "It was as if no umpire in World Series history had ever missed one before. As if the men in blue had caused the Cardinals to score their pitiful [Series total of] 13 runs."

In Game Seven, the Cardinals seemed to still be focused on the ninth inning of Game Six. It was a rout. The Royals won, 11–0. It was their third straight victory in the Series after trailing three games to one. Herzog was ejected, as was hot-tempered pitcher Joaquin Andujar. During the exchange of lineup cards prior to Game Seven, Herzog told Denkinger, "Try to have a good game tonight." Andujar was in the game in relief of starter John Tudor, who had been yanked after allowing four walks and five earned runs in just 2⅔ innings. During the pitching change, Herzog bellowed at Denkinger, "We shouldn't even be out here tonight! You know you blew that call!" Shortly thereafter, Tudor, his season over, stupidly decided to take out his frustrations by punching an electric fan in the visitors' clubhouse—a fan that was running at the time. Tudor watched the remainder of the game on television while receiving treatment at a local hospital.

"Moody?" Kirkpatrick sarcastically continued in his *SI* sidebar piece, "Why, of course. No wonder the Cardinals couldn't pitch or hit or steal or act like anything more charming than a bunch of John McEnroes. No wonder Tudor missed his changeup and hung his fastball, and K.C.'s George Brett and Steve Balboni … kept smashing rockets and Andujar went bananas." St. Louis had batted just .185 in the seven games. Kirkpatrick concluded, "The tragicomedic truth about this grand old franchise [is] that it was disgraced."

Regardless of how culpable the Cardinals were for their own demise, the plain fact remained that Don Denkinger had blown a critical call—and MLB had no remedy to correct the situation. No major professional sports league did at the time. The United States Football League had a challenge system earlier in 1985. The National Football League would begin using replay as an officiating tool the following year, but MLB was slow to adopt anything like it. With the 1985 World Series constantly cited as a blatant example of why a review system was necessary for the integrity of the game, video replay would be in the forefront of MLB rules changes for the next 30 years.

In 2010, when Jim Joyce became the updated version of Don Denkinger after his bad call cost Armando Galarraga a perfect game, Denkinger was suddenly in the news again at age 73, sought out for his opinion on Joyce's egregious goof. "I missed a call in the ninth inning," he stated from his home in Waterloo, IA. "There were plenty of opportunities to change the outcome of that game." Recalling the scary harassment his family members received in the subsequent days, Denkinger sadly remembered, "My mother-in-law was a basket case. People were calling and saying they were going to burn the house down."[3]

Fifteen years after the dramatic and traumatic 1985 World Series, the Cardinals organized a team reunion. Don Denkinger was invited to attend. He accepted the offer, to the surprise of many. He was roundly booed by the fans in attendance when he was announced as a special guest. Whitey Herzog presented him with a Braille wristwatch as a gag gift. Denkinger accepted the expected barbs with good humor and eventually won the crowd over with a funny speech.

Denkinger knows he will always be linked with one play for the rest of his life. "I retired in 1998 and people still always associate me with a mistake," Denkinger said in 2010, as part of his comments on Jim Joyce's troubles. "Jim has to know this is just another phase of what you signed up to do: officiate to the best of your ability. I'd tell him, 'That's what you were doing. Don't let it get you down. You just have to march on.'"[4]

St. Louis 1 at Kansas City 2

Game played on Saturday, October 26, 1985, at Royals Stadium

St. Louis Cardinals	ab	r	h	rbi	Kansas City Royals	ab	r	h	rbi
Smith ss	3	0	0	0	Smith lf	4	0	1	0
McGee cf	4	0	0	0	Wilson cf	3	0	1	0
Herr 2b	4	0	0	0	Brett 3b	4	0	0	0
Clark 1b	4	0	0	0	White 2b	4	0	1	0
Landrum lf	4	0	1	0	Sheridan rf	3	0	1	0
Pendleton 3b	4	1	1	0	Motley ph	0	0	0	0
Cedeno rf	2	0	1	0	Orta ph	1	0	1	0
Van Slyke pr, rf	0	0	0	0	Balboni 1b	3	0	2	0
Porter c	3	0	1	0	Concepcion pr	0	1	0	0
Cox p	2	0	0	0	Sundberg c	4	1	1	0
Harper ph	1	0	1	1	Biancalana ss	3	0	1	0
Lawless pr	0	0	0	0	McRae ph	0	0	0	0
Dayley p	0	0	0	0	Wathan pr	0	0	0	0
Worrell p	0	0	0	0	Leibrandt p	2	0	0	0
					Quisenberry p	0	0	0	0
					Iorg ph	1	0	1	2
Totals	31	1	5	1	Totals	32	2	10	2

| St. Louis | 000 000 010—1 5 0 |
| Kansas City | 000 000 002—2 10 0 |

St. Louis Cardinals	IP	H	R	ER	BB	SO
Cox	7.0	7	0	0	1	8
Dayley	1.0	0	0	0	1	2
Worrell L (0–1)	0.1	3	2	2	1	0
Totals 8.1		10	2	2	3	10
Kansas City Royals	IP	H	R	ER	BB	SO
Leibrandt	7.2	4	1	1	2	4
Quisenberry W (1–0)	1.1	1	0	0	0	1
Totals	9.0	5	1	1	2	5

E–None. DP–St. Louis 1, Kansas City 1. PB–Porter (1). 2B–Kansas City Smith (2, off Cox). SH–Leibrandt (2, off Cox). IBB–McRae (1, by Worrell). CS–White (1, 2nd base by Cox/Porter). IBB–Worrell (1, McRae). U–Jim Quick (NL), Don Denkinger (AL), Bill Williams (NL), Jim McKean (AL), John Shulock (AL), Bob Engel (NL). T–2:47. A–41,628.

October 3, 1995

Site: Yankee Stadium I, New York

Teams: Seattle Mariners vs. New York Yankees

Significance: First Post-Season Game Featuring a Wild Card Team

Impact: For the first time in modern MLB history, a team that did not finish first in the regular season played in a post-season game

"The more the playoffs expand, the greater the likelihood that the best team in baseball will not win the World Series. Nowadays, fully one-third of the teams in baseball go to the playoffs, compared to one-eighth in the pre-division era [prior to 1961], and one-seventh as recently as 1992."—Alex Remington of fangraphs.com

"I made my arguments and went down in flames. History will prove me right."—George W. Bush, then the owner of the Texas Rangers, after voting against realignment and a new wild-card system during a Major League Baseball owners meeting in September 1993 (The future president was the lone dissenter in a 27–1 vote.)

"Regular-season greatness is out of fashion these days, with the expanded postseason lowering the bar for entry and division titles reduced to what they are in the NBA, NFL, and NHL: little more than a means to a better playoff seeding. The new model for MLB teams? Be just good enough to squeak into the postseason, then see what happens in October."—Joe Sheehan in the February 2, 2015, issue of *Sports Illustrated*

"Time will tell. We believe in our research and that the positives far outweigh the negatives."—Bud Selig, president of the Milwaukee Brewers and acting commissioner, after owners approved the new system

For more than a century, MLB ensured that the only teams that qualified for its post-season were of championship mettle. Why have extra tiers of playoffs? They were not needed. Baseball's long regular season decisively whittled away the also-rans from the true kingpins. While other top professional sports leagues—particularly the NBA and NHL—watered down their regular seasons by allowing second-rate and even sub-.500 clubs to qualify for their playoffs, in MLB excellence remained the sole virtue. Every year from 1876 through 1968, a team had to be the champion of its entire league (based on the regular season) to gain a coveted post-season berth.

Well, almost. Beginning in 1894, the bloated 12-team National League held an annual postseason series featuring its top two teams squaring off in a best-of-seven format. They vied for a 30-inch-tall, silver trophy called the Temple Cup—named after William Chase Temple, the owner of the Pittsburgh Pirates who generously donated it. In 2010 baseball scholar Mike Rogers wrote of the whole Temple Cup concept, "the format just pitted the second-place team against the best team from the regular season. To say that is an absurd notion would be putting it mildly. After playing 130-plus games in a season, asserting your dominance of the league—and you then must play a team for the league championship that you already beat? It just doesn't jibe with me."[1] The team that finished first at the end of the NL's regular season was still considered the true NL champion regardless of which side won the Cup. Not too surprisingly, fans generally thought the playoff series was a pointless exercise. Players were largely unenthusiastic too. The last time the Temple Cup series was contested was 1897. By that time public interest in the event had waned considerably. The famous old Baltimore Orioles of John McGraw, Hughie Jennings and Willie Keeler played in every Temple Cup series and won the bauble twice; curiously the second-place team won three of the four series. After 1897, the gaudy, silver cup was reclaimed by the Temple family and vanished from public view until 1939, when *The Sporting News* located it in Florida in the possession of one of William Temple's descendants. It was acquired by the National Baseball Hall of Fame for $750. The old trophy still sits in a display case in Cooperstown, its historic significance understood only by the truly serious scholars of 19th-century baseball.

After 1897, MLB discontinued any sort of playoff system, unless a tie-breaker was needed to determine a league's pennant winner if two teams happened to finish in a first-place deadlock. From 1969 through 1993, thanks to expansion and realignment, the task to qualify for MLB's post-season was made marginally easier: a team just had to win its division within its league. Second place was still not good enough in MLB.

In September 1993, MLB, with more expansion in its future, believed that realignment and more teams in the post-season was the way to go. In a milestone decision, MLB's two-divisions-per-league format that had been in existence since 1969 was changed to three divisions. Instead of rewarding the best divisional champion with a bye, MLB became creative: A wild card team—the second place team with the best record—would qualify for the post-season along with the three divisional champions per league. It was uncharted territory for MLB—and traditionalists universally hated the idea. Writing in *Time* magazine, columnist Walter Shapiro declared, "Perhaps this latest wild-card wackiness will prove to be little more than an unfortunate rain delay, but don't wait till next year; this may be our last and best September."[2] (Atlanta and San Francisco did engage in one final, epic, winner-take-all battle for the NL West in 1993. The Giants won 103 games—one shy of the Braves' total of 104.) Years later Billy Beane, the *Moneyball* guru, explained, "The playoffs are a great thing for our sport—I want to make that clear," Beane said in an interview. "But let's call it what it is: we allow small sample sizes and random events to determine the champion. That's how it is in baseball."[3] Others firmly believed that the inclusion of more team's into MLB's post-season excitement could only be beneficial to everyone. It certainly would add more revenue to MLB's coffers, so nearly 12 decades of tradition were cavalierly discarded.

For most teams, the 1994 MLB season was slightly more than two-thirds complete when calamity struck: The season was shut down on August 12 due to a labor dispute. With no quick solution on the horizon, the entire post-season was cancelled, including the controversial debut of the two wild card teams. Some traditionalists, who continued to voice their objections to expanded post-season play, likened the work stoppage in 1994 to an act of God. Be that as it may, for the first time since 1904 the World Series was not played. Fans everywhere were understandably furious. Many vowed never to return to the game they had grown up loving. James Lincoln Ray, who wrote Don Mattingly's SABR biography, opined,

> It was the first time that a World Series had been cancelled in 90 years, and the fallout was mostly disgust. There was a feeling among many fans, who were paying a good deal of money to enable players and owners to make millions, that the players were no longer worth it. Overall, neither the owners, who were handing out money like candy, nor the players, whose average salary was almost $2 million per year, were getting much sympathy.[4]

The dispute between the players' union and the owners was so acrimonious that no deal was in place for the 1995 season. By the time the season did get underway on April 25, each team had lost 18 games from its schedule. Many fans were not in the forgiving mood. Demonstrations against the perceived greed of both players and owners were common at Opening Days across MLB. Some home teams were loudly booed when they took the field for the first time in 1995. Baseball's moguls hoped expanded post-season play would placate the masses.

In that first MLB season where second-best was now okay, the New York Yankees finished seven games behind the Boston Red Sox in the AL East, but still "won" the AL wild card race (much in the same way someone "wins" a silver medal in an Olympics). The Colorado Rockies—a team that had only been in existence since 1993—did the same in the NL despite finishing a game behind the NL West champion Los Angeles Dodgers. The only caveat to the new system was that the wild card team in each league could not face the first-place team from its own division in the opening round of the post-season (which MLB called the Division Series).

The eight-team, post-season tournament began with four night games on Tuesday, October 3, although it seemed as if MLB were trying to hide its new post-season wrinkle from as many fans as possible. Apparently baseball's honchos had not yet figured out the obvious benefits of spreading the Division Series games over the course of an entire day to a national audience to maximize viewership. Thus frustrated fans could watch only regional coverage of the ALDS and NLDS. *Sports Illustrated* wryly noted in its October 16 issue, "Riveting first-round games recall the sport's golden era. You had to read about it in the newspapers back then too." The periodical bluntly called The Baseball Network's coverage "idiotic" and "an embarrassment" and jokingly labeled the sport as "America's regional pastime." The four series were best-of-five contests that opened in the home ball parks of the lower-seeded teams. The higher-seeded clubs got the benefit of playing the final three games at home. Thus, by virtue of geography and time zones, the first wild card team to play was the New York Yankees, who hosted the Seattle Mariners. The Mariners, a 1977 AL expansion team, were in their 19th season of operation, but 1995 was their first championship campaign. They had never even had a winning season until 1991. The Colorado Rockies hosted the Atlanta Braves a few hours later.

The first post-season game in the history of the Seattle Mariners' franchise was a seesaw affair that saw numerous momentum swings even though the Yankees never trailed. Wade Boggs gave the home side a 2–0 lead with a rare home run in the third inning. The Mariners scored once in the fourth inning and again in the sixth inning to level matters temporarily. A two-run outburst put the Yankees ahead 4–2 in the bottom of the sixth. Ken Griffey, Jr., smashed his second home run in the seventh inning off Yankees starter David Cone as Seattle fought back to tie the game 4–4, but a Ruben Sierra home run was instrumental in New York's four-run reply in the bottom of the seventh. The Yankees eventually won, 9–6, surviving a rocky ninth inning in which Seattle got three hits and two runs off reliever John Wetteland. Rookie pitcher Mariano Rivera, who went 5–3 in 1995 mostly as a starter, remained on New York's bench. At the other end of the spectrum, 34-year-old Yankees first baseman Don Mattingly, in the last season of a terrific career, got a double, a single, and an RBI for the victors. He claimed that just taking the field on October 3, 1995—after being in the majors since 1982 without playing a single post-season game—was the highlight of his baseball career.

The debut of the Division Series had turned out to be excellent. All four series had their moments. Even the one-sided Cleveland-Boston ALDS had a compelling first game that Cleveland won in 13 innings on a walk-off home run by Tony Pena. A remarkable total of 50 home runs and four extra-inning contests scattered among the 15 games in the four series kept baseball fans riveted to their TV sets—if they could actually see the games they desired. Despite the deserved criticism of the inadequate television coverage, MLB had gotten what it wanted from its divisional realignment and the wild card teams— a renewed interest in post-season baseball. Fans who had hoped that wild card teams would go the way of the Temple Cup were not going to get their collective wish. There was no going back now to the simple times of "no prize for second place."

Seattle Mariners 6 at New York Yankees 9

Game played on Tuesday, October 3, 1995, at Yankee Stadium

Seattle Mariners	ab	r	h	rbi	New York Yankees	ab	r	h	rbi
Coleman lf	4	1	0	0	Boggs 3b	5	2	3	2
Cora 2b	4	1	0	0	Kelly pr,2b	0	1	0	0
Griffey, Jr., cf	5	3	3	3	Williams B. cf	5	2	3	2
Martinez E. dh	4	1	3	1	O'Neill rf	3	0	1	1
Martinez T. 1b	3	0	1	1	Sierra dh	5	1	1	2
Buhner rf	5	0	1	0	Mattingly 1b	4	1	2	1
Blowers 3b	4	0	0	0	James lf	3	0	1	0
Wilson c	3	0	0	1	Williams G. pr, lf	1	0	0	0
Sojo ss	4	0	1	0	Stanley c	4	0	1	1
Bosio p	0	0	0	0	Fernandez ss	3	0	0	0
Nelson p	0	0	0	0	Velarde 2b,3b	3	2	1	0
Ayala p	0	0	0	0	Cone p	0	0	0	0
Risley p	0	0	0	0	Wetteland p	0	0	0	0
Wells p	0	0	0	0					
Totals	36	6	9	6	Totals	36	9	13	9

Seattle	000 101 202—6	9 0
New York	002 002 41x—9	13 0

Seattle Mariners	IP	H	R	ER	BB	SO
Bosio	5.2	6	4	4	1	1
Nelson L (0–1)	0.1	1	1	1	0	0
Ayala	0.1	4	3	3	0	0
Risley	0.2	0	0	0	0	1
Wells	1.0	2	1	1	1	0
Totals	8.0	13	9	9	2	2

New York Yankees	IP	H	R	ER	BB	SO
Cone W (1–0)	8.0	6	4	4	6	5

New York Yankees	IP	H	R	ER	BB	SO
Wetteland	1.0	3	2	2	1	1
Totals	9.0	9	6	6	7	6

E–None. 2B–New York B Williams (1, off Ayala); Mattingly (1, off Ayala); Boggs (1, off Wells). HR–Seattle Griffey 2 (2, 4th inning off Cone 0 on, 0 out, 7th inning off Cone 1 on, 1 out), New York Boggs (1, 3rd inning off Bosio 1 on, 1 out); Sierra (1, 7th inning off Ayala 1 on, 1 out). SF–O'Neill (1, off Ayala). HBP–Velarde (1, by Nelson). HBP–Nelson (1, Velarde). U–Mike Reilly, Dale Scott, Jim McKean, Larry McCoy, Jim Joyce, Rich Garcia. T–3:38. A–57,178.

June 12, 1997

Site: The Ballpark in Arlington, Texas

Teams: San Francisco Giants vs. Texas Rangers

Significance: First Interleague Game

Impact: Interleague play ends the distinct separation of the AL and NL and profoundly affects balanced scheduling

> "Baseball is fast running out of traditions to bust up—like old furniture in a blizzard—and use to spark the fans' imagination. The people who play and own the game are learning the hard way they never should have put the fire out in the first place."—Jim Litke, *Associated Press*

> "In 1997, interleague baseball began. As we all know, interleague play sent baseball, and American culture, into an irreversible state of decline."—BaseballNation.com

In 1903 the rival National and American Leagues—two separate entities that had been warring since the AL declared itself a big-league outfit in 1901 and began raiding NL teams' rosters—made a noteworthy peace truce. In effect they agreed they were equal but distinct. They would play separate schedules and respect each other's player contracts. After the 1905 season they agreed to pit their champions against each other in an annual World Series. Beginning in 1933 the brightest stars of both circuits would square off in an annual All-Star Game. Other than that, the leagues kept a respectful distance from one another. They had separate umpiring crews, individual league presidents, and a handful of different playing rules that ranged the gamut from curfews to balks. The designated-hitter rule, which the AL adopted in 1973 and the NL still rejects, is the most prominent difference. Apart from meaningless spring training games, the idea of the two leagues playing any kind of intertwined schedule was seldom considered.

That is not to say the idea was not occasionally proffered. Veteran New York newspaper scribe Joe Vila seriously suggested it as early as 1920 as a substitute for the World Series. Vila's plan was dismissed without any official consideration. In the 1930s regular-season interleague play was discussed at owners' meetings but did not have anything close to enough support for it to happen. In 1933, Bill Veeck, Sr., of the Chicago Cubs wanted interleague play adopted as a novelty to combat the attendance woes of the Great Depression. When Veeck died that same year, the concept died with him—at least for a while.

Following the 1956 season, MLB owners considered a proposal by Cleveland general manager and minority-owner Hank Greenberg to implement limited interleague play beginning in 1958. Under Greenberg's proposal, each team would continue to play a 154-

game regular season, but have only 126 games within that team's league. The remaining 28 would be played against teams from the other circuit. Greenberg's plan presented an obvious mathematical problem: How would the 28 games be split among the eight clubs in the other league? It could not be done evenly and it would destroy the balanced schedule that MLB was proudly founded on in 1876. This issue was not fully addressed. According to Greenberg's plan, the interleague games would be played immediately following the All-Star Game. Greenberg's idea came to naught in his lifetime when the AL refused to consider it. Still, Bill Veeck, Jr., a man who never hesitated to think outside the box, accurately predicted in 1963 that MLB would have interleague play someday. He had resurrected his father's idea as early as 1953, when he owned the St. Louis Browns, but it met with no support whatsoever by the other 15 MLB owners.

As early as 1960 MLB planned to add two more teams—one in each league—which would have made interleague play absolutely necessary between what would have been two nine-team leagues. Instead the AL brought in two expansion teams in 1961 and the NL brought in another two the following year. Interleague play was off the table once again.

In 1973, the AL was apparently big on radical change. It endorsed interleague play at the same time it adopted the designated hitter. At the midsummer meetings, however, the NL voted no to the proposal. Commissioner Bowie Kuhn refused to cast a tie-breaking vote. Instead he appointed a committee to study the issue. The committee returned with various proposals, none of which were implemented.

After half-hearted discussions about the concept occurred infrequently during the 1970s, Bill Veeck, Jr.'s "someday" came to fruition in the mid–1990s as part of the fallout of the disastrous 1994 players' strike. In an attempt to win back disillusioned fans and rejuvenate its product, MLB instituted major changes. Along with an expanded postseason, interleague play would become a reality. On January 18, 1996, MLB's owners unanimously adopted interleague play, to begin in 1997. Its debut would come midway through that season. It would feature five three-game "rivalry" series between MLB's Eastern Division teams and Central Division teams in each league. In the leagues' Western Divisions, it would feature four two-game series. The designated hitter would be used in interleague games played at AL parks.

Such a drastic change to baseball tradition caused a great deal of passionate debate. Traditionalists argued that interleague play would certainly cause the annual MLB All-Star Game to lose whatever mystique it had. On a lesser level, they argued that the World Series would suffer the same fate. Intangibles and appeals to tradition aside, there were practical concerns too. AL pitchers were not used to batting or running the bases and NL teams did not have a roster space reserved for designated hitters. Of course, there was also the obvious problem of teams no longer playing anything close to a balanced schedule. Furthermore, meaningful and dramatic intra-divisional games were cut to make room for interleague games. Pennant races almost certainly would be decided because of the strength or weaknesses of individual teams' interleague opponents.

How would MLB's cherished records, so beloved by historians and stats geeks, be affected by these foreign interleague games? Record books divide MLB feats into separate AL and NL records. What happens if someone hits five triples in a Toronto-Atlanta game, for instance? Would there now be a third category of record-setting games? MLB had a ready answer prepared before June 12, 1997:

> For the first time in the history of Major League Baseball, Interleague games are to be played during the regular season. Breaking tradition always brings about controversy and the matter of baseball records is no exception.
>
> It is the opinion of Major League Baseball that there is no justification for compiling a new volume of records based on Interleague Play. On the contrary, the sovereignty of each league's records will be retained, and if a player or a team breaks a record against an Interleague opponent it will be considered a record in that league. In cases where two teams—as Interleague opponents—break a league or Major League record, that record will be annotated with the phrase "Interleague game." Streaks by both teams and individual will continue (or be halted) when playing Interleague opponents in the same manner as if playing against an intraleague opponent. In essence, records will be defined by who made them rather than against whom they were made.
>
> The official statistics of both leagues will be kept separately as they have in the past. This means statistics for each team and their individual players will reflect their performance in games within the league and also in Interleague games without differentiation.

Proponents of interleague play argued that it gave fans the chance to see players and teams it would otherwise miss. It was noted that baseball fans and writers in Detroit, for example, never had the chance to see Hall of Famers Ernie Banks, Stan Musial or Roberto Clemente play even a single game because of the two leagues' separation. Similarly, the Boston Red Sox had never played at Wrigley Field and had not played the Giants or Dodgers since they had met in the 1912 and 1916 World Series respectively. As for the World Series somehow being devalued because of interleague play, advocates noted that the two teams in the NBA finals always meet twice per year in the regular season. At the end of the six-team NHL era, the two Stanley Cup finalists were guaranteed to have already met 14 times during the regular season.

Calling interleague play "a commonsense idea whose time had come," *Sports Illustrated*'s Gerry Callahan, in his coverage of MLB's first weekend of such games, sarcastically mocked baseball fans who preferred tradition over gimmickry.

> This was only the beginning. You just wait. By next season major league teams will be handing out souvenir nose rings to the first 10,000 youngsters through the turnstiles. Marilyn Manson will be singing the national anthem before the All-Star Game and Billy the Marlin and the Phillie Phanatic will be cavorting together on top of the dugout.
>
> In the never-ending quest to make the game more stimulating, the baselines will be shortened to 85 feet, the strike zone will be shrunk to the size of Cecil Fielder's navel, and Ken Griffey Jr. will be allowed to bat twice an inning.
>
> Clearly, the radicals who are running baseball will not stop until the balls are painted red, white and blue and the bats are made of titanium. Look at what has happened in the last quarter century: First they foisted the designated hitter upon us, then they expanded the playoffs, and now they've introduced interleague play, the latest violation of the purity and sanctity of the game. It's an outrage.[1]

To back his assertion that there was nothing fundamentally wrong with interleague play, Callahan quoted the results from a Harris poll that found that a mere 20 percent of baseball fans disapproved of the concept. "[That] would be startlingly little opposition on any issue. Indeed, in this country you could probably get more than one out of five people to disapprove of the polio vaccine or child-labor laws."[2] Others weren't so smitten. Esteemed baseball writer Roger Angell derided the whole notion as "a gimmick"[3]—but it did not stop him from attending an interleague Red Sox-Mets game at Shea Stadium.

The actual first moment of interleague MLB play occurred at 7:11 p.m. local time in Arlington, TX. At that turning point in history, Texas Rangers pitcher Darren Oliver threw a low, inside fastball to San Francisco's Darryl Hamilton. "A strange thing happened," wrote Callahan. "The Ballpark in Arlington didn't collapse. Baseball as we know it didn't die. Babe Ruth didn't roll over in his grave."[4] More than 46,000 fans turned out for the game, which proved to be an entertaining 4–3 win for the visiting Giants. A three-run top of the seventh inning proved to be the difference in the game. Glenallen Hill earned a spot in the trivia books by being the first designated hitter for an NL team in a regular-season game. He batted seventh and went 0-for-3. Giants catcher Marcus Jensen probably did not like his first taste of interleague play. He struck out three times. On the other hand, San Francisco right fielder Stan Javier enjoyed his experience, having gone 3-for-4 with two RBI.

The strong attendance for the first interleague game was replicated everywhere as the novelty of seeing unfamiliar teams was definitely an enticement to buy tickets. The New York Yankees' first trip to Miami was especially celebrated by Florida Marlins fans. The aforementioned Red Sox–Mets series gave the home team a chance to relive and re-celebrate the 1986 World Series. When the Atlanta Braves hosted the Baltimore Orioles, youthful Braves third baseman Chipper Jones asked for and received autographs on two Orioles jerseys from his opposing hot-corner counterpart, Cal Ripken, Jr.

Even as staunch an advocate as Callahan wondered whether the intrigue provided by interleague play would have lasting popularity or would it be "this year's Macarena." Purists wrote in to *SI* to voice their counterpoints to what seemed to be the majority opinion. One New Jersey reader declared, "The thrill of interleague play will go the way of the exercise bicycle in the attic—great in the beginning but forgotten after a few weeks when the novelty wears off."[5] Others were angry, unabashed traditionalists, such as a reader from Virginia who sincerely asked, "Why can't baseball remain pristine? The owners, salivating over making a few extra bucks, can always think up gimmicks, but the game is the thing. No, volcanoes didn't erupt when the first interleague pitch was thrown, but the game was dumbed down just a little further. How sad."[6]

With interleague play blurring the lines between the two leagues, by 1999 two high-profile MLB jobs were deemed to be redundant and were eliminated: the offices of the AL president (last held by Gene Budig) and the NL president (Leonard S. Coleman Jr.). Similarly, beginning with the 2000 season, umpires no longer belonged to one of the two leagues—they were simply MLB umps. Nobody seemed to take issue with that residual effect of interleague play.

Starting in 2013, the MLB schedule was changed to mimic what the National Football had been doing since the NFL-AFL merger. Teams in one division would play the teams from a division in the other league that were not necessarily geographically close. Thus the AL East teams might play the NL Central clubs. "Rivalry matchups," however, continued between teams close in proximity. For example, the New York Yankees played the New York Mets every year—a point of contention to other AL East teams because the Yankees, overall, have been considerably better than the Mets since 1997. Through 2014, the Yankees have won more than 60 percent of their interleague games—the only MLB team to do so. The Yankees-Mets situation was not the only one that had fans questioning the schedule's apparent unfairness. From 1997 through 2012, the interleague schedule was often determined by "marquee matchups" for television and potential revenue—not by any sense of balance or equity. In a 2012 article, Jayson Stark of ESPN.com wrote of that season's upcoming interleague play,

In the NL East, the Braves have to play the Yankees six times. But how many times will the Marlins and Phillies play the Yankees? Zero, of course.

In the AL Central, the Tigers will play half of their 18 interleague games against the Pirates and Rockies. Want to guess how many games the White Sox will play against the Pirates and Rockies? Right you are. That would be none.

And in the NL Central, the Reds will play nine of their 15 interleague games against the two best teams in the AL Central—the Indians and Tigers. But the Brewers, naturally, won't play any games against those two teams.

For a decade and a half now, players, managers and general managers have been grumbling about bizarre, illogical interleague schedule glitches like these. And for a decade and a half, those complaints just sailed on out into space like a lost satellite.[7]

It took the divisional realignment of 2013—in which the Houston Astros became an AL team after 51 years in the NL—to make each league a 15-team circuit. The odd number per league meant that interleague games would have to occur throughout the year. (Furthermore, it makes it impossible to discontinue interleague play without more expansion, contraction, or again shifting one team to another league.) The NFL system of divisional scheduling proved to be fairer than what had occurred in the first 15 years of interleague play—but it was still not quite perfect.

On August 12, 2014—exactly 20 years to the day after the work stoppage of 1994 occurred—ESPN's Keith Olbermann offered this thoughtful editorial on his nightly sports program in which he tried to account for MLB's steadily declining television ratings and interest among young demographic groups:

After the [1994] strike, you know what [MLB] did to try to make up for the shooting of itself in the foot, and the leg, and two thighs, and the abdomen? It implemented—after literally 40 years of talking about it—interleague play. This was a cash bonanza, creating instantly profitable mid-season marquee matchups. And all it did was require that baseball destroy the reason its fans watched games even when their teams were not playing in them. It destroyed the concept of the two leagues.

In the old days—like 20 years ago yesterday—if you were a fan of the Boston Red Sox you virtually never saw the National League teams in person, so if they were on the Game of the Week you might watch them there. At All-Star Game time you had to watch the charming spectacle of guys from your league performing against the stars of its exotic rival.

Does any of this sound familiar to you? No? Of course not! Baseball killed all that off. It was called the reason to watch a game even if your team wasn't playing in it.

Whether you love interleague play, hate it, or are thoroughly ambivalent about its existence, it is a virtual certainty to remain in place for the foreseeable future. Fairness in scheduling will make the concept a little bit more palatable for traditionalists—but only a little bit.

San Francisco 4 at Texas 3

Game played on Thursday, June 12, 1997, at The Ballpark in Arlington

San Francisco Giants	ab	r	h	rbi	Texas Rangers	ab	r	h	rbi
Hamilton cf	4	0	1	0	Newson rf	5	0	0	0
Vizcaino ss	4	1	1	0	Rodriguez c	4	0	0	0
Kent 2b	4	1	1	0	Greer lf	4	0	3	0
Bonds lf	3	1	1	0	Gonzalez dh	4	0	1	0
Lewis 3b	4	0	1	1	Clark 1b	3	1	1	0
Mueller 3b	0	0	0	0	Palmer 3b	4	0	0	0
Hill dh	3	0	0	1	McLemore 2b	4	1	1	1
Javier rf	4	1	3	2	Buford cf	3	1	0	0
Snow 1b	3	0	1	0	Cedeno ph	1	0	0	0
Jensen c	4	0	0	0	Ripken ss	3	0	2	2
Gardner p	0	0	0	0	Stevens ph	1	0	0	0
Beck p	0	0	0	0	Oliver p	0	0	0	0
					Hernandez p	0	0	0	0
Totals	33	4	9	4	Totals	36	3	8	3

San Francisco   001 000 300—4 9 1
Texas   010 002 000—3 8 0

San Francisco Giants	IP	H	R	ER	BB	SO
Gardner W (7–2)	8.0	8	3	2	1	4
Beck SV (20)	1.0	0	0	0	0	0
Totals	9.0	8	3	2	1	4
Texas Rangers	IP	H	R	ER	BB	SO
Oliver L (3–8)	7.2	8	4	4	1	2
Hernandez	1.1	1	0	0	0	1
Totals	9.0	9	4	4	1	3

E–Kent (6). DP–Texas 1. 2B–San Francisco Javier (7, off Oliver); Bonds (5, off Oliver), Texas Greer (18, off Gardner). 3B–Texas McLemore (1, off Gardner). HR–San Francisco Javier (1, 3rd inning off Oliver 0 on, 0 out). SF–Hill (6, off Oliver). HBP–Bonds (4, by Oliver). IBB–Snow (5, by Oliver); W Clark (6, by Gardner). CS–Snow (1, 2nd base by Oliver/Rodriguez). SB–Buford (13, 2nd base off Gardner/Jensen); Greer (4, 2nd base off Gardner/Jensen). HBP–Oliver (4, Bonds). IBB–Gardner (3, W Clark); Oliver (2, Snow). U–HP–Jim McKean, 1B–Ted Hendry, 2B–Jim Joyce, 3B–Ed Hickox. T–2:23. A–46,507.

September 8, 1998

Site: Busch Stadium II

Teams: Chicago Cubs vs. St. Louis Cardinals

Significance: Mark McGwire's 62nd Home Run

Impact: One of MLB's touchstone records is decisively broken; PEDs first become a topic of conversation in baseball

> "I'm not here to talk about the past."—Mark McGwire, at the Congressional hearing investigating PED usage in MLB, March 17, 2005

> "The difference in Mark's game wasn't just the muscle mass he gained from steroids, it was the discipline, the strength, and the endurance he gained from the program. By 1996, Mark already had the body, the mindset, and the plan to make it all work. I'm convinced that his further use in '98 wasn't about getting big—it was about remaining well."—Jay McGwire, Mark's younger brother and steroid-using competitive bodybuilder, from his tell-all 2010 book titled *Me and Mark*

> "The reason it's still a dagger in the heart is because we fell in love. We wanted it to be romantic and pure and innocent and fun, but it wasn't."—Todd McFarlane, the owner of ten Mark McGwire home run balls from the 1998 season

> "Do I feel cheated?… All the non-users feel cheated. I think in a silent way, a lot of people who hadn't cheated over the years are happy with the way the media exposed the problem, and they're happy we're making progress toward evening the playing field."—Jeff Kent, quoted in the *San Francisco Chronicle*, March 3, 2005

We should have known better. All baseball fans everywhere—whether they were Cardinals fans, Cubs fans, Padres fans, Expos fans, whatever—should have known better. In the excitement and downright giddiness of the compelling, eye-popping Mark McGwire-Sammy Sosa home run derby of 1998, there were definite signs that something was not kosher.

Let's consider just the numbers involved and view them through the entirety of baseball's long, well chronicled, statistical history. MLB had been played since 1876. The 154-game schedule became the norm in the first decade of the 20th century and lasted until the early 1960s. In all those years, only one man—George Herman Ruth—was able to connect for 60 home runs in a single season. For more than a generation it was considered an untouchable record. In the nearly four decades since the expanded 162-game schedule became the norm, only one other man—Roger Maris—was able to match and overtake the Babe's feat. By 1998 more than 16,000 ballplayers had put on MLB uniforms and blasted baseballs beyond the deepest reaches of ballparks for more than a century, and only two had ever attained 60-home run seasons. Yet, in 1998, here were two men doing it in the same season. Sure, two new expansion teams that year had diluted the overall quality of MLB pitching, but the odds against it happening were astronomical. It was something akin to a man winning an enormous lottery jackpot and his next-door neighbor duplicating the feat on the very next drawing.

Then there was the long period of no one even coming close to threatening Ruth's or Maris' marks. During the 1980s, power numbers declined throughout MLB. In that decade, there were only 13 instances of players hitting 40 or more home runs in a season. Nobody had reached the 50-homer plateau in 12 years, not since George Foster whacked 52 in his 1977 MVP season for the Cincinnati Reds. Foster's feat was the first 50-home-run campaign since Willie Mays hit 52 in 1965. The Eighties were the first decade since the 1910s that no player had achieved a 50-home run campaign. A 50-home-run season was not attained until 1990 when Cecil Fielder accomplished it. Coming close, though, were Andre Dawson and an exciting newcomer named Mark McGwire. They both had 49 in 1987 to tie for the MLB lead that season. In 1998 alone, in stark contrast to the punchless 1980s, 13 players hit at least 40 home runs.

Then there were the startling physical traits. MLB players in 1998 were definitely a buffed bunch, looking far different from their counterparts of just a couple of decades before. Ballplayers of the 1970s looked not too much different from the average males one encountered in everyday life. None was on a weight-training program or even considered exercising in the manner of an Olympic athlete. (In *The Machine*, Joe Posnanski's excellent book about the fabulous 1975 Cincinnati Reds, the author tells the amusing story of a Nautilus machine being introduced to the Reds' clubhouse that season. The perplexed players did not know what it was or what to do with it. For the entire season it served not as a piece of exercise equipment but only as a handy receptacle from which the Reds cavalierly hung their sweaty jock straps!) Ballplayers of the 1990s started to resembled football linemen. Baseball writers thought they knew why home runs were on the rise in 1998—the balls were livelier! At least that was a widely held theory, and it was largely accepted as fact. In reality, few fans cared why more home runs were being hit—they just wanted to see more of them. MLB put on a collective happy face as baseball experienced one of its periodic surges in attendance and popularity.

Mark McGwire, who had played on the American Olympic baseball team in 1984, got a tiny taste of MLB action in 1986 with the Oakland Athletics. He played in just 18 games and batted an anemic .189 in 53 at-bats—but three of his ten hits were home runs. McGwire earned a spot on the A's roster during spring training in 1987, but he was not even the starting first baseman on Opening Day. Two veterans and another rookie were making it difficult to find a spot to insert the 23-year-old McGwire. Clearly McGwire, a right-handed power hitter, had undeniable talent, but Rob Nelson—who was seven months younger than McGwire and considered the better prospect—began the season as the team's regular first baseman. Carney Lansford was established at third base, so there was no room for McGwire at the hot corner, either. Veteran slugger Reggie Jackson, at age 41, winding up his career in Oakland for old-times' sake, was the A's designated hitter, so McGwire was originally used only as bench help. He got into a few games at first base, third base, DH, and even right field, but he was batting just .136 early on. Still, he did hit his first home run of the season off Donnie Moore on April 10.

Although McGwire was struggling, Rob Nelson had a monumentally rough start to the 1987 season too, striking out 12 times in his first 24 at-bats, so he was demoted to Oakland's AAA farm team in Tacoma. (He would never play another game for Oakland. In mid-season Nelson was dealt to San Diego. By 1990 Nelson's MLB career was over after just 76 games.) Thus, McGwire, by default, became Oakland's first baseman. It was a fortuitous happenstance. In an explosion of pure power, McGwire rocked 14 home runs in the team's next 22 games, including five in a single series versus Detroit. By the end of May, McGwire had recorded 19 home runs. At the All-Star break he had swatted 33 homers and was on pace with Roger Maris' famous 61-home run season of 1961. Everyone in MLB was suddenly talking about Oakland's rookie sensation.

McGwire's home runs kept coming. His 38th came on August 11. That tied him with Frank Robinson (1956) and Wally Berger (1930) for the most home runs ever hit by a rookie—and there were still seven weeks left on the A's schedule. Three nights later McGwire stood alone with 39 home runs after blasting one off veteran Don Sutton. His pace slowed to where he had "only" hit 49 homers by September 29. With the A's mathematically out of contention for the AL West title, McGwire eschewed his chance to hit number 50 so he could be with his wife when she gave birth to the couple's first child. Fans, in general, applauded McGwire's sense of priorities. When one looks at a photo of the 1987 Mark McGwire, he is a tall, gangly and lean ballplayer. There is no hint of the vast muscle mass he would carry 11 years later.

McGwire, with the help of 1986 AL Rookie of the Year Jose Canseco, collectively known as the "Bash Brothers," led the A's to AL pennants in 1988, 1989 and 1990. Oakland won the World Series in 1989 that is best remembered for an earthquake striking the San Francisco area and postponing play for 11 days. Although linked together in most news stories about the championship team, Canseco and McGwire were opposite personalities. Canseco was flashy, outspoken and craved attention. McGwire was more reserved and preferred quieter times.

The heady individual accomplishments continued for McGwire beyond his spectacular rookie campaign. In the three season following 1987, McGwire swatted 32, 33, and 39 homers respectively. In 1991 McGwire's home run total dipped to 22, but it rebounded to 42 in 1992. Injuries to his left heel in successive years severely derailed McGwire in 1993 and in the strike-shortened 1994 season, when his home run totals dipped to just nine each year.

Enter Jay McGwire, Mark's younger brother, who was a champion bodybuilder. According to Jay's revealing 2010 book, *Mark and Me*, late in 1994 he persuaded Mark to begin taking steroids as a means to quicken the healing time of the injuries that were threatening to severely shorten his baseball career at age 31. "You've got nothing to lose," Jay claims he told his brother. "Otherwise you'll need to become an expert at bunting the ball to get on base. That is, if you can run, because you won't be able to turn on [your heel]." Mark was reluctant at first. In his tell-all book, Jay says he managed to convince Mark that he would be doing nothing wrong because MLB had no policy whatsoever about steroids at the time, thus he was breaking no rules. Eventually Mark accepted that shaky premise and agreed. Jay wrote, "Somewhere in the course of a conversation between brothers, baseball history was changed. I know that he wouldn't have considered using the stuff if he wasn't injured. I was the one who convinced him to do it. Mark wouldn't trust anyone else. My heart told me I was simply trying to help a brother in need." Jay McGwire's book is subtitled "Mark McGwire and the Truth Behind Baseball's Worst-Kept Secret." Later, in his own tell-all book, Jose Canseco would claim that he and McGwire were both taking steroids in 1988, a charge that both McGwire brothers refute.

McGwire spectacularly rebounded with 39 homers in 1995 and 52 in 1996. In 1997, McGwire launched 34 home runs for Oakland in two-thirds of a season before being traded to the St. Louis Cardinals on July 31—where he promptly hit 24 more homers in just 51 games for a combined total of 58 for the 1997 season. Not since Hank Greenberg in 1938 had a right-handed hitter connected for 58 home runs in a season. Moreover, only Babe Ruth had ever recorded consecutive seasons with 50 or more homers. McGwire was now mentioned in the same breath as the famed Bambino. Because of the mid-season trade, McGwire quirkily became the first man to lead MLB in home runs, but not lead either league in that category. Ken Griffey, Jr., had 56. McGwire's trade to St. Louis (for relief pitcher T. J. Mathews and two minor league hurlers) was orchestrated by the A's because McGwire was going to be a free agent at the end of the season and would probably leave the team. Most fans expected McGwire to leave the Cardinals at the end of 1997 to pursue other suitors, but with ex-Athletics manager Tony LaRussa now in charge of the Cardinals, McGwire liked his new surroundings and chose to stay in Missouri for a while. A three-year contract for $28.5 million made him feel very much wanted.

The memorable 1998 MLB season began in spectacular fashion for McGwire. He hit a grand slam on Opening Day and one home run in each of his next three games. McGwire was off to the races—and so were a lot of MLB hitters. Home runs flew out of ballparks at a record rate. Analysts again credited the offensive outburst to livelier baseballs and better conditioned batters. More than a dozen MLB players would have spectacular home run totals in 1998. Early on it was Ken Griffey, Jr., who was chasing McGwire. At the end of May, McGwire had smacked 27 home runs and Griffey had belted 19. However, a new pursuer emerged in the season's third month to make it a three-way race: Sammy Sosa of the Chicago Cubs hit 20 home runs in June—breaking Rudy York's old mark of 18—establishing a monthly record that still stands and tying him with Griffey with 33 home runs. (York, largely forgotten by fans, had set the record as a 24-year-old rookie with the Detroit Tigers in 1937. York was one-eighth Cherokee and not much of a defensive stalwart, prompting one sportswriter to declare wittily, "He is part Indian and part first baseman.")[1] When July began, McGwire was four ahead of both his rivals with 37 homers.

As McGwire chased the late Roger Maris' record of 61 home runs in a season set back in 1961, Sosa and Griffey kept close on his heels. The McGwire-Sosa-Griffey home run derby became more important than the pennant races to many fans. The interest in the race to eclipse Maris became such that Dan Rather often opened his *CBS Evening News* broadcasts—which seldom dealt with sports stories of any kind—with updates on the sluggers' progress. Each time Sosa homered, he saluted the late, beloved Cubs' broadcaster Harry Caray, who had died that February. All the parts of the home run chase were combining to create a welcome, feel-good situation for MLB after the catastrophic work stoppage of just four years before.

All was not as it seemed, though. The first sign of trouble came in late August when a Seattle-based writer for the *Associated Press* named Steve Wilstein noticed something in plain view in the Cardinals' clubhouse. Wilstein—who would go on to investigate steroid use in a broad spectrum of sports, including the Iditarod—was quick to pounce on it. His August 21 story, when McGwire had notched 51 home runs, described in some quarters as the most important piece of baseball journalism ever written, said the following:

> Sitting in the top shelf of Mark McGwire's locker, next to a can of Popeye spinach and packs of sugarless gum, is a brown bottle labeled Androstenedione.
>
> For more than a year, McGwire says, he has been using the testosterone-producing pill, which is perfectly legal in baseball but banned in the NFL, Olympics and the NCAA.
>
> No one suggests that McGwire wouldn't be closing in on Roger Maris' home run record without the over-the-counter drug. After all, he hit 49 home runs without it as a rookie in 1987, and more than 50 each of the past two seasons.
>
> But the drug's abilities to raise levels of the male hormone, which builds lean muscle mass and promotes recovery after injury, is seen outside baseball as cheating and potentially dangerous.

Ironically, Wilstein was not even a regular baseball writer, but a general sports reporter. He had been captivated by the "Great American Home Run Chase" like many others who were simply enjoying the spectacle. One day, while drawn to the cute, Norman Rockwell–type image of McGwire's ten-year-old son—the Cardinals' batboy—sitting on the top shelf of his father's open locker, Wilstein noticed the container of Androstenedione and jotted the name down. It initially meant nothing to him. Later he asked a physician friend what the product (known colloquially as "Andro") was. He learned it was a precursor to testosterone and was often dangerous to the user's heart, liver and sex organs. His curiosity now aroused, Wilstein contacted John Lombardo, the NFL's steroid advisor, for further information about Andro. Lombardo told Wilstein the league had recently categorized Andro as an anabolic steroid—a performance-enhancing drug—and thus had made it illegal the previous year. Randy Barnes, the 1996 Olympic shot put gold medalist, had recently been banned for life for using it. The story of MLB's home run derby being fueled by a drug that was illegal in numerous other sports was just too big to ignore.

The reaction to Wilstein's article was mostly negative. He was accused of being a snoop for peering into McGwire's open locker and something of a party-pooper for casting doubt on the legitimacy of baseball's big happening. Cardinals manager Tony LaRussa was so irked by Wilstein's story that he considered banning reporters from his team's clubhouse. With MLB selling McGwire souvenirs in enormous quantities, the last thing anyone connected to the purse strings of the game wanted was a drug scandal. Andro was a legal product that anyone could buy in a drugstore. McGwire defended himself by saying, "Everyone I know in the game of baseball uses the same stuff I do."[2] MLB Commissioner Bud Selig, who, like the majority of the public, had never heard of Andro, allied himself with McGwire (and the cash flow he was generating) by saying, "I think what Mark McGwire has accomplished is so remarkable, and he has handled it all so beautifully, we want to do everything we can to enjoy a great moment in baseball history."[3] Still, fans began to look at MLB's home run orgy with a more critical eye, even if they were reluctant to do so. The manufacturers of Andro got a tremendous and unexpected boon because of Wilstein's story: By October, because of McGwire's connection with the drug, sales of Andro in the United States had increased by more than 1,000 percent.

The home runs kept coming at an astonishing rate. At the end of August, both Sosa and McGwire had opened up some distance on Griffey, who had missed some time with injuries. Each had 55 home runs to Griffey's 47. Roger Maris' 37-year-old record was in serious jeopardy of being shattered. Early in September, McGwire blasted four home runs in two games versus the Florida Marlins to assume a 59–56 lead over Sosa. McGwire's 59th home run gave him the all-time NL home run record that had been held by Hack Wilson since 1930. On September 7, in a home game versus the Cubs, McGwire hit his 61st home run to tie Maris. He also effectively put to rest the old Ruth-Maris "asterisk" controversy of 1961 by hitting 61 homers in well under 154 games. It occurred in the Cardinals' 144th game of the season.

The following day, Tuesday, September 8, again versus Chicago, Maris' coveted record fell. The Cubs jumped out to a 2–0 lead in the first inning on three singles. McGwire, plying first base and batting third, grounded out in his first plate appearance of the night to Chicago shortstop Jose Hernandez. In the bottom of the fourth inning, McGwire overtook Maris by hitting his shortest home run of the year, a 341-foot line drive off Chicago's Steve Trachsel, a 27-year-old right-hander. The ball barely cleared the left field fence a few feet to the right of the foul pole. There were two out with no runners on base. Veteran Cardinals broadcaster Jack Buck described the home run this way: "Down the left-field line. Is it enough? Gone! There it is! Sixty-two! Touch first, Mark. You are the new single-season home-run king!" (Buck's reminder to touch first base was made because McGwire had originally missed the base; Cardinals first-base coach Dave McKay demonstratively alerted McGwire to the missed base and he quickly retreated to correct the oversight.)

McGwire's home run whittled the Cubs' 2–0 lead in half and sparked the Cardinals to a 6–3 comeback win. McGwire came to the plate twice more. In the sixth inning he was intentionally walked. In the eighth inning he walked again. Despite losing, the Cubs outhit St. Louis 12–5 that night. The attendance at Busch Stadium was 43,688.

MLB made sure the Maris family was in attendance for the historic occasion, which was a classy gesture by all concerned. (McGwire, in a nifty coincidence, was born on October 1, 1963—exactly two years after Roger Maris had hit his 61st home run in 1961.) Sosa raced from his position in the outfield to congratulate McGwire as soon as the umpires had signaled the home run. During an on-field ceremony, McGwire praised Sosa for pushing him towards the record. Sosa was equally complimentary towards McGwire all season long. *Saturday Night Live* would parody the two men's open admiration for each other in a memorable sketch in which the two sluggers (portrayed by Will Ferrell and Tracy Morgan) concluded the routine with a romantic slow dance.

Often forgotten in the hoopla surrounding McGwire's 62nd homer is that Sosa briefly regained the lead in the home run chase with his 66th clout of the season on September 25. Thus for a brief period—a few hours—Sosa held the MLB single-season home run record. McGwire, however, tied Sosa and regained the record that night with two home runs as part of the five he hit versus the Montreal Expos on the season's final weekend. The Great American Home Run Chase ended with McGwire edging Sosa, 70 to 66. (Who even remembers that Ken Griffey, Jr., smacked 56 home runs in 1998?)

Another largely forgotten bit of home run derby esoterica from the 1998 season that bordered on the absurd: McGwire was victimized by a bad call by umpire Bob Davidson, who incorrectly declared fan interference on what should have been home run number 66 in Milwaukee on September 20. Television replays clearly showed the spectator in question—a 45-year-old, disabled Iowan named Alan Riesbeck, who was sitting in a motorized scooter—did not reach over the fence to grab the ball as Davidson had ruled. Video review was not a tool MLB umpires had at their disposal in 1998, so McGwire unfortunately had to settle for a two-base hit.

Although McGwire's 62nd home run was the most replayed of his 70, each subsequent home run set a new record or tied it, depending on how many homers Sosa had hit. Thus McGwire's 70th home run of 1998—hit off Montreal right-hander Carl Pavano on September 27—was the true historic milestone. McGwire was named the NL's MVP, but it was Sosa's Chicago Cubs who won the NL Central Division in 1998. The Atlanta Braves swept the Cubs in the NLDS.

Months later, still exuberant over what had occurred during the MLB season, *Sports Illustrated* declared 1998 to be the greatest sports year of all time—which is no trifling acclamation—and noted that the compelling McGwire-Sosa home-run chase had been the lynchpin for the excitement. Accordingly, the twosome jointly shared the honor as the magazine's "Sportsmen of the Year." On the cover of the year-end issue, McGwire and Sosa were photographed as ancient godlike figures wearing togas and wreaths of laurel. Andro was not mentioned anywhere in the accompanying story.

The next season, McGwire almost matched his 1998 record. This time he connected for 65 home runs. (Sosa launched 63 homers in 1999.) His 135 home runs in two consecutive seasons is a feat that has never been approached. However, Mark McGwire's tenure as the single-season home run champion lasted only three seasons. Barry Bonds, who had never hit more than 49 home runs in a single season, suddenly clouted the scarcely believable total of 73 in 2001 at the advanced age of 37. A ballplayer having the peak year of his career in his late 30s was more than a statistical aberration. It seemed to defy the normal realities of human physiology. All open-minded baseball fans now had to face the reality that something was terribly amiss.

So far from the norm were the MLB home run totals in recent years that the United States government felt compelled to look into the matter in 2005 and investigate the prevalence of performance-enhancing drugs in baseball. In a congressional hearing held on March 17, 2005, McGwire—who had been out of the public eye since retiring from baseball in 2001—famously refused to answer any specific questions, declaring he did not want to "talk about the past." Of course, that was the precise reason McGwire had been summoned to testify. He further stated, "Asking me or any other player to answer questions about who took steroids in front of television cameras will not solve the problem…. My lawyers have advised me that I cannot answer these questions without jeopardizing my friends, my family and myself. I intend to follow their advice."

McGwire's elusiveness only served to heighten the doubts about his slugging achievements. In reporting McGwire's non-cooperation, journalists noted that McGwire looked considerably trimmer than he had in his playing days with the St. Louis Cardinals. Sosa, who had been summoned along with Rafael Palmeiro and Jose Canseco, looked even worse. He seemed not to understand the questions despite having an interpreter translating the hearing's goings-on from English to Spanish. (Curiously, Sosa seldom required the services of a translator for routine baseball interviews throughout his career.) His lawyer made statements on Sosa's behalf.

Dave Sheinin of the *Washington Post* described the remarkable spectacle that unfolded in front of a national television audience:

> On an extraordinary day of words and images, a House committee investigating steroids in baseball forced the sport to confront its past and rethink its future—encountering resistance on both counts—and the most extraordinary image of all was that of Mark McGwire, once the game's most celebrated slugger but now the face of the steroid scandal, reduced to a shrunken, lonely, evasive figure whose testimony brought him to the verge of tears.

McGwire, whose Ruthian feats on the field in the late 1990s made him a national folk hero, sat on the same panel but never made eye contact with [Jose] Canseco, whose recent tell-all book gave voice to the long-rumored view that McGwire's accomplishments—along with those of many other contemporaries— were done with the help of steroids.

McGwire, who has been estimated to be 30 to 40 pounds lighter than at the end of his career, appeared on the verge of tears at least twice as he read his opening statement. The first time came as he referred to some of the participants of an earlier panel—the parents of two amateur baseball players whose suicides were attributed to steroid use.

The tone of the day was set by Sen. Jim Bunning (R–Ky.), whose previous career was as a Hall of Fame pitcher in the 1950s and '60s.

Apparently referring to modern sluggers like McGwire and Bonds, whose physiques expanded and whose home run totals began skyrocketing in their mid- to late-thirties, Bunning told the panel: "When I played with Henry Aaron, Willie Mays and Ted Williams, they didn't put on 40 pounds … and they didn't hit more home runs in their late thirties than they did in their late twenties. What's happening in baseball is not natural, and it's not right."

Bunning went a step beyond those who say the records of steroid-users should be marked by an asterisk, arguing that the records should be thrown out of the book. "If they started in 1992 or '93 illegally using steroids," Bunning said, "wipe all their records out. Take them away. They don't deserve them."

Nearly five years passed. On January 11, 2010, Mark McGwire finally came clean— metaphorically speaking—in an interview with Bob Costas on the MLB Network. For the first time, he openly admitted using steroids when he broke baseball's home-run record in 1998, but he also insisted he did not need performance-enhancing drugs to attain the feat. "I was given a gift to hit home runs," he told Costas.

In a statement he sent to the *Associated Press*, McGwire said he had used steroids on and off for nearly a decade. During the Costas interview, McGwire said he had achieved his 70-home-run season mostly by studying opposing pitchers and shortening his swing. When specifically asked by Costas if steroids had made the difference in his surpassing of Maris' mark, McGwire responded that he could have hit all his home runs without PEDs.

"I truly believe so," McGwire insisted. "I believe I was given this gift. The only reason I took steroids was for health purposes."

Fox News reported McGwire's revelation this way:

Finally willing to talk about the past, Mark McGwire sobbed and sniffled, giving the missing—and unsurprising—answer to the steroids question.

Ending more than a decade of denials and evasion, McGwire admitted Monday that steroids and human growth hormone helped make him a home run king.

That same day McGwire telephoned Pat Maris, Roger's widow, and tearfully apologized to her.

Chicago 3 at St. Louis 6

Game played on Tuesday, September 8, 1998, at Busch Stadium II

Chicago Cubs	ab	r	h	rbi	St. Louis Cardinals	ab	r	h	rbi
Johnson cf	5	0	0	0	DeShields 2b	4	1	2	1
Hernandez ss	4	1	0	1	Tatis 3b	4	0	0	0
Grace 1b	4	1	2	1	McGwire 1b	2	2	1	1
Sosa rf	4	0	1	0	Lankford cf	4	1	1	3
Hill lf	5	0	2	0	Gant lf	3	1	1	1
Gaetti 3b	4	0	2	1	Croushore p	0	0	0	0
Morandini 2b	2	0	0	0	Painter p	0	0	0	0
Mieske ph	1	0	0	0	Frascatore p	0	0	0	0
Maxwell 2b	0	0	0	0	Lampkin c	0	0	0	0
Wengert p	0	0	0	0	Mabry rf	3	0	0	0

Chicago Cubs	ab	r	h	rbi
Heredia p	0	0	0	0
Merced ph	1	0	0	0
Servais c	4	1	3	0
Trachsel p	3	0	1	0
Mulholland p	0	0	0	0
Alexander ph,2b	1	0	1	0
Totals	38	3	12	3

St. Louis Cardinals	ab	r	h	rbi
Ordaz ss	3	0	0	0
Mercker p	1	0	0	0
Drew ph, lf	2	0	0	0
Marrero c	2	1	0	0
Acevedo p	0	0	0	0
Totals	28	6	5	6

Chicago	200 000 010—3 12 1
St. Louis	000 105 00x—6 5 0

Chicago Cubs	IP	H	R	ER	BB	SO
Trachsel L (14–8)	5.2	5	6	6	2	6
Mulholland	1.1	0	0	0	0	1
Wengert	0.2	0	0	0	1	1
Heredia	0.1	0	0	0	0	0
Totals	8.0	5	6	6	3	8

St. Louis Cardinals	IP	H	R	ER	BB	SO
Mercker W (10–11)	6.0	8	2	2	3	2
Croushore	0.2	1	0	0	2	0
Painter	0.2	2	1	1	0	0
Frascatore	0.2	0	0	0	0	0
Acevedo SV (7)	1.0	1	0	0	0	1
Totals	9.0	12	3	3	5	3

E–Hill (1). DP–St. Louis 1. 2B–Chicago Hill (4, off Acevedo). HR–St. Louis McGwire (62, 4th inning off Trachsel 0 on, 2 out); Lankford (27, 6th inning off Trachsel 2 on, 2 out); Gant (23, 6th inning off Trachsel 0 on, 2 out). IBB–McGwire (28, by Trachsel). WP–Mercker (6). BK–Trachsel (2), Mercker (4). IBB–Trachsel (5, McGwire). U-HP–Steve Rippley, 1B–Larry Poncino, 2B–Mike Winters, 3B–Gary Darling. T–2:46. A–43,688.

July 9, 2002

Site: Miller Park, Milwaukee

Teams: American League All-Stars vs. National League All-Stars

Significance: All-Star Game Tie

Impact: Future All-Star Games must be played to a finish; the game's winner gets home field advantage in the World Series

> "The only bad thing about winning the pennant is that you have to manage the All-Star Game the next year. I'd rather go fishing for three days."—former AL manager Whitey Herzog

> "In 2002 the All-Star Game crumbled before Commissioner Bud Selig's eyes, right in his hometown of Milwaukee. The game ended … after 11 innings of play, a 7–7 tie, and no more players to use. Selig called the game a tie, and the decision rocked baseball."—Thom Loverro

For 11 innings, the 2002 MLB All-Star Game was as good as any of the 73 Midsummer Classics that had been played since 1933. There was stellar defense. (One play was so spectacular that it was deemed the MLB defensive gem of the year at the end of the season.) The game also featured generally decent pitching and plenty of offense, and was a hard-fought, tight battle. Instead of a fitting climax, though, baseball fans around the world saw a strange, inconclusive, unsatisfactory and tepid conclusion. The disappointment of fans and sponsors was so profound that MLB strongly reacted—some would say overre-acted—and decided to up the ante and give the annual exhibition game considerably higher stakes starting in 2003.

Milwaukee's Miller Park was the setting. MLB commissioner Bud Selig was a huge factor in securing the game for the National League Milwaukee Brewers' home park. Mil-waukee was Selig's home. The Brewers had last hosted the ASG in 1975, when they were an AL club and played at County Stadium. It should have been a triumphant night for the MLB commissioner. Through no fault of Selig's—a point which could be and has been debated—it turned into anything but that.

The origins of what happened at Miller Park on July 9, 2002, could be traced back nine years to the 1993 ASG in Baltimore. Camden Yards was hosting the game. Orioles pitcher Mike Mussina was expected to make an appearance in front of the hometown fans for at least an inning of work. However, AL manager Cito Gaston of the Toronto Blue Jays chose not to use Mussina in the ninth inning of an easy 9–3 AL victory. Gaston was in a tough spot. His Toronto Blue Jays were battling the Orioles for the AL east title. No matter how he used Mussina in the ASG, somebody would complain. He feared overworking Mussina and being accused of deliberately overusing a rival team's star hurler. Gaston actually thought he was doing the Orioles a favor by saving Mussina's arm, but the local fans were outraged that they had been deprived of seeing their best pitcher take the mound in the ASG. Gaston was roundly criticized far and wide for "snubbing" the Orioles and the city of Baltimore in general—and Mussina specifically. Mussina did his best to fan the flames of discontent by warming up in the AL bullpen before the top of the ninth inning without being told to do so. He also played to the Bal-timore crowd by tipping his cap to them when the game ended without him being sum-moned to pitch. From that day forward, managers at the annual ASG have done their best to get every player into the game to avoid the criticism leveled against Gaston in 1993. In some ways, the ASG started to resemble a softball game at a church picnic; every-body gets to play so no one's feelings will get hurt. The days of Willie Mays playing every inning of an All-Star Game (which he did 11 times) were now a thing of the romantic past.

The 2002 ASG began on a somber note as baseball great Ted Williams had passed away the previous week at the age of 83. During a pre-game ceremony, a red number 9 was unveiled in the left field grass as a tribute to the late Red Sox star who had patrolled that same section of outfield at Boston's Fenway Park from 1939 to 1960 (excepting the war years). Three of the Boston players in the AL lineup—Nomar Garciaparra, Johnny Damon and Ugueth Urbina—performed the honors. After that fitting salute to the Splen-did Splinter, it was game on.

Curt Schilling was the National League's starting pitcher. His outing was strong. Schilling whiffed three AL batters in just two innings of work. In the past, ASG starters typically lasted for three innings (unless they were shelled), but the memories of 1993 still lingered. Players were moved in and out of the lineup with dizzying frequency regard-less of how well they were doing.

The most memorable defensive play in the 2002 ASG—perhaps in any ASG—occurred in the bottom of the first inning. San Francisco's Barry Bonds hit a long fly ball off AL starter Derek Lowe. It looked deep enough to be a home run. However, center fielder Torii Hunter of the Minnesota Twins made a sensational play. He chased down Bonds' blast and, at the last instant, reached over the fence to make a run-saving grab.

The startled Bonds showed a rare playful side of his personality by affectionately lifting Hunter off the ground when the NL took the field for the second inning.

The NL opened the scoring in the bottom of the second inning when Mike Piazza's groundout scored Vladimir Guerrero from third base. Three more NL runs crossed the plate in the third inning. Todd Helton's single brought home Jimmy Rollins. Bonds atoned for missing a home run by inches in the first inning with a two-run shot. The NL was up by a 4–0 score.

Undaunted, the AL fought their way back into the game. Manny Ramirez's fourth-inning RBI single cut the NL lead to 4–1. The AL further cut into the home side's lead courtesy of Alfonso Soriano's solo home run off Eric Gagne in the top of the fifth inning. The seesaw contest continued with the NL getting one run back in the home half of the fifth inning on an RBI double by Damian Miller. After five innings the score was 5–2 in favor of the NL. The 41,871 fans at Miller Park and television audiences far and wide were being treated to an exciting ASG.

The sixth inning produced no runs—the first frame in which zeroes prevailed since the opening inning. In the top of the seventh, the AL scored four runs to take the lead for the first time in the game. An RBI groundout by Garret Anderson, a run-scoring base hit by Tony Batista, and a two-run double by Paul Konerko accounted for the four AL scores. Temporarily the visitors held a 6–5 advantage. It did not last long. In the bottom of the seventh inning, Lance Berkman's two-run single scored Mike Lowell and Damian Miller. The lead shifted back to the NL by a 7–6 count.

No lead was safe in this ASG. In the top of the eighth inning, Omar Vizquel's RBI triple tied the score at 7–7. Vizquel was stranded on base. From that point onward, there would be no more scoring, but the player changes continued unabated. By the time extra innings were necessary to decide the game's winner, both teams were down to just one pitcher. Accordingly, Vicente Padilla of the NL and Freddy Garcia of the AL worked two innings in relief. Neither man surrendered a run.

If the game proceeded beyond 11 innings, there would be a problem. Neither manager (Bob Brenly of the NL and Joe Torre of the AL) wanted to expend the energies of Padilla or Garcia. No other pitcher in the game had thrown more than two innings. Certainly neither man wished to see the game decided by putting a non-pitcher on the mound. As Garcia warmed up for the bottom of the 11th inning, Brenly, Torre, and the six-man umpiring crew were summoned to Commissioner Selig's field-level box seat to discuss their limited options. As far as everyone was concerned, there was just one option: Call the game a tie if the NL did not score in the home half of the 11th inning.

Word of that decision filtered up to Fox broadcasters Joe Buck and Tim McCarver, who both thought the decision was a sensible one. "I think that everybody can accept that if the National League doesn't score it will be a 7–7 tie," Buck naïvely opined to the TV audience. "The sun will come out tomorrow." An announcement over Miller Park's PA system informed the crowd of it after the first NL batter was retired. Buck and McCarver had been sorely mistaken: The paying customers were overwhelmingly displeased with the proposition of a tied ASG. Chants of "Ripoff," "Refund!" and "Bud must go!" echoed throughout Miller Park. At one point the fans began chanting "Let them play!"—which Joe Buck quickly recognized as dialogue from the 1977 movie *The Bad News Bears in Breaking Training*. Unlike the kids' ballgame in the motion picture, MLB had no intention of letting the 2002 ASG go on indefinitely. With one out, Mike Lowell of the Florida Marlins singled to give the NL a glimmer of hope of breaking the deadlock.

With Padilla batting—yes, the rosters on both teams were so depleted that the pitchers were batting—Lowell took second base on a Garcia wild pitch. However, the Seattle right-hander bore down and struck out both Padilla and Benito Santiago to conclude the game. When plate umpire Gerry Davis emphatically signaled strike three against Santiago, the 2002 ASG sputtered to an end without a winner three hours and 29 minutes after it began.

Despite witnessing 11 innings of high-caliber baseball, the fans felt cheated by the strange outcome. Debris was tossed on the field in protest of the game being stopped. An ASG ending in a tie was not unprecedented. The second game of 1961 (two ASG were played each season from 1959–1962), played at Fenway Park, was rained out after nine innings with the teams locked in a 1–1 tie. Nobody squawked too much as rainouts are common, though undesirable occurrences that baseball fans have learned to tolerate. A game terminated because of poor roster management was apparently something else entirely. Curiously, no player was named the game's MVP—quite likely because the now very unpopular Bud Selig wished to avoid having to oversee an on-field award ceremony in front of thousands of loud, unhappy customers.

The participants tried to put a positive spin on what had occurred. "Obviously, nobody wanted it to end like this, but it really was the right move," declared Minnesota Twins reliever Eddie Guardado. "The fans got to see the stars. They got to see good pitching, good hitting, and great plays. The only thing they didn't get to see was a winner."[1] Others tried to make light of the situation. Chicago's Paul Konerko, upon learning that he had tied an ASG record by hitting two doubles, commented with a smile, "Somehow I don't think this game will be remembered for that—except maybe by me."[2]

Was anyone to blame for the outcome? Sports fans, even those who followed baseball only vaguely, generally thought so. Some singled out Selig for agreeing to the convenient draw. Others blamed the two managers for mismanaging their lineups in order to get everyone into the game. Longtime fans recalled past All-Star Games when starting pitchers went four or five innings and other starters played the entire game. It was more typical for many players selected to play the game to see no action whatsoever. There were always plenty of substitutes on the bench ready to enter the game whenever necessary. Journalist Thom Loverro, writing for theatlantic.com website, took the scholarly and historic approach and squarely blamed the 1993 Cito Gaston-Baltimore situation for the fiasco.

Selig and MLB as a whole were surprised by the level of hostility displayed by both the fans and the media. The commissioner had seen the television ratings for the ASG drop significantly from their gaudy peak in 1970. Fearing the backlash from the 7–7 tie would further erode public interest in the game, he announced that all future ASG would be played to a decisive finish—and the winning league would get home-field advantage for that year's World Series. (It had alternated between the two leagues since the end of the Second World War.) It was a drastic—some would say desperate—act designed to expunge the 7–7 tie from the memory of fans who were not likely to forget it. "This time it counts!" became the slogan and MLB's rallying cry for the 2003 ASG at Chicago's U.S. Cellular Field.

The important prize that now comes with winning the ASG has been hotly debated. Some fans approve because they want the MLB All-Star Game to regain the stature it once had on the American sports landscape. Declining interest has severely affected the viewership of the NBA's and NHL's All-Star Games. There is occasional talk of scrapping the NHL All-Star Game altogether because of the lack of intensity shown by the players—

a mindset clearly reflected in the ridiculous double-digit scores it regularly produces. The 2015 NHL ASG saw 29 goals scored. Similarly, defense was just a rumor at the 2015 NBA ASG; it ended in a score of 163–158. In 2013 the NFL basically abandoned its long-time AFC-NFC format for the Pro Bowl in an attempt to renew viewer interest in what was once a premier event. Hardly anyone cared enough to object or approve. Other baseball fans maintain that the ASG is not the proper forum to decide something as potentially important as home-field advantage for the World Series. One interesting suggestion is that the ASG should remain a glamorous exhibition contest while the overall results of the entire season's interleague play should be used to determine home-field advantage for the World Series. Critics of this plan say that regular-season interleague play is a large part of the problem, claiming it has eroded the uniqueness and charm the ASG once possessed.

When asked about the controversial 2002 ASG 11 years later during a press conference for the 2013 ASG in New York City, Selig remained unapologetic, even defiant. Prefacing his comment with a warning that he was about to use profanity, the usually imperturbable Selig exclaimed, "We ran out of f*&%$ pitchers!" When the laughter in the room subsided, Selig continued, "It happened—and the fate of western civilization, by the way, wasn't changed one iota as a result of that tie, lest anybody get too concerned about it."[3]

Has Selig's gimmick rekindled fan interest in the MLB All-Star Game? Apparently not. The 2014 ASG was soundly beaten in that night's TV ratings by *America's Got Talent.*

American League 7 at National League 7

Game played on Tuesday, July 9, 2002, at Miller Park

American League	ab	r	h	rbi	National League	ab	r	h	rbi
Suzuki rf	2	0	0	0	Vidro 2b	2	0	0	0
Winn rf	2	1	1	0	Spivey 2b	2	0	0	0
Urbina p	0	0	0	0	Nen p	0	0	0	0
Rivera p	0	0	0	0	Smoltz p	0	0	0	0
Garcia p	1	0	0	0	Santiago ph-c	2	0	1	0
Hillenbrand 3b	2	0	0	0	Helton 1b	2	1	1	1
Ventura 3b	1	0	0	0	Berkman lf-1b	3	0	1	2
Batista ph,3b	3	1	1	1	Bonds lf	2	1	1	2
Rodriguez ss	2	0	0	0	Sexson 1b	1	0	0	0
Tejada ss	2	1	1	0	Dunn lf	1	0	0	0
Garciaparra ph, ss	1	0	0	0	Sosa rf	2	0	1	0
Giambi 1b	2	1	1	0	Green rf	3	0	1	0
Konerko 1b	2	0	2	2	Guerrero cf	2	1	1	0
Sweeney 1b	1	0	0	0	Jones ph-cf	3	0	0	0
Ramirez lf	2	0	2	1	Piazza c	2	0	0	1
Buehrle p	0	0	0	0	Gagne p	0	0	0	0
Pierzynski ph-c	3	0	0	0	Hernandez ss	3	0	0	0
Posada c	3	0	0	0	Rolen 3b	3	0	0	0
Zito p	0	0	0	0	Castillo 2b	2	0	0	0
Guardado p	0	0	0	0	Rollins ss	2	2	2	0
Sasaki p	0	0	0	0	Hoffman p	0	0	0	0
Fick ph-rf	2	1	1	0	Remlinger p	0	0	0	0
Hunter cf	2	0	0	0	Kim p	0	0	0	0
Damon cf	3	1	1	0	Lowell ph-3b	3	1	2	0
Soriano 2b	2	1	1	1	Schilling p	0	0	0	0
Vizquel 2b	2	0	1	1	Williams p	0	0	0	0

American League	ab	r	h	rbi		National League	ab	r	h	rbi
Lowe p	0	0	0	0		Gonzalez ph	1	0	0	0
Jeter ph	1	0	0	0		Perez p	0	0	0	0
Halladay p	0	0	0	0		Miller c	3	1	2	1
Anderson lf	4	0	0	1		Padilla p	1	0	0	0
Totals	45	7	12	7		Totals	45	7	13	7

American League 000 110 410 00—7 12 0
National League 013 010 200 00—7 13 0

American League	IP	H	R	ER	BB	SO
Lowe	2.0	2	1	1	0	0
Halladay	1.0	3	3	3	0	1
Buehrle	2.0	2	1	1	0	2
Zito	0.1	0	0	0	0	0
Guardado	0.2	0	0	0	0	2
Sasaki	1.0	3	2	2	1	2
Urbina	1.0	0	0	0	0	1
Rivera	1.0	1	0	0	0	0
Garcia	2.0	2	0	0	0	3
Totals	11.0	13	7	7	1	11

National League	IP	H	R	ER	BB	SO
Schilling	2.0	1	0	0	0	3
Williams	1.0	0	0	0	0	2
Perez	1.0	2	1	0	0	2
Gagne	1.0	2	1	1	0	1
Hoffman	1.0	1	0	0	0	1
Remlinger	0.2	1	2	2	1	0
Kim	0.1	3	2	2	0	0
Nen	1.0	2	1	1	0	2
Smoltz	1.0	0	0	0	0	1
Padilla	2.0	0	0	0	1	0
Totals	11.0	12	7	6	2	9

E–None. 2B–American Winn; Konerko 2, National Miller 2. 3B–Vizquel. HR–American Soriano, National Bonds. LOB–American 7, National 6. SB–American Damon; Winn; Fick, National Berkman; Green. WP–Garcia. BK–Lowe. PB–Piazza. U–Gerry Davis, Tim Tschida, Chuck Meriwether, Jerry Meals, Marty Foster, Paul Emmel. T–3:29. A–41,871.

October 14, 2003

Site: Wrigley Field, Chicago

Teams: Florida Marlins vs. Chicago Cubs

Significance: Game Six of the 2003 NLCS

Impact: A fan's life is forever negatively impacted because of one foul ball

"Baseball, it is said, is only a game. True. And the Grand Canyon is only a hole in Arizona."—George Will

"This was bigger than baseball, this story; this was human. As the documenter of a historical event, I had to do my job. As a human being, I don't know if I'm even proud of it. If we had something to do with how this young man has had to live his life, I feel bad about that."[1]—Jeff Gowen, producer of FOX-TV's coverage of the 2003 NLCS

It was such an ordinary occurrence. Any casual baseball fan will see it happen dozens of times in a typical MLB season. A foul fly ball heads toward the first few rows of the stands. An infielder gives chase just in case it doesn't fall into the crowd, just in case the wind pushes it back and he can make a catch. Most often it falls beyond the fielder's reach and among the spectators—but sometimes the ball stays in play. Sometimes the fielder falls headlong into the crowd in pursuit of the ball. That's why TV cameras follow those batted balls into the stands. There just might be something extraordinary to see.

In this case it was the circumstances that made everything extraordinary. It was Game Six of the 2003 NLCS. The Chicago Cubs led the Florida Marlins, three games to two. One more win would get them into the World Series for the first time since 1945. 1945! Leading the series three games to one, the Cubs had a chance to wrap up the National League pennant two days earlier in Florida in Game Five, but they lost badly, 4–0. Chicago got just two hits off Josh Beckett, who also recorded 11 strikeouts in the complete-game shutout. Cubs fans, confident despite their history of disappointment, shrugged off the setback. At least, they said, the Cubs can win the NL pennant at home— at the "Friendly Confines" of Wrigley Field. It can be a feel-good moment filled with rejoicing, optimism and civic pride. They could wait two days for Game Six on October 14. After all, they had waited 58 years for the Cubs to capture a pennant and 95 years for a Cubs' World Series championship. What difference could another 48 hours make? Plenty, as it turned out.

Everything seemed to be going according to the script for the Cubs. Mark Prior was doing a masterful job pitching. The Cubs held a 3–0 lead going into the top of the eighth inning. With one out and Juan Pierre on second base for Florida, the most famous foul ball in the history of baseball was hit. Luis Castillo, batting with a full count, lofted a fly ball that was clearly drifting foul well past third base. It flew over the unoccupied on-field bullpen and toward the elevated seating area. In Aisle 4, Row 8, Seat 113—a front-row chair—was 26-year-old Steve Bartman, a youth baseball coach and a lifelong Cubs fan. Bartman and several other fans attempted to catch the foul ball—utterly unaware that Cubs left fielder Moises Alou had drifted over to the wall in an attempt to make the catch.

Alou approached the high wall and jumped for the ball with his glove extended. Whether the ball was over the stands or over the field at that moment has been hotly debated. Bartman, like several fans sitting near to him, tried to catch the approaching souvenir. His hands touched the ball momentarily, but he fumbled it. As soon as Bartman touched the ball, Alou could not legally catch it. Alou, an average defensive player at best, maintains to this day that he absolutely would have caught the ball had Bartman not stuck his hands in front of his glove. The ball fell away from Bartman into the stands to his left, where it was scooped up by another spectator. Frustrated and angry, Alou slapped his glove against his thigh and shouted at the fans, convinced he had a play on the ball. Thom Brennaman described the incident on FOX-TV this way: "Again in the air … down the left-field line…. Alou, reaching into the stands … and couldn't get it … and is livid with a fan!"

A six-man umpiring crew was working the NLCS. Left field umpire Mike Everitt ruled the play simply to be a foul ball—and not fan interference. A ruling of fan interference (which would have had the effect of Castillo being called out) could only be made if a spectator had reached over the field of play and touched the ball. It cannot be called if a fielder reaches over the stands. In Everitt's opinion, the ball was over the stands—

not the field—when Bartman made contact with it. Both Alou and Prior argued for fan interference to be called but to no avail. Chicago manager Dusty Baker was in no position to dispute the call as his seat in the Cubs' dugout did not give him a decent view of the play. In practice, an umpire will only call fan interference if there is absolutely no doubt that a fan has reached over the imaginary vertical "plane" that separates the stands from the field. In Bartman's case it was borderline but not conclusive. The count remained 3–2 on Castillo. After seeing the replay, Steve Lyons, doing color commentary for FOX, said prophetically, "This could be huge." Many cynical Cubs fans felt the same way.

For the moment, what would go down in baseball lore as the "Bartman Incident" was just another foul ball. However, the Cubs proceeded to unravel spectacularly. Mike Lowell, Florida's third baseman, recalled saying to his teammates in the visitors' dugout, "Let's make that guy [Bartman] famous!"[2] Prior's next pitch to Castillo was wild for ball four and rolled to the backstop. Pierre advanced to third base while Castillo went to first. Ivan Rodriguez singled. Pierre crossed the plate to make the score 3–1 while Castillo moved to second base. The most critical at-bat of the inning came next. Miguel Cabrera hit a routine, high-bouncing ground ball to sure-handed shortstop Alex Gonzalez, who had made just ten errors in 625 chances in 2003. It looked to be a tailor-made double-play situation—but Gonzalez booted it. Instead of the Cubs being out of the inning with a two-run lead, the score was still 3–1, but the Marlins had the bases loaded with just one out. The next batter, Derrek Lee, smacked a double. The game was tied, 3–3. Wrigley Field fell ominously quiet. Florida now had runners at second and third bases. Prior was removed from the game in favor of reliever Kyle Farnsworth.

Mike Lowell was intentionally walked to load the bases. Jeff Conine hit a sacrifice fly to Cubs right fielder Sammy Sosa that scored Cabrera. Florida now led, 4–3. Sosa's throw missed the cutoff man, which allowed Lowell to advance to second base and Lee to third. Todd Hollandsworth, was intentionally walked to load the bases. Mike Mordecai made the Cubs pay severely for their miscues with a bases-clearing double. The visitors now led, 7–3. Mike Remlinger was summoned to pitch in place of the ineffective Farnsworth. Juan Pierre, batting for the second time in the inning, singled Mordecai home. Florida now held an 8–3 advantage. Luis Castillo, the man who had hit the foul ball towards Steve Bartman, concluded the memorable inning by popping out to Cubs second baseman Mark Grudzielanek. Florida had sent 12 men to the plate in the top of the eighth inning. The game ended, 8–3. Florida had leveled the Series at three games apiece. A seventh game would be needed the following night to decide the 2003 NLCS.

While the disastrous events were unfolding for the Cubs and their fans, FOX-TV was fixated on Bartman. Several times he was shown in close-ups to baseball fans everywhere. Wearing a Cubs cap, a headset connected to a transistor radio, eyeglasses, and a green turtleneck under his dark sweatshirt, Bartman was singled out from his fellow fans. In the eyes of the television world, he was culpable for the Cubs' epic meltdown. He was already being verbally harassed by nearby spectators for preventing Alou's catch on Castillo's foul ball. Bartman was shown sitting stoically with his attention turned to the diamond, trying to be inconspicuous—but failing. Wrigley Field had no video scoreboard, but numerous fans in the stands were receiving cellphone calls from fans watching the telecast at home identifying Bartman as the villain of the debacle that had unfolded. Within a short time things began to turn ugly at the Friendly Confines.

Several fans descended upon the area to threaten Bartman and throw garbage at him. The crowd trying to get into Aisle 4 grew steadily. An obscene chant began that engulfed the ballpark. "Did I do anything wrong?"[3] Bartman pitifully asked two strangers seated behind him. They kindly assured him he had not, but the hostility elsewhere continued unabated. One miffed fan managed to dump a cup of beer on him. Security personnel moved in to assist Bartman and take him to a safe area. With the anger of the ever-increasing mob descending upon his tiny section of Wrigley Field, he sensibly acquiesced. Enclosed in a protective circle of ballpark staff, Bartman and the two friends he came to the game with were ushered away to a secure place somewhere deep in the bowels of the old ballpark. The last view the public got of Steve Bartman was of him covering his head to escape the barrage of debris being thrown his way in Wrigley Field's concourse.

Things got exponentially worse for Bartman. His companions were able to leave Wrigley Field without incident because no one was looking for them. Bartman, however, was the target for the wrath of numerous fans who stayed long after the game's last pitch to hunt him down. Bartman was eventually smuggled out of the ballpark in a security staff member's uniform and was temporarily transported to the home of the head of Wrigley Field's security department. Bartman lingered there for several hours. He watched the replay of the incident several times on ESPN and on local Chicago news broadcasts, before the situation had apparently calmed down enough for him to proceed back to his own house. But in truth, things were not calming down. Anger was rising in the city— a city that had not seen a Cubs team participate in a World Series in nearly six decades. Chicagoans who personally knew Bartman and recognized him from FOX's television coverage identified him by name via online posts on numerous baseball website chatrooms. Bartman was no longer just the anonymous "headset guy." His suburban address was published too—in the next day's *Chicago Sun-Times*. It was not long before harassing phone calls were coming into the home that Bartman shared with his parents. At one point six police cars surrounded the house to provide protection to the Bartman family. The next morning a local TV news helicopter hovered over their home.

Bartman became the most talked-about man in the United States—and likely the most reclusive. Debate centered on whether Bartman was at fault at all. *Sun-Times* columnist Jay Mariotti thought so, at least to some extent. He wrote, "A fan in that situation should try his best to get out of the way, even if he isn't of the mind to see Alou approaching, as Bartman claims. Still, he's also a human being who was reacting in a tense, unusual moment. And the resulting verbal abuse and trash-hurling, followed by the Neanderthal threats and creepy reaction on the Internet, hasn't reflected well on Chicago's sports culture."[4] Meanwhile the Cubs issued a formal statement absolving Bartman of any blame in the team's loss. Most Cubs players quickly blamed themselves for the horrendous eighth inning that suddenly turned the game in Florida's favor. Shortstop Alex Gonzalez, whose misplay of Miguel Cabrera's easy ground ball was the costliest blunder of the inning, was happily content that he was not the focus of the fans' anger.

Despite many people not assigning fault to Bartman, the abuse continued unabated. Bartman was skewered in Jay Leno's monologue on the *Tonight Show*. Illinois governor Rod Blagojevich suggested Bartman be put in the state's witness protection program. No one was entirely certain if the governor was serious or not. Conversely, Florida governor Jeb Bush cheerfully offered Bartman speedy asylum in the Sunshine State if he wanted it. Bartman's father defended his son's instinctive reaction to reporters. "He's a huge Cubs fan. I'm sure I taught him well. I taught him to catch foul balls when they come near him."[5] A longtime neighbor and family friend, who was appalled by the media frenzy, added, "He's a good kid, a wonderful son, never in any trouble. I don't think he should be blamed at all. People reach for balls. This just happened to be a little more critical. If Florida didn't score all the runs, you wouldn't be standing here."[6]

Bartman's Wrigley Field misadventure and the passions it incited could not be contained within the baseball community or even the North American continent. Because of its intensely human element, the story progressed to world news. The British website BBC Sport, which normally paid scant attention to baseball, told its readers about Bartman's woes, although it was readily apparent the BBC's correspondent did not know a whole lot about the sport:

Baseball Fan Feels Chicago's Fury

Chicago hates him, Florida loves him, and Alaska maybe awaits him—it has been a bad week for Chicago Cubs baseball fan Steve Bartman.

By trying to catch a foul ball from his seat in the stands, Mr. Bartman denied his team the chance of a winning catch against the Florida Marlins.

The Cubs' dream of winning their first World Series since 1908 rapidly receded—and with it Mr. Bartman.

He has been in hiding since Tuesday's match to escape his city's anger.

During that game, he stuck his hand out just as a Cubs' fielder was poised to catch an out ball.

He blocked the catch, and the shaken Cubs proceeded to drop from a 3–0 lead to an 8–3 defeat…. Mr. Bartman's ill-fated intervention—for which he has humbly apologised—has brought down a wave of contempt on his head, from abuse and spitting by fellow fans in Wrigley Field stadium as he was escorted out on Tuesday to a campaign to ridicule him on the internet.

One Cubs fan parodied an FBI "Ten most wanted" poster on the net with Mr. Bartman's picture on it.

"Considered ignorant and extremely stupid," the poster reads. "Wanted for "interfering with crucial play … breaking the heart of an entire city.""[7]

Through a family friend, Bartman issued the following public statement to the media in which he accepted blame for what had transpired:

There are few words to describe how awful I feel and what I have experienced within these last 24 hours. I've been a Cub fan all my life and fully understand the relationship between my actions and the outcome of the game. I had my eyes glued on the approaching ball the entire time and was so caught up in the moment that I did not even see Moises Alou, much less that he may have had a play. Had I thought for one second that the ball was playable or had I seen Alou approaching I would have done whatever I could to get out of the way and give Alou a chance to make the catch. To Moises Alou, the Chicago Cubs organization, Ron Santo, Ernie Banks, and Cub fans everywhere I am so truly sorry from the bottom of this Cubs fan's broken heart. I ask that Cub fans everywhere redirect the negative energy that has been vented towards my family, my friends, and myself [sic] into the usual positive support for our beloved team on their way to being National League champs.[8]

There was still Game Seven to be played on Wednesday night to settle to NLCS. Florida jumped out to a quick 3–0 advantage in the top of the first inning, but the Cubs led 5–3 after three innings, giving some hope that Bartman's dubious place in MLB lore would be minimized. By the time the fifth inning was over, however, Florida was back on top, 6–5. They would extend their lead to 9–5. Chicago managed to get one run back, but the final score was 9–6 in favor of the Marlins. Florida advanced to the 2003 World Series, where they beat the New York Yankees. It was their second World Series title in the franchise's 11-year history, which hardly seemed fair given the Cubs' long championship drought.

The Cubs' defeat in the NLSC meant the heat was now fully on Bartman as he was widely perceived as the fan who cost the Cubs the 2003 NL pennant. His family got an unlisted phone number. For a time, Bartman, fearing for his safety, could not and would not leave his house or go to his job as a financial services advisor. He refused all interview requests and even opportunities to cash in substantially on his infamy. A business that specialized in sports collectibles offered Bartman $25,000 for a single autograph. Bartman also refused a six-figure payday to appear in a Super Bowl commercial. At the end of October, Steve Bartman–themed Halloween costumes—typically comprised of eyeglasses, a green turtleneck, a Cubs cap, and a transistor radio headset—were all the rage in Chicago. After some months had passed, false rumors circulated that Bartman had moved out of the country, perhaps to England, to start life anew. He had not. In 2005, an ESPN journalist stealthily tracked Bartman down to a parking lot adjacent to his place of employment in hopes of getting an interview. Bartman politely declined. Bartman, as of 2014, is reputedly still living in the Chicago area, is still a devoted Cubs fan, but has understandably never returned to Wrigley Field since Game Six of the 2003 NLCS.

The ball that Bartman had touched for a mere fraction of a second was sold to Harry Caray's restaurant that December for $113,824. Two months later the ball was symbolically tried and sentenced to death. Before it met its doom, the ball was amusingly given a last day of pampering at a luxury hotel—where it received a massage, among other niceties. On February 26, 2004, it was destroyed in a well-attended public ceremony at Harry Caray's at the hands of Michael Lantieri, a special-effects expert. In 2005, the tattered remnants of the ball were boiled. The steam was captured and used in preparing a special spaghetti sauce made by the restaurant.

As the Cubs' pennant drought continued for another decade—their last post-season win was Game Four of the 2003 NLCS—the anniversary of Bartman's moment in the spotlight was acknowledged each year. Numerous stories recounting what had happened in 2003 were rehashed on the Bartman Incident's tenth anniversary in 2013. Updates confirmed that Bartman remained as reclusive as ever. "He's happy and healthy and he's still a Cubs fan," said Frank Murtha, a longtime friend whom the *New York Times* identified as a spokesman for Bartman. "He values his privacy."[9] At that time, Cubs general manager Theo Epstein wanted to reach out to Bartman as a goodwill gesture in the hope of ending his decade-long public exile. Some fans think a Bartman public appearance at Wrigley Field, endorsed by the team, would be something of a cleansing ritual that might remove the bad mojo cursing MLB's oldest operating club. One anonymous poet contributed this sextain in the comments section of the *New York Times* after its tenth anniversary story appeared:

> A Cubs fan may yearn
> for Steve Bartman's return
> to Wrigley to banish the curse.
> But Steve's comeback won't help
> and the fans will still yelp
> and the team will get even worse.[10]

Others were not so magnanimous, or at least sensibly wondered about the type of reception Bartman would receive at Wrigley Field despite the passage of time. In a tenth-anniversary piece in the *New York Times*, *Chicago Sun-Times* columnist Rick Telander said of Cubs fans: "They'd rip him apart. He can't just waltz in when the Cubs are still losers and expect to be cheered."[11] Michael Wilbon, a passionate Cubs fan and a co-host on ESPN's popular *Pardon the Interruption*, was aghast at such an idea. "A Steve Bartman night? Are you kidding me?" Wilbon asked. "What does the organization have to gain by that? I'll tell you: Nothing!"[12]

To date, the Bartman Incident has been the focus of two documentary films: *Catching Hell*, produced by ESPN in 2011, and *5 Outs*, produced by Chicago's Comcast station in 2013. So compelling was Bartman's story that *Catching Hell* was one of the first documentaries produced in ESPN's acclaimed *30 for 30* series.

Some Cubs fans simply want to put the Bartman Incident aside and move on altogether. They believe the regular references and allusions to Steve Bartman are akin to cyberbullying. In response to the *New York Times*' 2013 story, one Bartman sympathizer in Hawaii replied, "Here's a story that didn't need to be written. At least Mr. Bartman is forewarned that the *Times* will write about him in 2023, 2033, 2043 and (the big one!) 2053—you know, just in case the world needs a reminder because it's moved on and put this silly matter in perspective. [The *Times*' anniversary story was] pointless, petty and mean-spirited, in a passive-aggressive way."[13]

Other fans firmly believe that the hand Bartman has been dealt is fully justified. "The guy deserves it," wrote one commenter on an online news story from October 2014 titled "Where is Steve Bartman?" "as he is everything that is typically wrong with humans—too self-centered. Keep your grubby little paws to yourself and back your team. You call yourself a lifelong fan and yet you're interfering with your own player? Anyone that does that no longer has the right to claim they [*sic*] are a fan."[14]

Plenty of baseball fans firmly believe that Bartman will be haunted by his one moment of baseball infamy to his grave and beyond, much like Fred Merkle has been since his famous 1908 baserunning blunder—a truly historic mistake that started a chain reaction that led to the most recent Chicago Cubs' World Series triumph. A 2012 post made on the Obstructedview.net sports website predicted, "Someday, at Steve Bartman's funeral, there will be some prick with an ESPN microphone shoving it in the face of any friend or family member too slow to avoid them, asking if Steve died regretting what he did in Game Six. Bank on it."[15]

Florida 8 at Chicago 3

Game played on Tuesday, October 14, 2003, at Wrigley Field

Florida Marlins	ab	r	h	rbi	Chicago Cubs	ab	r	h	rbi
Pierre cf	5	1	3	1	Lofton cf	5	1	1	0
Castillo 2b	4	1	1	0	Grudzielanek 2b	3	0	1	1
Rodriguez c	4	1	1	1	Sosa rf	4	1	3	1
Cabrera rf	5	1	1	0	Alou lf	4	0	2	0
Encarnacion rf	0	0	0	0	Ramirez 3b	4	0	1	0
Lee 1b	5	1	1	2	Simon 1b	2	0	0	0
Lowell 3b	3	1	0	0	Karros ph,1b	1	0	0	0
Conine lf	2	0	1	1	Gonzalez ss	3	0	0	0
Gonzalez ss	3	0	0	0	Alfonseca p	0	0	0	0
Fox p	0	0	0	0	Bako c	4	1	2	0
Hollandsworth ph	0	1	0	0	Prior p	2	0	0	0
Urbina p	0	0	0	0	Farnsworth p	0	0	0	0
Pavano p	2	0	0	0	Remlinger p	0	0	0	0
Willis p	0	0	0	0	Martinez ss	1	0	0	0
Mordecai ss	2	1	1	3					
Totals	35	8	9	8	Totals	33	3	10	2

Florida	**000 000 080—8 9 0**	
Chicago	**100 001 100—3 10 2**	

Florida Marlins	IP	H	R	ER	BB	SO
Pavano	5.2	7	2	2	1	5

Florida Marlins	IP	H	R	ER	BB	SO
Willis	1.0	1	1	1	1	2
Fox W (1–0)	0.1	2	0	0	0	0
Urbina	2.0	0	0	0	0	2
Totals	9.0	10	3	3	2	9
Chicago Cubs	IP	H	R	ER	BB	SO
Prior L (1–1)	7.1	6	5	3	3	6
Farnsworth	0.1	1	3	3	2	0
Remlinger	0.1	1	0	0	0	0
Alfonseca	1.0	1	0	0	0	0
Totals	9.0	9	8	6	5	6

E–Grudzielanek (2), Gonzalez (1). DP–Florida 2, Chicago 1. PB–Bako (2). 2B–Florida Pierre (1, off Prior); Lee (1, off Prior); Mordecai (1, off Farnsworth), Chicago Sosa (1, off Pavano). SF–Conine (2, off Farnsworth). IBB–Lowell (1, by Farnsworth); Hollandsworth (1, by Farnsworth). SH–Grudzielanek (2, off Pavano); Prior (3, off Willis). CS–Pierre (3, 2nd base by Prior/Bako). WP–Willis (1), Prior (1). IBB–Farnsworth 2 (2, Lowell, Hollandsworth). U–Mike Reilly, Jerry Crawford, Chuck Meriwether, Fieldin Culbreth, Larry Poncino, Mike Everitt. T–3:00. A–39,577.

August 7, 2007

Site: AT&T Park, San Francisco

Teams: Washington Nationals vs. San Francisco Giants

Significance: Barry Bonds' 756th Career Home Run

Impact: Baseball's most cherished record falls to a player widely suspected of using performance-enhancing drugs

> "[Barry] Bonds inspires a like amount of passion from both sides of the fence. For many, Bonds belongs beside Babe Ruth and Hank Aaron in baseball's holy trinity; for others, he embodies all that is wrong with the modern athlete: aloof, arrogant, alienated."—part of a reader's online review of Jeff Pearlman's 2006 book, *Love Me, Hate Me: Barry Bonds and the Making of an Antihero*

> "How had it come to this? Once a spindly 185-pound leadoff hitter, Bonds had reinvented himself as the second coming of Babe Ruth. Three years earlier he had been an afterthought in the race between [Mark] McGwire and Sammy Sosa to break Roger Maris's single-season home-run mark. Now he was altering the modern definition of a power hitter."—baseball author Jeff Pearlman, describing Barry Bonds in 2001

> "Doctors ought to quit worrying about what ballplayers are taking. What players take doesn't matter. It's nobody else's business. The doctors should spend their time looking for cures for cancer. It takes more than muscles to hit homers. If all those guys were using stuff, how come they're not all hitting homers?"—Barry Bonds, as quoted in a May 21, 2002, *Associated Press* story

> "I think a lot of people are watching too much Court TV and they think the only way that something is established as fact is if you have a DNA test or a confession. Those things are helpful. But people have gone to jail, with no doubt, for long periods of time without either of those two factors if you have enough evidence that is substantial and convincing. There is a mountain of said evidence against Barry Bonds. If you are a reasonable person—not a malicious person and not living in San Francisco and blinded by your own fandom—you already know."—renowned baseball announcer Bob Costas on MSNBC's July 30, 2007, *Morning Joe* program, when asked, "Will we ever know for a fact that Barry Bonds took steroids?"

Never had a more important event in MLB history been treated with such contempt and disdain.

In 1974 Hank Aaron's breaking of Babe Ruth's career home run record was widely celebrated throughout baseball. Apart from the vitriolic racist element who resented a black man surpassing a notable white man in any endeavor, Aaron was overwhelmingly lauded as a sports hero. He received record amounts of fan mail and earned a place in baseball history.

Thirty-three years later, the atmosphere was markedly different as Barry Bonds eclipsed Aaron's record. The whole escapade was something of an embarrassment to MLB, and when it did occur there was little celebration outside of San Francisco. Fans, for the most part, smelled a rat and could not stomach another one of MLB's touchstone records falling amid the specter of performance-enhancing drugs.

Barry Bonds himself was not exactly a warm and embraceable personality. Taciturn, standoffish, moody, short-tempered, petulant, self-centered, truculent and arrogant were apt adjectives that best described him during the final decade of his unique MLB career. Certainly other baseball stars from the past had been far from beloved figures—Ty Cobb easily comes to mind—but Bonds was reviled in many MLB cities for his dramatic and highly suspect slugging statistics that came at a time in Bonds' life when most MLB players are in decline because of advancing age. The one-of-a-kind Bonds seemed to be uniquely improving as he approached his 40th birthday. His numbers were either unbelievable in the positive sense of the word or not to be believed in the negative sense. In an interview on MSNBC's *Morning Joe* program, Bob Costas explained what was deeply troubling him and many other passionate baseball fans as Bonds moved within striking distance of Hank Aaron's cherished record of 755 career homers in the summer of 2007:

> You're not supposed to go, at age 38, from a lifetime batting average of .290 and all of a sudden hit .370 and .362. You're not supposed to have a lifetime slugging percentage of .556—which is good but nowhere near the top of the list—then slug .863, and have two other seasons over .800 and one at .799 in your late thirties and early forties. It's incredible to maintain a high level of performance when most players are declining, let alone to improve stratospherically over anything you've ever done with an established pattern of performance for 13 or 14 years or anyone in the whole history of the game has ever done. If those statistics can be taken at face value, Barry Bonds is not only the greatest baseball player of all time, he is a greater baseball player than Michael Jordan was a basketball player or Tiger Woods was a golfer. I choose not to believe them.

Seven years later, in an especially scathing rant, ESPN's Keith Olbermann opined on his nightly program that Bonds' stats were "as meaningless as video-game numbers" and "as dishonest as the North Korean presidential-election results."

Barry Bonds certainly arrived on this planet having the DNA of outstanding athletic potential within him and waiting to be tapped. His father, Bobby, was a longtime MLB outfielder, spending time on the rosters of nine teams in a 14-year career that ended in 1981. The senior Bonds compiled a lifetime batting average of .268 and hit 332 home runs. Ten times Bobby surpassed the 20-home-run mark in a season. (In a marvelous coincidence, Bobby watched as Hank Aaron's 755th and final home run sailed over his head in 1976.) Barry's aunt, Rosie Bonds, was a member of the 1964 U.S. Olympic team. She finished eighth in the 80-metre hurdles in Tokyo. Hall of Fame slugger Reggie Jackson is a distant cousin of Bonds. Although there is no direct family connection between them, Willie Mays—a former teammate of Bobby—is Barry Bonds' godfather.

Bonds' baseball skills were obvious even when he was a high school student. He batted .467 in his senior year. The San Francisco Giants drafted him as an 18-year-old in 1982, but Bonds insisted on a $75,000 deal—$5,000 more than the Giants were prepared to pay him. Unable to reach an agreement, Bonds opted to attend Arizona State University, a school known for producing MLB-caliber players. Bonds continued that tradition, batting .367 in one NCAA season and .368 in another. As a sophomore, Bonds connected for a record-tying seven consecutive hits in the 1984 College World Series. He graduated with a degree in criminology.

In the 1985 MLB draft, Bonds was selected by the woeful Pittsburgh Pirates, who won just 57 games that season. He was the sixth overall pick. In 1986 he rapidly advanced up the Pirates' minor-league ladder. After short stints with the Prince William Pirates of the Carolina League and the Hawaii Islanders of the Pacific Coast League, on May 30, 1986, Bonds made his MLB debut with Pittsburgh. By the end of that debut season, Bonds had swatted 16 home runs and stolen 36 bases. Judging by his 65 bases on balls, Bonds had quickly acquired the deserved reputation of a batter who was best avoided, if at all possible. He finished sixth in the NL Rookie of the Year voting. Bonds was certainly a key figure in resurrecting baseball interest in Pittsburgh. After two dismal seasons at the turnstiles when the Pirates drew fewer than 10,000 fans per game to Three Rivers Stadium, Bonds was an exciting star attraction. In 1986 the Pirates drew slightly over one million people to watch their home games. Record crowds were on hand for the team's home openers in both 1987 and 1988. In 1990 and 1991, Pittsburgh drew in excess of two million fans, smashing the club's old attendance record of more than 1.7 million customers set in the World Series championship season of 1960.

As a rookie, Bonds initially played center field and typically batted leadoff as he was tabbed a stolen-base threat. In 1987 Bonds was shifted to left field to make room in center for another promising newcomer, Andy Van Slyke. The Pirates were a talented bunch, but they somewhat resembled the battling Oakland A's from the early 1970s. They played superbly and won a lot of games, but they did not especially get along well with one another. Despite the chilly interpersonal relationships on the team, Pittsburgh won National League East titles in 1990, 1991, and 1992, ending a long championship drought dating back to the Pirates' 1979 World Series triumph. However, they failed each time to advance to the World Series. In the final game of the 1992 NLCS, Bonds was the last Pirate to throw a baseball, coming up short in his effort to gun down Atlanta's Sid Bream at the plate as he slid home with the dramatic series-winning run. Thus concluded Barry Bonds' tenure with the Pittsburgh Pirates.

Bonds was often perceived as greedy and overpaid, both in Pittsburgh and beyond. During the Gulf War, a newspaper cartoon graphically compared how little an average American soldier was paid—alongside a list of the selfless and important tasks he was expected to fulfill—compared to Bonds' demand for $10 million per season just to play baseball. Bonds' lone job skill was succinctly listed as "Hits ball with stick."

Still, if any one ballplayer deserved to be paid exorbitantly, it was Barry Bonds. He put up consistently solid numbers each year in winning the National League MVP Award in both 1990 and 1992. With Pittsburgh unwilling to match Bonds' escalating salary demands, Bonds opted for free agency and signed with the San Francisco Giants in 1993. His contract paid him a record $43.75 million for six seasons. In a spectacular moment of hubris, Bonds asked for uniform number 24—the number Willie Mays had famously worn for more than 20 seasons as the Giants' greatest star. It, of course, had been retired by the team. Mays himself was okay with the idea of permitting his godson to ·wear his old number, but the public was not. The overwhelming negative sentiment caused Bonds to withdraw the request. Instead he would opt for number 25—the number his father had worn as a Giant.

From 1993 to 2000, Bonds recorded steady *and* spectacular numbers with the Giants. He smacked 46 homers and drove in 123 runs in his first season with San Francisco, good enough for his third NL MVP award. He had 37 home runs in 1994 when the season was canceled in mid–August because of a labor dispute. In 1995 Bonds declined to a mere 33 home runs and finished 12th in MVP voting. In 1996 Bonds became the first NL member of baseball's rare 40/40 club (accruing at least 40 home runs and 40 stolen bases in a single season). By 1999 Bonds was recognized as one of the truly elite baseball players ever to take the field. Bill James, SABR's most esteemed number-cruncher, rated Bonds as the best player of the 1990s. "When people begin to take in all of his accomplishments," James declared in 1999, "Bonds may well be rated among the five greatest players in the history of the game." High praise, indeed.

Individual achievements were always in the forefront of Bonds' MLB career—and he had plenty of trophies to put on his mantel and staggering batting stats that dominated record books. He was a 14-time All-Star and an eight-time Gold Glove Award winner. Seven times Bonds was named the NL's MVP, including a remarkable string of four consecutive awards from 2001 through 2004. No one else has ever done that. Bonds, of course, holds numerous MLB offensive records. Most prominent are most home runs in a single season (73), most career walks received (2,558), and most career intentional walks received (688). Bonds' crowning achievement is most career home runs (762).

Like most major leaguers, Bonds became a less productive home-run hitter in his mid-thirties. He recorded 37 and 34 home runs in 1998 and 1999 respectively, but injuries could account for this power decline. Then something peculiar started to happen: Bonds seemed rejuvenated. He put up numbers that were far different than one would expect from a typical aging slugger. In 2000 he hit 49 home runs, a career high to that point. In 2001, at age 37, Bonds broke Mark McGwire's single-season home-run record set just three years before with the unworldly total of 73. It was a 49 percent increase over his previous best total. Eyebrows were raised—and for good reason. Anyone could plainly see that the buffed Barry Bonds of 2001 did not resemble the tapered Bonds who had patrolled the outfield for Pittsburgh. Few athletes in the history of sports had ever reached the peak of their prowess so late in life. (Boxer Archie Moore, whose true age had always been a bit of a mystery, had won the world light heavyweight title at age 36—or perhaps 39. Even then—and with a decade-long title reign ahead of him—Moore was certainly not the fighter he had been a few years earlier.) In baseball Mickey Mantle and Joe DiMaggio had both retired before their 38th birthdays because they could no longer be the ballplayers they once were. Bonds' surliness was highlighted by *Sports Illustrated* that season with a cover photo of Bonds alongside the telling caption "I'm Barry Bonds … and you're not."

As the 2007 MLB season progressed, more and more attention was focused on how Bonds was inching towards the all-time home-run record of 755 held by Hank Aaron. Much of it was innuendo, but it was damning innuendo to be sure. Based on records obtained from the Giants' and Pirates' clubhouse attendants, in May ESPN announced that over the course of Barry Bonds' MLB career from age 22 to 43, his shirt size had ballooned from 42" to 52", his shoe size had grown from 10½ to 13, and his hat size had expanded from 7⅛ to 7¾. The general consensus among baseball fans was that Bonds had turned himself into a human chemistry experiment. Bonds credited his improved physique to flaxseed oil.

In 2006 and 2007, at just about every MLB ballpark (with the exception of San

Francisco's, where Bonds adulation was unabated) Bonds was heckled mercilessly, verbally and via creative signage. Critics held up placards featuring syringe motifs. One enormous banner that extended across dozens of outfield seats posed this question: "Ruth did it on hot dogs and beer. Aaron did it with class. How did you do it?" A Mets fan displayed a sign that said, "Hey Barroid…. Not in our park!" Some fans preferred minimalism: Placards with giant asterisks. Others showed their contempt for the soon-to-be all-time home run champ by conspicuously snubbing him. They simply turned their backs towards the field whenever Bonds came to bat. Bonds seemed unmoved and undaunted. He steadfastly kept on homering and equaled Hank Aaron's career mark of 755 homers in San Diego on August 4 with a shot off pitcher Clay Hensley. The soon-to-be-deposed, 73-year-old Aaron graciously refused to become embroiled in any PED debates, but nevertheless Aaron was not especially interested in being on hand when his record fell.

The history-making moment occurred on a Tuesday night, August 7, 2007, at San Francisco's AT&T Park at 8:51 p.m. The unfashionable Washington Nationals were the visiting team, but it did not matter which NL club was the opposition—the ballpark was going to be sold out. Bonds had a perfect night at the plate (3-for-3). He doubled and singled and scored two runs as the Nats and Giants headed to the bottom of the fifth inning locked in a 4–4 tie. Mike Bacsik, a 29-year-old, journeyman left-hander who was back in the majors after a two-year absence, was on the mound for Washington. Bacsik's pitch to Bonds on a full count sailed down the pipe. Bonds got all of it and sent it to the deepest part of right field. There was no doubt it was gone. The next day on National Public Radio, Jon Miller, who had called the game for ESPN, recalled the scene when it became obvious that Bonds had connected for home run number 756: "Thousands of camera flashes lit up the ballpark. There was an armada of nautical craft—kayaks, rowboats, motorboats—out in McCovey Cove in San Francisco Bay [with fans] hoping to catch the ball. Fireworks shot off … and the place just basically went nuts for a while."

Here's how NPR's website, in a story written by Richard Gonzalez, reported the happening the next morning:

Barry Bonds hit his 756th career home run Tuesday night, surpassing Hank Aaron and landing himself in the Major League baseball record books.

The San Francisco Giants' slugger made the record-breaking hit at AT&T Park in San Francisco, shattering Aaron's record that stood for more than 30 years.

After tying the record at Petco Park in San Diego over the weekend, Bonds said the hard part was over, but on his first night back in San Francisco Monday, Bonds went hitless in three at-bats with one walk against the Washington Nationals.

Then, in Tuesday's game, with a capacity crowd of more than 45,000 people standing every time he approached the batter's box, Bonds hit a double in the second inning and a single in the third.

Then, in the fifth inning he launched a three-ball-two-strike pitch to the deepest part of park, some 435 feet from home plate—a solo home run.

As Bonds rounded the bases suppressing a smile, his teammates and family streamed out to greet him. Fireworks showered the field and an errant fan ran across left field, only to be mercilessly tackled by a group of security guards.

The game was stopped for 10 minutes for a tribute to Bonds, highlighted by a videotaped congratulatory message from the man whose home-run record had been surpassed.

Aaron was barely audible above the crowd's cheers and surprise. The former all-time home-run leader had let it be known that he had little interest in being present when Bonds broke his 33-year-old record. Yet, graciously offering his best wishes, Aaron said he hoped Bonds' "achievement would inspire others to chase their own dreams."

In a news conference after the game, a relaxed and smiling Bonds was obviously moved.

Aaron's congratulations "meant everything. It meant absolutely everything," Bonds said. "We all admire

Hank Aaron. We all have a lot of respect for him. Right now, everything is just hitting me so fast. I'm lost for words … but it was absolutely the best," he said.

Conspicuous in his absence was Baseball Commissioner Bud Selig. Instead, he sent Hall-of-Famer Frank Robinson as his representative. Selig did phone in his congratulations to Bonds, a gesture the slugger said he accepted.

If the message of the commissioner's absence was to suggest that Bonds' record is tainted by allegations of steroid use, it was flatly rejected by the new record-holder.

"This record is not tainted at all. At all. Period," Bonds said.

As for the man who delivered the decisive pitch, Washington's Mike Bacsik said he was disappointed to give up the home run. Bacsick said he was trying to challenge Bonds by throwing down and away, but left the ball over the plate.

"I dreamed of this as a kid. Unfortunately, I dreamed that I would be the one hitting the home run," he said.

As for the ball itself, it wound up in the hands of 22-year-old Matt Murphy of Queens, NY. He was bloodied and his clothes torn as security guards hustled him and his prize ball out of the park. The ball is estimated to be worth at least $500,000.

Bonds left the game after the historic swat, being removed in a double-switch. The home run gave the Giants a 5–4 lead which they increased to 6–4 after seven innings. However, Washington rallied for four runs off three Giants pitchers in the top of the eighth inning to win the game, 8–6. (Bacsik, who got a no-decision instead of a loss because of his team's late rally, asked for and got an autographed bat from Bonds after the game. Bacsik would vanish from MLB after the 2007 season. Today he is a proud advocate of nudism.) Four other players hit homers that Tuesday night in San Francisco—but nobody was especially interested in those home run balls. Bonds went on to hit six more home runs in 2007 to up his lifetime total to 762, but an odyssey surrounded the home run ball that Bonds whacked on August 7.

Matt Murphy, the bloodied and battered fan who ended up with the valuable baseball, sold it to the highest bidder via an online auction. The winner was a fashion designer and New York Yankees fan named Marc Ecko, who paid more than three-quarters-of-a-million dollars for it. Ecko—who was absolutely no admirer of the Giants' star outfielder—wanted to make a personal statement about the authenticity of Bonds' achievement. Ecko told ESPN.com,

I was in the middle of a late night here in my office with a little too much to drink and my friends around me debating the record and its validity. We were yelling at each other and getting emotional about it. I said, "Guys, I'm getting that ball and we'll let America settle the debate." It was clear that MLB wasn't going to make a statement on the ball, so we decided we were going to make a statement.

Accordingly Ecko conducted an online poll to determine what should be done with the ball. More than ten million electronic votes were registered before the announced deadline. The majority of voters chose Option #1: Engrave an asterisk on the ball and donate it to the National Baseball Hall of Fame in Cooperstown, NY. (The other two, less-popular options were to donate the ball to Cooperstown unmarked or blast it to the moon.) The poll's results were announced on NBC's *The Today Show* on September 26. When Bonds learned of the voting public's red-asterisk decision, he angrily denounced Ecko as "an idiot" and vowed to boycott the Hall of Fame.

There was some dispute over whether the Hall of Fame would accept a deliberately "defaced" artifact, and whether Ecko was loaning or donating the item. In the end the Hall accepted the ball, knowing full well it would not have been donated otherwise. It features a prominent red asterisk just above the MLB logo, inscribed by a master engraver. Hall of Fame president Dale Petroskey said accepting the ball did not mean the Hall of

Fame necessarily endorsed Ecko's viewpoint that Barry Bonds had used performance-enhancing drugs to attain the home-run record. "This ball wouldn't be coming to Cooperstown if Marc hadn't bought it from the fan who caught it and then let the fans have their say," Petroskey told the *Associated Press*. "We're delighted to have the ball. It's a piece of baseball history."[1]

As the 2007 season wound down, the Giants announced they would not be re-signing Bonds for 2008. Accordingly, Bonds filed for free agency in late October. "I am anticipating widespread interest from every MLB team,"[2] Bonds' agent, Jeff Borris, optimistically told the media. Despite Bonds being within reasonable striking distance of attaining more important career milestones—including the MLB records for most career extra-base hits and most runs scored—not a single MLB team offered Bonds a contract for 2008.

Washington 8 at San Francisco 6

Game played on Tuesday, August 7, 2007, at AT&T Park

Washington Nationals	ab	r	h	rbi	San Francisco Giants	ab	r	h	rbi
Lopez ss	4	1	3	2	Davis cf, lf	5	1	2	0
Belliard 2b	3	1	1	0	Klesko 1b	5	0	0	0
Zimmerman 3b	4	0	1	1	Winn rf	5	0	1	1
Young 1b	5	0	0	0	Bonds lf	3	3	3	1
Rauch p	0	0	0	0	Sanchez p	0	0	0	0
Cordero p	0	0	0	0	Correia p	0	0	0	0
Kearns rf	4	2	2	2	Messenger p	0	0	0	0
Church lf	3	0	0	0	Molina c	4	1	2	3
Langerhans lf	1	0	0	0	Durham 2b	3	1	0	0
Schneider c	4	2	1	1	Feliz 3b	4	0	2	0
Logan cf	4	1	1	1	Frandsen ss	4	0	0	0
Bacsik p	2	0	0	0	Zito p	2	0	0	1
Flores ph	1	0	0	0	Roberts cf	2	0	0	0
Schroder p	0	0	0	0					
Batista ph,1b	1	1	1	1					
Totals	36	8	10	8	Totals	37	6	10	6

Washington	003 100 040—8	10 1
San Francisco	022 010 100—6	10 1

Washington Nationals	IP	H	R	ER	BB	SO
Bacsik	5.0	7	5	5	1	5
Schroder W (1–0)	2.0	2	1	1	0	2
Rauch	1.0	1	0	0	0	1
Cordero SV (24)	1.0	0	0	0	0	0
Totals	9.0	10	6	6	1	8

San Francisco Giants	IP	H	R	ER	BB	SO
Zito	5.0	6	4	4	3	2
Sanchez	2.1	1	2	2	2	2
Correia L (1–6)	0.0	3	2	2	1	0
Messenger	1.2	0	0	0	0	1
Totals	9.0	10	8	8	6	5

E–Lopez (10), Feliz (6). 2B–Washington Kearns (24, off Sanchez); Lopez (20, off Correia), San Francisco Bonds (12, off Bacsik); Davis (3, off Schroder); Feliz (18, off Rauch). 3B–Washington Zimmerman (3, off Zito). HR–Washington Lopez (7, 3rd inning off Zito 0 on 0 out); Kearns (9, 3rd inning off Zito 1 on 2 out); Schneider (6, 4th inning off Zito 0 on 0 out), San Francisco Molina (12, 3rd inning off Bacsik 1 on 2 out); Bonds (22, 5th inning off Bacsik 0 on 1 out). SF–Zimmerman (3, off Messenger). IBB–Kearns (4, by Zito); Belliard (1, by Correia). SH–Sanchez (1, off Schroder). SB–Lopez (16, 3rd base off Zito/Molina); Belliard (2, 2nd base off Zito/Molina); Logan (15, 3rd base off Correia/Molina). U-HP–John Hirschbeck, 1B–Wally Bell, 2B–Laz Diaz, 3B–Bill Welke. T–3:12. A–43,154.

June 2, 2010

Site: Comerica Park, Detroit

Teams: Cleveland Indians vs. Detroit Tigers

Significance: Jim Joyce's Blown Call

Impact: An inopportune blown call heightens the demand for use of video review to assist MLB umpires to get calls right

> "A baseball diamond is, most simply, the intersecting of four 90-foot baselines—and, most powerfully, the intersecting of seemingly random lives. At first base at Comerica Park on June 2, [2010], [Jim] Joyce and Detroit pitcher Armando Galarraga, the ball in his glove and his right foot on the bag after taking a throw from first baseman Miguel Cabrera, met for what should have been the 27th out of the 21st perfect game in baseball history. Only the formality of the out call by Joyce, the first base umpire, remained. What happened next changed their lives and may well do the same to baseball, at least to the sacrosanct manner in which out and safe have been determined since the game's inception."—Tom Verducci, *Sports Illustrated* (June 14, 2010)

> "If by now you are not in favor of Major League Baseball drastically overhauling its instant replay protocols, you are as blind as Jim Joyce was Wednesday night."—Jeff Passan, Yahoo! Sports

> "While the human element has always been an integral part of baseball, it is vital that mistakes on the field be addressed. Given last night's call and other recent events, I will examine our umpiring system, the expanded use of instant replay and all other related features."—MLB Commissioner Bud Selig (June 3, 2010)

> "That game changed baseball history. It's easy to argue we don't have instant replay today without that game, and that call."—Will Leitch, of sportsonearth.com, on the fourth anniversary of Jim Joyce's infamously bad call

The most talked-about MLB game of the 2010 season was not a World Series clash or even any post-season matchup. It occurred at Detroit's Comerica Park on Wednesday, June 2, 2010, before a small gathering of 17,738 fans who had come to see their Detroit Tigers, the second-place team in the American League Central division, play the bottom-rung Cleveland Indians. Before the night was over, a little-known Detroit pitcher and a veteran MLB umpire would be the talk of the entire sports world. Remarkably, instead of a horribly bad situation mushrooming, within 17 hours both men would be widely championed as displaying the best ideals of sportsmanship. Moreover, the villain would oddly transform into a heroic figure.

Both teams' starting pitchers were strong that night. Cleveland's Fausto Carmona, a right-hander, was looking to regain the form he had shown in 2007 when he won 19 games for the Tribe. (Interestingly, Carmona was guarding a secret: his true name was Roberto Hernandez. He was using the pseudonym as a ruse to play under a false birth certificate to chop three years off his age. He would use his real name starting in 2012.) Through seven innings Carmona had allowed just one run—a second-inning solo homer by Miguel Cabrera. Even better was Detroit's Armando Galarraga, a 28-year-old native of Venezuela. A journeyman of sorts, Galarraga, also a right-hander, had meandered his way through the farm systems of the Montreal Expos and Texas Rangers before being dealt to Detroit. He had compiled a mediocre 20–18 record through his first three seasons in the majors. On this night, though, Galarraga was untouchable.

Through eight innings, Cleveland had failed to get a runner safely to first base. Galarraga was three outs from the rarest and most coveted of all pitching achievements— a perfect game. The Tigers scored twice in the bottom of the eighth inning to pad their lead to 3–0. With Galarraga pitching so well, the insurance runs seemed to seal the win for Detroit. Now everyone's attention was focused on the lanky hurler's attempt to add his name to the pages of MLB's history books.

The perfect game at the major league level is elusive because it requires a combination of both excellence and luck. No hurler can be expected simply to overpower a lineup of MLB hitters as a Little Leaguer with a blazing fastball might. The quality of the opposition dictates that balls will often be put into play and patient hitters may be disciplined enough to draw an occasional walk. Add into the equation the possibility of bad bounces, fielding miscues, and human nervousness, and the perfect game becomes even less likely. Although there has been a recent glut in their frequency—there were three during the 2012 season alone—MLB perfect games are treasured because of their overall infrequency. Entire decades have come and gone without a perfect game occurring. None occurred in the 1930s, 1940s or 1970s. Going into June 2, 2010, there had been just 20 perfect games in all MLB history, although remarkably there had already been two in 2010. Roy Halladay of the Philadelphia Phillies had thrown one just four days earlier in Miami versus the Florida Marlins. Dallas Braden of the Oakland A's had also thrown one on May 9 versus the Tampa Bay Rays.

Detroit made a defensive change to start the ninth inning. To bolster Galarraga's defensive support, Tigers manager Jim Leyland inserted the more mobile Don Kelly in left field to replace aging veteran Johnny Damon. The first batter, Mark Grudzielanek, playing in the next-to-last game of his 15-year MLB career, drove the first pitch he saw not to left field, but to deep center field. Speedy Tigers center fielder Austin Jackson chased the ball down and made a spectacular, over-the-shoulder catch at the edge of the warning track to preserve Galarraga's perfect game. Although few people recall it now, had things unfolded as they should have, Jackson's catch would be remembered today as one of the truly clutch grabs in MLB history.

Next up was Cleveland's 39-year-old catcher, Mike Redmond. (Redmond's MLB career would also conclude shortly.). Redmond hit a routine ground ball to Tigers shortstop Ramon Santiago. Santiago fielded the ball cleanly and fired it to first baseman Miguel Cabrera in plenty of time. The soon-to-be-infamous Jim Joyce called Redmond out. Galarraga was one out away from baseball immortality.

The crowd was understandably in a frenzy. No Detroit Tigers pitcher had ever achieved a perfect game in the team's 110-year history, although two had come within one out of the rare feat. The Tigers had once been on the losing end of a perfect game. Back on April 30, 1922, Charlie Robertson of the Chicago White Sox retired all 27 batters he faced at Detroit's Navin Field. Detroit's lineup that day featured Ty Cobb and Harry Heilmann. It was an especially surprising feat. Robertson, a very mediocre MLB pitcher who compiled a career 49–80 won-lost record, was strongly accused of doctoring the ball with an oily substance that day. Six days after Don Larsen became the next AL pitcher to achieve the feat during the 1956 World Series, the 60-year-old Robertson was recruited from his home in Texas to be a contestant on the popular TV show *What's My Line?*

Jason Donald, Cleveland's 25-year-old, rookie shortstop, was the next batter. In Donald's two previous at-bats he had grounded out and lined out. On a 1–1 count, Donald hit a soft ground ball between second and first base. Tigers first baseman Miguel Cabrera moved well to his right, deftly fielded the ball, and made a careful sidearmed toss to Galarraga, who had alertly hustled over to cover first base. Replays show that Donald was out by close to a step. Fifty-four-year-old Jim Joyce, an MLB umpire since 1987 and rated as one of the sport's best officials, inexplicably muffed the call even though he was in the ideal position to see the play clearly. He emphatically signaled Donald safe at first base. *Sports Illustrated*'s Tom Verducci called it "the most heartbreaking call in baseball history."

MLB history records several other occasions where perfect games had been cruelly thwarted by the 27th batter. In two of them umpiring was a key factor. On July 4, 1908, in the first game of a doubleheader at Philadelphia, Hooks Wiltse of the New York Giants retired the first 26 Phillies who came to bat before facing the opposing pitcher, George McQuillan, who also had pitched scoreless baseball. On a 1–2 pitch, Wiltse threw what appeared to be strike three. However, it was controversially called a ball by plate umpire Cy Rigler, who later admitted that he blew the call. Wiltse's next pitch plunked McQuillan to end his bid for perfection. Wiltse settled for a ten-inning no-hitter when the Giants finally scored a run for him. Rigler reputedly spent years buying Wiltse cigars to atone for his mistake. On September 2, 1972, Milt Pappas of the Chicago Cubs lost his perfect game by surrendering a debatable walk to San Diego's Larry Stahl. (To his dying day Pappas maintained that three of the four balls called by second-year umpire Bruce Froemming should have been ruled strikes.) Video of the game shows Froemming smirking at the enraged Pappas. Aside from Rigler's admitted blunder and Pappas' long-standing beef with Froemming, neither of those two games nor any of the other half dozen close-but-no-cigar pitching efforts unraveled in the egregious manner that Galarraga's did, though.

Under the limited replay rules of 2010, Jim Joyce's call could not be changed despite the overwhelming video evidence that it was wrong. The perfect game—and even the lesser no-hitter—instantly vanished. Instead, Galarraga became the tenth pitcher in MLB history to lose a perfect game with two out in the ninth inning. Official scorer Chuck Klonke had to rule the play a hit. Without an obvious bobble or mishandling of the ball, there was little else he could call. An error would have preserved the no-hitter, but there was nothing to suggest a defensive error had occurred. The only error involved in the play was Jim Joyce's faulty call.

Galarraga was ready to celebrate his terrific achievement when the impact of Joyce's call hit him. Maintaining an admirable sense of poise and grace, Galarraga gave Joyce a perplexed look and then a wry smile. "I wanted to argue but I was in shock," the pitcher said afterward. "I'm serious."[1] Other members of the Tigers were not nearly as cheerful about the obvious mistake. At first manager Leyland—who had recently stated in an interview that he was opposed to managers arguing judgment calls simply for the sake of arguing them—slowly came onto the field to contest the play with Joyce in a respectfully restrained manner. He, of course, had not yet seen the replay to know for certain that Joyce had booted the call badly. One batter later, after Trevor Crowe grounded out to end the game, civility broke down. Third baseman Brandon Inge was sprawled on the ground in despair as if the Tigers had just lost a crucial game.

By that time everyone in the Tigers' dugout had been informed that Donald should have been ruled out. The fans were furious and Joyce was besieged by angry Tigers. (How often to you see a team livid after winning a home game, 3–0?) Stadium security personnel were mustered to get the umpires safely to their dressing room. Once he was away from the howling mob, Joyce knew what he had to do: he asked to see a replay of Jason Donald's grounder. "After I heard from the Tigers, who had obviously seen a replay, I asked the guy in the [video] room to cue up the play as soon as we got in," Joyce said, "and I missed it from here to that wall. I had a great angle, and I missed the call."[2] Joyce had deprived a struggling young pitcher of a deserved spot in baseball history. He was devastated. He watched the replay only once. He did not have to see it multiple times.

To his everlasting credit, Joyce did not shy away from the responsibility of being held accountable. "It was the biggest call of my career," an emotional Joyce told reporters shortly thereafter, "and I kicked it. I just cost that kid a perfect game. This wasn't just *a* call; this was a history call."[3]

Indeed, Joyce felt so awful about his blunder that after the game was over he asked to meet with Galarraga—a highly irregular action. Given the circumstances, though, it was totally understandable. Tigers president/general manager Dave Dombrowski personally brought Galarraga from the Tigers' clubhouse into the umpires' room. Dombrowski stayed for the short meeting.

"He [Joyce] asked if he could see Armando and I brought Armando in there," Dombrowski said later, "and [Joyce] apologized profusely to him and he said he just felt terrible. They hugged each other and Armando said, 'I understand.'" "When I saw him," Galarraga told *SI*, "he was red, like a tomato. He hugged me right away. Not even one word."

Dombrowski was one of the first people to sympathize with Joyce's plight. "I feel terrible. I don't know why life works this way, but sometimes life just isn't fair for people. He's a good umpire."[4] Dombrowski's opinion of Joyce was backed up by an ESPN poll that was released later that month. A survey of 100 MLB players ranked Joyce as the best umpire by a fairly wide margin. Joyce got 53 percent of the vote. Tim McClelland had the second-highest total with a distant 34 percent.

Galarraga continued to be gracious far beyond what might have been expected. Said Galarraga, "He [Joyce] understands. I give him a lot of credit for coming in and saying, 'Hey, I need to talk to you to say I'm sorry.' That doesn't happen. You don't see an umpire after the game come out and say, 'Hey, let me tell you I'm sorry.' He apologized to me and he felt really bad. He didn't even shower. He was in the same clothes. He gave me a couple hugs."[5] Galarraga's "imperfect game" was making him far more famous than many hurlers who were actually credited with achieving the rare feat.

Things would get more interesting for Joyce over the next few hours. The Indians and Tigers concluded their series with a day game on Thursday. Joyce was scheduled to work the plate. He and his family were already receiving threats from irate baseball fans everywhere. Joyce left the ballpark and drove to his elderly mother's home in Toledo, OH, as he always did when working a series in Detroit. Because the game had lasted only 104 minutes, 86-year-old Ellouise Joyce was surprised to see her son at her door so early. She had not watched the game. She knew nothing about what had occurred a few hours earlier at Comerica Park.

"Ellouise may have been the last person on earth who hadn't heard," noted *SI*'s Verducci with a smidgen of hyperbole. "Her previously anonymous son had become the hottest search item on Google, displacing a porn actor who allegedly murdered a colleague with a samurai sword." Hate-filled rants directed towards Joyce flooded cyberspace. An anti–Joyce Facebook page was created shortly after the game ended. Similarly, the website firejimjoyce.com was launched. "I worked with Don Denkinger, and I know what he went through, but I've never had a moment like this,"[6] Joyce said. Denkinger's blown call in the 1985 World Series remains the most ill-timed umpiring miscue ever, but the Internet was not around in the mid–1980s to torment him.

Opinions about Jim Joyce and "The Call" flooded in from the sports world and points beyond. It became the lead story on NBC's *Today Show*. President Obama expressed his desire that MLB would adopt greater use of instant replay to avoid similar calamities. The Iron Sheik, a former professional wrestling villain, professed in a profanity-laced video rant on YouTube a strong desire to physically abuse the arbiter and "make him humble." St. Louis Cardinals manager Tony LaRussa weighed in too; he hoped MLB Commissioner Bud Selig would take the extraordinary and unprecedented step of reversing the erroneous call.

MLB Security was providing assistance to Joyce, his mother in Toledo, and his family back in Oregon, but for the most part, the majority of baseball fans were amazingly supportive of Joyce because he had openly admitted his mistake and was willing to stand by the resulting consequences. The shift in public opinion was both unexpected and welcome. ESPN broadcaster Ken Rosenthal noted, "Jim Joyce's stature has risen dramatically in this sport for owning up to [the mistake] immediately. People make mistakes all the time in every walk of life. People will have more respect for him than they ever had before."

Before Thursday's game, Joyce was in tears at a press conference in which he thanked the public for its surprising support. Jason Beck, a reporter for MLB.com, wrote,

> Longtime Major League umpire Jim Joyce, whose incorrect call Wednesday night thwarted what would've been a perfect game for Tigers' pitcher Armando Galarraga, was just as remorseful and just as emotional when he discussed it again Thursday morning.
>
> Joyce told reporters gathered outside the tunnel at Comerica Park that while he appreciates the support he has received from around baseball, his family has been hearing it from fans since his call.
>
> "I wish my family was [kept] out of this," Joyce said, "and I wish they would just direct it all to me. It's a big problem. My wife is a rock. My kids are very strong, but they don't deserve this. I'll take it. I'll take whatever you can give me, and I'll handle it like a man, and I'll do the best I can."
>
> Joyce stood by his statements from Wednesday night, when he apologized profusely for his call. He asked to meet with Galarraga after the game and apologize personally, and ended up exchanging hugs.
>
> He teared up Thursday morning as he talked about the feedback he has received.
>
> "I cannot believe the outpouring of support I've gotten, not only from my fellow umpires, but all my friends, my family and, frankly, you guys," Joyce said. "I can't thank you enough. I can't thank the people enough. I'm a big boy. I can handle this. It's the hardest thing I've ever had to go through in my professional career, without a doubt."

No one was quite sure what the fan reaction at Comerica Park would be when Joyce and his three colleagues took the field for Thursday afternoon's game, some 17 hours after the hullaballoo of the previous night. It was a memorable entrance. Amid a scattering of boos, there were mostly cheers. Joyce was an emotional wreck; he walked to the plate teary-eyed but with a certain dignity about him. There to greet him with the Tigers' lineup card was Armando Galarraga, to whom Leyland had specially dispatched to do the honors. (Moments earlier General Motors had awarded the pitcher a red Corvette as an expensive consolation prize.) The two men exchanged pats on the back. Joyce saluted him and the Tigers when he returned to the Tigers' dugout. Somehow Joyce had been transformed into a folk hero for being man enough to admit he had erred in a crucial situation. The sudden morphing of Joyce's mistake from a potentially ugly situation to a feel-good story had taken just about everyone by surprise—especially Joyce.

More remarkable moments followed. Joyce's crew was next assigned to a weekend series between the Padres and Phillies in Philadelphia. MLB had another security detail escort the crew through the airport in Detroit after Thursday's game. It proved to be completely unnecessary. "People were walking up and shaking my hand and telling me, 'Great job,'" recalled the amazed umpire. A security officer with a dog also thanked Joyce, who was utterly perplexed by his new status as a 21st-century folk hero. "This guy puts his life on the line every day and I'm ... just me. We do this for a living, but it's fun. I couldn't believe this officer *had thanked me*. It was heartfelt; he wasn't blowing smoke. That's what this has turned into. I'm glad it has, but I can't understand it."

After conducting an interview with Joyce, Philadelphia baseball reporter Scott Palmer eloquently offered his take on the public's positive perception of the umpire: "Here's why Jim Joyce has people thanking him: In this day when we can't stop an oil leak and we can't start the economy—a time when no one seems ready to stand up and take the blame—Jim Joyce has stepped forward holding himself accountable. In a profession that demands judgment calls, this was his best."

Still there were lingering issues from the bad call that MLB would have to face. Tyler Kepner of the *New York Times,* while praising Joyce for courageously making the call that he thought was right regardless of its importance, noted, "The problem, of course, is that Joyce's decision is easily the most egregious blown call in baseball over the last 25 years."[7]

The voices calling for expanded use of replay to correct obvious errors grew exponentially. In 2010, only decisions pertaining to home runs were subject to video review. Longtime opponents of replay—mostly avid traditionalists—suddenly saw the wisdom of employing replay more widely to address certain situations where not only games but baseball history could be adversely affected by a bad call. San Diego Padres manager Bud Black admitted, "I'm a traditionalist who's been against it, but I've come around to think we need it. The technology just has gotten too good to ignore."[8]

One blogger on a website called Front Office Fans opined, "Bud Selig and Major League Baseball need to take this chance to expand instant replay in baseball. Any call should be up for review. Worried about taking up time? Just use the NFL's system of limiting appeals. We've seen botched calls greatly affect playoff game outcomes, and now we've seen them take away one of the finest accomplishments a pitcher can ever achieve. I don't want to see it again."[9] Even on the Cleveland Indians' blog, Let's Go Tribe, one fan penned, "This game will go down in history, but unfortunately not in the type of history that shows baseball in a good light. This call will reawaken the cries for NFL-style instant replay, but, in my mind, if any good should come of this game, it will provide an impetus for a new evaluation process for umpires."[10]

Since Joyce's bad call took away what should have been the game's final out, some fans lobbied for MLB to take the unprecedented step of correcting the call in this one important instance. While this idea appealed to some fans, others were not so eager for such a radical move to occur. "But that is baseball," wrote blogger Randy Booth on another fan site called Over the Monster. "And it's not that we should 'learn to live with it.' It's that we have always been living with it and for such a long time. Baseball is not a new sport and making mistakes in baseball is not foreign. In every game it happens. This time it was just on a very big stage with many eyes peering down. If Selig reverses the call and gives Galarraga the 21st complete game in baseball history, it is like taking a giant eraser to baseball history. It's also like taking a lighter to the baseball rulebook."[11]

Politicians seemed to hold a contrary view. Michigan lawmakers quickly got into action, lobbying Selig to reverse the call and recognize Galarraga as having thrown a perfect game. Governor Jennifer Granholm bypassed Selig altogether and issued a record-keepers-be-damned proclamation declaring that Galarraga *had* indeed pitched a perfect game. Meanwhile, a federal politician, John D. Dingell, said he would introduce a congressional resolution in the House of Representatives asking MLB to overturn Joyce's blown call. No doubt many of the resolutions were just opportunistic displays of political grandstanding. Nevertheless, the dramatic events of June 2, 2010, at Comerica Park and the aftermath clearly showed how steadfastly passionate Americans from all walks of life were about their national pastime.

In the end, MLB decided to do nothing about Jim Joyce's bad call, but the seeds were definitely planted to expand replay as a tool for umpires at some time in the near future. With the challenge system instituted by MLB for the 2014 season, such egregious umpiring errors in historically important moments are less likely to ever happen again. Tom Verducci accurately commented, "If Joyce provided a tipping point toward baseball's embracing more technology, the irony is that baseball never seemed so human and empathetic as it did in the aftermath of his blunder."[12]

Several months after the "imperfect game," Joyce and Galarraga were reunited to serve as co-presenters of an ESPY Award. Joyce told the audience, "Every umpire strives for the same thing: not to be noticed. So much for that."

In 2012, Joyce and Galarraga teamed up to co-write a book about the episode. Its title is *Nobody's Perfect*.

Cleveland 0 at Detroit 3

Game played on Wednesday, June 2, 2010, at Comerica Park

Cleveland Indians	ab	r	h	rbi	Detroit Tigers	Ab	r	h	rbi
Crowe cf	4	0	0	0	Jackson cf	4	1	3	0
Choo rf	3	0	0	0	Damon lf	4	1	1	0
Kearns lf	3	0	0	0	Kelly lf	0	0	0	0
Hafner dh	3	0	0	0	Ordonez rf	4	0	1	1
Peralta 3b	3	0	0	0	Cabrera 1b	4	1	2	1
Branyan 1b	3	0	0	0	Boesch dh	3	0	1	0
Grudzielanek 2b	3	0	0	0	Guillen 2b	3	0	0	0
Redmond c	3	0	0	0	Inge 3b	3	0	0	0
Donald ss	3	0	1	0	Avila c	3	0	1	0
Carmona p	0	0	0	0	Santiago ss	3	0	0	0
Galarraga p	0	0	0	0					
Totals	28	0	1	0	Totals	31	3	9	2

Cleveland	000 000 000—0 1 1
Detroit	010 000 02x—3 9 0

Cleveland Indians	IP	H	R	ER	BB	SO
Carmona L(4–4)	8.0	9	3	2	0	3
Totals	8.0	9	3	2	0	3

Detroit Tigers	IP	H	R	ER	BB	SO
Galarraga W(2–1)	9.0	1	0	0	0	3
Totals	9.0	1	0	0	0	3

E–Choo (3). DP–Cleveland 2. Carmona-Donald-Branyan, Peralta-Grudzielanek-Branyan. HR–Detroit Cabrera (15, 2nd inning off Carmona 0 on 0 out). U-HP–Marvin Hudson, 1B–Jim Joyce, 2B–Jim Wolf, 3B–Derryl Cousins. T–1:44. A–17,738.

May 25, 2011

Site: AT&T Park, San Francisco

Teams: Florida Marlins vs. San Francisco Giants

Significance: Buster Posey's Injury

Impact: The incident provides impetus for a new rule to restrict runners from violently crashing into catchers

> "Buster Posey lay in the dirt around home plate, dazed, writhing in pain and curling up in a ball. AT&T Park fell silent, fans covering their mouths in disbelief."—*Associated Press* report as it appeared online in The Huffington Post
>
> "It's a baseball play. I feel bad for Buster Posey, I really do. I'm going to send a message over there to them."—Florida Marlins Scott Cousins, the baserunner who flattened Posey
>
> "That is the way this game is meant to be played: Ask no quarter and give none."—longtime Orioles announcer Chuck Thompson's opinion of Baltimore's Dave Johnson flattening Pittsburgh's Manny Sanguillen at home plate during Game Two of the 1971 World Series.

It was a play that is very familiar to generations of baseball fans: a baserunner is desperately trying to score a key run in a ballgame while the catcher is equally trying his best to apply a run-saving tag. There's a bone-crunching collision near home plate. The catcher and runner are both the worse for wear. One of the two is severely shaken up. This time it was the catcher, whose left ankle was twisted beyond where it is supposed to bend. Along with damage to the ankle, X-rays would later reveal a broken bone in the catcher's left leg. (Adding insult to injury, the catcher never tagged the runner, thus the go-ahead run scored.) But it was no ordinary catcher who took the brunt of the crash. It was Buster Posey of the defending World Series champion San Francisco Giants, the very popular, humble-to-a-fault, 2010 National League Rookie of the Year—one of MLB's new shining stars.

It was the night of Friday, May 25, 2011. The play occurred in the top of the 12th inning of a game between the visiting Florida Marlins and the hometown San Francisco Giants at picturesque AT&T Park. The score was tied, 6–6. With Guillermo Mota pitching for the Giants, the Marlins had runners at first base and third base with one out. With the count at 2–2, a high, medium-deep fly ball was launched into center field by Emilio Bonifacio. Clearly the Marlins would risk sending the runner from third base—Scott Cousins—to try to score the go-ahead run on a sacrifice fly. The Giants knew it too. The fly ball had such a high loft to it that Giants right fielder Nate Schierholtz, who had a better arm than center fielder Andres Torres, had adequate time to take charge of the play. He made the catch moving forward, giving himself added momentum. He unleashed a throw to catcher Posey, who was positioned slightly in front of home plate.

Schierholtz's throw was reasonably accurate. It bounced in the dirt area in front of home plate. Posey, pressed for time, attempted to field it on one hop and make a quick sweep tag on the charging Cousins. Posey never quite got control of the ball; it was lying on the ground between his feet when Cousins, in keeping with decades of hard-nosed baseball tradition, lowered the boom—more specifically, his right shoulder—blasting into the helpless Giants catcher. Posey absorbed the severe jolt. The force of the collision knocked Posey's hockey-style catcher's mask off his head.

Cousins may or may not have touched the plate initially, but after taking Posey out of the play he was smart enough to go back and touch it with his left hand. The dazed and battered Posey was certainly in no position to retrieve the ball and make a tag. Plate umpire Joe West properly called Cousins safe at home and called time so Posey could be attended to by the Giants' medical staff. Although the crowd at AT&T Park booed their collective disapproval over what had occurred, no one on the Giants took exception with Cousins' aggressive baserunning. Such collisions had always been part of the sport, at least at the professional level. Posey was gingerly moved into a sitting position. Looking very much like a boxer who had been felled by a knockout blow, Posey shook his head to clear the cobwebs. Within a minute two trainers were helping Posey to the Giants' clubhouse. "That is a sobering sight for any Giants' fans—and for any baseball fan," stated Giants broadcaster Jon Miller. Having suffered a serious injury to his left leg, Posey clearly could not continue. Eli Whiteside replaced Posey defensively. The Marlins retired the Giants in the bottom of the 12th inning to preserve their 7–6 victory.

Not surprisingly, the Cousins-Posey collision far overshadowed what had been a wildly entertaining game at AT&T Park. (The Marlins had scored three runs in the top of the ninth inning to expand their lead to 6–2, but San Francisco rallied with four runs of their own in the home half of the frame to force extra innings.) The *Huffington Post*'s headline declared the incident to be "brutal," but its correspondent admitted it was not unlike dozens of other home plate collisions that occur every year in MLB. Nevertheless, the *Huffington Post* rightly concluded, "the night would belong to a play that could have serious implications for San Francisco's season." The story continued,

> Cousins, who went to the University San Francisco, lives in the Bay Area and had almost a dozen friends and family in attendance, said he felt sorry for injuring Posey but believed it was a clean baseball play.
>
> "I felt like he was blocking the dish. It's the go-ahead run to win the game, I've got to do whatever I can to score," Cousins said. "I'm not trying to end anybody's season or anything like that. I just was trying to play hard and score the go-ahead run. He [Posey] didn't say much and you could tell he was in pain. And when their manager came out, he was pretty frustrated. I didn't want to make things any more tense."
>
> After several minutes of being attending to at the plate, with fans finally chanting "Posey! Posey!," he was helped off the field by two team trainers holding his left leg and looking stunned.
>
> "It's the toughest play in baseball. You hate to see it," Giants manager Bruce Bochy said. "As a [former] catcher you know what it's like, and you don't like it. Believe me. When I see him lying there, it's certainly not a good feeling."

Some amateur and youth baseball leagues strictly outlaw deliberate contact at the plate. All levels of softball—even international-caliber, fast-pitch softball—have for decades outlawed baserunners crashing into defensive players "with great force." Change has always occurred slowly in MLB circles, though. Addressing dangerous collisions at home plate was no exception. Clearly, the Buster Posey situation provided the impetus to create a safer environment for all MLB catchers. It took nearly three years of deliberations among MLB reps and the Major League Baseball Players Association (MLPBA), but an experimental rule was finally added to the sport's rule book before spring training games began in 2014:

Official Baseball Rule 7.13: Collisions at Home Plate

> A runner attempting to score may not deviate from his direct pathway to the plate in order to initiate contact with the catcher (or other player covering home plate). If, in the judgment of the umpire, a runner attempting to score initiates contact with the catcher (or other player covering home plate) in such a manner, the umpire shall declare the runner out (even if the player covering home plate loses possession of the ball). In such circumstances, the umpire shall call the ball dead, and all other baserunners shall return to the last base touched at the time of the collision.

Rule 7.13 comment: The failure by the runner to make an effort to touch the plate, the runner's lowering of the shoulder, or the runner's pushing through with his hands, elbows or arms, would support a determination that the runner deviated from the pathway in order to initiate contact with the catcher in violation of Rule 7.13. If the runner slides into the plate in an appropriate manner, he shall not be adjudged to have violated Rule 7.13. A slide shall be deemed appropriate, in the case of a feet first slide, if the runner's buttocks and legs should hit the ground before contact with the catcher. In the case of a head first slide, a runner shall be deemed to have slid appropriately if his body should hit the ground before contact with the catcher. Unless the catcher is in possession of the ball, the catcher cannot block the pathway of the runner as he is attempting to score. If, in the judgment of the umpire, the catcher without possession of the ball blocks the pathway of the runner, the umpire shall call or signal the runner safe. Notwithstanding the above, it shall not be considered a violation of this Rule 7.13 if the catcher blocks the pathway of the runner in order to field a throw, and the umpire determines that the catcher could not have fielded the ball without blocking the pathway of the runner and that contact with the runner was unavoidable.

Here's what the legalese in Rule 7.13 boiled down to:

- A runner may not run out of a direct line to the plate in order to initiate contact with the catcher or any other player who is covering the plate. If he does, the umpire can call him out even if the player taking the throw loses possession of the ball. (Interestingly, the rule only applies to collisions at home plate. An infielder covering third base or second base is accorded no similar protection from being knocked silly by an oncoming baserunner.)
- The catcher may not block the pathway of a runner attempting to score unless he has possession of the ball. If the catcher blocks the runner before he has the ball, the umpire may call the runner safe. (A defensive player blocking a base or home without possession of the ball has technically always been guilty of obstruction, although it is seldom enforced at home plate.)
- All calls will be based on the umpire's judgment. The umpire will consider such factors as whether the runner made an effort to touch the plate and whether he lowered his shoulder or used his hands, elbows, or arms when approaching the catcher.
- Runners are not required to slide, and catchers in possession of the ball are allowed to block the plate. However, runners who do slide and catchers who provide the runner with a lane will never be found in violation of the rule.
- The expanded instant replay rules, which went into effect in 2014, are available to review potential violations of Rule 7.13.

Tony Clark of the MLBPA explained the need for Rule 7.13 and the inherent difficulty in drafting it. "There is nothing more sacred in the game than home plate, and baserunners want to do all they can to score a run, while catchers want to do their best to defend the plate—in many cases, at all costs. Therefore, as one might imagine, the issue of home-plate collisions is one that generates spirited debate among the players. Because of this, coming up with a rule change that allows both the runner and catcher a fair and equal opportunity to score and defend was our mandate."

Clark continued, "We believe the new experimental rule allows for the play at the plate to retain its place as one of the most exciting plays in the game while providing an increased level of protection to both the runner and the catcher. We will monitor the rule closely this season before discussing with the Commissioner's Office whether the rule should become permanent."[1]

MLB's executive vice president of baseball operations Joe Torre was quick to add that MLB has the right to issue supplemental discipline in the form of fines or suspensions for flagrant acts.

> There will be discipline that will be my call. The umpires are going to look at replay on this thing, too. It's going to be a little tricky because if the manager comes out and wants to question the safe-out call, then he uses the challenge. If he wants to check if he violated the collision rule, then that's not a challenge. It's like a home run; the umpire has the discretion [to use replay for assistance]. The umpire has the right to eject [a player] from the game if it's blatant, and he'd be automatically out. Different umpires will view it differently.[2]

Information packages pertaining to Rule 7.13 were distributed to all MLB clubs before spring training began. Several teams incorporated the anticipated changes into their workouts. One of them was the Toronto Blue Jays. "We did a little bit of that [on the first Sunday]. I said, 'This is what I think it's going to be,'" said Blue Jays manager John Gibbons, himself a former catcher. "In a lot of ways, I really don't know if it's going to be a big difference. A lot of catchers don't hold their ground at the plate anymore anyway. A lot of them leak out and use the swipe tag to begin with. It will be a small adjustment. I don't think it will be that big a deal."[3]

The mere fact that some home-plate collisions were verboten and some were okay, depending upon the circumstances and the baserunner's intent, perplexed and annoyed some sports journalists. Steve Simmons of the *Toronto Sun* wrote, "Does anyone understand what you can and cannot do at home plate anymore? The home plate story has become the pass interference of baseball."

Pete Rose, who famously clobbered Ray Fosse at home plate to score the winning run on the final play of the 1970 MLB All-Star Game, to no one's great surprise, publicly opposed Rule 7.13. When the hard-nosed Rose heard about the proposed rule change, he asked a reporter, "What's the game coming to?" and wondered whether MLB would soon outlaw breaking up a double play. However, Rose's former Cincinnati teammate, Hall of Fame catcher Johnny Bench, heartily approved of it. Bench declared via social media that the new rule "was long overdue."

Still, some former catchers were curiously opposed to the new rule. Prior to the Toronto Blue Jays' 2014 Opening Day telecast from Tampa Bay, Gregg Zaun, a studio analyst for Canada's Sportsnet, cynically opined that Rule 7.13 was adopted only because of Buster Posey's superstar status. Zaun further stated that MLB's newfound concern about catchers' well-being reminded him of the preferential protective treatment that NFL quarterbacks receive compared to other football players. One active catcher, Jonathan Lucroy of the Milwaukee Brewers, did not approve of Rule 7.13 either. His objection was based solely on baseball tradition. "I'm a conservative-type guy. I like keeping things the way they are, although I do understand where they're coming from. I understand the importance of [avoiding] concussions. I get it. It's just really hard to break old habits."[4]

The "Buster Posey Protection Rule" still had a few kinks to be worked out—a fact that was patently obvious on July 31, 2014, in Miami. That Thursday night in a game versus Cincinnati, the Reds, by virtue of replay review, were awarded what turned out to be a game-winning run on a bizarre obstruction call that had the vast majority of baseball fans shaking their heads in disbelief. On a play in which Reds runner Zack Cozart was at least ten feet from home plate when Marlins catcher Jeff Mathis got possession of the ball, Mathis applied an easy tag. Up until the 2014 season, no one would have even questioned the out. Nevertheless Cozart was awarded home plate because Mathis had not provided a pathway for Cozart to try to score in accordance with rule 7.13. It was generally agreed that the intent of the Buster Posey Protection Rule was not to deny outs on cases where the runner had absolutely no chance of scoring. Even though MLB defended its replay officials' decision, most longtime fans thought the call was preposterous. Baseball blogger Craig Calcaterra of NBC's Hardball Talk website rightly called it "a hyper-technical reading of the rule" and deemed it to be "clown shoes." In August 2014, ESPN's Keith Olbermann, in a skit where he had been named the new MLB Commissioner, declared he was scrapping the Buster Posey Rule because "so far I have yet to meet any two people who think it means the same thing." In September the rule was sensibly tweaked to permit a catcher—or any other defensive player covering the plate—to "block" the runner's lane if he arrives at or near the plate and possesses the ball well ahead of the runner's arrival. Ironically, the revised, common-sense interpretation of the rule came into play during Game Four of the 2014 NLDS between San Francisco and Washington— with Buster Posey the runner being tagged out.

Undoubtedly the "Buster Posey Rule" was a factor in a later and similar rule change prior to the 2016 MLB season. Malicious slides into other bases were limited after Chase Utley, in the 2015 NLDS against the New York Mets, broke the leg of shortstop Ruben Tejada with a hard slide into second base.

In 2011, Buster Posey's leg injury was severe enough to sideline him for the remainder of the season. His loss greatly impacted San Francisco's chances to repeat as World Series champions. The Giants finished in second place in the NL West standings with a disappointing 86–76 record, eight games behind the division-leading Arizona Diamondbacks. The team missed qualifying for the post-season altogether. In 2012 a healthy Posey returned to San Francisco's lineup. He picked up where he had left off in May 2011. Posey won the NL batting title in 2012 with a .336 average, becoming only the third NL catcher to achieve the feat—the others being Cincinnati backstops Bubbles Hargrave in 1926 and Ernie Lombardi in 1938. Lombardi won another batting title with the Boston Braves in 1942. Posey was named the league's MVP. The 2012 Giants also won their second World Series in a span of three years.

Florida 7 at San Francisco 6

Game played on Wednesday May 25, 2011, at AT&T Park

Florida Marlins	ab	r	h	rbi	San Francisco Giants	ab	r	h	rbi
Coghlan cf	5	2	2	0	Torres cf	5	1	1	1
Badenhop p	0	0	0	0	Sanchez 2b	6	1	4	0
Ramirez ss	3	1	0	1	Huff 1b	6	0	1	2
Mujica p	0	0	0	0	Posey c	5	0	1	0
Nunez p	0	0	0	0	Whiteside c	1	0	0	0
Dobbs 3b	1	0	1	0	Ross lf	5	0	0	0
Morrison lf	5	2	3	0	Wilson p	0	0	0	0
Sanchez 1b	5	0	1	1	Mota p	1	0	0	0
Stanton rf	6	0	4	4	Schierholtz rf	5	1	2	0
Buck c	5	0	1	0	Fontenot ss	2	0	0	0
Helms 3b	5	0	0	0	Burriss ss	2	0	1	0
Webb p	0	0	0	0	Tejada 3b	5	2	2	0
Cousins ph, cf	1	1	0	0	Bumgarner p	1	0	0	0
Infante 2b	6	0	2	0	Ramirez p	0	0	0	0
Volstad p	3	0	0	0	Rowand ph	1	0	0	0
Dunn p	0	0	0	0	Romo p	0	0	0	0
Choate p	0	0	0	0	Lopez p	0	0	0	0
Hensley p	0	0	0	0	Affeldt p	0	0	0	0

Florida Marlins	ab	r	h	rbi	San Francisco Giants	ab	r	h	rbi
Bonifacio ph, ss	1	1	0	1	Burrell ph, lf	2	1	1	1
Totals	46	7	14	7	Totals	47	6	13	4

Florida	200 010 003 001—7 14 0	
San Francisco	002 000 004 000—6 13 0	

Florida Marlins	IP	H	R	ER	BB	SO
Volstad	6.0	6	2	2	2	6
Dunn	1.0	0	0	0	0	0
Choate	0.1	0	0	0	0	0
Hensley	0.2	0	0	0	0	0
Mujica	0.1	2	2	2	0	0
Oviedo	0.2	4	2	2	0	1
Webb W(1–3)	2.0	1	0	0	0	0
Badenhop SV(1)	1.0	0	0	0	0	0
Totals	12.0	13	6	6	2	7

San Francisco Giants	IP	H	R	ER	BB	SO
Bumgarner	6.0	8	3	3	2	4
Ramirez	1.0	1	0	0	1	1
Romo	1.0	0	0	0	0	3
Lopez	0.2	1	3	3	2	1
Affeldt	0.1	0	0	0	0	0
Wilson	2.0	2	0	0	0	1
Mota L(2–1)	1.0	2	1	1	0	0
Totals	12.0	14	7	7	5	10

E–None. DP–San Francisco 1. Tejada-Huff. PB–Buck (5). 2B–Florida Stanton 2 (11, off Bumgarner, off Lopez); Coghlan (14, off Bumgarner), San Francisco Torres (8, off Volstad); Tejada (8, off Mujica); F. Sanchez (11, off Nunez). SH–Coghlan (1, off Lopez); Bumgarner (5, off Volstad); Burriss (1, off Webb). SF–Bonifacio (2, off Mota). HBP–Coghlan (2, by Bumgarner); Ramirez (1, by Lopez). IBB–G. Sanchez (2, by Ramirez). SB–Ramirez (10, 2nd base off Bumgarner/Posey); Coghlan 2 (6, 3rd base off Bumgarner/Posey, 2nd base off Ramirez/Posey); Torres (4, Home off Volstad/Buck). U–HP–Joe West, 1B–Angel Hernandez, 2B–Angel Campos, 3B–Chad Fairchild. T–4:06. A–41,037.

October 5, 2012

Site: Turner Field, Atlanta

Teams: St. Louis Cardinals vs. Atlanta Braves

Significance: First Wild-Card Play-In Game

Impact: Divisional champions are now rewarded by not having to play an extra game; conversely each league's wild-card berth must be earned by winning a one-game playoff

When MLB first instituted a three-divisional setup per league in 1995 and the necessity of one wild-card team per league, traditionalists were irked that a team that did not win its division could win the World Series. The possibility happened often in its first 17 years of existence. The Florida Marlins won the World Series twice as the NL's wild-card team. The 2002 World Series featured both leagues' wild-card teams, the Anaheim Angels and the San Francisco Giants. When the Boston Red Sox won it all as the AL wild-card team in 2004, it marked the third straight season a wild-card team had captured the World Series. It did not happen again until the St. Louis Cardinals went all the way in

2011, but from 2002 through 2007, at least one wild-card team was in the World Series each October. A dubious first was achieved in 2014. That year's World Series featured two wild-card teams that failed to win 90 games during the regular season.

Opponents of the wild-card system complained with considerable justification that such occurrences devalued what it meant to be a divisional champion. Of course they were right. One season New York Yankees general manager Brian Cashman told a reporter that the Yankees were not especially interested in winning the American League East as long as they qualified for the post-season as the American League's wild-card team.

Cashman declared there was almost no tangible benefit to being a divisional winner instead of the wild-card team "except that you might get a commemorative t-shirt." MLB realized that Cashman's flippant remark was based in fact. Instead of scrapping the wild-card system and returning to some form of "champs only" system for the playoffs, in 2012 MLB instituted another tier of post-season play. Now the two best non-divisional winners in each league would have to play a one-game showdown to determine the "real" wild-card team. That way there was a benefit to being a first-place team—an anything-might-happen, single-game elimination was avoided. Casual fans loved the idea since more teams remained in the running late in the season. Purists ruefully absorbed it as another hit to their sport's uniqueness and integrity. Accordingly, on Friday, October 5, 2012, the St. Louis Cardinals and Atlanta Braves—two second-place teams—met in a late-afternoon game at Atlanta's Turner Field for the historic first National League "wild-card" game or "play-in" game. Given the stakes, the game turned out to be a beauty and was much discussed. As it turned out, very little discussion centered on the concept of a winner-takes-all diamond battle.

The wild-card game between the Cardinals and Braves was as advertised—wild! The fans at home and at Turner Field witnessed two huge talking points. The subsequent controversies indicated that while many fans have a passion for the game, darn few have ever bothered to read a baseball rule book.

Incident number one went the way of the home team. In the bottom of the second inning, with two out, a runner on base, and the score tied 0–0, David Ross of the Braves was batting. With the count 1–2, Ross requested time while Cardinals pitcher Kyle Lohse was in the stretch. Plate umpire Jeff Kellogg granted time—although not as quickly as everyone would have preferred. Ross was unsure if time had been given. He remained in the batter's box as Lohse's changeup sailed toward the plate. Ross swung at the off-speed pitch and missed for an apparent strikeout. It was not a whiff, of course, as Kellogg had killed the play. Given a second life, Ross blasted a two-run homer to give the Braves an early 2–0 edge. The Cards felt they had gotten the short end of the stick, but baseball rules empower an umpire to call or grant time whenever he thinks it is appropriate. The non-strikeout normally would have been fodder for sports radio shows, but it was greatly overshadowed six innings later by the most famous infield-fly call in MLB history. (In truth, it was probably the *only* famous infield-fly call in MLB history.)

The necessity of having an "infield-fly rule" dates back to baseball's first professional team—the Cincinnati Red Stockings of 1869. They were true sports pioneers: men who openly received salaries to play a team game. They traveled anywhere where they could draw a sizable paying crowd and collect a huge chunk of the gate. Only one of the Red Stockings was actually from Cincinnati. The Red Stockings found a flaw in baseball's rules and exploited it on several occasions. If the opposing team had the bases loaded or runners at first and second bases with less than two out, and the batter hit an infield pop-up, the Red Stockings would do something no team before had ever thought of doing. Knowing the runners would be forced to stick close to their bases, assuming the ball would be easily caught, the Cincinnati crew would allow the ball to fall to the infield, grab it, and quickly turn a double play! Sheer genius! However, the rules-makers of the day did not think this sneaky way of attaining a double play (or even, on occasion, a triple play) was particularly sporting, so they designed the "infield-fly rule" which exists to this day. Once that rule was established, the umpires were required to call an infield fly in similar circumstances. The batter would be automatically out if the ball landed fair, which eliminated any force plays on the runners already on base. (Runners could stay put or advance at their own peril.) It would be solely up to an umpire's judgment to determine if an infielder could make a catch with "ordinary effort." Where the infielder happened to be standing would make no difference in the implementation of the rule. In fact, even an outfielder could attempt to make a catch on an infield fly if an umpire believed an infielder could make the same play with routine effort.

Fast-forward 143 years: It is the bottom of the eighth inning in Atlanta. The Cardinals and Braves are locked in their one-game, winner-take-all shot at the real MLB playoffs. The Cards lead, 6–3, but the Braves are trying to mount a rally. There is one out. Dan Uggla is Atlanta's runner at second base, and David Ross is at first base. Given the number of outs and where the runners are stationed, the potential for an infield fly exists and is acknowledged by the six-man umpiring crew assigned to the game. The batter, Alex Simmons, lofts a high fly ball to very shallow left field. St. Louis shortstop Peter Kozma backpedals into the outfield. At the same time, left fielder Matt Holliday charges toward the infield. The ball is so high that Kozma has plenty of time to stop, stare at the ball in the sky, and position himself for what appears to be a very routine play for an MLB middle infielder. Left field umpire Sam Holbrook looks at the situation. Like most of the fans in Turner Field or watching on television, Holbrook reasonably assumes Kozma should make the catch. He raises his right hand with his finger pointing skyward—quite properly judging the play to be an infield fly. Seconds later third-base umpire Jeff Nelson does the same. For whatever reason—the clamor of the crowd, miscommunication between teammates, who knows?—Kozma suddenly gives up on the ball and it falls to the ground between the stationary shortstop and the onrushing left fielder. Holliday retrieves the ball but he has no play on any baserunner as Uggla and Ross both frantically advance. The bases are loaded. The hometown fans cheer in anticipation of a big inning. One problem: By rule Simmons is out on the infield-fly rule. The advancements of the two other runners are perfectly legal, but the application of the infield-fly rule means that instead of having three runners on base with one out, the Braves have just runners at second and third base with two outs. Simmons abandons first base without complaint, but he is in the minority. The rest of his teammates are not a happy bunch—and neither are their aroused fans.

When the realization that an infield fly had been called—albeit correctly—on a batted ball that fell untouched in shallow left field, neither the Braves nor their fans are in any mood for a lecture on the subtleties of Rules 2.0 and 6.05e which address the play in great detail. Atlanta manager Fredi Gonzalez rages against umpires Nelson and Holbrook. He puts the game under protest. His chances of winning are nil. The decision to invoke the infield-fly rule cannot be protested because it is a judgment call, not a misapplication of a rule. (The Braves' protest is denied by MLB almost immediately.)

Miffed fans start using Turner Field as an enormous refuse receptacle. As missiles fly onto the diamond from every direction, the Cardinals sensibly take refuge in their dugout for their own safety. The game is delayed 19 minutes while groundskeepers and security staff try to make the field playable again. The interruption is so long that Cardinals pitcher Mitchell Boggs is removed from the game because he is no longer warm. He is replaced by Jason Motte. Once some semblance of order is restored, Atlanta pinch-hitter Brian McCann draws a walk to load the bases, but leadoff hitter Michael Bourn strikes out to end the inning. The Braves fail to score. Despite getting two hits in the bottom of the ninth inning to bring the tying run to the plate, Atlanta cannot score off Motte, who earns a four-out save. St. Louis wins, 6–3, to advance to the National League Division Series. When the final out is made, both teams scurry to their clubhouses to escape another bombardment of litter from the irked ticketholders. With the Braves' loss, the game marked the last MLB appearance by Chipper Jones, Atlanta's 40-year-old third baseman, who was the team's most identifiable and popular player. He went out quietly, notching a single in five at-bats. Sadly he left the field under a shower of debris—hardly a distinguished way to conclude a fine career.

Typical for the new age of social media, the reaction in cyberspace to the important infield-fly call was instantaneous but not necessarily well-informed. A headline on the sports website Deadspin.com blustered, "Braves fans attack umpires with garbage after worst infield fly call ever."[1] Never mind that most of the accompanying comments from learned baseball fans—many claiming to have amateur and professional umpiring experience on their side—wholly agreed with the call. Those posters who did not know the rule, did not understand the rule, could not understand the rule, had absolutely no intention of ever wanting to understand the rule, or were blinded by sheer homerism, echoed TBS commentator and former MLB pitcher Ron Darling, who incredibly declared to a continental television audience, "You cannot call that an infield fly; it's too deep." Darling also strangely insinuated that the call was baseball's version of too many cooks spoiling the broth. "You know," he opined, "this is what happens occasionally when you add extra umpires down the right-field and left-field lines. You have extra umpires and sometimes you have extra calls."

One poster, who claimed to be a longtime employee of the Kansas City Royals, honestly did not know what all the fuss was about and was thoroughly exasperated by the complainers. "Plays where a shortstop drifts into shallow left field to make a catch happen hundreds of times a year," he wrote. "The umpires always signal infield fly when the situation calls for it. The only difference here was that he [Kozma] didn't make the catch. That call was totally correct."[2]

One other poster stated, "Imagine if the umps hadn't called the play an infield fly, and the ball fell in front of Kozma, and he started an inning-ending double play. Those same fans who think today's call was wrong would have been screaming bloody murder!"[3]

Whether one believes the infield-fly call was controversial or a no-brainer, Major League Baseball got what it desired: an intense one-game playoff that had fans across the world abuzz. The Cardinals went on to beat the Washington Nationals in a five-game NLDS before losing to San Francisco in the National League Championship Series. The Cards won three of the first four games versus the Giants before faltering. The Giants easily swept the Detroit Tigers to win the 2012 World Series.

St. Louis 6 at Atlanta 3

Game played on Friday, October 5, 2012, at Turner Field

St. Louis Cardinals	ab	r	h	rbi		Atlanta Braves	ab	r	h	rbi
Jay cf	4	0	0	0		Bourn cf	5	0	1	1
Beltran rf	4	1	1	0		Prado lf	5	0	1	0
Holliday lf	3	2	2	1		Heyward rf	5	0	1	0
Motte p	0	0	0	0		Jones 3b	5	0	1	0
Craig 1b	4	1	2	1		Freeman 1b	4	0	3	0
Molina c	4	0	0	1		Uggla 2b	4	1	0	0
Freese 3b	2	0	0	1		Ross c	4	1	3	2
Chambers pr	0	1	0	0		Simmons ss	4	0	1	0
Mujica p	0	0	0	0		Medlen p	2	0	0	0
Rzepczynski p	0	0	0	0		Durbin p	0	0	0	0
Boggs p	0	0	0	0		Venters p	0	0	0	0
Robinson lf	1	0	0	0		Constanza ph	1	1	1	0
Descalso 2b	3	0	0	0		O'Flaherty p	0	0	0	0
Kozma ss	4	1	0	0		McCann ph	0	0	0	0
Lohse p	2	0	0	0		Pastornicky pr	0	0	0	0
Lynn p	0	0	0	0		Kimbrel p	0	0	0	0
Carpenter ph,3b	1	0	1	1						
Totals	32	6	6	5		Totals	39	3	12	3

St. Louis	000 301 200—6	6 0
Atlanta	020 000 100—3	12 3

St. Louis Cardinals	IP	H	R	ER	BB	SO
Lohse W(1–0)	5.2	6	2	2	1	6
Lynn	0.1	0	0	0	0	0
Mujica	0.2	2	1	1	0	0
Rzepczynski	0.1	1	0	0	0	0
Boggs	0.2	1	0	0	1	0
Motte SV(1)	1.0	2	0	0	1	1
Totals	9.0	12	3	3	3	7

Atlanta Braves	IP	H	R	ER	BB	SO
Medlen L(0–1)	6.1	3	5	2	0	4
Durbin	0.0	0	1	0	0	0
Venters	0.2	1	0	0	0	0
O'Flaherty	1.0	2	0	0	0	0
Kimbrel	1.0	0	0	0	0	1
Totals	9.0	6	6	2	0	5

E–Jones (1), Uggla (1), Simmons (1). DP–Atlanta 2. Simmons-Freeman, Jones-Uggla-Freeman. 2B–St. Louis Craig (1, off Medlen), Atlanta Heyward (1, off Rzepczynski); Freeman (1, off Motte). 3B–Atlanta Constanza (1, off Mujica). HR–St. Louis Holliday (1, 6th inning off Medlen 0 on 1 out), Atlanta Ross (1, 2nd inning off Lohse 1 on 2 out). SH–Descalso (1, off Medlen). SF–Freese (1, off Medlen). HBP–Holliday (1, by Medlen). U–Jeff Kellogg, Mike Winters, Gary Cederstrom, Jeff Nelson, Sam Holbrook, Rob Drake. T–3:09. A–52,631.

March 31, 2014

Site: PNC Park, Pittsburgh

Teams: Chicago Cubs vs. Pittsburgh Pirates

Significance: First Use of the Video-Review Challenge System

Impact: Umpiring an MLB game is changed forever; most erroneous calls can now be reversed with the new video challenge system

> "Progress has never been a bargain. You've got to pay for it. Sometimes I think there's a man behind a counter who says, 'All right, you can have a telephone, but you'll have to give up the charm of distance. Mister, you may conquer the air, but the birds will lose their wonder and the clouds will smell of gasoline.'"—Henry Drummond, on the price of progress, from the 1960 film *Inherit the Wind*

> "Major League Baseball officially entered the 21st century on March 31, 2014 with the debut of an expanded replay system that allowed managers to challenge calls in games."—BleacherReport.com

In its April 1, 2014, edition, *USA Today* humorously reported, "In a dazzling clash of time-honored baseball tradition with the sport's latest innovation, the Chicago Cubs lost MLB's first-ever replay challenge on Monday." The Cubs joke aside, it was nevertheless a historic occasion. For the first time in MLB history, a team could request a video review to verify the accuracy of a call on a play other than a disputed home run. The idea of relying on photographic or video evidence to ensure a correct call was basically more than 60 years in the making.

During the fifth game of the 1952 World Series, umpire Art Passarella made an egregiously bad call that went against the New York Yankees and in favor of the Brooklyn Dodgers on a play at first base. It was the bottom of the tenth inning at Yankee Stadium. With the Series tied two games apiece and the score tied, 5–5, New York's Johnny Sain led off the inning. He hit a slow roller to second baseman Jackie Robinson, who fielded the ball but threw late to first baseman Gil Hodges. At least it appeared late to everyone but Passarella, who quickly signaled out—perhaps too quickly. A large argument ensued. Quickly developed news photos—the closest technology to video review available in 1952—showed Sain's left foot firmly planted on the bag with the ball still on its way to Hodges' mitt. The Yankees failed to score and Brooklyn won, 6–5, in 11 innings. Before the game concluded, reporters showed MLB Commissioner Ford Frick the damning photographic evidence of Passarella's bad call. Unable and unwilling to defend the indefensible, Ford remarked, "If I owned a newspaper, I'd blow that picture up to six or eight columns!"[1] The *New York Times* did just that. The Yankees recovered from the blown call to win the 1952 World Series in seven games.

Eighteen years later, during the 1970 World Series, Ken Burkhart made a call so comically bad that it has been used in umpires' instructional videos to stress the importance of positioning and game awareness. The infamous play occurred in the bottom of the sixth inning of the first game. The Baltimore Orioles were tied with the hometown Cincinnati Reds, 3–3. With one out, Bernie Carbo was at third base for the Reds, representing the go-ahead run. Ty Cline hit a high chopper in front of home. Plate umpire Burkhart moved from his position a few feet down the third-base line to rule on whether the ball was fair or foul. He apparently forgot about Carbo, who was barreling down the line towards home plate. With Burkhart unintentionally blocking the plate, Carbo was forced to attempt a hook slide around the umpire. By this time Orioles catcher Elrod Hendricks had fielded the fair ball with his bare hand. He lunged at Carbo in an attempted to tag him. The jostled Burkhart had no idea what had occurred literally behind his back. He inexplicably called Carbo out—even though he was in no position to make such a call. Moreover, television replays clearly showed Hendricks had the ball in his throwing hand and had tagged Carbo with an *empty* catcher's mitt. Furthermore, Carbo had actually missed the plate with his wide slide; he touched it only by accident when he rushed back towards Burkhart to argue the bad call. The Reds failed to score in the inning. Baltimore got a run in the top of the seventh inning and won the game, 4–3. The Orioles took the World Series in five games.

Another historically important but largely forgotten blown call occurred in the fifth game of the best-of-five 1972 ALCS between the Oakland A's and Detroit at Tiger Stadium. In the top of the fourth inning, Oakland's first batter, George Hendrick, was called safe at first base as umpire John Rice ruled that shortstop Dick McAuliffe's low throw pulled Detroit's Norm Cash off the bag. Television replays showed Cash's foot had maintained contact with the base and McAuliffe's throw had beaten Hendrick. Detroit journalist Bill Dow, who had skipped school as a 17-year-old to attend the game, wrote about the play in 2011, describing Rice's call as "horrible." He further stated, "[Tigers outfielder Jim] Northrup actually told me that the call was so blatantly wrong that he even wondered if Rice was on the take."[2] A long, bitter argument ensued. Rice—an ex-Marine who had fought on Guadalcanal during the Second World War—found himself under fire again, this time from irate Tigers. Frank Howard, an aging slugger who had been acquired by Detroit from the Texas Rangers in mid-season and was only on the field as the Tigers' interim first-base coach, was ejected by Rice for his persistent complaining. "The umpire knew he blew the play,"[3] grumbled Howard afterward. Hendrick eventually came around to score on Gene Tenace's base hit to break a 1–1 tie. There was no further scoring in the game. "We got beat on a little old technicality,"[4] Cash strangely observed. Thus the A's advanced to the World Series for the first time since 1931—when they were the Philadelphia Athletics—in a somewhat controversial fashion.

A year later, in Game Two of the 1973 World Series, the Athletics again got the benefit of what was generally perceived to be an awful call by veteran NL umpire Augie Donatelli. With one out in the top of the tenth inning, New York Mets shortstop Bud Harrelson attempted to score the go-ahead run on a fly ball hit to medium left field by Felix Millan. The ball was caught by A's outfielder Joe Rudi, who had a good arm. Rudi's throw was fairly accurate, but it pulled catcher Ray Fosse up the line slightly. Harrelson never slid, but he appeared to elude the sweeping tag of Fosse. Nevertheless Donatelli—who was oddly positioned low to the ground, nearly on his stomach—called Harrelson out on what became known as the "phantom tag" play. The Mets were livid. On-deck batter Willie Mays, nearing the end of his fabulous career, was famously photographed on his knees pleading with Donatelli to change his call. The Mets had a legitimate beef. Television replays seemed to indicate that Fosse's mitt had not touched Harrelson. Even longtime A's broadcaster Monte Moore thought Oakland had caught a break. (A photo later published in *Baseball Digest*, however, seemed to show that Fosse's tag may have nicked Harrelson's right arm.) Interestingly, when Mets manager Yogi Berra strenuously argued the play, Donatelli told the irate manager that Fosse had tagged Harrelson on his rear end—not his arm. Fortunately for the Mets, they won the game, 10–7, in 12 innings. Donatelli, who umpired his first MLB game in 1950, retired at the end of the 1973 World Series at age 59.

The most infamous blown call in the history of the World Series occurred in 1985 when umpire Don Denkinger badly fluffed a play at first base which very well could have cost the St. Louis Cardinals the title. An entire chapter in this book is devoted to what transpired on that wild night in Kansas City.

More controversy ensued in later post-season baseball. The 1992 World Series saw the Toronto Blue Jays deprived of a triple play when umpire Bob Davidson missed a clear tag that Kelly Gruber applied on Atlanta's Deion Sanders, who was scrambling back to second base in a rundown. In 1996, 12-year-old Jeffrey Maier became the most famous baseball fan in America when he reached from his seat in the right field bleachers at Yankee Stadium and interfered with outfielder Tony Tarasco's likely catch in an ALCS game. Umpire Rich Garcia wrongly ruled the play a Derek Jeter homer, giving the New York Yankees a horribly tainted scoring play versus the Baltimore Orioles. Video review was not permitted to assist the umpires in any of the above cases.

By 2008, public opinion finally forced MLB to embrace 21st-century technology. It became the last of the four major sports leagues to introduce some version of video review to assist its officials. Starting in 2009, disputed home runs—and only home runs—could be checked via replay to see if the ball was fair or foul, if it went over the fence or not, or if fan interference did or did not play a part. An August 26, 2008, story written by Alyson Footer for MLB.com discussed the decision. Footer wrote,

> The new use of technology doesn't sit well with some baseball purists, but the majority of players and managers surveyed across the league agreed on two points: It's important to get the call right, and instant replay should be limited to home runs only. Leave the other calls—balls and strikes, safe or out—up to the umpires, without the help of a television screen.
>
> "I think they made the right decision when it comes to home runs—foul or fair," [Washington] Nationals' manager Manny Acta said. "The new dimensions and the way stadiums are built [make] it very tough on the umpires. The good part is they are not taking the human element away. I like it. The human element has been around for 100 years and you just can't take it away. Maybe in 100 years, you may have a machine calling balls and strikes, but I don't want to see that."
>
> Neither does [Los Angeles] Dodgers' manager Joe Torre.
>
> "I think if it just stands like this, [it is good]," he said. "It's tough to overturn safe and out. Then you'll get into balls and strikes; then all of a sudden people have to pack more than a lunch to get here to the ballpark."[5]

While reviews on home runs generally settled all arguments in those cases, other plays were still being adjudicated the old-fashioned way—using umpires' judgment alone. No call was more replayed or rehashed than Jim Joyce's unfortunate blunder in Detroit in 2010 which deprived Armando Galarraga of a rare perfect game. If any single call in the history of MLB was the catalyst for expanded use of video review, Joyce's horribly inopportune decision was it. (Another full chapter in this book describes the Jim Joyce call.) Still, change did not come overnight. Three more years would pass before expanded video review was given the green light by MLB.

Beginning with the 2014 season, as an addendum to the Official Rules of Baseball, MLB instituted a "challenge system" in which each team is permitted to challenge virtually any play except balls and strikes. The disputed play is analyzed by a team of officials in New York. Their decision is relayed through a headset to the umpires on the field. If the challenge proves the umpire's call was correct, that team loses any further right to challenge a play during the remainder of the game. Opening Day at PNC Park in Pittsburgh, March 31, 2014, was the first time the new system was put into use. In the bottom of the fifth inning, Chicago Cubs pitcher Jeff Samardzija attempted a sacrifice bunt. It was a poor one. The Pirates turned it into a double play in which the putout on Samardzija at first base was extremely close. Cubs manager Rick Renteria challenged the play—an MLB first. After video review was consulted, umpire Bob Davidson's call was upheld. The throw had beaten Samardzija to the bag. The system had worked exactly as it had been designed to do. It clearly was not the Cubs' day. In the top of the tenth inning, with the score deadlocked 0–0, the first MLB replay reversal saw Cubs runner Emilio Bonifacio picked off first base by relief pitcher Bryan Morris after initially being called safe by Davidson. The Pirates dramatically won the game, 1–0, on a walkoff homer by Neil Walker in the bottom of the tenth inning.

After video review's initial success, a few gremlins appeared in the system. Cagey managers discovered the benefits of strategic dawdling. If they delayed or extended an argument with an umpire long enough, someone in their dugout could view a TV replay to see if the play ought to be challenged or not and signal the manager accordingly. Within a short time, stalling for time became standard operating procedure for all managers. In contrast to tennis matches, where a challenge on a line call must be initiated within seconds, MLB's video-review system was far from "instant" replay. Keith Olbermann noted on his ESPN program that once a challenge is made during an MLB game, the fans at home and at the ballpark are forced to endure "the antiseptic tedium of two umpires wearing giant headphones like they were having their hearing examined."

What became abundantly clear was that the nature of baseball made the use of video review not nearly as simple as it is in tennis, hockey or football. Those three sports use replay for a single cut-and-dried call: Was the ball in or out? Did the puck cross the goal line? Did the receiver make a legal catch? However, the continuation of plays and action away from the ball make replay in baseball far more complex. Two particular games in 2014 highlighted the problem.

An utterly absurd situation arose in a Toronto-Oakland game on Thursday, July 3, that only video review could create. The quirky incident happened in the top of the second inning with the bases loaded and one out. Blue Jays outfielder Anthony Gose hit a sharp grounder to first base. A's first baseman Nate Freiman fielded the ball cleanly and attempted to make a tag on baserunner Munenori Kawasaki, who was running past him. First-base umpire Vic Carapazza wrongly ruled that Kawasaki had avoided the tag and immediately gave an emphatic safe sign. Oakland accepted Carapazza's call at face value. That meant the force play at home on Edwin Encarnacion could still be made. Oakland catcher Stephen Vogt recorded the putout when he caught Freiman's accurate throw while stepping on the plate. Vogt did not even consider tagging Encarnacion because he did not need to—if the play at home really was a force play.

Toronto manager John Gibbons took the unorthodox approach of suggesting that Kawasaki—his own player—should have been ruled out on Freiman's tag! Gibbons challenged, and when the play was reviewed, it was determined that Kawasaki had indeed been tagged. That prompted the umpires to overturn the ruling on the field. Kawasaki was called out. As a result, Encarnacion was ruled safe at home because the putout on Kawasaki killed the force play at the plate and Vogt never applied a tag on Encarnacion— because he did not think it was necessary based on Carapazza's original call! Yikes!

"When [the replay decision] came back, our hands are tied," crew chief Bill Miller explained. "There's only so much we can do. We can't put runners back. We have to go with what happened on the field, and what happened on the field was the guy [Vogt] tagged home plate but he did not tag the runner. Unfortunately that was in direct relation to the call on the field at first base, and that's something we just can't explain."[6] When the Blue Jays were credited with a run, vexed A's manager Bob Melvin played the game under protest. Melvin contended that the rules were not being correctly interpreted and that it should be up to the umpire's discretion whether Encarnacion was called safe at home. In this particular case, that would have resulted in Encarnacion being called out because he was still at least several feet from home plate when the throw arrived in Vogt's mitt. The call did not end up having an impact in the game because Oakland went on to win, 4–1. Thus the A's protest died without having to be considered. Oakland's win disappointed many scholarly fans who were quite keen to see how the protest would have progressed.

"That's probably the first time that's happened in that fashion," Melvin said. "My understanding now is you can't protest anything that has to do with replay, so I don't know that it was a legitimate protest or not. And you're going to come up with plays like that over the course of the season based on replay being brand new, and you're gonna find some ones that are some tweeners. They did the best they could with it."[7]

"Replay's a new dimension to this game and there are going to be quirks and funny plays like this that happen," Miller apologetically said after the game. "Unfortunately it happened to us."[8]

Comments on MLB.com from baseball fans far and wide echoed the same terrible fear in one way or another: Imagine if a similar play had scored the winning run in the seventh game of a World Series!

An exponentially more important video-review controversy occurred on Saturday, September 20, at Kansas City's Kaufman Stadium in a critical game between the Detroit Tigers and the hometown Royals. In the end, nobody doubted that the correct call was eventually made, but there was considerable controversy about the roundabout method of how that decision was made. With the score tied, 1–1, in the bottom of the sixth inning, Kansas City mounted a threat. With one out and runners on second and third, Kansas City's Omar Infante lined out to second baseman Ian Kinsler. Eric Hosmer, the Royals' runner at second base, hustled back toward the bag. Kinsler attempted to double him up. Tigers shortstop Eugenio Suarez did not expect a throw from Kinsler. He never reached his glove toward the ball, which sailed into left field. The blunder appeared to give the runner at third base, Salvador Perez, an easy opportunity to sprint home with the go-ahead run. The problem was that Perez had not bothered to tag up after Infante's line drive was caught. "I never thought about tagging,"[9] an embarrassed Perez later confessed to reporters.

Inside the Tigers' dugout, another Perez—a rookie named Hernan Perez—cleverly noticed his namesake's silly baserunning gaffe. He alerted Detroit manager Brad Ausmus to the oversight. When play resumed, Detroit pitcher Max Scherzer started an appeal play by stepping off the rubber and throwing the ball to third baseman Nick Castellanos, who stepped on the base. Larry Vanover, the third base umpire and crew chief, wrongly ruled Perez safe. Ausmus requested a video review. Vanover suspected video review could not be used on an appeal play—but he wanted to verify this with the "war room" video officials in New York City. (Note: Whether or not a runner leaves his base too early on a caught fly ball *is not* subject to video review, but whether or not a runner misses a base *is*. There was some dispute about whether the play in question was the former or the latter.) As Andy McCullough of the *Kansas City Star* noted, "Thus began a convoluted process that left [Kansas City manager Ned] Yost confounded, his players furious, Perez out, and the inning over." McCullough continued,

The umpires convened. Vanover conferred with MLB headquarters in Manhattan to make sure the play could not be reviewed.

As Vanover communicated with his bosses, the replay rolled on the screen above center field, revealing Perez deserved to be out. In general, the videoboard operator is instructed to show the replay as soon as an umpire goes to the headset connecting to New York. After another conference with his three fellow umpires, Vanover made a fist. He would later say the decision came from their "consensus" that Perez never touched the bag, and not from peeks at the screen or a challenge by Ausmus.

"We took a consensus of the information," Vanover said to a pool reporter. "Out of that crew consultation, we came up with the answer that he didn't tag up."

Yeah. Uh-huh. Detroit ended up winning the game, 3–2. At the time, the victory gave the Tigers a two-game lead over the Royals atop the AL Central division. The umpires' curious way of getting the call right completely overshadowed Perez's amateurish baserunning blunder—probably to his great relief. As it turned out, both the Tigers and the Royals qualified for post-season play. Detroit accrued 90 wins, one more victory than Kansas City, but it did give the Tigers the luxury of avoiding the perilous one-game AL wild-card game. The Royals beat Oakland in the one-game showdown and subsequently romped undefeated through both the ALDS versus the Los Angeles Angels and the ALCS versus the Baltimore Orioles. They came within one run of winning the 2014 World Series, losing to the San Francisco Giants, 3–2, in the seventh game.

One consistent critic of expanded video review is Joe Posnanski of NBCSports.com, who penned a wonderfully thoughtful online column on April 18, 2014—not even three weeks into MLB's new "review era." He presented the quote from *Inherit the Wind* that appears atop this chapter to lament what high-level sports have lost since they became overly dependent on video review to ensure the correctness of each and every close call.

Posnanski argued that common sense has gone out the window in some cases. He cited a play in a Baltimore-Detroit game from early April in which a force out at second base was not given after the Tigers' second baseman, Andrew Romine, lost control of the ball in attempting to pull it out of his glove to make a double play. The umpires on the field ruled everybody safe. Most people in the park and watching at home expected the call to be overturned by video review. It was not. Replay officials in New York City ruled, according to the strictest definition of "possession," that Romine did not have control of the ball when he stepped on second base. As a mere fan, Ponanski was livid.

It was clearly a blown call—at least it was the wrong call as viewed through the eyes of millions of life-long baseball fans who had seen countless versions of this play through the years. If the guy catches the ball, steps on the bag, and fumbles it in the exchange, the runner is out. That's how it was in 1950. That's how it was in 1970. That's how it was in 1990. By the eyes, the ball was snug in Romine's glove, he stepped on second base, open and shut, and if you watch the [TV replay] again, you will note that both announcers were confident that call would be overturned.

And now we are getting to the heart of what replay costs.

We are now arguing about the very meaning of what it means to catch a baseball.

Nobody ever wondered about what constituted a catch before all this legal wrangling. We all just knew. It was in our blood as baseball fans. We were all in the same sports time zone; we all worked off more or less the same internal spectator clock. But now with replay, the catch is an abstract concept, like justice, or infinity, or what it is to be a Kardashian.

And that is the cost of replay because this sort of ambiguity pops up again and again in our games. Stuff that was always blindly obvious to us now comes down to intensive review. Every moment in every game, it seems, is played back and forth, back and forth, like the Zapruder film. Every moment in every game is argued about like the Dreyfuss Affair. Nothing is real anymore.

Point is: All of the replay scrutiny is making our games a lot less fun. To get the calls right we are willing to sacrifice time. We are willing to sacrifice the power of the moment. We are willing to sacrifice the simplicity that had charmed us about sports in the first place.

Chicago 0 at Pittsburgh 1

Game played on Monday, March 31, 2014, at PNC Park

Chicago Cubs	ab	r	h	rbi
Bonifacio cf,2b	5	0	4	0
Lake lf	4	0	1	0
Villanueva p	0	0	0	0
Castro ss	3	0	0	0
Rizzo 1b	4	0	0	0
Olt 3b	3	0	0	0
Valbuena ph,3b	0	0	0	0
Castillo c	2	0	0	0
Schierholtz rf	4	0	1	0
Barney 2b	2	0	0	0
Sweeney ph, cf	1	0	0	0
Samardzija p	3	0	0	0
Strop p	0	0	0	0
Grimm p	0	0	0	0
Russell p	0	0	0	0
Kalish ph, lf	1	0	0	0
Totals	32	0	6	0

Pittsburgh Pirates	ab	r	h	rbi
Marte lf	3	0	1	0
Snider rf	3	0	0	0
McCutchen cf	3	0	1	0
Alvarez 3b	4	0	0	0
Martin c	4	0	1	0
Walker 2b	4	1	1	1
Ishikawa 1b	3	0	2	0
Mercer ss	3	0	0	0
Liriano p	2	0	0	0
Watson p	0	0	0	0
Melancon p	0	0	0	0
Harrison ph	1	0	0	0
Grilli p	0	0	0	0
Morris p	0	0	0	0
Totals	30	1	6	1

Chicago   000 000 000 0—0 6 0
Pittsburgh   000 000 000 1—1 6 1

Chicago Cubs	IP	H	R	ER	BB	SO
Samardzija	7.0	5	0	0	2	3
Strop	1.0	0	0	0	0	1
Grimm	0.1	0	0	0	1	1
Russell	0.2	0	0	0	0	1
Villanueva L (0–1)	0.0	1	1	1	0	0
Totals	9.0	6	1	1	3	6

Pittsburgh Pirates	IP	H	R	ER	BB	SO
Liriano	6.0	4	0	0	3	10
Watson	1.0	0	0	0	0	0
Melancon	1.0	1	0	0	0	0
Grilli	1.0	0	0	0	1	0
Morris W(1–0)	1.0	1	0	0	0	1
Totals	10.0	6	0	0	4	11

E–Ishikawa (1). DP–Chicago 3. Barney-Castro-Rizzo, Bonifacio-Rizzo, Castro-Rizzo, Pittsburgh 1. Liriano-Alvarez-Walker. 2B–Chicago Bonifacio (1, off Melancon), Pittsburgh Marte (1, off Samardzija). HR–Pittsburgh Walker (1, 10th inning off Villanueva 0 on 0 out). SH–Lake (1, off Melancon); Castillo (1, off Grilli). SB–Bonifacio (1, 2nd base off Liriano/Martin). U-HP–John Hirschbeck, 1B–Bob Davidson, 2B–James Hoye, 3B–John Tumpane. T–3:16. A–39,833.

April 29, 2015

Site: Oriole Park at Camden Yards, Baltimore

Teams: Chicago White Sox vs. Baltimore Orioles

Significance: First MLB Game Played with Zero Paid Attendance

Impact: MLB showed it could still be willing to forsake gate receipts to ensure that a community stays safe

> "If a tree falls in the forest and there's no one to hear it, does it really make a noise? And if you play a Major League Baseball game and there are no fans in the stands, does it really count? The answer is yes."—Joe Angel, WJZ-FM, at the beginning of the radio pre-game show

On Thursday, September 28, 1882, two woebegone National League clubs, the seventh-place Troy (NY) Trojans and the eighth-place Worcester (MA) Ruby Legs, met in a meaningless late-season game at the latter's home ballpark, the Worcester Driving Park Grounds.

Neither team was financially viable. In fact, the NL had already informed both clubs that they would be dissolved at the end of the 1882 season and be replaced by teams in larger and more lucrative population centers for the 1883 campaign. Accordingly, there were few compelling reasons for fans in Worcester to shell out 50 cents to watch the Trojans-Ruby Legs game; in fact, there were only six paying customers present when the first pitch was thrown. At the time it was the smallest paid attendance at any MLB game. Troy won the game, 4–1. The following day attendance more than quadrupled as a crowd of 25 fans paid to see the last NL game these two lame-duck teams would ever play. The Trojans won that game too, by a 10–7 count, and then faded into MLB history along with their hosts. The core of the Troy team included five future Hall of Famers who would be part of the 1883 New York Gothams—later renamed the Giants. The Philadelphia Quakers—today known as the Phillies—would also join the NL in 1883 to replace the departed Ruby Legs. None of the Ruby Legs was on the Quakers' roster the following season.

Much like Cy Young's career win total, it was generally assumed that the record low MLB attendance from September 28, 1882, would never be broken or seriously challenged. The mark lasted for more than 132 years until the Chicago White Sox played the Baltimore Orioles in front of zero paid customers on Wednesday, April 29, 2015. Unlike the 1882 situation, fan apathy was not to blame for the empty ballpark. It was civil unrest in the neighborhood near Baltimore's Camden Yards that caused MLB, in an utterly unprecedented move, to order the game played behind locked doors.

The cause was utterly unrelated to baseball. On Sunday morning, April 12, 2015, the Baltimore Police Department took 25-year-old Freddie Carlos Gray, Jr., into custody in the Gilmor Homes housing project for possession of an illegal switchblade. Gray, an African American with a sizable, drug-related criminal record dating back to his teenage years, fell into a coma while in custody in a police van. He died a week later on April 19. The subsequent medical investigation determined that Gray had expired due to a spinal cord injury sustained while in transport. (It was later learned that Gray had recently undergone back surgery.) In inner-city Baltimore, the police force had long been perceived by its residents as overzealous and oppressive. After the unusual and suspicious cause of Gray's death became public knowledge, anti-police protests were organized within Baltimore. Six police officers involved in Gray's arrest—three of them African American—were put on administrative leave pending an investigation. Eventually they would be indicted by a Grand Jury on May 21. Nevertheless, demonstrations quickly turned violent following Gray's funeral on Monday, April 27.

To prevent confrontations with the city's law enforcement personnel, Stephanie Rawlings-Blake, Baltimore's 45-year-old mayor, controversially ordered the police to "stand down" and not intervene in the rioting. Predictably, the mayhem escalated exponentially. Oriole Park at Camden Yards was situated not too far from the violence, which was spreading dangerously close to the Orioles' home grounds. Parked vehicles and local businesses became the targets of vandals and thieves. The participants in the crime spree were overwhelmingly black youths who perceived the Freddie Gray situation as racially motivated. The fact that Baltimore had a black mayor, a predominantly black city council and a large black representation in the municipal police force did not seem to matter.

Bystanders were indiscriminately assaulted. A new seniors' center, built by a local church to serve the elderly people of the impoverished inner city, was senselessly gutted as the mob ran amok.

The unsettling scenes featured prominently in national and international news for days. The *Chicago Sun-Times* and the *New York Daily News*, both tabloid newspapers, featured fiery front-page images of angry protesters attacking police vehicles, looting, and burning buildings. Larger broadsheet newspapers, including the *New York Times* and *Seattle Times*, printed images of police in riot gear and tense standoffs between law enforcement and the unruly mob. The rioting was the lead story on the BBC's world newscasts for three days running. "Anarchy" and "chaos" were two words frequently used to describe the unfolding mayhem from across the Atlantic.

An initial estimate of the total property damage—thought to be a conservative guess by some analysts—was $9 million. Approximately 200 businesses suffered at least some loss. Many of the worst-hit shops were unlikely to reopen. It was a major economic blow to a city that was hardly in a position to absorb such a setback. *Fortune* magazine noted in its website coverage of the unrest that even before the riots in Baltimore occurred, the city was already perceived as a difficult locale for business enterprises to succeed. In 2015 it was the biggest city in America that did not have a major corporation headquartered within its municipal borders. Baltimore had suffered a crippling blow to its image. The negative repercussions from lost tourism dollars would undoubtedly be felt for many months. Indeed, many baseball fans discussing the developments on MLB.com commented that they had shelved their plans to attend any games in Baltimore for the foreseeable future.

In seemed nearly irrelevant at the time, but the Chicago White Sox were scheduled to play a three-game series at Baltimore's Oriole Park at Camden Yards from April 27–29. Due to the quirks of MLB's unbalanced schedule, this was to be the Pale Hose's only trek to Baltimore that season. This made things complicated.

About a thousand fans were already inside Oriole Park on the evening of Monday, April 27, anticipating the first game of the Orioles-White Sox series, when MLB decided it was in the best interest of public safety to postpone that night's contest. There were few complaints when people realized the seriousness of what was unfolding not too far away. The next night's game was also postponed as the violence continued at a slightly diminished level. Both games were rescheduled as a doubleheader set for Thursday, May 28, a mutual off-day for the two squads. However, because MLB's Collective Bargaining Agreement prohibits triple-headers—there had not been one since 1920—the April 29 game could not be re-scheduled for the same date. With sporadic rioting continuing throughout Baltimore on April 28 and the Maryland National Guard summoned to restore order by Governor Larry Hogan, MLB undertook the unprecedented move of playing Wednesday's game without paid spectators.

"After conferring with local officials, it was determined that Wednesday afternoon's game should be played without fan admittance in order to minimize safety concerns," Major League Baseball announced.[1] "All of the decisions in Baltimore were driven first by the desire to insure the safety of fans, players, umpires and stadium workers," MLB's new commissioner Rob Manfred wrote in an email to the *Associated Press*. "Only after we were comfortable that those concerns had been addressed did we consider competitive issues and the integrity of the schedule."[2] Fans would not be allowed into the ballpark for their own protection. (Presumably their journeys to and from Oriole Park was the primary safety concern.) Moreover, police resources that would normally be assigned to the ballgame could be dispatched elsewhere in the city if further trouble arose. MLB's move was not met with universal acclaim. Hall of Fame first baseman Frank Thomas, obviously unaware of the underlying and complex schedule issues that prompted the decision, tweeted, "They should just cancel this series and make it up later! Playing in front of a [sic] empty house makes no sense!"[3]

Thus the April 29 game went forward, although it was moved from a night game to a 2:05 p.m. start to ensure there was virtually no chance of it violating the 10:00 p.m. curfew that had been put into effect throughout Baltimore until the violence completely abated. With no ticket-holders to consider, a day game made the most sense logistically anyway. It was vaguely reminiscent of situations in South America and Europe where important soccer games have occasionally been played behind locked doors as a way of punishing fans for hooligan violence. This was a North American first, however.

Broadcasters managed to maintain some sense of humor about the unprecedented situation. Veteran Baltimore announcer Joe Angel stated on WJZ-FM, "What a beautiful day for a ballgame! Wish you could be here!" He was right. At game time there were sunny skies and a perfect temperature of 73 degrees. Sadly no one was permitted to be in the ballpark on such a splendid afternoon unless he/she was a member of the media, a scout, or other personnel deemed necessary. Even longtime Orioles employees were banned from entering the venue. At game time, three scouts were conspicuously present behind home plate.[4] Due to the uniqueness of the situation, there were odd sights aplenty. Dozens more media than usual for a typical late April game in Baltimore were on hand to witness the curious and historic scene. The game was televised nationally on Sportsnet in Canada—a rarity for a weekday day game. One Orioles staffer was assigned to retrieve foul balls that ended up in the grandstands. Fans could be seen watching the game from the balconies of the nearby Hilton Baltimore or peering through the bars of a stadium gate. One male held a placard encouraging his fellow fans to "Remember Freddie Gray"— as if they needed to be reminded why they were milling about outside a locked ballpark. The throng's cheers could be heard sporadically throughout the game whenever the home team did something positive.

Players, umpires, and staff brought some levity to the proceedings as well. Orioles manager Buck Showalter, in his radio pre-game show, openly wondered whether he'd actually need to use the telephone to communicate with his relief pitchers or if he could just shout his instructions to the distant bullpen. Plate umpire Jerry Layne jokingly waved to the thousands of empty green seats as he walked onto the field. Fielders continued the pleasant custom—utterly pointless on this day—of throwing balls from third outs into the stands when innings concluded. Music was still played between innings to entertain no one. (One appropriate selection was Simon & Garfunkel's "The Sound of Silence.") The national anthem and the seventh-inning stretch were both observed as usual. In keeping with longstanding Orioles tradition, John Denver's recording of "Thank God I'm a Country Boy" was also played. Only the Kiss-Cam and the Guess the Attendance contest were shelved. About an inning into the game, Joe Angel told his radio audience that the quiet atmosphere reminded him of an intra-squad spring-training contest.

The game did not begin well for the White Sox: A catastrophic Jose Abreu throwing error led to six Baltimore runs on six hits as the home team sent 11 batters to the plate in the bottom of the first. The White Sox never recovered from the early deficit. Chris Davis walloped a three-run home run off Chicago starter Jeff Samardzija. The ball sat lonely on Eutaw Street as nobody was permitted in that area to claim the souvenir. Another unusual occurrence: On the Davis home run, Orioles broadcaster Gary Thorne's call could clearly be heard in the background of the White Sox' television broadcast because there was no crowd noise to drown it out.[5] Similarly, fans listening to the either team's radio broadcast could hear the distinct thumps of foul balls cashing into empty seats along both foul lines. After only two hours and three minutes of baseball played before MLB's first empty house, the final out was recorded in an easy, 8–2 Orioles victory. Both starters lasted just five innings. Ubaldo Jimenez got the win for the home team to raise his record to 2–1. Samardzija's record dropped to 1–2 with the loss. The White Sox managed just four hits, all singles. In contrast, four of Baltimore's 11 hits went for extra bases. Third baseman Manny Machado had three hits and scored three runs for the victors.

The Orioles' following series against the Tampa Bay Rays, also scheduled for Camden Yards, was moved to Tampa's Tropicana Field. (As the official "home team," the Orioles still batted last and kept all gate receipts less the costs incurred by the Rays in their role as hosts.) An interesting note about those re-scheduled contests: The average length of the games in Tampa was two hours and 32 minutes—times much more in line with games of yesteryear than the four-hour marathons that permeate many modern MLB contests. It was as if the two teams were trying to get the awkward situation over with as soon as possible. On May 14 the Orioles announced that Camden Yards staff, such as ushers, vendors and ticket-takers—who had lost several days' wages through no fault of their own—would be paid as if those games had been played in Baltimore as originally scheduled.

After the Orioles' strange home stand in Tampa (where Baltimore won two out of three games), the team embarked on their scheduled road trip to New York City, where they dropped five of six games to the Mets and Yankees. Monday, May 11, was the first Baltimore home game with paid spectators at Camden Yards since the civil unrest occurred. There were more than 20,000 fans in attendance. To open the Orioles' pre-game radio show, Joe Angel casually joked, "We're back in Baltimore. Back home. Back at Oriole Park at Camden Yards. It does look familiar. I know I've been here before. It's all coming back to me." Manager Showalter echoed those thoughts, saying it seemed weird to be back in Baltimore after the long, unplanned absence. He commented that the ballpark's grass had become greener since he had last seen it in late April.

That night the Orioles faced their AL East rivals, the Toronto Blue Jays, in a game described by fans Chris McDaniels and Jerie Shaw as "business as usual." Shaw remarked, "We didn't even know [it was the first game back for Baltimore] until we looked it up." McDaniels believed the normal atmosphere of a typical MLB game was important to establish. He opined, "The Orioles did not necessarily sweep [the circumstances of their long absence] under the rug, but with so much tension around the city, you never know. One wrong step could ignite something else."[6]

The Orioles won in their return to Camden Yards by a score of 5–2. As was the case on April 29, Baltimore jumped out to an early lead and held it throughout the game. Coincidentally, Ubaldo Jimenez was again the Orioles' starting pitcher. He struck out nine Blue Jays and got credit for the home team's win. A louder cheer than usual erupted from the crowd when Jimenez's first pitch of the game was called a strike. Normalcy—at least from a baseball standpoint—had returned to MLB and to the city of Baltimore.

Chicago 2 at Baltimore 8

Game played on Wednesday, April 29, 2015, at Oriole Park at Camden Yards

Chicago White Sox	ab	r	h	rbi		Baltimore Orioles	ab	r	h	rbi
Eaton cf	3	0	0	0		De Aza lf-rf	3	1	1	0
Bonifacio ph	1	0	1	0		Paredes dh	4	1	0	0
M Cabrera lf	4	0	1	0		Young rf	4	1	1	0
Abreu 1b	4	0	0	0		Lough lf	0	0	0	0
LaRoche dh	3	1	0	0		Jones cf	3	0	1	0
Garcia rf	3	1	2	0		Davis 1b	4	1	1	3
Gillaspie 3b	3	0	0	0		Machado 3b	4	3	3	1
Ramirez ss	3	0	0	0		E Cabrera ss	4	1	2	1
Soto c	3	0	0	1		Joseph c	4	0	2	2
Johnson 2b	3	0	0	0		Navarro 2b	4	0	0	0
Samardzija p	0	0	0	0		Jimenez p	0	0	0	0
Carroll p	0	0	0	0		Gausman p	0	0	0	0
Rodon p	0	0	0	0		Britton p	0	0	0	0
Totals	30	2	4	1		Totals	34	8	11	7

Chicago	000 020 000—2	4 1
Baltimore	601 010 00X—8	11 1

Chicago White Sox	IP	H	R	ER	BB	SO
Samardzija L(1–2)	5.0	10	8	7	1	5
Carroll	2.0	1	0	0	0	1
Rodon	1.0	0	0	0	0	1
Totals	8.0	11	8	7	1	7

Baltimore Orioles	IP	H	R	ER	BB	SO
Jimenez W(2–1)	7.0	3	2	0	1	6
Gausman	1.0	0	0	0	0	2
Britton	1.0	1	0	0	0	1
Totals	9.0	4	2	0	1	9

E–Abreu (2), Machado (5). DP–Chicago 1. Samardzija-Ramirez-Abreu. Baltimore 2. Navarro-Machado-Davis, Machado-Navarro-Davis. 2B–Baltimore: Machado (4), E Cabrera 2 (2), Jones (6). HR–Baltimore: Davis (5), Machado (4). SF–Jones (2). U-HP–Jerry Layne, 1B–Hunter Wendelstedt, 2B–Bob Davidson, 3B–David Rackley. T–2:03. A–0

Appendix: Games That Didn't Quite Make the Cut

This project began with an original session of brainstorming by the authors that, not surprisingly, led to a very cumbersome list of 132 "historically significant MLB games." It was first pared down to a more manageable total of 61 games. (Why 61 games? We thought 61 also was a cute number as it exactly matched Roger Maris' home run total in 1961.) That number was later reduced to 51 games and finally to the 43 games which appear in this text. Here is a list of those 10 games that were culled in the second cut:

- First game played at Yankee Stadium
- John McGraw's final game as New York Giants manager
- Joe DiMaggio's hitting streak ends
- Connie Mack's final game as Philadelphia A's manager
- Bob Sheppard's first game as Yankees' P.A. announcer
- Vin Scully's first game as a broadcaster
- Game Seven of the 1955 World Series
- The first LCS game
- First night game at Wrigley Field
- Game Five of the 1995 Mariners-Yankees ALDS

And the eight games that were removed in the third cut:

- The first game after the Black Sox scandal came to light
- The last tie game in the World Series
- Babe Ruth's 60th home run of 1927
- The game that ended Lou Gehrig's consecutive-games-played streak
- The first televised World Series game
- Ten-Cent Beer Night in Cleveland
- The first game at Oriole Park at Camden Yards in Baltimore
- Game Seven of the 2004 ALCS

Notes

April 22, 1876

1. John M. Rosenburg, *They Gave Us Baseball* (Harrisburg, PA: Stackpole Books, 1989), 14.
2. Ibid., 20.

August 17, 1877

1. Bill Mooney, "The Tattletale Grays," *Sports Illustrated*, June 10, 1974 (SI online archives).
2. Ibid.
3. Ibid.
4. Ibid.
5. Ibid.
6. Ibid.
7. Ibid.
8. Ken Burns, *Baseball*, PBS Documentary, 1994.
9. Ibid.
10. Michael Haupert, SABR Biography Project, "William Hulbert," SABR.org.

September 4, 1884

1. John R. Husman, SABR Biography Project, "Fleet Walker," SABR.org.
2. Ibid.
3. Ibid.
4. Ibid.
5. Ibid.
6. Ibid.
7. Ibid.
8. Ibid.

April 19, 1890

1. Ethan M. Lewis, "A Structure to Last Forever: The Players' League and the Brotherhood War of 1890," EthanLewis.org.
2. Ibid.
3. Ibid.
4. Ibid.
5. Ibid.
6. Ibid.
7. Ibid.
8. Ibid.
9. Ibid.

10. Ibid.
11. Ibid.
12. Ibid.
13. Ibid.
14. Ibid.
15. Ibid.
16. Ibid.

April 27, 1893

1. Ralph Berger, SABR Biography Project, "Amos Rusie," SABR.org.
2. Ibid.
3. Jonathan Stilwell, "An Analysis of Pre-Modern Pitchers," SABR.org.

April 24, 1901

1. "Ban Johnson" biography, Baseballhall.org.
2. Ibid.
3. Ibid.
4. Ibid.
5. Ibid.
6. John M. Rosenburg, *They Gave Us Baseball*, 68.

October 1, 1903

1. Sam Bernstein, SABR Biography Project, "Barney Dreyfuss," SABR.org.
2. Ibid.
3. Roger I. Abrams, *The First World Series and the Baseball Fanatics of 1903* (York, PA: Maple Press, 2003), 52.
4. Irwin Cohen, "The Jewish Father of the World Series," jewishpress.com, October 9, 2013.
5. Frank Sleeper, "The Series That Almost Never Got Played," *Sports Illustrated*, September 30, 1968 (SI online archives).
6. Ibid.
7. Andy Dabilis and Nick Tsiotis, *The 1903 World Series* (Jefferson, NC: McFarland, 2004), 64.
8. Ibid., 67.
9. Ibid., 69.
10. Ibid., 71.
11. Ibid., 72.

12. Ibid., 73.
13. Frank Sleeper, "The Series That Almost Never Got Played," *Sports Illustrated*, September 30, 1968 (SI online archives).
14. Ibid.
15. Joseph L. Reichler, *The World Series: A 75th Anniversary* (New York: Simon & Schuster, 1978), 11.

September 23, 1908

1. John P. Carmichael, *My Greatest Day in Baseball* (New York: Grosset & Dunlap, 1951), 37.
2. David Shiner, SABR Biography Project, "Johnny Evers," SABR.org.
3. Gordon H. Fleming, *The Unforgettable Season* (New York: Holt, Reinhart and Winston, 1981), 22.
4. Dan McComb, "1908: The Greatest Baseball Year Ever?" thedailynewsonline.com, December 5, 2009.
5. Charles Dryden, "Game Ends in Tie, May Go to Cubs," *Chicago Daily Tribune*, September 24, 1908, 12.
6. Leonard Koppett, "Giants Can Win One for Merkle," nytimes.com, September 29, 1989.
7. Gabriel Schechter, SABR Biography Project, "Hooks Wiltse," SABR.org.
8. Cait Murphy, *Crazy '08: How a Cast of Cranks, Rogues, Boneheads and Magnates Created the Greatest Year in Baseball History* (New York: HarperCollins, 2007), 193.
9. Original letter from the National Baseball Library in Cooperstown, NY.
10. Harold Seymour, *Baseball: The Golden Age* (New York: Oxford University Press, 1971), 151.
11. Arthur D. Hittner, *Honus Wagner: The Life of Baseball's "Flying Dutchman"* (Jefferson, NC: McFarland, 1996), 174.
12. David W. Anderson, SABR Biography Project, "Hank O'Day," SABR.org.

October 3, 1915

1. Robert C. Cottrell, *Blackball, the Black Sox, and The Babe: Baseball's Crucial 1920 Season* (Jefferson, NC: McFarland, 2002), 19.
2. Stuart Banner, *The Baseball Trust: A History of Baseball's Antitrust Exemption* (New York: Oxford University Press, 2013), 54.
3. Marc Okkonen, *The Federal League of 1914–1915: Baseball's Third Major League* (Garrett Park, MD: Society for American Baseball Research, 1989), 15.
4. Eric Lutz, "Tale of the Whales: The Forgotten Story of Chicago's Original North Side Ballclub," Newcity.com.

October 1, 1919

1. Ken Burns, *Baseball*, PBS Documentary, 1994.
2. Ibid.

April 14, 1920

1. Graham Womack, "Graham Womack's 25 Most Important People in Baseball History Survey," RadicalBaseball.blogspot.ca.
2. Ken Burns, *Baseball*, PBS Documentary, 1994.
3. Donald Honig, *Baseball America* (New York: Macmillan, 1985), 133.

August 16, 1920

1. "Beaned By a Pitch, Ray Chapman Dies," *New York Times*, August 18, 1920.
2. Vince Guerrieri, "League, City Plunged into Mourning After Chapman's Death," Didthetribewinlastnight.com.
3. Susan Jacoby, "Death on the Mound," *New York Times*, September 17, 1989 (online archives).

May 16, 1921

1. S. A. Paolantonio, "Reuben Rule Gives Souvenir-Seeking Fans a Reason to Attend," *Orlando Sentinel*, September 9, 1986 (online archives).
2. Ibid.
3. Kevin Reichard, "Bloomberg: 1,750 Fans Injured Annually by Foul Balls at MLB Ballparks," BallparkDigest.com, September 11, 2014.

August 5, 1921

1. "Harold W. Arlin Dead; An Early Radio Figure," *New York Times*, March 18, 1986 (online archives).

July 6, 1933

1. Lew Freedman, *The Day All the Stars Came Out: Major League Baseball's First All-Star Game* (Jefferson, NC: McFarland), 10.

May 24, 1935

1. Oscar Eddleton, "Under the Lights," SABR Research Journals Archive (online).
2. Ibid.
3. Ibid.
4. Ibid.
5. Ibid.

August 26, 1939

1. Evan Andrews, "Major League Baseball Makes Television Debut, 75 Years Ago," history.com, August 26, 2014.
2. Ibid.
3. Ibid.

April 15, 1947

1. *Ghosts of Flatbush*, HBO Video, 2007.
2. Neil Lanctot, *Negro League Baseball: The Rise and Ruin of a Black Institution* (Philadelphia: University of Pennsylvania Press, 2004), 314.
3. Jules Tygiel, *Baseball's Great Experiment: Jackie Robinson and His Legacy* (New York: Oxford University Press, 1983), 211.

4. Calvin W. Boaz, "Larry Doby: The Forgotten Pioneer," bleacherreport.com, July 5, 2009.

5. Ibid.

August 19, 1951

1. Bill Veeck, *Veeck—As in Wreck* (Chicago: University of Chicago Press, 1962), 12.

2. Ibid.

3. Jim Sargent, SABR Biography Project, "Jim Delsing," SABR.org.

4. Matt Snyder, "The Bobblehead Project: Little Person Eddie Gaedel Steps In," CBSsports.com, August 15, 2013.

5. "Eddie Gaedel Makes History," dantheman trivia.wordpress.com, August 19, 2009.

6. Bill Christine, "This Fan Knew the Browns Didn't Have a No. 1/8," articles.latimes.com, August 19, 1991.

7. Ibid.

8. *The Sporting News*, August 29, 1951.

9. Jim Sargent, SABR Biography Project, "Jim Delsing," SABR.org.

10. Paul Dickson, *Bill Veeck: Baseball's Greatest Maverick* (New York: Walker, 2012), 192–193.

11. Ibid.

12. Ibid., 192.

13. *The Sporting News*, August 29, 1951.

14. Paul Dickson, *Bill Veeck*, 193.

15. Bill Christine, "This Fan Knew the Browns Didn't Have a No. 1/8," articles.latimes.com, August 19, 1991.

16. Richard Bak, "Sixty Years Ago: Detroit Tiger Bob Cain Pitched to Midget Eddie Gaedel," blog.detroitathletic.com, August 19, 2011.

17. "Eddie Gaedel Midget Pinch Hitter," yourememberthat.com.

October 3, 1951

1. Heywood Hale Broun, "Brooks, Bums, Dodgers, Men," *Chicago Times*, February 27, 1972, J4.

2. Ken Burns, *Baseball*, PBS Documentary, 1994.

3. James S. Hirsch, *Willie Mays: The Life, The Legend* (New York: Scribner, 2010), 134.

4. Ray Robinson, *The Home Run 'Heard Round the World: The Dramatic Story of the 1951 Giants-Dodgers Pennant Race* (New York: HarperCollins, 1991), 227.

5. Lindsay Berra, "Branca Doesn't Let One Pitch Define Career," MLB.com, February 20, 2014.

6. Ken Burns, *Baseball*, PBS Documentary, 1994.

7. *Ball Talk*, J2Communications (video documentary), 1989.

April 14, 1953

1. David M. Jordan, *Closing 'Em Down: Final Games at Thirteen Classic Ballparks* (Jefferson, NC: McFarland, 2010), 32.

2. *The Sporting News*, March 25, 1953.

September 24, 1957

1. Henry D. Fetter, "The Queens Dodgers?" *New York Times* (online archives), August 14, 2005.

2. "On This Day: Dodgers and Giants Receive Permission to Move to California," findingdulcinea.com, May 28, 2011.

3. Ibid.

4. Curt Smith, *Pull Up a Chair: The Vin Scully Story* (Dulles, VA: Potomac Books, 2009), 48.

5. "On This Day: Dodgers and Giants Receive Permission to Move to California," findingdulcinea.com, May 28, 2011.

6. Curt Smith, *Pull Up a Chair*, 88.

7. *The Sporting News*, April 5, 1969.

8. Michael Coffey, *27 Men Out: Baseball's Perfect Games* (New York: Atria Books, 2004), 76.

9. Ibid.

10. Ibid., 77.

11. Joseph M. Sheehan, "They Took Our Hearts Too," *New York Times* (online archives) May 28, 1957.

12. Ibid.

13. Ibid.

14. Kathryn Jay, *More Than Just a Game: Sports in American Life Since 1945* (New York: Columbia University Press, 2004), 85.

15. James S. Hirsch, *Willie Mays: The Life, The Legend* (New York: Scribner, 2010), 268.

16. "May 28, 1957: Baseball Owners Allow Dodgers and Giants to Move," history.com.

17. Edward J. Reilly, *Baseball: An Encyclopedia of Popular Culture* (Lincoln, NE: University of Nebraska Press, 2000), 200.

18. Michael D'Antonio, *Forever Blue* (New York: Riverhead Books, 2009).

19. Curt Smith, *Pull Up a Chair*, 60.

20. Michael Coffey, *27 Men Out*, 72.

October 1, 1961

1. Wayne Stewart, (ed., *The Gigantic Book of Baseball Quotations* (New York: Skyhorse, 2007), 107.

2. Joseph Durso, "Roger Maris Is Dead at 51, Set Home Run Records," *New York Times* (online archives), December 15, 1985.

3. Ibid.

4. Ibid.

5. Ibid.

6. Ken Burns, *Baseball*, PBS Documentary, 1994.

7. Dan Shaughnessy, "Tracy Stallard: He Yielded No. 61 To Roger Maris," *Baseball Digest*, January 1992.

April 12, 1965

1. "Colt Stadium," Ballparksofbaseball.com.

2. "A History of the Astrodome," HoustonAstros.mlb.com.

3. Ibid.

4. "Could Have Pitched 20 Years in Dome—Satch Paige," *Jet*, May 27, 1965, 53.

5. *The Sporting News*, April 25, 1965.

April 14, 1969

1. "Curt Flood Raps Field," *Montreal Gazette*, April 15, 1969, 10.
2. "Crime Doesn't Pay on Soft Track," *Montreal Gazette*, April 15, 1969, 10.

October 13, 1971

1. Gene Collier, "The 1971 World Series Was Played in a Different World," *Pittsburgh Post-Gazette* (online version), June 19, 2011.

April 6, 1973

1. "Ron Blomberg," *Yankee Magazine*, December 1993.
2. Ibid.
3. Ibid.
4. Ibid.
5. Ibid.
6. Ibid.
7. Ibid.
8. Dan Schlossberg, "First Designated Hitter Ron Blomberg Proud to Be Father of Position," usatoday.com, April 10, 2013.

April 8, 1974

1. "Darrell Evans Stats," baseball-almanac.com.
2. "Hank Aaron, Two Fans Reunite," espn.com, August 27, 2010.
3. Ken Burns, *Baseball*, PBS Documentary, 1994.
4. Mark Inabinett, "Hank Aaron Reminisces with Al Downing," al.com, January 26, 2014.
5. Mike Axisa, "Hank Aaron Compares Republicans Who Oppose Obama to KKK," cbssports.com, April 9, 2014.
6. "Baseball Legend Hank Aaron Compares Obama Critics to KKK," BlackNews.com, April 17, 2014.

April 9, 1974

1. Gene Wojciechowski, "San Diego Chicken Deserves Call to Hall," espn.com, June 30, 2009.
2. Bruce Newman, "Some Wild and Krazy Guys," *Sports Illustrated* (online version), September 17, 1979.
3. Ibid.
4. Patricia Lee Murphy, "Looking for Some Chicken Delight? Just Order Up Ted Giannoulas, Who's Sure Not to Lay an Egg," people.com, September 25, 1978.
5. Bruce Newman, "Some Wild and Krazy Guys," *Sports Illustrated* (online version), September 17, 1979.
6. Ibid.
7. Ibid.
8. Patrick Hruby, "The Phanatic Speaks," espn.com, December 4, 2006.
9. Ibid.
10. Ibid.

11. Gene Wojciechowski, "San Diego Chicken Deserves Call to Hall," espn.com, June 30, 2009.

October 21, 1975

1. Ken Burns, *Baseball*, PBS Documentary, 1994.
2. Ibid.
3. Ibid.
4. Ibid.
5. Geoffrey C. Ward and Ken Burns, *Baseball: An Illustrated History* (New York: Alfred A. Knopf, 2010), 442.

September 9, 1979

1. Dan Gutman, *The Way Baseball Works* (New York: Simon & Schuster, 1996), 36.
2. Bill Dow "Detroit Legends Howe & Cochrane Nearly Died from Head Injuries," detroitathletic.com, March 30, 2011.

October 26, 1985

1. Curry Kirkpatrick, "K.C. Had a Blast," *Sports Illustrated*, November 4, 1985, 25.
2. Ibid.
3. Wayne Coffey, "Don Denkinger, Ump Best Known for Blown Call in 1985 World Series, Has Words of Advice for Jim Joyce," nydailynews.com, June 3, 2010.
4. Ibid.

October 3, 1995

1. Mike Rogers, "Revisiting the 1894 Temple Cup," beyondtheboxscore.com, December 12, 2010.
2. "Division Series," Baseball-almanac.com.
3. Alex Remington, "Should MLB Eliminate its Entire Playoffs?" fangraphs.com, May 2, 2013.
4. James Lincoln Ray. SABR Biography Project, "Don Mattingly," SABR.org.

June 13, 1997

1. Gerry Callahan, "Nice to Meet You," *Sports Illustrated*, June 23, 1997, 63.
2. Ibid., 64.
3. Ibid., 63.
4. Ibid.
5. "Letters," *Sports Illustrated*, August 4, 1997, 4.
6. Ibid.
7. Jayson Stark, "Even More Interleague Intrigue," espn.com, May 19, 2012.

September 8, 1998

1. "Rudy York," baseballlibrary.com.
2. Joe Drape, "McGwire Admits Taking Controversial Substance," nytimes.com, August 22, 1998.
3. Marc Johnson, "Not Guilty as Sin," manythingsconsidered.com, June 19, 2012.

July 9, 2002

1. Adam McCalvy, "All-Star Game Finishes in Tie," mlb.com, July 9, 2002.
2. Jim Maloney, "Konerko Enjoys All-Star Game," mlb.com, July 10, 2002.
3. "MLB Set for More Instant Replay," espn.com, July 17, 2013.

October 14, 2003

1. *Catching Hell*, ESPN "30-for-30" documentary series, 2011.
2. Ibid.
3. Ibid.
4. Jay Mariotti, "Time for Fan to Reach Out, Have Say," *Chicago Sun-Times*, October 28, 2003, 110.
5. Annie Sweeney, "Infamous Fan: I'm Truly Sorry," *Chicago Sun-Times*, October 16, 2003, 9.
6. Ibid.
7. "Baseball Fan Feels Chicago's Fury," news.bbc.co.uk, October 17, 2003.
8. Annie Sweeney, "Infamous Fan: I'm Truly Sorry," *Chicago Sun-Times*, October 16, 2003, 9.
9. Ben Strauss, "Ten Years Later, Infamous Cubs Fan Remains Invisible," nytimes.com, October 13, 2013.
10. Ibid.
11. Ibid.
12. Ibid.
13. Ibid.
14. Ibid.
15. Ibid.

August 7, 2007

1. "Designer to Brand Asterisk on Ball; Hall of Fame to Accept It," espn.com, September 26, 2007.
2. "Bonds Files for Free Agency," mlb.com, October 31, 2007.

June 2, 2010

1. "The Perfect Mistake," saintsational.net, June 3, 2010.
2. Jesse Sanchez, "Jim Joyce's Legacy Now Includes Imperfect Call," espn.com, June 3, 2010.
3. Ibid.
4. Jason Beck, "Missed Call Ends Galarraga's Perfect Bid," espn.com, June 3, 2010.
5. Ibid.
6. Ibid.
7. Tyler Kepner, "Perfect Game Thwarted by Faulty Call," nytimes.com, June 3, 2010.
8. Tom Verducci, "A Different Kind of Perfect," *Sports Illustrated*, June 14, 2010, 47.
9. "Bloggers React to Armando Galaragga's [sic] 'Perfect' Game," sbnation.com, June 3, 2010.
10. Ibid.
11. Ibid.

12. Tom Verducci, "A Different Kind of Perfect," *Sports Illustrated*, June 14, 2010, 47.

May 25, 2011

1. Paul Hagen, "New Rule on Home-Plate Collisions Put into Effect," mlb.com, February 24, 2014.
2. Ibid.
3. Ibid.
4. Jerry Nowak, "Mixed Reaction from Players, Managers to Collision Rule," mlb.com, February 24, 2014.

October 5, 2012

1. "Braves Fans Attack Umpires with Garbage after Worst Infield Fly Call Ever," deadspin.com, October 5, 2012.
2. Ibid.
3. Ibid.

March 31, 2014

1. John Billheimer, *Baseball and the Blame Game: Scapegoating in the Major Leagues* (Jefferson, NC: McFarland, 2007), 186.
2. Bill Dow, "How Milly Martin and Umpire John Rice Cost the Tigers the 1972 Pennant," detroitathletic.com, October 1, 2011.
3. Brian Murphy, "Wild Tigers-A's Series Reminiscent of their Meeting in 1972 ALCS—Just in Reverse," archive.freep.com, October 11, 2012.
4. Ibid.
5. Alyson Footer, "Most Players, Skippers in Favor of Replay," mlb.com, August 26, 2008.
6. Gregor Chisholm, "Odd Challenge Starts Domino Effect for A's, Blue Jays," mlb.com, July 4, 2014.
7. Ibid.
8. Ibid.
9. Blair Kerkhoff, "Crazy, Confusing Play Costs Royals in Loss to Tigers," kansascity.com, September 20, 2014.

April 29, 2015

1. Almasy, Steve. "Orioles game on Wednesday will have no fans," cnn.com, April 28, 2015.
2. ESPN.com news services. "White Sox-Orioles game will be played Wednesday, closed to public," espn.com, April 29, 2015.
3. Thomas, Frank. "https://twitter.com/TheBig Hurt_35/status/593137465608826880," twitter.com, April 28, 2015.
4. Axisa, Mike. "SIGHTS & SOUNDS: Orioles, White Sox play in empty Camden Yards," CBSSports.com, April 29, 2015.
5. Ibid.
6. Shaw, Jerie & McDaniels, Christopher. Personal interview, May 14, 2015.

Bibliography

Books and Published Articles

Abrams, Roger I. *The First World Series and the Baseball Fanatics of 1903.* York, PA: Maple Press, 2003.

Akin, William E. "William A. Hulbert," in *Nineteenth Century Stars.* Kansas City: Society for American Baseball Research, 1989.

Allen, Lee. *The National League Story.* New York: Hill & Wang, 1965 [revised edition].

Anson, Adrian C. *A Ball Player's Career.* Chicago: Era Publishing, 1900.

Appel, Marty. *Slide, Kelly, Slide.* Lanham, MD: Scarecrow Trade, 1999.

Asinof, Eliot. *The Black Sox and the 1919 World Series.* New York: Henry Holt, 1977.

Banner, Stuart. *The Baseball Trust: A History of Baseball's Antitrust Exemption.* New York: Oxford University Press, 2013.

Biegel, Brian. *Miracle Ball.* New York: Three Rivers Press, 2009.

Billheimer, John. *Baseball and the Blame Game: Scapegoating in the Major Leagues.* Jefferson, NC: McFarland, 2007.

Brunell, F. H. *1890 Players' National League Baseball Guide.* Chicago: W. J. Jefferson Printing, 1889.

Carmichael, John P., et al. *My Greatest Day in Baseball.* New York: Grosset & Dunlap, 1951.

Clavin, Tom, and Danny Peary. *Gil Hodges.* New York: New American Library, 2012.

Coffey, Michael. *27 Men Out: Baseball's Perfect Games.* New York: Atria Books, 2004.

Cottrell, Robert C. *Blackball, the Black Sox, and The Babe: Baseball's Crucial 1920 Season.* Jefferson, NC: McFarland, 2002.

Creamer, Robert W. *Babe: The Legend Comes to Life.* Open Road Integrated Media (online version), 1974.

Crehan, Herb. *Red Sox Heroes of Yesteryear.* Cambridge, MA: Rounder Books, 2005.

Dabilis, Andy, and Nick Tsiotos. *The 1903 World Series.* Jefferson, NC: McFarland, 2004.

D'Antonio, Michael. *Forever Blue.* New York: Riverhead Books, 2009.

DeValeria, Dennis, and Jeanne Burke DeValeria. *Honus Wagner: A Biography.* New York: Henry Holt, 1996.

Dickson, Paul. *Bill Veeck: Baseball's Greatest Maverick.* New York: Walker, 2012.

Einstein, Charles, ed. *The Baseball Reader.* New York: Bonanza Books, 1989.

Elliott, Bob. *The Northern Game.* Toronto: Sports Media Publishing, 2005.

Fleming, Gordon H. *The Unforgettable Season.* New York: Holt, Reinhart and Winston, 1981.

Freedman, Lew. *The Day All the Stars Came Out: Major League Baseball's First All-Star Game, 1933.* Jefferson, NC: McFarland, 2010.

Frommer, Harvey. *Five O'Clock Lightning.* Hoboken, NJ: John Wiley & Sons, 2008.

Frost, Mark. *Game Six.* New York: Hyperion, 2009.

Gallagher, Danny, and Bill Young. *Remembering the Montreal Expos.* Toronto: Scoop Press, 2005.

Golenbock, Peter. *Bums: An Oral History of the Brooklyn Dodgers.* New York: Contemporary Books, 2000.

_____. *Dynasty: The New York Yankees 1949–1964.* New York: Prentice Hall, 1975.

Gutman, Dan. *Banana Bats and Ding-Dong Balls: A Century of Unique Baseball Inventions.* New York: Macmillan, 1995.

_____. *The Way Baseball Works.* New York: Simon & Schuster, 1996.

Halfon, Mark S. *Tales from the Deadball Era.* Lincoln, NE: Potomac Books, 2014.

Hirsch, James S. *Willie Mays: The Life, the Legend.* New York: Scribner, 2010.

Hittner, Arthur D. *Honus Wagner: The Life of Baseball's "Flying Dutchman."* Jefferson, NC: McFarland, 1996.

Honig, Donald. *Baseball America.* New York: Macmillan, 1985.

Hynd, Noel. *The Giants of the Polo Grounds.* Dallas, TX: Taylor, 1995.

Jay, Kathryn. *More Than Just a Game: Sports in American Life Since 1945*. New York: Columbia University Press, 2004.

Jordan, David M. *Closing 'Em Down: Final Games at Thirteen Classic Ballparks*. Jefferson, NC: McFarland, 2010.

Kennedy, Kostya. *56: Joe DiMaggio and the Last Magic Number in Sports*. New York: Sports Illustrated Books, 2011.

Keri, Jonah. *Up, Up, & Away*. USA: Random House Canada, 2014.

Koppett, Leonard. *Koppett's Concise History of Major League Baseball*. Philadelphia: Temple University Press, 1998.

Lanctot, Neil. *Negro League Baseball: The Rise and Ruin of a Black Institution*. Philadelphia: University of Pennsylvania Press, 2004.

Lieb, Frederick G. *Connie Mack: Grand Old Man of Baseball*. Kent, OH: Kent State University, 2012 (reprint of Lieb's 1945 biography of Mack).

Lupica, Mike. *Summer of '98: When Homers Flew, Records Fell and Baseball Reclaimed America*. New York: Contemporary Books, 1999.

Markusen, Bruce. *The Team that Changed Baseball: Roberto Clemente and the 1971 Pittsburgh Pirates*. Yardley, PA: Westholme Publishing, 2006.

McGwire, Jay. *Mark and Me*. Chicago: Triumph Books, 2010.

Mead, William B. *The Official New York Yankees Hater's Handbook*. New York: Perigree Books, 1983.

Merrell, David B. "Rusie, Amos Wilson, 'The Hoosier Thunderbolt.'" In *Biographical Dictionary of American Sports: Baseball,* edited by David L. Porter, Rev. ed. Vol. 3. Westport, CT: Greenwood Press, 2000.

Murphy, Cait. *Crazy '08: How a Cast of Cranks, Rogues, Boneheads and Magnates Created the Greatest Year in Baseball History*. New York: HarperCollins, 2007.

Nathan, Daniel A. *Saying It's So: A Cultural History of the Black Sox Scandal*. Urbana-Champaign, IL: University of Illinois Press, 2003.

Neyer, Rob. *Rob Neyer's Big Book of Baseball Legends*. New York: Fireside Books, 2008.

Okkonen, Marc. *The Federal League of 1914–15: Baseball's Third Major League*. Garrett Park, MD: Society for American Baseball Research, 1989.

Okrent, Daniel, and Steve Wulf. *Baseball Anecdotes*. New York: Oxford University Press, 1989.

O'Nan, Stewart, and Stephen King. *Faithful*. New York: Scribner, 2004.

Pearlman, Jeff. *Love Me, Hate Me: Barry Bonds and the Making of an Antihero*. New York: HarperCollins, 2006.

Pearson, Daniel M. *Baseball in 1889: Players vs. Owners*. Bowling Green, OH: Bowling Green State University Popular Press, 1993.

Porter, David L., ed. *Biographical Dictionary of American Sports,* vol. 2. Westport, CT: Greenwood Publishing, 2000.

Posnanski, Joe. *The Machine*. New York: HarperCollins, 2009.

Reichler, Joseph L., ed. *The World Series: A 75th Anniversary*. New York: Simon & Schuster, 1978.

Reilly, Edward J. *Baseball: An Encyclopedia of Popular Culture*. Lincoln, NE: University of Nebraska Press, 2000.

Ritter, Lawrence S. *The Glory of Their Times*. New York: Vintage Books, 1985.

Robinson, Ray. *Iron Horse: Lou Gehrig in His Time*. New York: W.W. Norton, 1990.

_____. *The Home Run Heard 'Round the World: The Dramatic Story of the 1951 Giants-Dodgers Pennant Race*. New York: HarperCollins, 1991.

Rosenburg, John M. *They Gave Us Baseball*. Harrisburg, PA: Stackpole Books, 1989.

Seymour, Harold, and Dorothy Seymour Mills. *Baseball: The Golden Age*. New York: Oxford University Press, 1971.

Shatzkin, Mike, ed. *The Ballplayers*. New York: William Morrow, 1990.

Simon, Tom, ed. *Deadball Stars of the National League*. Washington, DC: Brassey's, 2004.

Simon, Tom, ed. *Green Mountain Boys of Summer: Vermonters in the Major Leagues 1882–1993*. Shelburne, VT: New England Press, 2000.

Smith, Curt. *Pull Up a Chair: The Vin Scully Story*. Dulles, VA: Potomac Books, 2009.

Sons of Sam Horn, *Win It For....* Champaign, IL: Sports Publishing, 2005.

Sowell, Mike. *The Pitch That Killed: The Story of Carl Mays, Ray Chapman, and the Pennant Race of 1920*. New York: Macmillan, 1989.

Thornton, Patrick K. *Legal Decisions that Shaped Modern Baseball*. Jefferson, NC: McFarland, 2012.

Tygiel, Jules. *Baseball's Great Experiment: Jackie Robinson and His Legacy*. New York: Oxford University Press, 1983.

Veeck, Bill. *Veeck—As in Wreck*. Chicago: University of Chicago Press, 1962.

Walker, M. F. *Our Home Colony: A Treatise on the Past and Future of the Negro Race in America*. Steubenville, OH: Herald Printing, 1908.

Ward, Geoffrey C, and Ken Burns. *Baseball: An Illustrated History*. New York: Alfred A. Knopf, 2010.

Zang, David. W. *Fleet Walker's Divided Heart: The Life of Baseball's First Black Major Leaguer*. Lincoln, NE: University of Nebraska Press, 1995.

Online Reference Sources

Al.com.
Armchairqb.com
Athomeplate.com
BallparkDigest.com
Ballparksofbaseball.com
Baseball-Almanac.com
BaseballLibrary.com
BaseballNation.com
Baseballparks.com
BaseballReference.com
Baseballreliquary.org
BaseballsSteroidEra.com
Beyondtheboxscore.com
BlackNews.com
BleacherReport.com
Boston.com
CBSsports.com.
Centerfieldgate.com
Cleveland.com
Danallen.com
Deadspin.com
Detroitathletic.com
DodgerBlues.com
ESPN.com
Ethanlewis.org
Fangraphs.com
Freep.com
Futilityinfielder.com
History.com
I70basbeball.com
Jewishpress.com
Kansascity.com
Latimes.com
Manythingsconsidered.com
MLB.com
NBCSports.com
Newcity.com
News.bbc.co.uk
Npr.org
Nydailynews.com
Obstructedview.net
Orlandosentinel.com
Padres360.com
PaperofRecord.com
Pastimepost.com
People.com
Phillies.com
Philly.com
Quotegarden.com
RadicalBaseball.blogspot.ca
Retrosheet.org
SABR.org
Saintsational.net
SI.com
Sfia.org
Sourcefed.com
Sportsoneearth.com
Stuffnobodycaresabout.com
Theatlantic.com
Thedailynewsonline.com
TheDeadballEra.com
TheMick.com
Thestlbrowns.com
Todayinbaseball.com
USAToday.com
Washingtonpost.com
Yourememberthat.com
19cbaseball.com

Video Sources

Ball Talk. J2Communications, 1989.
Baseball (produced by Ken Burns). PBS Home Video, 1994.
Catching Hell. ESPN 30-for-30 series, 2011.
Four Days in October. ESPN 30-for-30 series, 2009.
Ghosts of Flatbush. HBO Sports, 2007.

Index

Numbers in **_bold italics_** refer to pages with photographs.

Aaron, Estella 165
Aaron, Gaile 165
Aaron, Henry "Hank" 161–167, 169–170, 202, 215–216, 218–220
Abreu, Jose 250
Acta, Manny 241
Adams, Franklin P. 48
Alexander, Grover Cleveland 59
Allen, Dick 142, 145
Allenson, Gary 181
Alou, Felipe 159
Alou, Jesus 150
Alou, Matty 159
Alou, Moises 209–212
Altrock, Nick 169
Anaheim Angels 234; _see also_ Los Angeles Angels
Anderson, Dave 128
Anderson, Garret 205
Anderson, Sparky 173–176
Angel, Joe 245, 248–249
Anson, Cap 6, 15, 17–19, **_19_**, 26, 33, 180
Appel, Marty 26, 160
Arizona Diamondbacks 233
Arlin, Harold 88–89, **_90_**, 91
Arnold, Benedict 128
Ashburn, Richie 143
Asinof, Eliot 10
AT&T Park 215, 219, 221, 229–230, 233
Atlanta Braves 147, 150, 161–167, 168, 170, 187, 188, 191, 193, 201, 217, 234–237, 241
Atlanta-Fulton County Stadium 161, 163, 166
Attell, Abe 70
Auker, Elden 179
Aulick, W.W. 54
Ausmus, Brad 243–244
Autostade (Montreal) 149–150
Averill, Earl 94

Bacsik, Mike 219–220
Bailey, Bill 66
Bailey, Pearl 164
Baker, Dusty 210

Baker, John Franklin (Home Run) 93
Baker Field (Columbia University) 102, 104
Balboni, Steve 183–184
The Ballpark in Arlington 190, 192, 194
Baltimore Colts 149
Baltimore Orioles (AA-NL) 29, 32, 187
Baltimore Orioles (current AL) 116, 152–156, 181, 193, 204, 239–241, 245–249
Baltimore Orioles (IL) 62
Baltimore Orioles (original AL) 36, 123
Baltimore Terrapins 62
Banks, Ernie 192, 212
Barber, Red 102–104, 120, 140
Barclay, Curt 130
Barlick, Al 122
Barnes, Randy 199
Barnes, Ross 6, 9
Barrier, Smith 109
Bartell, Dick 94
Bartman, Steve 209–214
Batista, Tony 205
Battey, Earl 180
Beane, Billy 187
Beaumont, Ginger 42
Beck, Jason 226
Beckett, Josh 209
Belanger, Mark 154
Bench, Johnny 174–175, 232
Beniquez, Juan 178
Berger, Wally 197
Berkman, Lance 205
Berman, Leonard 85
Berman, Reuben 84–86
Bernard, E.S. 37
Berry, Connie 116
Bertrand, Jean-Jacques 151
Biegel, Brian 119
Billingham, Jack 150, 163
Birmingham, Joe 49
Bisher, Furman 163
Black, Bud 227
Black, Joe 122

Blackman, Ted 151
Blagojevich, Rod 211
Blair, Paul 154
Blass, Steve 153
Blomberg, Ron 157–160
Bochy, Bruce 230
Boggs, Mitchell 237
Boggs, Wade 188
Bonds, Barry 166, 201–202, 204–205, 215–221
Bonds, Bobby 166, 216
Bonds, Rosie 216
Bonifacio, Emilio 229
Borris, Jeff 221
Bosk, Joe 179
Boston Americans/Pilgrims/Red Sox 35–45, **_40_**, 68–69, 73–76, 78, 91, 101, 106, 121, 133, 136–137, 139, 157, 159–160, 173–178, 181, 188, 189, 192, 194, 204, 234
Boston Red Caps/Beaneaters/Doves/Braves 3–5, 7, 9, 11–14, 32, 37, 42, 57, 63, 91, 105, 109, 121–124, 127, 134, 180, 233
Boston Red Stockings (NA) 6, 7
Boston Reds 24, 26
Bourn, Michael 237
Bouton, Jim 1
Bowman, John S. 3, 33
Bracker, Milton 131
Braden, Dallas 223
Bradley, George 9
Bramham, W.G. 107–108
Branca, Ralph 117, 119–120
Bransfield, Kitty 42, 45
Braves Field 121–123, **_123_**
Breadon, Sam 100
Bream, Sid 217
Breard, Stan 109
Breitenstein, Ted 32
Brenly, Bob 205
Brennaman, Thom 209
Brennan, Bill 66
Bresnahan, Roger 52, 179
Brett, George 184
Bridwell, Al 46, 52–54, 56
Briggs Stadium 101

Briles, Nelson 151
Broeg, Bob 114, 116
Bronfman, Charles 149
Brooklyn Bridegrooms (AA) 27
Brooklyn Robins/Dodgers 46, 47, 81, 83, 100, 101–107, 109–112, 117–120, 122–132, 148, 179–180, 239
Brooklyn Tip Tops 62, 65–66
Brooklyn Ward's Wonders (PL) 26–27
Brotherhood Park 25, 28; *see also* Polo Grounds
Broun, Heywood 118
Brouthers, Dan 32
Brown, Jonathan 26–27
Brown, Mordecai 69
Browning, Pete 24, 27
Brunell, Frank H. 23
Brush, John T. 22
Bruton, Bill 124
Bucca, Gaetano 131
Buck, Jack 200
Buck, Joe 205
Buckley, Jack Boyd 144
Buckner, Bill 46, 165
Budig, Gene 193
Buffalo Bisons 20, 21, 23–26
Buffalo Buffeds/Blues 62–63, 65–66
Bulkeley, Morgan G. 7
Bunning, Jim 139, 202
Burdette, Lew 122
Burke, Eddie 49
Burket, Harlan 16
Burkhart, Ken 239–240
Burns, Bill 70, *71*
Busch Stadium 195, 200, 202
Bush, Donie 68–69
Bush, George W. 168, 186
Bush, Jeb 211

Cabrera, Miguel 210–211, 222–224
Cahill, George F. 98–99
Cain, Bob 114–116
Calcaterra, Craig 233
Caldwell, Ray 79
Callahan, Gerry 192–193
Callahan, Jimmy 34
Callison, Johnny 159
Camden Yards 147, 204, 245–247, 249–251
Campanella, Roy 122, 127
Canseco, Jose 197–198, 201–202
Carapazza, Vic 242
Caray, Harry 198, 213
Carbo, Bernie 174–175, 239
Carmona, Fausto (Roberto Hernandez) 222
Carter, Jimmy 164
Cartwright, Alexander 68
Cash, Norm 180, 240
Cashman, Brian 235
Castellanos, Nick 243
Castillo, Luis 209–210
Catton, Bruce 2
Cepeda, Orlando 159–160
Chadwick, Henry 4, 10, 24
Chamberlain, Wilt 157

Chance, Frank 52, 54, 56, 81, 179
Chapman, Jack 12
Chapman, Kathleen 80, 83
Chapman, Rae 83
Chapman, Ray 77–83, *83*
Chase, Charles E. 12–13
Chicago Pirates 25, 27
Chicago Whales 60, 62–63, 65–66
Chicago White Sox (AL) 10, 33–34, 47, 67–72, *71*, 83, 93, 110, 115, 135, 193, 223, 245–249
Chicago White Stockings (NA) 6, 11
Chicago White Stockings/Colts/Orphans/Cubs 6, *8*, 9, 17–19, 22, 25–26, 29, 30, 32, 34, 46–52, 54–58, 69, 85–87, 94, 112, 143, 166, 179, 190, 195, 198, 200–201, 208–214, 224, 238–239, 241–242
Chylak, Nestor 155
Cicotte, Eddie 10, 70–72, *71*
Cimoli, Gino 132
Cincinnati Red Stockings 5, 235–236
Cincinnati Reds 7, 9, 10, 12, 26, 29, 31–32, 34, 57, 63, 67–68, 70, *71, 72*, 84–85, 93, 96–104, *100, 102*, 110, 124, 130, 146, 154–155, 163–164, 166, 173–176, 178, 194, 196, 232–233, 239–240
Clark, Jack 183–184
Clark, Tony 231
Clarke, Fred 38–39, 42
Clemente, Roberto 154–155, 192
Clendenon, Donn 150
Cleveland Blues (NL) 16
Cleveland Blues/Indians (AL) 33–35, 49, 77–83, *79, 83*, 93, 110, 112, 135, 164, 178, 189–190, 194, 222–225, 227, 251
Cleveland Infants 20, 24, 27
Cline, Ty 239
Cobb, Ty 44, 47, 63, 93, 134, 168, 216, 223
Cochrane, Mickey 179
Coffey, Michael 1, 132
Colavito, Rocky 138
Coleman, Leonard S., Jr. 193
Collins, Eddie 70
Collins, Jimmy 35, 39–40
Collins, Shano 70–72
Colorado Rockies 188, 193
Colt Stadium 142–143, 145, 151
Comerica Park 222, 225–226, 228
Comiskey, Charles 31, 34, 36, 70, *71*, 98
Comiskey Park 92–95, 115
Como, Perry 140
Concepcion, Dave 178
Concepcion, Onix 183–184
Cone, David 189
Connally, John 144
Connolly, Tommy 79–81
Conroy, Pat 133
Coon, William 4
Cooper, Samuel 20
Cooper, Walker 122
Corum, Bill 108

Costas, Bob 157, 202, 215–216
County Stadium (Milwaukee) 120–121, 124–125, 204
Courtenay, Cliff 165
Cousins, Scott 229–230
Coveleski, Stan 80
Cowan, Tommy 89
Cox, Danny 182–183
Cox, W.N. 109
Cozart, Zack 232
Cravath, Gavvy 74
Craver, Bill 13–14
Crawford, Sam 93
Crehan, Herb 181
Criger, Lou 40, 42
Cronin, Joe 94, 137, 149
Crosley Field 96, 97, 99–101, *100*, 130, 146
Crotty, Burke 103
Crowder, General 94
Crowe, Trevor 224
Cuban Giants 105

Daly, Dan 78
Daly, Martin B. 80
Damon, Johnny 204, 223
Daniel, Dan 107, 122
D'Antonio, Michael 127–128, 132
Darcy, Pat 175
Dark, Alvin 118
Darling, Ron 156, 237
Davidson, Bob 200, 241–242
Davidson, Satch 175
Davis, Chris 248–249
Davis, Gerry 206
Davis, Sammy, Jr. 164
Dawson, Andre 196
Dayley, Ken 183
Delahanty, Ed 24, 35
Delsing, Jim 113–114, 116
Denkinger, Don 160, 182–185, 226, 240
Denver, John 248
Derringer, Paul 99
Desjardines, Marcel 109
Detroit Tigers *32*, 33, 44, 47, 58, 63, 68–69, 81, 112–116, 138–139, 174, 179, 192–194, 197–198, 222–227, 237, 240–241, 243–244
Detroit Wolverines 21
Devlin, Art 52
Devlin, Jim (pitcher) 11–14
Dilone, Miguel 81
DiMaggio, Joe 112, 114, 251
Dingell, John D. 228
Dinneen, Bill 39, 44–45, 77
Dobson, Pat 154
Doby, Larry 110–111
Doheny, Ed 41
Dombrowski, Dave 225
Donald, Jason 224–225
Donatelli, Augie 240
Donlin, Mike 52
Dow, Bill 240
Downing, Al 164–166
Doyle, Barney 129
Doyle, Denny 175
Doyle, Jack 130
Doyle, Larry 130

Drago, Dick 175
Drapeau, Jean 148–150
Drebinger, John 126, 139
Dressen, Chuck 119
Dreyfuss, Barney 38–40, *40*, 42–45, 50–51
Drummond, Henry 239
Dryden, Charles 54
Drysdale, Don 130, 164
Duffy, Hugh 32, 35, 123
Dugan, Joe 75–76
Duncan, James 133
Durante, Sal 139–140
Durocher, Leo 103, 109, 119
Dwyer, Jim 181

Eastern Park 26
Eastwick, Rawly 174
Ebbets Field 15, 100–105, 107, 109–111, 122, 125–130, 132, 140, 168, 169, 180
Ecko, Marc 220–221
Eddleton, Oscar 96–97, 99
Edison, Thomas 97
Eggler, Dave 4–5
Elliott, Bob (infielder) 110
Elysian Fields 68
Emslie, Bob 46, 52, 54, *55*, 56
Encarnacion, Edwin 242
Enron Field 147
Epstein, Theo 213
Errickson, Dick 180
Evans, Darrell 164
Evans, Dwight 175
Everitt, Mike 209
Evers, Johnny 46, 48–50, *48*, 52, 54–56, 59
Ewing, Buck 26
Exposition Park 38, 48–50

Faber, Red 70
Face, Roy 132
Falls, Joe 38
Fanning, Jim 150
Farnsworth, Kyle 210
Farrell, Turk 144
Feller, Bob 29, 115
Felsch, Happy 10, 70
Fenway Park 2, 76, 91, 101, 106, 121, 123, 157, 159–160, 173–174, 176–177, 181, 204, 206
Ferrell, Rick 94
Ferrell, Wes 158
Ferrell, Will 200
Ferris, Hobe 42
Fewster, Chick 81
Fielder, Cecil 192, 196
Fimrite, Ron 162, 164
Finley, Charlie O. 149, 157
Fisher, Chauncey 49
Fisher, Cherokee 9
Fisher, Jack 139
Fisk, Carlton 159–160, 173–176
Fisler, Wes 4–5
Fitzgerald, William S. 81
Flack, Max 66
Fleischmann, Bill 60
Flood, Curt 150
Florida/Miami Marlins 193, 200, 205, 208–212, 223, 229–230, 232, 234
Fondy, Dee 132
Footer, Alyson 241
Forbes Field 86, 88, 91, 168
Force, Davy 4–5, 9
Ford, Gerald R. 88
Ford, Whitey 135
Fosse, Ray 232, 240
Foster, George 174–175, 196
Fouser, Bill 4–5
Frazee, Harry 74–76
Freedman, Andrew 56
Freeman, Sara 20
Freiman, Nate 242
Frick, Ford 99–100, 128, 133, 136–137, 139, 239
Friedman, Elliotte 182
Friend, Bob 131
Frisch, Frankie 93
Froemming, Bruce 224
Frost, Mark 173, 175–176
Furillo, Carl 127

Gaedel, Eddie 112–116
Gaedele, Kyle 116
Gagne, Eric 205
Galarraga, Armando 185, 222–228
Gandil, Chick 10, 70–71
Garagiola, Joe 154, 174
Garcia, Freddy 205–206
Garcia, Rich 241
Garciaparra, Nomar 204
Gardner, J. Alvin 108
Gardner, Larry 78
Gardner, Steve 157
Garfield, James 82
Garver, Ned 158
Gaston, Britt 165
Gaston, Cito 204, 206
Gehrig, Lou 94, 137, 251
Gehringer, Charlie 94
Gerard, Lou 176
Geronimo, Cesar 178
Giannoulas, Ted 168–172
Gibbons, John 232, 242
Gibson, Bob 159
Gibson, Josh 107
Giles, Warren 124, 150
Gill, Warren 49–50, *50*, 54, 59
Gilliam, Jim 132
Gilman, Richard 126
Gilmore, James 61, 63, 67
Giusti, Dave 154
Gleason, Kid 68, 70–71, *72*
Gleich, Frank 76
Golenbock, Peter 129
Gomez, Lefty 94
Gonzalez, Alex 210–211
Gonzalez, Fredi 236
Gonzalez, Richard 219
Gonzalez, Tony 180
Gooding, Gladys 126
Gordon, Sam 140
Gorman, Tom 122
Gose, Anthony 242
Goslin, Goose 98
Gowdy, Curt 154–155, 176, 178
Gowen, Jeff 208
Granholm, Jennifer 228
Gray, Freddy Carlos, Jr. 246–248
Greenberg, Hank 190–191
Greene, Sam 179
Grieve, Curly 126
Griffey, Ken, Jr. 189, 192, 198–200
Griffey, Ken, Sr. 174–175, 178,
Griffin, Doug 160
Griffith, Clark 34–35, 96
Grillo, J. Ed 38
Grimes, B.T. 3, 88
Groat, Dick 131
Groth, Johnny 114
Grove, Lefty 94
Gruber, Henry 24
Gruber, John H. 43
Gruber, Kelly 241
Grudzielanek, Mark 210, 223
Guardado, Eddie 206
Guerrero, Vladimir 205
Guinn, Skip 150
Gutman, Dan 178

H.A. Lott Inc. 144
Hadley, Bump 179
Hafey, Chick 93–94
Hague, Bill 12
Haldeman, John A. 13
Halfon, Mark S. 69
Hall, George 4, 11–14
Halladay, Roy 223
Hallahan, Bill 94
Hamilton, Darryl 192
Hamilton, Milo 164–166
Hample, Zack 87
Harding, Warren 67
Hargrave, Bubbles 233
Harper, Brian 182–183
Harrah, Toby 133
Harrelson, Bud 240
Harridge, Will 33, 92–93, 99–100, 112, 115–116
Harrist, Earl 110
Hart, James 69
Hartford Dark Blues 7, 9, 11–12
Hartung, Clint 118
Haupert, Michael 14
Hawke, Bill 32
Hawkins, Chris 59
Hebner, Richie 156
Heitz, Tom 85
Helfer, Al 104
Helton, Todd 205
Hendrick, George 240
Hendricks, Elrod 239
Hensley, Clay 219
Hermon Lloyd & W. B. Morgan 144
Hernandez, Jose 200
Hernandez, Roberto (Fausto Carmona) 222
Herr, Tommy 183
Herrmann, Garry *40*, 98
Herzog, Buck 52
Herzog, Whitey 183–185, 203
Heydler, John 39
Hill, Glenallen 193
Hitler, Adolf 132
Hodges, Gil 118, 127, 239

Hodges, Russ 119–120
Hoffer, Bill 33–34
Hofheinz, Roy 143–145, 150
Hofman, Art 54–56
Hogan, Larry 247
Hogriever, George 49
Holbrook, Sam 236
Hollandsworth, Todd 210
Holliday, Matt 236
Holmes, Oliver Wendell 64
Holmes, Tommy (player) 122
Holmes, Tommy (writer) 180
Honig, Donald 29–30, 68, 121, 133, 161–162
Hooper, Harry 74–75
Hopper, Clay 109
Horner, Jack 108
Hornsby, Rogers 138
Hosmer, Eric 243
Houk, Ralph 135, 138, 159
Houston Astrodome 141–147, *145*
Houston Colt .45s/Colts/Astros 134, 137, 141–145, 147, 150, 166, 167, 169, 194
Houston Oilers 147
Howard, Elston 160
Howard, Frank 240
Howser, Dick 183
Hubbell, Carl 130
Huggins, Miller 74, 79
Hulbert, William A. 3, 6–7, 9–11, 13–14
Hunt, George W. 117
Hunter, Jim "Catfish" 1
Hunter, Torii 204–205
Huntington Avenue Baseball Grounds 37, 42, 45
Hurley, Ed 113–114, 116
Husman, John R. 15–16
Hynd, Noel 131

Indianapolis Clowns 162
Indianapolis Colts 149
Indianapolis Hoosiers (FL) 63
Indianapolis Hoosiers (NL) 22
Indianapolis Millers (Western League) 49
Infante, Omar 243
Inge, Brandon 224
Iorg, Dane 184
Iron Sheik 226
Irsay, Robert 149
Irvin, Monte 118, 130
Irwin, John 24
Isaminger, James C. 76

Jackson, Austin 223
Jackson, Maynard 164
Jackson, Reggie 184, 196, 216
Jackson, "Shoeless" Joe 10, 70, 72
Jacobs Field 147
Jaffe, Chris 153
James, Bill 81, 218
Jarry Park (Parc Jarry) 148, 150–152
Jaster, Larry 151
Javier, Stan 193
Jefferson Street Grounds 3, 4, 9
Jennings, Hughie 31, *32*

Jensen, Marcus 193
Jeter, Derek 241
Jimenez, Ubaldo 249
Johnson, Albert L. 24
Johnson, Ban 33–37, 39, 44, 67, 81
Johnson, Bill 83
Johnson, Chief 62
Johnson, Claude B. 98
Johnson, Darrell 175
Johnson, Davey 154, 229
Johnson, Lady Bird 145
Johnson, Lyndon 145
Johnson, Randy 29
Johnson, Walter 29, 63, 81, 93, 158
Johnson, Will 24
Johnstone, Jim 66
Jones, Chipper 193, 237
Jones, Mack 151
Jones, Sam 75
Jorda, Lou 119
Jordan, Michael 216
Joss, Addie 21, 93
Joyce, Ellouise 225
Joyce, Jim 185, 222–228, 241
Jurges, Billy 130
Just, Ward S. 101

Kansas City Athletics 135, 149
Kansas City Monarchs 105–106
Kansas City Packers 61–62, 65–66
Kansas City Royals 149, 182–185, 237, 240, 243–244
Kauff, Benny 63
Kaufman Stadium 243; *see also* Royals Stadium
Kavanagh, Jack 30
Kawasaki, Munenori 242
Keeler, Willie 35, 187
Kellogg, Jeff 235
Kelly, Don 223
Kelly, Emmett 169
Kelly, King 26, *27*, 123
Kent, Jeff 195
Kepner, Tyler 227
Keri, Jonah 150
Keyser, E. Lee 98
Kiley, John 176
Killilea, Henry 39–40, 45
Kilroy, Matt 29–30, 32
King, Joe 130, 138, 142
King, Larry 110
King, Silver 25
Kinsler, Ian 243
Kirby, Clay 175
Kirkpatrick, Curry 184–185
Kison, Bruce 154
Klem, Bill 56, 94
Klonke, Chuck 224
Knetzer, Elmer 66
Knight, Lon 5, 7, 27
Konerko, Paul 205–206
Koppett, Leonard 3, 158–159
Koufax, Sandy 1, 29, 132, 164
Kozma, Peter 236–237
Krapp, Gene 63
Kroc, Ray 169
Kruk, John 92
Kubek, Tony 155, 174

Kuhn, Bowie 150–151, 153, 155, 163–164, 191

Labine, Clem 118
Laboy, Coco 151
Lajoie, Napoleon 35, *36*
Land, Grover 66
Landis, Kenesaw Mountain 37, 64, 68, 72, 89
Lansford, Carney 196
Lardner, Ring 68
Larsen, Don 1, 223
LaRussa, Tony 198–199, 226
Layne, Jerry 248
Leach, Tommy 38, 42
League Park (Cincinnati) 29, 32
League Park (Cleveland) 93
League Park (Toledo) 15, 20
Lee, Bill 175
Lee, Derrek 210
Leever, Sam 41
Leibrandt, Charlie 182
Leno, Jay 211
Leonard, Dutch 68, 75
Levesque, Jean Louis 149
Levy, George 130
Lewis, Duffy 75
Lewis, Ethan M. 21, 28
Leyland, Jim 223–224, 226
Lieb, Fred 134
Litke, Jim 190
Lockman, Whitey 118
Lohse, Kyle 235
Lombardo, John 199
Los Angeles Angels/California Angels/Anaheim Angels/Los Angeles Angels of Anaheim 134, 234, 244
Los Angeles Dodgers 126, 128, 132, 143, 146, 148, 161, 164, 188, 241
Los Angeles Rams 149
Louisville Colonels 38
Louisville Eclipse 16–17
Louisville Grays 7, 9–15, 68
Loverro, Thom 203, 206
Low, Nat 109
Lowe, Derek 204
Lowell, Mike 205–206, 210
Luciano, Ron 168
Lucroy, Jonathan 232
Lunte, Harry 80, 83
Lutz, Eric 65
Lynn, Fred 174–175
Lyons, Steve 210

Machado, Manny 249
Mack, Connie 24, *25*, 35, 93, 101, 251
MacPhail, Larry 99–100, 102, 180
Maier, Jeffrey 241
Maislin, Syd 151
Manassau, Al 49
Manfred, Rob 247
Manning, Jack 5
Manson, Marilyn 192
Mantle, Mickey 112, 135–140, 144, 160, 218
Maranville, Rabbit 123
Mariotti, Jay 211, 256

Maris, Pat 202
Maris, Roger 133, 135–141, 196–200, 202, 215, 251
Marquard, Rube 130
Marshall, Mike 166
Martin, Billy 135
Martin, Ned 175
Martin, Pepper 94
Martinez, Dennis 1
Martinez, Pedro 154
Mathews, Denny 183
Mathews, Eddie 163–164
Mathews, T.J. 198
Mathewson, Christy 51–52, 54, 56, 59
Matlin, Sam 148
Mattingly, Don 188–189
Mauch, Gene 150–151
Maxvill, Dal 151
Mays, Carl 75, 78–82, 178
Mays, Willie 119, 128, 132, 196, 202, 204, 216–217, 240
Mazeroski, Bill 2
McAleer, Jimmy 93
McAllister, Jack 79
McAuley, Ed 108, 151
McAuliffe, Dick 240
McCann, Brian 237
McCarthy, Michael 156
McCarver, Tim 138, 205
McClelland, Tim 225
McCormick, Mike 110
McCormick, Moose 51–52, **53**, 54, 56–57, 130
McCullough, Andy 243
McDaniels, Chris 249
McDevitt, Danny 132
McEnaney, Will 178
McFarlane, Todd 195
McGinley, Tim 4, 9
McGinn, Dan 150–151
McGinnity, Joe 54–56
McGowan, Bill 94
McGowan, James F. 82
McGowan, Lloyd 109
McGraw, Blanche 130
McGraw, John 35–36, 46, **48**, 51, 56–59, 93, 130, 187, 251
McGraw, Tug 142
McGwire, Jay 195, 197–198
McGwire, Mark 195–202, 215, 218
McHale, John 87, 150
McKay, Dave 200
McKechnie, Bill 65, 137
McLean, William 4, 7
McMullin, Fred 10, 70–71
McQuillan, George 224
McRae, Hal 183
McVey, Cal 6
Medwick, Joe 180
Melvin, Bob 242–243
Mercer, Sid 51
Merkle, Fred 46, **48**, 50–59, 214
Metropolitan Stadium 145
Meyerle, Levi 4–5, 9
Miami Marlins *see* Florida/Miami Marlins
Michaels, Al 183
Millan, Felix 240

Miller, Bill 242
Miller, Damian 205
Miller, Jon 219, 230
Miller Park 203–205, 207
Mills, Rupert 65
Milwaukee Braves 2, 120–125, 131, 150, 162–163
Milwaukee Brewers 186, 194, 204, 232
Minneapolis Millers 119, 129
Minnesota Twins 134–135, 142, 145, 155, 180, 204, 206
Minute Maid Park 147
Mogridge, Frank 178
Montreal Alouettes 149
Montreal Expos 148–152, 195, 200, 223
Montreal Royals 19, 107–109, 148–149
Moore, Archie 218
Moore, Donnie 197
Moore, Monte 240
Mooty, Jake 179
Moran, Pat 68, 179
Mordecai, Mike 210
Moret, Roger 174
Morgan, Bobby 122
Morgan, Joe 175–176
Morgan, Tracy 200
Morris, Bryan 242
Morton, Alfred P. 104
Morton, Charlie 18
Moses, Robert 127–128
Mota, Guillermo 229
Motte, Jason 237
Muchnick, Isadore 106
Mueller, Don 118–119
Mullane, Tony 18
Mullin, Pat 114
Municipal Stadium (Cleveland) 112
Munzel, Edgar 129
Murcer, Bobby 159
Murnane, Tim 4, **5**, 7, 42, 44
Murphy, Cait 54–55
Murphy, Charley 56
Murphy, Matt 220
Murtaugh, Danny 154
Murtha, Frank 213
Mussina, Mike 204
Myers, Billy 99

Naman, Israel A. 144
Nash, Bruce 165
Navin Field 68, 223
Nelson, Jeff (umpire) 236
Nelson, Rob 196–197
Nemec, David 26, 35, 58
Nessy, Santiago 59
Nettles, Graig 159
New York Giants (PL) 25–28, 49
New York Gothams/Giants (NL) 21, 25, 28–30, 36, 46–59, 75, 84–86, 89, 112, 117–120, 126, 128–132, 224, 246, 251
New York Mets 29, 134, 137, 139, 142, 150, 192–193, 219, 240, 249
New York Yankees 37, 46, 69, 73–79, 81–82, 89, 94, 112, 115, 119,

112, 122–124, 126, 132–136, 138–140, 144–145, 157–160, 164, 179, 186, 188–189, 193, 212, 220, 235, 239, 241, 249, 251
Newark Peppers 65–67, 137
Newcombe, Don 118
Newman, Bruce 169
Newton, Doc 49
Neyer, Rob 66
Nichols, Al 12–14
Nightengale, Bob 166
Nolan, Gary 174
Northrup, Jim 240

Oakland Athletics 149, 155, 157, 163, 174, 196–198, 217, 223, 240, 242–244
Obama, Barack 166, 226
O'Connell, Jack 172
O'Day, Hank 49–50, **50**, 54–57, 59
Office, Rowland 164
Okkonen, Mark 60, 63
Okrent, Daniel 72, 173
Olbermann, Keith 46, 135, 137–138, 194, 216, 233
Oliva, Tony 180
Oliver, Al 154
Oliver, Darren 192
Olympic Park (Buffalo) 20, 24, 29
O'Malley, Walter 127–130, 132, 149
O'Neill, Steve 80
O'Rourke, Jim 4, 9
Orta, Jorge 182–184
Owens, Jesse 106

Padilla, Vicente 205–206
Paige, Satchel 107, 144
Palmeiro, Rafael 201
Palmer, Jim 154, 183
Palmer, Scott 227
Pappas, Milt 224
Parent, Freddy 41, 44–45
Parizeau, Paul 109
Parker, Dan 108
Parker, Edwin L. 137
Parks, Bill 9
Parrott, Harold 103
Parsley, Al 105
Passan, Jeff 222
Passarella, Art 239
Patkin, Max 169
Pavano, Carl 201
Pearlman, Jeff 215
Pearson, Daniel M. 21
Pena, Tony 189
Pendleton, Terry 182
Pennock, Herb 75
Peppers Park 65
Perez, Hernan 243
Perez, Salvador 243
Perez, Tony 174
Perini, Lou 121–124
Petco Park 219
Petrocelli, Rico 174–175
Petroskey, Dale 220–221
Pfeffer, Jeff 81
Pfiester, Jack 51–52
Philadelphia Athletics (AL) **25**,

35, 40, 63, **64**, 73, 76–78, 100, 121, 127, 179, 251
Philadelphia Athletics (NA) 6
Philadelphia Athletics (NL) 3–5, 7–9, 11
Philadelphia Quakers/Phillies (NL) 25, 28, 35–36, **64**, 88–89, 96, 99–100, 110, 118, 132, 139, 141, 145–146, 150, 155–156, 171, 179–180, 193, 223, 224, 227, 246,
Phillippe, Deacon 38, 43
Piazza, Mike 205
Pierre, Juan 209–210
Pillette, Duane 114
Pinson, Vada 151
Pipp, Wally 79
Pittsburgh Alleghenys 15, 18
Pittsburgh Pirates 2, 21, 25, 27, 34, 36–45, 47–51, 54–55, 57, 59, 69, 86, 88–89, 99, 122, 125–126, 131–132, 134, 152–155, 166, 174, 187, 193, 217–218, 238, 241–242
Pittsburgh Rebels 60, 65–66
Pittsburgh Steelers 154
PNC Park 238, 241, 244
Polo Grounds 25, 28–29, 46, 49–52, 54–59, **58**, 69, 76–82, 84–87, 89, 95, 117–118, 120, 126, 128–132; *see also* Brotherhood Park
Popowski, Eddie 175
Porter, Darrell 183–184
Posey, Buster 229–230, 232–233
Posnanski, Joe 196, 244
Powers, Maurice (Doc) 78
Powers, Patrick 65
Presley, Elvis 171
Prince, Bob 89, **90**, 91, 154–155
Prior, Mark 209–210,
Providence Grays 16, 21, 30
Pulliam, Harry C. 41, 44, 46, 55, 57

Quinn, Jack 62

Racine, Hector 109
Radbourn, Charles "Hoss" 30, 32
Raines, Tim, Sr. 180
Ramirez, Manny 205
Ramos, Pedro 135
Rath, Morrie 71
Rather, Dan 198
Rawlings-Blake, Stephanie 246
Ray, James Lincoln 188
Raymond, Dave 171
Redland Field 67, 70, 73
Redmond, Mike 223
Reese, Pee Wee 127, 179
Reichler, Joseph, L. 39
Remington, Alex 186
Remlinger, Mike 210
Renteria, Rick 241
Rettenmund, Merv 154
Rhodes, Dusty 131
Rice, Grantland 89
Rice, Jim 174
Rice, John 155, 240
Rice, Sam 158
Richard, J.R. 29
Richter, Frank 34

Rickards, Tex 126
Rickey, Branch 106–110, **106**
Riesbeck, Alan 200
Rigler, Cy 224
Rigney, Bill 119, 130–131
Ripken, Cal, Jr. 156, 193
Risberg, Swede 10, 70
Ritter, Lawrence S. 1, 74
Rivera, Mariano 189
Rizzuto, Phil 115, 139
Robertson, Charlie 223
Robinson, Frank 197, 220
Robinson, Jackie 15–16, 19–20, 74, 105–111, 118–119, 122, 124, 127, 148, 239
Robinson, Mack 106
Robinson, Rachel 110
Robinson, Ray 119
Rockefeller, John D. 82
Rodriguez, Alex 87
Rodriguez, Ivan 210
Roenicke, Gary 181
Rollins, Jimmy 205
Romine, Andrew 244
Roosevelt, Franklin D. 99
Roosevelt Stadium 128
Rose, Pete 173–174, 176, 232
Rosenburg, John M. 6, 37
Rosenthal, Ken 226
Ross, David 235–236
Roth, Mark 81
Rothstein, Arnold 70
Roush, Edd 60, 65
Rowe, Jack 21
Rowswell, Albert 89
Royals Stadium 182, 185; *see also* Kaufman Stadium
Rubin, Bob 170
Ruhle, Vern 174
Ruppert, Jacob 75, 77
Rusie, Amos 29–32, **31**
Russell, Bill 164
Russell, Lillian 30
Ruth, Babe 62, 69, 73–77, **75**, 93–95, 114, 116, 123, 133, 135–140, 158, 161–165, 168–169, 192, 196, 198, 200, 215–216, 219, 251
Ryan, Bob 173
Ryan, Jimmy 30
Ryan, Nolan 29–30
Ryan, Rosy 130
Ryder, Jack 96

Sain, Johnny 110, 239
St. Louis Browns (AL) 35, 61, 69, 77, 97, 100, 112–116, 121, 124, 127, 158, 191
St. Louis Browns/Perfectos/Cardinals 7–9, 32, 47, 51, 61, 69, 94, 100, 117, 120–121, 124, 128, 138, 140, 148, 150, 155, 159, 182–185, 195, 198–201, 226, 234–237, 240
St. Louis Terriers 60–61, 63, 65–66
St. Paul Saints (Western League) 49
Samardzija, Jeff 241, 248–249
San Diego Padres 86, 116, 149, 151, 163, 167–171, 195, 197, 219, 224, 227

San Diego Stadium 167, 169–170, 172
San Francisco Giants 29, 132, 187, 190, 192–193, 204, 215–221, 229–230, 233–234, 237, 244
Sanders, Deion 241
Sanguillen, Manny 229
Santiago, Benito 206
Santiago, Ramon 223
Santo, Ron 212
Saucier, Frank 113, 115–116
Schafer, Harry 4–5, 9
Schalk, Ray 70
Schang, Wally 75
Scherzer, Max 243
Schierholtz, Nate 229
Schilling, Curt 204
Schultz, Howie 110
Schumacher, Garry 131
Scully, Vin 102, 132, 161, 251
Seattle Mariners 186, 188–189, 206, 251
Seattle Pilots 149
Seaver, Tom 150
See, Charlie 85
Selig, Bud 167, 186, 199, 203–207, 220, 222, 226–228
Sewell, Joe 83
Seymour, Cy 52
Shapiro, Walter 187
Shaughnessy, Frank J. 149
Shaw, Jerie 249
Shea Stadium 29, 150, 192
Sheinin, Dave 201
Shibe Park 73, 76, 77, 78, 101, 168
Shiner, David 48
Shore, Ernie 75
Short, Chris 145
Shotton, Burt 109
Showalter, Buck 248–249
Sierra, Ruben 189
Simmons, Alex 236
Simmons, Lon 128
Simmons, Steve 232
Sinclair, Harry 67
Sisler, George 158
Smallwood, Percy 80
Smith, Lester 123
Smith, Red 119
Smith, Reggie 159
Snider, Duke 119, 127, 132
Snyder, Gerry 148–149
Soriano, Alfonso 205
Sosa, Sammy 195, 198–201, 210, 215
South End Grounds (Boston) 9, 12, 14
South Side Park (Chicago) 33, 37
Sowell, Mike 77
Spahn, Warren 123–124
Spalding, Albert 3, 6, 13–14, 22–28, **23**
Speaker, Tris 63, 79–80, 82, 93
Spies, Harry 49
Sportsman's Park 100, 112, 115–116
Stahl, Chick 42
Stahl, Larry 224
Staley, Gerry 124
Stalin, Josef 132

Stallard, Tracy 139–140
Stargell, Willie 154
Stark, Jayson 193
Start, Joe 16
Staub, Rusty 142–143, 150
Stearns, Frederick 21
Steinfeldt, Harry 56
Stengel, Casey 134–135
Stevens, Chris 15
Stifel, Otto 61
Stilwell, Jonathan 32
Stockton, Dick 176
Stoneham, Horace 128–131
Stovey, George 19
Street, Gabby 93
Styles, Mary Sue 171
Suarez, Eugenio 243
Suehsdorf, A.D. 34
Sukeforth, Clyde 109
Sullivan, Billy 96
Sullivan, Ed 115, 120, 176
Sullivan, Sport 70
Sundberg, Jim 183–184
Sutherland, Donald 126
Sutherland, Gary 151
Sutton, Don 197
Sutton, Ezra 4–5
Swift, Bob 114, 116
Swope, Tom 99
Symington, Stuart 149

Taft, William Howard 34
Tampa Bay Rays 155, 223, 232, 249
Tarasco, Tony 241
Taylor, Jack 69
Taylor, Tony 180
Taylor, Zack 113–114
Tejada, Ruben 233
Telander, Rick 213
Temple, William Chase 187
Tenace, Gene 240
Tenney, Fred 51
Terry, Ralph 2
Texas Rangers 186, 190, 192, 223, 240
Thomas, Frank 248
Thompson, Chuck 229
Thomson, Bobby 112, 117–120, 131
Thorne, Gary 249
Three Rivers Stadium 152–156, 217
Thurber, James 112, 114
Tinker, Joe 48, 52, 56
Todd, Al 99
Toledo Blue Stockings 15, 17–18
Torgeson, Earl 110
Toronto Blue Jays 191, 204, 232, 241–242, 249
Torre, Joe 151, 205, 231, 241

Torres, Andres 229
Totten, Hal 94
Trachsel, Steve 200
Tropicana Field 249
Trout, Dizzy 115
Troy Trojans 246
Tudor, John 184
Turner, Ted 168, 170
Turner Field 234–236, 238
Twain, Mark 3

Uggla, Dan 236
Union Grounds (Brooklyn) 12
Urbina, Ugueth 204
U.S. Cellular Field 206
Utley, Chase 233

Valentine, Ellis 181
Vanover, Larry 243–244
Van Slyke, Andy 184, 217
Vargo, Ed 154
Veeck, Bill 110, 112–116, 124, 191
Veeck, William, Sr. 190
Verducci, Tom 222, 224
Veterans Stadium 171
Vila, Joe 50, 56, 74, 76, 190
Vincent, Fay 141
Vizquel, Omar 205
Vogt, Stephen 242–243

Wagner, Honus 39, 39, 41–42, *41*, 44, 47
Walker, James R. 88
Walker, Luke 154
Walker, Moses Fleetwood 15–20
Walker, Neil 242
Walker, Sherman 99
Walker, Welday 15–16, 18–19
Wallace, Bobby 93
Walsh, Ed 21
Walter P. Moore Engineers and Consultants 144
Walters, Bucky 103
Ward, Arch 92–93
Ward, Geoffrey C. 33
Ward, John Montgomery 20–24, *22*, 26, 28, 62
Wardlow, Calvin 163
Warrington, Robert D. 78
Washington Nationals 215, 219–220, 233, 237, 241
Washington Senators (1960s) 134, 142
Washington Senators (original) 33, 35, 63, 93, 96, 98, 134, 142
Waslewski, Gary 151
Watt, Eddie 154
Weaver, Buck 10, 70, 72

Webb, Del 126
Weeghman Park 60, 62, 65–67; *see also* Wrigley Field
Welch, Louie 144
West, Joe 230
Wetteland, John 189
White, Deacon 6, 21
White, Frank 184
White, Gordon 104
White, Sol 105
White, William Edward 16
Whiteside, Eli 230
Wilbon, Michael 213
Will, George 208
Williams, Lefty 10, 70, 72
Williams, Ted 202, 204
Williamson, Ned 137
Wills, Maury 150–151
Wilson, Hack 200
Wilson, Morris, Crain and Anderson 144
Wilstein, Steve 199
Wiltse, Hooks 55, 224
Wise, Rick 157
Wojciechowski, Gene 168
Womack, Graham 74
Wood, Smokey Joe 93
Woods, Tiger 216
Worcester Driving Park Grounds, 246
Worcester Ruby Legs 246
Worrell, Todd 183
Wright, George 4, 7
Wright, Harry 7
Wrigley Field 61–62, 87, 101, 179, 192, 208–214, 251; *see also* Weeghman Park
Wynn, Jimmy 143, 165

Yankee Stadium 119, 133, 135, 139–141, 186, 189, 239
Yastrzemski, Carl 139, 174, 178
York, Rudy 198
Yost, Ned 243
Young, Cy 1, 23, 32, 35, 39–40, 42–43, *43*, 61, 246
Young, Dick 136
Young, Nick 23

Zachary, Tom 139
Zang, David W. 15, 19
Zaun, Gregg 232
Zimmer, Don 123
Zoss, Joel 3, 33
Zullo, Allan 168
Zwilling, Dutch 66